AF710238

Object-Oriented Programming via Fortran 90/95

Learn how to write technical applications in a modern object-oriented approach using Fortran 90 or 95. This book will teach you how to stop focusing on the traditional procedural abilities of Fortran and to employ the principles of object-oriented programming (OOP) to produce clear, highly efficient, executable codes. Get ready now to take advantage of all the features of the finalized, fully object-oriented Fortran 200X!

In addition to covering the OOP methodologies, the book covers the basic foundation of the language and good programming skills, making the book valuable also as a good migration tool for experienced Fortran programmers who want to pick up the OOP paradigm smoothly. The author highlights common themes by using comparisons with MATLAB and C++ and uses numerous cross-referenced examples to convey all concepts quickly and clearly. Complete code for the examples is included on the accompanying CD-ROM.

Ed Akin is Professor of Mechanical Engineering and Professor of Computational and Applied Mathematics at Rice University.

Object-Oriented Programming via Fortran 90/95

ED AKIN

Rice University

CAMBRIDGE
UNIVERSITY PRESS

PUBLISHED BY THE PRESS SYNDICATE OF THE UNIVERSITY OF CAMBRIDGE
The Pitt Building, Trumpington Street, Cambridge, United Kingdom

CAMBRIDGE UNIVERSITY PRESS
The Edinburgh Building, Cambridge CB2 2RU, UK
40 West 20th Street, New York, NY 10011-4211, USA
477 Williamstown Road, Port Melbourne, VIC 3207, Australia
Ruiz de Alarcón 13, 28014 Madrid, Spain
Dock House, The Waterfront, Cape Town 8001, South Africa

http://www.cambridge.org

First published 2003

Printed in the United States of America

Typefaces Times Ten 9.5/12 pt. *with* Helvetica Neue, Optima, *and* Lucida Typewriter
System LaTeX 2ε [TB]

A catalog record for this book is available from the British Library.

Library of Congress Cataloging in Publication data available

ISBN 0 521 52408 3 paperback

Contents

Preface

There has been an explosion of interest in, and books on, object-oriented programming (OOP). Why have yet another book on the subject? In the past a basic education was intended to result in mastery of the three r's: reading, 'riting, and 'rithmetic. Today a sound education in engineering programming leads to producing code that satisfies the four r's: readability, reusability, reliability, and real efficiency. Although some object-oriented programming languages have some of these abilities, Fortran 90/95 offers all of them for engineering applications. Thus, this book is intended to take a different tack by using the Fortran 90/95 language as its main OOP tool. With more than 100 pure and hybrid object-oriented languages available, one must be selective in deciding which ones merit the effort of learning to utilize them. There are millions of Fortran programmers, and so it is logical to present the hybrid object-oriented features of Fortran 90/95 to them to update and expand their programming skills. This work provides an introduction to Fortran 90 as well as to OOP concepts. Even with the current release (Fortran 95) we will demonstrate that Fortran offers essentially all of the tools recommended for OOP techniques. It is expected that Fortran 200X will offer additional object-oriented capabilities such as declaring "extensible" (or virtual) functions. Thus, it is expected that the tools learned here will be of value far into the future.

It is commonly agreed that the two-decade-old F77 standard for the language was missing several useful and important concepts of computer science that evolved and were made popular after its release, but it also had a large number of powerful and useful features. The following F90 standard included many improvements that have often been overlooked by programmers. It is fully compatible with all old F77 standard code, but it declared several features of that standard obsolete. That was done to encourage programmers to learn better methods even though the standard still supports those now obsolete language constructs. The F90 standards committee brought into the language most of the best features of other more recent languages like Ada, C, C++, Eiffel, and so forth. In part those additions included structures, dynamic memory management, recursion, pointers (references), and abstract data types along with their supporting tools of encapsulation, inheritance, and the overloading of operators and routines. Equally important for those involved in numerical analysis, the F90 standard added several new features for efficient array operations that are very similar to those of the popular MATLAB environment. Most of those features include additional options to employ logical filters on arrays. All of the new array features were intended for use on vector or parallel computers and allow programmers to avoid the bad habit of writing numerous serial loops. The current standard, F95, went on to add more specific parallel array tools, provided "pure" routines for general parallel operations, simplified the use of pointers, and made a few user-friendly refinements of some F90 features. Indeed, at this time one can view F90/95 as the only cross-platform international standard language for parallel computing. Thus, Fortran continues to be an important programming language that richly rewards the effort of learning to take advantage of its power, clarity, and user friendliness.

We begin that learning process in Chapter 1 with an overview of general programming techniques. Primarily the older "procedural" approach is discussed there, but the chapter closes with an outline of the newer "object" approach to programming. An experienced programmer may want to skip directly to the last section of Chapter 1, where we outline some object-oriented methods. In Chapter 2, we introduce the concept of the abstract data types and their extension to classes. Chapter 3 provides a fairly detailed introduction to the concepts and terminology of object-oriented programming. A much larger supporting glossary is provided as a supplement.

For the sake of completeness, Chapter 4 introduces language-specific details of the topics discussed in the first chapter. The Fortran 90/95 syntax is used there, but in several cases cross references are made to similar constructs in the C++ language and the MATLAB environment. Although some readers may want to skip Chapter 4, it will help others learn the Fortran 90/95 syntax, or they may read related publications that use C++ or MATLAB. All of the syntax of Fortran 90 is also given in an appendix.

Since many Fortran applications relate to manipulating arrays or doing numerical matrix analysis, Chapter 5 presents a very detailed coverage of the powerful intrinsic features Fortran 90 has added to provide for more efficient operations with arrays. It has been demonstrated in the literature that object-oriented implementations of scientific projects requiring intensive operations with arrays execute much faster in Fortran 90 than in C++. Since Fortran 90 was designed for operations on vector and parallel machines, that chapter encourages the programmer to avoid unneeded serial loops and to replace them with more efficient intrinsic array functions. Readers not needing to use numerical matrix analysis may skip Chapter 5.

Chapter 6 returns to object-oriented methods with a more detailed coverage of using object-oriented analysis and object-oriented design to create classes and demonstrates how to implement them using OOP in Fortran 90. Additional Fortran 90 examples of inheritance and polymorphism are given in Chapter 7. Object-oriented programs often require the objects to be stored in some type of "container" or data structure such as a stack or linked list. Fortran 90 object-oriented examples of typical containers are given in Chapter 8. Some specialized topics for more advanced users are given in Chapter 9, and so beginning programmers may skip that chapter.

To summarize the two optional uses of this text: it is recommended that experienced Fortran programmers wishing to learn to use OOP cover Chapters 2, 3, 6, 7, 8, and 9, whereas persons studying Fortran for the first time should cover Chapters 1, 2, 3, and. Anyone needing to use numerical matrix analysis should also include Chapter 5.

An OO glossary is included to aid in reading this text and the current literature on OOP. Another appendix on Fortran 90 gives an alphabetical listing of its intrinsic routines, a subject-based list of them, a detailed syntax of all the F90 statements, and a set of examples demonstrating the use of every statement. Selected solutions for many of the assignments are included in another appendix, along with comments on those solutions. The final appendix gives the C++ versions of several of the F90 examples in the text. They are provided as an aid to understanding other OOP literature. Since F90 and MATLAB are so similar, the corresponding MATLAB versions often directly follow the F90 examples in the text.

Acknowledgments

We are all indebted to the hundreds of programmers who labor on various standards committees to improve all programming languages continuously. Chapter 1 is a modification of introductory programming notes developed jointly with Prof. Don Johnson at Rice University. I would like to thank Tinsley Oden and the Texas Institute for Computational Mathematics for generously hosting my sabbatical leave, during which most of this work was developed, and Rice University for financing the sabbatical. Special thanks go to my wife, Kimberly, without whose support and infinite patience this book would not have been completed.

Source Codes

All of the program examples and selected solutions are included on the CD-ROM provided with the book. To be readable on various platforms they have been written with the ISO9660 standard format. Additional files are provided to relate the ISO standard short file names to the full-length program names used in the book. Of course, the source files will have to be processed through a Fortran 90 or 95 or 2000 compiler to form executables. All of the figures are also provided as encapsulated PostScript® files.

Ed Akin, Rice University, 2002

CHAPTER ONE

Program Design

1.1 Introduction

The programming process is similar in approach and creativity to writing a paper. In composition, you are writing to express ideas; in programming, you are expressing a computation. Both the programmer and the writer must adhere to the syntactic rules (grammar) of a particular language. In prose, the fundamental idea-expressing unit is the sentence; in programming, two units – *statements* and *comments* – are available.

Composition, from technical prose to fiction, should be organized broadly, usually through an outline. The outline should be expanded as the detail is elaborated and the whole reexamined and reorganized when structural or creative flaws arise. Once the outline settles, you begin the actual composition process using sentences to weave the fabric your outline expresses. Clarity in writing occurs when your sentences, both internally and globally, communicate the outline succinctly and clearly. We stress this approach here with the aim of developing a programming style that produces efficient programs humans can easily understand.

To a great degree, no matter which language you choose for your composition, the idea can be expressed with the same degree of clarity. Some subtleties can be better expressed in one language than another, but the fundamental reason for choosing your language is your audience: people do not know many languages, and if you want to address the American population, you had better choose English over Swahili. Similar situations happen in programming languages, but they are not nearly so complex or diverse. The number of languages is far fewer, and their differences minor. Fortran is the oldest language among those in use today. The C and C++ languages differ from it somewhat, but there are more similarities than not (see Bar-David [6], Barton and Nackman [7], Hanly [22], Hubbard [24], and Nielsen [30]). MATLAB, written in C and Fortran, was created much later than these two, and its structure is so similar to the others that it can easily be mastered (see Hanselman and Littlefield [23], and Pratap [33]). The C++ language is an extension of the C language that places its emphasis on object-oriented programming (OOP) methods. Fortran added object-oriented capabilities with its F90 standard, and additional enhancements for parallel machines were issued with F95(see Adams et al. [1], Gehrke [17], Hahn [21], Kerrigan [25], and Press et al. [34]). The Fortran 200X standard is planned to contain more user-friendly constructs for polymorphism and will thus enhance its object-oriented capabilities. This creation of a new language and its similarity to more established ones are this book's main points: more computer programming languages will be created during your career, but these new languages will probably not be much different than ones you already know. Why should new languages evolve? In the case of MATLAB, the desire to express matrix-like expressions easily motivated its creation. The difference between MATLAB and Fortran 90 is infinitesimally small compared with the gap between English and Swahili.

An important difference between programming and composition is that in programming you are writing for two audiences: people and computers. As for the computer audience, what you write is "read" by interpreters and compilers specific to the language you used. They are very rigid about syntactic rules, and perform exactly the calculations you say. It is like a document you write being read by the most detailed, picky person you know; every pronoun is questioned, and if the antecedent is not perfectly clear, then they throw up their hands, rigidly declaring that the entire document cannot be understood. Your picky friend might interpret the sentence "Pick you up at eight" to mean that you will literally lift him or her off the ground at precisely 8 o'clock and will then demand to know whether the time is in the morning or afternoon and what the date is.

Humans demand even more from programs. This audience consists of two main groups whose goals can conflict. The larger of the two groups consists of *users*. Users care about how the program presents itself, its *user interface*, and how quickly the program runs that is, how efficient it is. To satisfy this audience, programmers may use statements that are overly terse because they know how to make the program more readable by the computer's compiler, enabling the compiler to produce faster but less human-intelligible programs. This approach causes the other portion of the audience – programmers – to boo and hiss. The smaller audience, of which you are also a member, must be able to read the program to enhance or change it. A characteristic of programs that further distinguishes it from prose is that you and others will seek to modify your program in the future. For example, in the 1960s, when the first version of Fortran was created, useful programs by today's standards (such as matrix inversion) were written. Back then, the user interface possibilities were quite limited, and the use of visual displays was limited. Thirty years later, you would (conceivably) want to take an old program, and provide a modern user interface. If the program is structurally sound (a good outline and organized well) and is well written, reusing the "good" portions is easy accomplished.

The three-audience situation has prompted most languages to support both computer- and human-oriented "prose." The program's meaning is conveyed by statements and is what the computer interprets. Humans read this part, which in virtually all languages bears a strong relationship to mathematical equations, and also read *comments*. Comments are not read by the computer at all but are there to help explain what might be expressed in a complicated way by programming language syntax. The document or program you write today should be understandable tomorrow, not only by you, but also by others. Sentences and paragraphs should make sense after a day or so of gestation. Paragraphs and larger conceptual units should not contain assumptions or leaps that confuse the reader. Otherwise, the document you write for yourself or others serves no purpose. The same is true with programming; the program's organization should be easy to follow, and the way you write the program, using both statements and comments, should help you and others understand how the computation proceeds. The existence of comments permits the writer to express the program's outline directly in the program to help the reader comprehend the computation.

These similarities highlight the parallels between composition and programming. Differences become evident because programming is, in many ways, more demanding than prose writing. On one hand, the components and structure of programming languages are far simpler than the grammar and syntax of any verbal or written language. When reading a document, you can figure out the misspelled words and not be bothered about every little imprecision in interpreting what is written. On the other hand, simple errors, akin to misspelled words or unclear antecedents, can completely undermine a program, rendering it senseless or causing it to go wildly wrong during execution. For example, there is no real dictionary when it comes to programming. You can define variable names containing virtually any combination of letters (upper- and lowercase), underscores, and numbers. A typographical error in a variable's name can therefore lead to unpredictable program behavior. Furthermore, computer execution speeds are becoming faster and faster, meaning that increasingly complex programs can run very quickly. For example, the program (actually groups of programs) that runs NASA's space shuttle might be comparable in size to Hugo's *Les Misérables*, but its complexity and immediate importance to the "user" far exceed that of the novel.

As a consequence, program design must be extremely structured and have the ultimate intentions of performing a specific calculation efficiently with attractive, understandable, efficient programs. Achieving these general goals means breaking the program into components, writing and testing them separately, and then merging them according to the outline. Toward this end, we stress *modular programming*. Modules can be on the scale of chapters or paragraphs and share many of the same features. They consist of a sequence of statements that by themselves express a meaningful computation. They can be merged to form larger programs by specifying what they do and how they interface to other packages of software. The analogy in prose is agreeing on the character's names and what events are to happen in each paragraph so that events happen to the right people in the right sequence once the whole is formed. Modules can be reused in two ways. As with our program from the 1960s, we would "lift" the matrix inversion routine and put a different user interface around it. We can also reuse a routine within a program several times. For example, solving the equations of space flight involves the inversion of many matrices. We would want our program to use the matrix inversion routine over and over, presenting it with a different matrix each time.

The fundamental components of good program design are

1. Problem definition, leading to a program specification;
2. Modular program design, which refines the specification;
3. Module composition, which translates specification into executable program;
4. Module and program evaluation and testing, during which you refine the program and find errors; and
5. Program documentation, which pervades all other phases.

The result of following these steps is an efficient, easy-to-use program that has a user's guide (to enable someone else run your program) and internal documentation so that other programmers can decipher the algorithm.

Today it is common in a university education to be required to learn at least one foreign language. Global interactions in business, engineering, and government make such a skill valuable to one's career. So it is in programming. One often needs to be able to read two or three programming languages – even if you compose programs in only one language. It is common for different program modules, in different languages, to be compiled separately and then brought together by a "linker" to form a single executable. When something goes wrong in such a process it is usually helpful to have a reading knowledge of the programming languages being used.

When one composes to express ideas there are, at least, two different approaches to consider: poetry and prose. Likewise, in employing programming languages to create software distinctly different approaches are available. The two most common ones are "procedural programming" and "object-oriented programming." The two approaches are conceptually

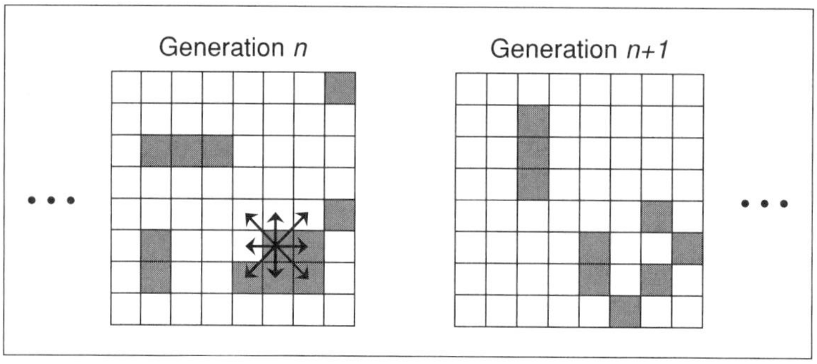

Figure 1.1: Here, the game is played on an 8×8 square array, and the filled squares indicate the presence of life. The arrows emanating from one cell radiate to its eight neighbors. The rules are applied to the *n*th generation to yield the next. The row of three filled cells becomes a column of three, for example. What is going to happen to this configuration in the next generation?

sketched in Figure 1.1. They differ in the way that the software development and maintenance are planned and implemented. Procedures may use objects, and objects usually use procedures called *methods*. Usually the object-oriented code takes more planning and is significantly larger, but it is generally accepted to be easier to maintain. Today when one can have literally millions of users active for years or decades, maintenance considerations are very important.

1.2 Problem Definition

The problem the program is to solve must be well specified. The programmer must broadly frame the program's intent and context by answering several questions.

- *What must the program accomplish?*
  From operating the space shuttle to inverting a small matrix, some thought must be given to *how* the program will do what is needed. In technical terms, we need to define the *algorithm* employed in small-scale programs. In particular, numeric programs need to consider well how calculations are performed. For example, finding the roots of a general polynomial demands a numeric (non-closed form) solution. The choice of algorithm is influenced by the variations in polynomial order and the accuracy demanded.
- *What inputs are required and in what forms?*
  Most programs interact with humans and other programs. This interaction needs to be clearly specified as to *what* format the data will take and *when* the data need to be requested or arrive.
- *What is the execution environment and what should be in the user interface?*
  Is the program a stand-alone program, calculating the quadratic formula for example, or do the results need to be plotted? In the former case, simple user input is probably all that is needed, but the programmer might want to write the program so that its key components could be used in other programs. In the latter, the program probably needs to be written so that it meshes well with some prewritten graphics environment.
- *What are the required and optional outputs, and what are their formats (printed, magnetic, graphical, audio)?*
  In many cases, output takes two forms: *interactive* and *archival*. Interactive output means that the programs results must be provided to the user or to other programs. The data

format must be defined so that the user can quickly see or hear the programs results. Archival results need to be stored on long-term media, such as disk, so that later interpretation of the file's contents is easy (recall the notion of being able to read tomorrow what is written today) and the reading process is easy.

The answers to these questions help programmers organize their thoughts and can lead to decisions about programming language and operating environment. At this point in the programming process, the programmer should know what the program is to do and for whom the program is written. We do not yet have a clear notion of how the program will accomplish these tasks; that comes down the road. This approach to program organization and design is known as *top–down* design. Here, broad program goals and context are defined first with additional detail filled in as needed. This approach contrasts with *bottom–up* design, where the detail is decided first and then merged into a functioning whole. For programming, top–design makes more sense, but you as well as professional programmers are frequently lured into writing code immediately, which is usually motivated by the desire to get something running and figure out later how to organize it all. That approach is prompted by expediency but usually winds up being more inefficient than a more considered, top–down approach that takes longer to get off the ground but has increased likelihood of working more quickly. The result of defining the programming problem is a *specification*: how the program is structured, what computations it performs, and how it should interact with the user.

An Extended Example: The Game of Life

To illustrate how to organize and write a simple program, let us structure a program that plays *The Game of Life*. Conway's "Game of Life" was popularized in Martin Gardner's Mathematical Games column in the October 1970 and February 1971 issues of *Scientific American*. This game is an example of what is known in computer science as *cellular automata*. An extensive description of the game can be found in *The Recursive Universe* by William Poundstone (Oxford University Press, 1987).

The rules of the game are quite simple. Imagine a rectangular array of square cells that are either empty (no living being present) or filled (a being lives there). As shown in Figure 1.1, each cell has eight neighboring cells. At each tick of the clock, a new generation of beings is produced according to how many neighbors surround a given cell.

- If a cell is empty, fill it if three of its neighboring cells are filled; otherwise, leave it empty.
- If a cell is filled, it
  dies of loneliness if it has zero or one neighbors,
  continues to live if it has two or three neighbors, or
  dies of overcrowding if it has more than three neighbors.

The programming task is to allow the user to "play the game" by letting him or her define initial configurations, start the program, which applies the rules and displays each generation, and stop the game at any time the user wants, returning to the initialization stage so that a new configuration can be tried. To understand the program task, we as programmers need to pose several questions, some of which might be

- What computer(s) are preferred, and what kind of display facilities do they have?
- Is the size of the array arbitrary or fixed?
- Am I the only programmer?

No matter how these questions are answered, we start by forming the program's basic outline. Here is one way we might outline the program in a procedural fashion.

1. Allow the user to initialize the rectangular array or quit the program.
2. Start the calculation of the next generation.
   (a) Apply game rules to the current array.
   (b) Generate a new array.
   (c) Display the array.
   (d) Determine whether the user wants to stop or not.
      i. If not, go back to 2a.
      ii. If so, go to step 1.

Note how the idea of reusing the portion of the program that applies game rules arises naturally. This idea is peculiar to programming languages, having no counterpart in prose (it's like being told at the end of a chapter to reread it!). This kind of *looping* behavior also occurs when we go back and allow the user to restart the program.

This kind of outline is a form of *pseudocode*:* a programming–language-like expression of how the program operates. Note that at this point, the programming process is language independent. Thus, *informal pseudocode* allows us to determine the program's broad structure. We have not yet resolved the issue of how, or if, the array should be displayed: Should it be refreshed as soon as a generation is calculated, or should we wait until a final state is reached or a step limit is exceeded? Furthermore, if calculating each generation takes a fair amount of time, our candidate program organization will not allow the user to stop the program until a generation's calculations have been finished. Consequently, we may, depending on the speed of the computer, want to limit the size of the array. A more detailed issue is how to represent the array internally. These issues can be determined later; programmers frequently make notes at this stage about how the program would behave with this structure. Informal pseudocode should remain in the final program in the form of comments.

Writing a program's outline is not a meaningless exercise. How the program will behave is determined at that point. An alternative would be to ask the user how many generations should be calculated and then calculate all generations and display the results as a movie, allowing the user to go backward, play in slow motion, freeze-frame, and so forth. Our outline will not allow such visual fun. Thus, programmers usually design several candidate program organizations, understand the consequences of each, and determine which best meets the specifications.

1.3 Modular Program Design

We now need to define what the routines are and how they are interwoven to archieve the program's goals. (We will deepen this discussion to include objects and messages when we introduce object-oriented formulations in Sec. 1.7.) What granularity – how large should a routine be – comes with programming experience and depends somewhat on the language

* The use of the word *code* is interesting here. It means program as both a noun and a verb: From the earliest days of programming, what the programmer produced was called code, and what he or she did was "code the algorithm." The origin of this word is somewhat mysterious. It may have arisen as an analogy to Morse code, which used a series of dots and dashes as an alternative to the alphabet. This code is tedious to read but ideal for telegraphic transmission. A program is an alternate form of an algorithm better suited to computation.

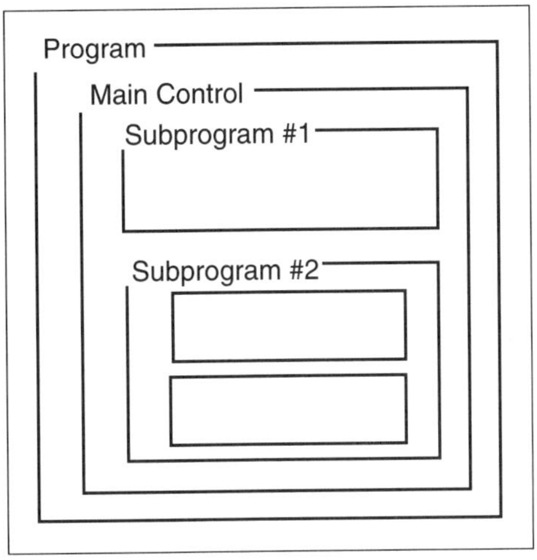

Figure 1.2: Modular program organization relies on self-contained routines in which the passage of data (or messages) from one to the other is very well defined and each routine's (or objects) role in the program becomes evident.

used to express it. A program typically begins with a main segment that controls or directs the solution of the problem by dividing it into subtasks (see Figure 1.2). Each of these may well be decomposed into other routines. This stepwise refinement continues as long as necessary and as long as it benefits program clarity and efficiency. This *modular program design* is the key feature of modern programming design practice. Furthermore, routines can be tested individually and replaced or rewritten as needed. Before actually writing each routine, a job known in computer circles as the *implementation*, the program's organization can be studied: Will the whole satisfy design specifications? Will the program execute efficiently? As the implementation proceeds, each routine's *interface* is defined: How does it interact with its master – the routine that called it – and how are data exchanged between the two? In some languages, this interface can be *prototyped*: the routine's interface – what it expects and what values it calculates – can be defined and the whole program merged and compiled to check for consistency without performing any calculations. In small programs, where you can have these routine definitions easily fitting onto one page, this prototyping can almost be performed visually. In complex programs, where there may be hundreds or thousands of routines, such prototyping really pays off. Once the interfaces begin to form, we ask whether they make sense: Do they exchange information efficiently? Does each routine have the information it needs, or should the program be reorganized so that data exchange can be accomplished more efficiently?

From another viewpoint, you should develop a programming style that "hedges your bets:" programs should be written in such a way that allows their components to be used in a variety of contexts. Again, using a modular programming style, the fundamental components of the calculation should be expressed as a series of subroutines or functions, the interweaving of which is controlled by a main program that reads the input information and produces the output. A modular program can have its components extracted and used in other programs (program reuse) or interfaced to environments. So-called monolithic programs, which tend not to use routines and express the calculation as a single, long-winded program, should not be written.

We emphasize that this modular design process proceeds without actually writing program statements. We use a programming-like language known as *formal pseudocode* to express in prose what routines call others and how. This prose might reexpress a graphic representation of program organization such as that shown in Figure 1.2. In addition, expressing the program's design in pseudocode eases the transition to program composition, the actual programming process. The components of formal pseudocode at this point are few:

- *comments* that we allow to include the original outline and to describe computational details;
- *functions* that express each routine, whether it be computational or concerned with the user interface;
- *conditionals* that express changing the flow of a program; and
- *loops* that express iteration.

Comments. A comment begins with a comment character, which in our pseudocode we take to be the exclamation point `!`, and ends when the line ends. Comments can consume an entire line or the right portion of some line.

```
! This is a comment: you can read it, but the computer won't
statements
statement ! From the comment character to end of this line is a comment
statements
```

The statements cited in the lines above share the status of the sentence that characterizes most written languages. They are made up of components specific to the syntax of the programming language in use. For example, most programming books begin with a program that does nothing but print "Hello world" on the screen (or other output device). The pseudocode for this might have the following form:

```
! if necessary, include the device library
initiate my program, say main
    send the character string ''Hello world'' to the output device library
terminate my program
```

Figure 1.3 illustrates this in three common languages beginning with F90. At this point it is possible to say we are multilingual in computer languages. Here, too, we may note that, unlike the other two languages shown, in Fortran, when we begin a specific type of software construct, we almost always explicitly declare where we are ending its scope. Here the construct pair was `program` and `end program`, but the same style holds true for `if` and `end if` pairs, for example. All languages have rules and syntax to terminate the scope of some construct, but when several types of different constructs occur in the same program segment, it may be unclear in which order they are terminating.

Functions. To express a program's organization through its component routines we use the notation of mathematical *functions*. Each program routine accepts inputs expressed as arguments of a function, performs its calculations, and returns the computational results as functional values.

```
output_1 = routine (input_1,...,input_m)
```

or

```
call routine (input_1,..., input_m, output_1,..., output_n)
```

```
!  This is a comment line in Fortran 90

program  main                    ! a program called main
                                 ! begin the main program
  print *,"Hello, world"         ! * means default format
end program main                 ! end the main program
```

```
// This is a comment line in C++
#include <iostream.h>    // standard input output library

main ()                                   // a program called main
                                          // begin the main program
  cout << "Hello, world" << endl ;        // endl means new line
  return 0;                               // needed by some compilers
                                          // end the main program
```

```
%  This is a comment line in MATLAB

function main ()                 %  a program called main
                                 %  begin the main program
  disp ('Hello, world');         %  display the string
                                 %  end the main program
```

Figure 1.3: 'Hello World' program and comments in three languages.

In Fortran, a routine evaluating a single-output object, as in the first style, is called a *function* and, otherwise, it is called a *subroutine*. Other languages usually use the term function in both cases. Each routines's various inputs and results are represented by *variables*, which, in sharp contrast to mathematical variables, have text-like names that indicate what they contain. These names contain no spaces but may contain several words. There are two conventions for variable names containing two or more words: either words are joined by the underbar character "_" (like `next_generation`) or each word begins with an uppercase letter (like `NextGeneration`). The results of a routines's computation are always indicated by a sequence of variables on the left side of the equals sign =. The use of an equals sign does not mean mathematical equality; it is a symbol in our pseudocode that means "assign a routines's results to the variables (in order) listed on the left."

Conditionals. To create something other than a sequential execution of routines, conditionals form a test on the values of one or more variables and continue execution at one point or another depending on whether the test was true or false. That is usually done with the `if` statement. It either performs the instruction(s) that immediately follow (after the `then` keyword) if some condition is valid (like `x> 0`) or those that follow the `else` statement if the condition is not true.

```
if test then
  statement group A ! executed if true
else
  statement group B ! executed if false
end if
```

The test here can be very complicated but is always based on values of variables. Parentheses should be used to clarify exactly what the test is. For example,

```
((x > 0) and (y = 2))
```

One special statement frequently found in `if` statements is `stop`: This command means to stop or abort the program – usually with a fatal error message.

Conditionals allow the program to execute nonsequentially (the *only* mode allowed by statements). Furthermore, program execution order can be data-dependent. In this way, how the program behaves – what output it produces and how it computes the output – depends on what data, or messages, it is given. *This means that exact statement execution order is determined by the data, messages, or both, and the programmer – not just the programmer.* It is this aspect of programming languages that distinguishes them from written or spoken languages. An analogy might be chapters in a novel being read in the order specified by the reader's birthday; what that order might be is determined by the novelist through logical constructs. The tricky part is that, in programming languages, each execution order must make sense and not lead to inconsistencies or, at worst, errors: the novel must make sense in all the ways the novelist allows. This data- and message-dependent execution order can be applied at all programming levels from routine execution to statements. Returning to our analogy with the novel, we recall that chapter (routine) and sentence (statement) order depend on the reader's birthday. Such complexity in prose has little utility but does in programming. How else can a program be written that informs the user on what day of the week and under what phase of the moon he or she was born given the birth date?

Loops. Looping constructs in our formal pseudocode take the form of *do loops*, where the keyword do is paired with the key phrase end do to mean that the expressions and routine invocations contained therein are calculated in order (from top to bottom), then calculated again starting with the first, then again, then again, . . . , forever. The loop ceases only when we explicitly exit it with the `exit` command. The pseudocode loop shown below on the left has the execution history shown on the right.

```
do
  y = routine_1(x)            y = routine_1(x)
  z = routine_2(y)            z = routine_2(y)
  x = routine_3(z)            x = routine_3(z) [let's say x=-1]
  if x > 0 then               y = routine_1(x)
    exit                      z = routine_2(y)
  end if                      x = routine_3(z) [let's say x=1]
end do                        [program ends]
```

Infinite loops occur when the Boolean expression always evaluates to true; these are usually not what the programmer intended and represent one type of program error – a "bug."* The constructs enclosed by the loop can be anything: statements, logical constructs, and other loops! Because of this variety, programs can exhibit extremely complex behaviors. How a program behaves depends entirely on the programmer and how his or her definition of the program flows based on user-supplied data and messages. The pseudocode loops are defined in Table 1.1.

* This term was originated by Grace Hopper, one of the first programmers. In the early days of computers, they were partially built with mechanical devices known as relays. A relay is a mechanical switch that controls which way electric current flows: the realization of the logical construct in programming languages. One day, a previously working program stopped being so. Investigation revealed that an insect had crawled into the computer and had become lodged in a relay's contacts. She then coined the term "bug" to refer not only to such hardware failures but to software ones as well since the user becomes upset no matter which occurs.

Table 1.1: Pseudocode Loop Constructs

Loop	Pseudocode

Indexed loop	`do index = b,i,e`
	  `statements`
	`end do`

Pretest loop	`while (test)`
	  `statements`
	`end while`

Posttest loop	`do`
	  `statements`
	  `if (test) exit`
	`end do`

1.4 Program Composition

Composing a program is the process of expressing or translating the program design into computer language(s) selected for the task. Whereas the program design can often be expressed as a broad outline, each routine's algorithm must be expressed in complete detail. This writing process elaborates the formal pseudocode and contains more explicit statements that more greatly resemble generic program statements.

Generic programming language elements fall into five basic categories: the four we had before – comments, loops, conditionals, and functions – and statements. We will expand the variety of comments, conditionals, loops, and functions/subroutines that define routines and their interfaces. The new element is the statement, the workhorse of programming. It is the statement that actually performs a concrete computation. In addition to expanding the repertoire of programming constructs for formal pseudocode, we also introduce what these constructs are in MATLAB, Fortran, and C++. As we shall see, formal pseudocode parallels these languages; the translation from pseudocode to executable program is generally easy.

1.4.1 Comments

Comments need no further elaboration for pseudocode. However, programmers are encouraged to make heavy use of comments.

1.4.2 Statements

Calculation is expressed by *statements*, which share the structure (and the status) of the sentence that characterizes virtually all written language. Statements are always executed one after the other as written. A statement in most languages has a simple, well-defined structure common to them all such as

```
variable = expression
```

Statements are intended to bear a great resemblance to mathematical equations. This analogy with mathematics can appear confusing to the first-time programmer. For example, the statement `a = a+1`, which means "increment the variable `a` by one" makes perfect sense as a programming statement but no sense as an algebraic equality since it seems to say that $0 = 1$. Once you become more fluent in programming languages, what is mathematics and what is programming become easily apparent. Statements are said to be *terminated* when a certain character is encountered by the interpreter or the compiler. In Fortran, the termination character is a carriage return or a semicolon (`;`). In C++, all statements must be terminated with a semicolon or a comma; carriage returns do not terminate statements. MATLAB statements may end with a semicolon '`;`' to suppress display of the calculated expression's value. Most statements in MATLAB programs end thusly.

Sometimes, statements become quite long, becoming unreadable. Two solutions to improve clarity can be used: decompose the expression into simpler expressions or use *continuation markers* to allow the statement to span more than one line of text. The first solution requires you to use intermediate variables, which only results in program clutter. Multiline statements can be broken at convenient arithmetic operators, and this approach is generally preferred. In C++, there is no continuation character; statements can span multiple text lines and end only when the semicolon is encountered. In MATLAB, the continuation character sequence comprises three periods '`...`' placed at the end of each text line (before the carriage return or comment character). In Fortran, a statement is continued to the next line when an ampersand `&` is the last character on the line.

Variables. A *variable* is a named sequence of memory locations to which values can be assigned. As such, every variable has an address in memory, which most languages conceal from the programmer so as to present the programmer with a *storage model* independent of the architecture of the computer running the program. Program variables correspond roughly to mathematical variables that can be integer, real, or, complex-valued. Program variables can be more general than this, being able in some languages to have values equal to a user-defined data type or object which, in turn, contains sequences of other variables. Variables in all languages have *names*: a sequence of alphanumeric characters that cannot begin with a number. Thus, `a`, `A`, `a2`, and `a9b` are feasible variable names (i.e., the interpreter or compiler will not complain about these), whereas `3d` is not. Since programs are meant to be read by humans as well as interpreters and compilers, such names may not lead to program clarity even if they are carefully defined and documented. The compiler and interpreter do not care whether humans can read a program easily or not, but you should: *Use variable names that express what the variables represent.* For example, use `force` as a name rather than `f`; use `i`, `j`, and `k` for indices rather than `ii` or `i1`.

In most languages, variables have *type*: the kind of quantity stored in them. Frequently occurring data types are integer and floating point, for example. Integer variables would be chosen if the variable were only used as an array index; floating point if the variable might have a fractional part.

In addition to having a name, type, and address, each variable has a value of the proper type. The value should be assigned before the variable is used elsewhere. Compilers should indicate an error if a variable is used before it has been assigned a value. Some languages allow variables to have aliases, which are usually referred to as "pointers" or "references." Most higher-level languages also allow programmers to create "user-defined" data types.

Assignment Operator. The symbol = in a statement means *assignment* of the expression into the variable provided on the left. This symbol does not mean algebraic equality; it means that once `expression` is computed, its value is stored in the `variable`. Thus, statements that make programming sense, like `a=a+1`, make no mathematical sense because '=' means different things in the two contexts. Fortran 90 and other languages allow the user to extend the meaning of the assignment symbol (=) to other operations. Such advanced features are referred to as "operator overloading."

Expressions. Just as in mathematics, expressions in programming languages can have a complicated structure. Most encountered in engineering programs amount to a mathematical expression involving variables, numbers, and functions of variables, numbers, or both. For example, the following are all valid statements:

```
A = B
x = sin (2*z)
force = G * mass1 * mass2 / (r*r)
```

Thus, mathematical expressions obey the usual mathematical conventions but with one added complexity: vertical position cannot be used help express what the calculation is; program expressions have only one dimension. For example, the notation $\frac{a}{b}c$ clearly expresses to you how to perform the calculation. However, the one-dimensional equivalent obtained by smashing this expression onto one line becomes ambiguous: Does a/bc mean divide a by b then multiply by c or divide a by the product of b and c? This ambiguity is relieved in program expressions in two ways. The first, the human-oriented way, demands the use of parentheses – grouping constructs – to clarify what is being meant, as in $(a/b)c$. The language-oriented way makes use of *precedence rules*: What an expression means is inferred from a set of rules that specify what operations take effect first. In our example, because division is stronger than multiplication, a/bc means $(a/b)c$. Most people find that frequent reliance on precedence rules leads to programs that take a long time to decipher; the compiler/interpreter is "happy" either way.

Expressions make use of the common arithmetic and relational operators. They may also involve function evaluations; the `sin` function was called in the second expression given in the previous example. Programming expressions can be as complicated as the arithmetic or Boolean algebra ones they emulate.

1.4.3 Flow Control

If a program consisted of a series of statements, statements would be executed one after the other in the order they were written. Such is the structure of all prose, where the equivalent of a statement is the sentence. Programming languages differ markedly from prose in that statements can be meaningfully executed over and over with details of each execution differing each time (the value of some variable might be changed) or some statements skipped with statement ordering dependent on which statements were executed previously or upon external events (the user clicked the mouse). With this extra variability, programming languages can be more difficult for the human to trace program execution than the effort it takes to read a novel. In written languages, sentences can be incredibly complex, much more so than program statements; in programming, the sequencing of statements – program flow – can be more complex.

The basic flow control constructs present in virtually all programming languages are *loops* – repetitive execution of a series of statements – and *conditionals* – diversions around statements.

Loops. Historically, the loop has been a major tool in designing the flow control of a procedure, and one would often code a loop segment without giving it a second thought. Today, massively parallel computers are being widely used, and one must learn to avoid coding explicit loops in order to take advantage of the power of such machines. Later we will review which intrinsic tools are included in F90 for use on parallel (and serial) computers to offer improved efficiency over explicit loops.

The loop allows the programmer to repeat a series of statements, and parameter – the *loop variable* – takes on a different value for each repetition. The loop variable can be an integer or a floating-point number. Loops can be used to control iterative algorithms such as the Newton–Raphson algorithm for finding solutions to nonlinear equations, to accumulate results for a sequential calculation, or merely to repeat a program phrase such as awaiting for the next typed input. Loops are controlled by a `logical expression`, which when evaluated to `true` allows the loop to execute another iteration and when false terminates the loop and commences program execution with the statement immediately following those statements enclosed within the loop.

There are three basic kinds of looping constructs, the choice of which is determined by the kind of iterative behavior most appropriate to the computation. The *indexed loop* occurs most frequently in programs. Here, one loop variable varies across a range of values. In pseudocode, the index's value begins at b and increments each time through the loop by `i`; the loop ends when the index exceeds e. For example,

```
do j = b, e, i
```

or through the default increment of unity:

```
do j = b, e
```

As an example of an indexed loop, let us explore summing the series of numbers stored in the array A. If we know the number of elements in the array when we write the program, the sum can be calculated explicitly without using a loop as follows:

$$\text{sum} = A_1 + A_2 + A_3 + A_4$$

However, we have already said that our statements must be on a single line, and so we need a way to represent the subscript attached to each number. We develop the convention that a subscript is placed inside parentheses like

```
sum = A(1) + A(2) + A(3) + A(4)
```

Such programs are very inflexible, and this *hard-wired* programming style is discouraged. For example, suppose in another problem the array contains 1,000 elements. With an indexed loop, a more flexible, easier to read program can be obtained. Here, the index assumes a succession of values, its value tested against the termination value *before* the enclosed statements are executed with the loop terminating once this test fails to be true. The following generic indexed loop also sums array elements but in a much more flexible, concise way.

```
sum = 0
for i = 1, n
  sum = sum + A(i)
end for
```

Here, the variable n does *not* need to be known when the program is written; this value can wait until the program executes and can be established by the user or after data are read.

In F90 the extensive support for matrix expressions allows *implicit loops*. For example, consider the calculation of $\sum_{i=1}^{N} x_i y_i$. The language provides at least three ways of performing this calculation. If it is assumed the vectors x and y are column vectors,

```
1.  sum_xy = 0
    N = size (x)
    do i = 1,N
       sum_xy = sum_xy + x(i)*y(i)
    end do
```

```
2.   sum_xy = sum (x*y)
```

```
3.   sum_xy = dot_product (x,y)
```

The first method is based on the basic loop construct and yields the slowest-running program of the three versions. In fact, avoiding the do statement by using implicit loops will almost always lead to faster running programs. The second and third statements employ intrinsic functions, operators designed for arrays, or both. In many circumstances, calculation efficiency and clarity of expression must be balanced. In practice, it is usually necessary to set aside memory to hold subscripted arrays, such as `x` and `y` above, before they can be referenced or used.

Conditionals. Conditionals test the veracity of logical expressions and execute blocks of statements accordingly (see Table 1.2). The most basic operation occurs if we want to execute a series of statements when a logical expression, say `test`, evaluates to `true`. We call that a simple if conditional; the beginning and end of the statements to be executed when `test` evaluates to `true` are enclosed by special delimiters, which differ according to language. When only one statement is needed, C++ and Fortran allow that one statement to end the line that begins with the if conditional. If you want one group of statements to be executed when `test` is `true` and another set to be executed when `false`, you use the if-else construct. When you want to test a series of logical expressions that are not necessarily complementary, the nested-if construct allows for essentially arbitrarily complex structure to be defined. In such cases, the logical tests can interlock, thereby creating programs that are quite difficult to read. Here is where program comments become essential. For example, suppose you want to sum only the positive numbers less than or equal to 10 in a given sequence. Let us assume the entire sequence is stored in array A. In informal pseudocode, we might write

```
loop across A
  if A(i) > 0 and A(i) < = 10 add to sum
end of loop
```

More formally, this program fragment as a complete pseudocode would be

Table 1.2: Syntax of Pseudocode Conditionals

Conditional	Pseudocode
if	`if (test) statement`

if	`if (test) then`
	  statements
	`end if`

if-else	`if (test) then`
	  statements A
	`else`
	  statements B
	`end if`

nested if	`if (test1) then`
	  statements A
	  `if (test2) then`
	    statements B
	  `end if % end of test2`
	`end if`

```
sum = 0
do i=1, n
  if (A(i) > 0) & (A(i) <= 10)
    sum = sum + A(i)
  end if
end do
```

Several points are illustrated by this pseudocode example. First of all, the statements that can be included with a loop can be arbitrary – that is, composed of simple statements, loops, and conditionals in any order. This same generality applies to statements within a conditional as well. Secondly, logical expressions can themselves be quite complicated. Finally, note how each level of statements in the program is indented, visually indicating the subordination of statements within higher-level loops or conditionals. This stylistic practice lies at the heart of *structured programming*: explicit indication of each statement within the surrounding hierarchy. In modern programming, the structured approach has become the standard because it leads to greater clarity of expression, allowing others to understand the program more quickly and the programmer to find bugs more readily. Employing this style only requires the programmer to use the space key liberally when typing the program. Since sums are computed so often you might expect that a language would provide an intrinsic function to compute it. For F90 and MATLAB you would be correct.

1.4.4 Functions

Functions, which define subprograms having a well-defined interface to other parts of the program, are an essential part of programming languages. For, if properly developed, these functions can be included in future programs, and they allow several programmers to work on complex programs. The function takes an ordered sequence of messages, objects, or variables as its arguments and returns to the calling program a value (or set of values) that can be assigned to an object or variable. Familiar examples of a function are the mathematical ones: the `sin` function takes a real-valued argument, uses this value to calculate the trigonometric sine, and returns that value, which can be assigned to a variable.

```
y = sin (x)
```

Note that the argument need not be a variable: a number can be explicitly provided or an expression can be used. Thus, `sin (2.3)` and `sin (2*cos (x))` are all valid. Functions may require more than one argument. For example, the `atan2` function, which computes the arctangent function in such a way that the quadrant of the calculated angle is unambiguous, needs the `x` and `y` components of the triangle.

```
z = atan2 (x, y)
```

Note that the order of the arguments – the `x` component must be the first – and the number of arguments – both `x` and `y` are needed – matter for all functions: The calling program's argument ordering and number must agree with those imposed by the function's definition. Said another way, the interface between the two must agree. This is analogous to the relationship between plugs and electric sockets in the home: a three-prong plug will not fit into a two-hole socket, and, if you have a two-prong plug, you must plug it in the right way. A function is usually defined separately outside the body of any program or other function. We call a program's extent its *scope*. In MATLAB, a program's scope is equivalent to what is in a file; in C and C++, scope is defined by brace pairs; and in Fortran, scope equals what occurs between function declaration and its corresponding `end` statement. Variables are also defined within a program's and a function's scope. What this means is that a variable named x defined within a function is available to all statements occurring within that function, and different functions can use the same variable name without any conflict occurring. What this means is that two functions `f1` and `f2` can each make use of a variable named x, and the value of x depends on which function is being referred to. In technical terms, the scope of every variable is limited to its defining function. At first, this situation may seem terribly confusing ("There are two variables both of which are named x?"); further thought brings the realization that this convention is what you want. Because each function is to be a routine – a program having a well-defined interface – execution of the function's internal statements must not depend on the program that uses it. This convention becomes especially important when different people write the programs or functions. Thus, such local variables – those defined locally within a function – do not conflict, and they are stored in different memory locations by the compiler or interpreter.

This limited scope convention can be countermanded when you explicitly declare variables to be *global*. Such variables are now potentially available to all functions, and each function cannot define a variable having the same name. For example, you may well want a variable pointedly named `pi` to be available to all functions; you can do so by declaring it to be a global variable. To demonstrate scope, consider the following simple example. Here, we want to clip the values stored in the array x and store the results in the array y.

Main Pseudocode Program

```
! Clip the elements of an array
limit = 3
do i=1,n
  y(i) = clip(x(i), limit)
end do
```

Function Pseudocode Definition

```
! function clip(x, edge)
! x - input variable
! edge - location of breakpoint
function clip(x, edge)
if abs(x) > edge then
   y = sign (x) * edge
else
   y = x
end if
end
```

The clipping function has the generic form show in Figure 1.4. Thus, values of the argument that are less than L in magnitude are not changed, and those exceeding this limit are set equal to the limiting value. In the program example, note that the name of the array in the calling program – x – is the same as the argument's name used in the definition of the function. Within the scope of a program or function, an array and a scalar variable cannot have the same name. In our case, because each variable's scope is limited to the function or program definition, no conflict occurs: Each is well defined, and the meaning should be unambiguous. Also note that the second argument has a different name in the program than

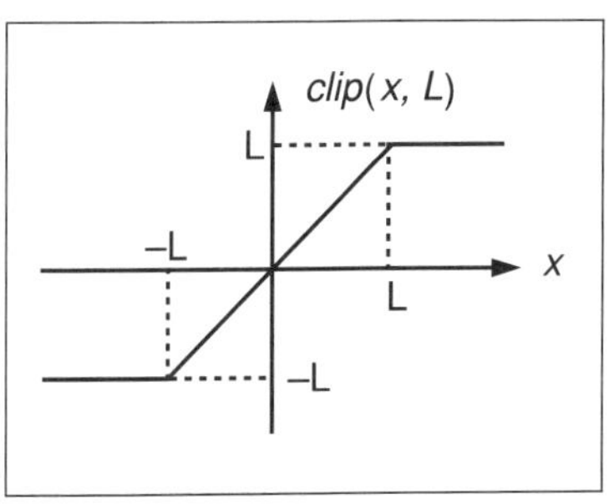

Figure 1.4: Input–output relationship for the function clip(x). So long as $|x| < L$, this function equals its argument; for larger values, the output equals the clipping constant L no matter how large the input might be.

in the function. No matter how the arguments are defined, we say that they are *passed* to the function with the function's variables set equal to values specified in the calling program. These interface rules allow the function to be used in other programs, which means that we can reuse functions whenever we like!

1.4.5 Modules

Another important programming concept is that of packaging a group of related routines, selective variables, or both into a larger programming entity. In the Ada language they are called *packages*, whereas C++ and MATLAB call them *classes*. The F90 language has a generalization of this concept that it calls a *module*. As we will see later, the F90 module includes the functionality of the C++ classes as well as other uses such as defining global constants. Therefore, we will find the use of F90 modules critical to our object-oriented programming goals. In that context modules provide us with the means to take several routines related to a specific data type and to encapsulate them into a larger programming unit that has the potential to be reused for more than one application.

1.4.6 Dynamic Memory Management

From the very beginning, several decades ago, there was a clear need to be able to allocate and deallocate segments of memory dynamically for use by a program. The initial standards for Fortran did not allow for this. It was necessary to invoke machine language programs to accomplish that task or to write tools to manage arrays directly by defining "pseudo-pointers" to move things around manually in memory or to overwrite space that was no longer needed. It was very disappointing that the F77 standard failed to offer that ability, although several "nonstandard" compilers offered such an option. Beginning with the F90 standard a full set of dynamic memory management abilities is now available within Fortran. Dynamic memory management is mainly needed for arrays and pointers. Both of these will be considered later with a whole chapter devoted to arrays. Both of these entities can be declared as ALLOCATABLE, and later one will ALLOCATE and then DEALLOCATE them. There are also new "automatic arrays" that have the necessary memory space supplied and then freed as needed.

Pointers are often used in "data structures," abstract data types, and objects. To check on the status of such features one can invoke the ALLOCATED intrinsic and use ASSOCIATED to check on the status of pointers and apply NULLIFY to pointers that need to be freed or initialized. Within F90 allocatable arrays cannot be used in the definitions of derived types, abstract data types, or objects. However, allocatable pointers to arrays can be used in such definitions. To assist in creating efficient executable codes, entities that might be pointed at by a pointer must have the TARGET attribute.

Numerous examples of dynamic memory management will be seen later. Specific addition discussion will be given in Chapter 9. Persons who write compilers suggest that, in any language, it is wise to deallocate dynamic memory in the reverse order of its creation. The F90 language standard does not require that procedure, but you see that advice followed in most of the examples.

1.5 Program Evaluation and Testing

Your fully commented program, written with the aid of an editor, must now come alive and be translated into another language that more closely matches computer instructions; it must be executed or run. Statements expressed in MATLAB, Fortran, or C++ may not directly correspond to computational instructions. However, the Fortran syntax was designed to match mathematical expressions more clearly. These languages are designed to allow humans to define computations easily and also allow easy translation. Writing programs in these languages provides some degree of *portability*: a program can be executed on very different computers without modification. So-called assembly languages allow more direct expression of program execution but are very computer specific. Programmers that write in assembly language must worry about the exquisite details of computer organization – so much so that writing of what the computation is doing takes much longer. What they produce might run more rapidly than the same computation expressed in Fortran, for example, but no portability results and programs become incredibly hard to debug.

Programs become executable machine instructions in two basic ways. They are either *interpreted* or *compiled*. In the first case, an interpreter reads your program and translates it to executable instructions "on the fly." Because interpreters essentially examine programs on a line-by-line basis, they usually allow instructions and accept typed user instructions as well as fully written programs. MATLAB is an example of an interpreter.* It can accept typed commands created as the user thinks of them (plot a graph, see that a parameter must have been typed incorrectly, change it, and replot, for example) or entire programs. Because interpreters examine programs locally (line-by-line), program execution tends to be slower than when a compiler is used.

Compilers are programs that take your program in its entirety and produce an executable version of it. Compiler output is known as an *executable* file that, in UNIX for example, can become a command essentially indistinguishable from others that are available. The C++ language is an example of one that is frequently compiled rather than interpreted. Compilers will produce much more efficient (faster running) programs than interpreters, but if you find an error, you must edit and recompile before you can attempt execution again. Because compilation takes time, this cycle can be time-consuming if the program is large.

Interpreters are themselves executable files written in compiled languages: MATLAB is written in C. Executable programs produced by compilers are stand-alone programs: everything (user input and output, file reading, etc.) must be handled by the user's program. In an interpreter, you can supplement a program's execution by typed instructions. For example, in an interpreter you can type a simple command to make the variable `a` equal to 1; in a compiled program, you must include a program that asks for the value of `a`. Consequently, users frequently write programs in the context of an interpreter, understand how to make the program better by interacting with it, and then reexpress it in a compiled language.

Interpreters and compilers make extensive use of what are known as *library* commands or functions. A natural example of a library function is the `sin` function: users typically do not want to program the computation of the trigonometric sine function explicitly. Instead, they want to be able to pull it "off the shelf" and use as need be. Library modules are just programs written in a computer language one would write. Consequently, both interpreters and compilers allow user programs to become part of the library, which is usually written by many programmers over a long period. It is through modules available in a library that programming teams cooperate. Library modules tend to be more extensive and do more things in an interpreter. For example, MATLAB provides a program that produces pseudo-three-dimensional plots of functions. Such routines usually do not come with a compiler but may be purchased separately from graphics programming specialists. For compiled languages, we

* This statement is only partially true. MATLAB does have some features of a compiler such as looking ahead to determine if interface errors exist with respect to functions called by the main program.

refer to *linking* the library routines to the user's program (in interpreters, this happens as a matter of course). A linker is a program that takes modules produced by the compiler, be they yours or others, associates the modules, and produces the executable file we mentioned earlier. Most C++ compilers "hide" the linking step from you; you may think you are typing just the command to compile the program, but it is actually performing that step for you. When you are compiling a module not intended for stand-alone execution, a compiler option that you type can prevent the compiler from performing the linking step.

Debugging is the process of discovering and removing program errors. Two main types of errors occur in writing programs: what we would generally term "typos" and what are design errors. The first kind may readily be found (where is the function `sni`?) or more subtle (you type `aa` instead of `a` for a variable's name and `aa` also exists!). The second kind of error can be hard or subtle to find. The main components of this process are

1. Search the program module by eye as you do a "mental run through" of its task. This kind of error searching begins when you first think about program organization and continues as you refine the program. Why write a program that is logically flawed?
2. If written in a compiled language, compile the program to find syntax errors or warnings about unused or undefined variables. If in an interpreted language, attempt preliminary execution to obtain similar error messages. Linking can also locate modules or libraries that are improperly referenced.
3. Running the executable file with typical data sets often causes the program to abort – a harsh word that expresses the situation in which the program goes crazy and ceases to behave – and the system to supply an error message such as division by zero. Error messages *may* help locate the programming error.

Easy errors to find are *syntactic* errors: You have violated the language's rules of what a well-formed program must be. Usually, the interpreter or compiler complains bitterly on encountering a syntax error. Compilers find these at compile time (when the program is compiled), interpreters at run time. Design errors are only revealed when we supply the program with data. The programmer should design test data that exercise each of the program's valid operations. Invalid user input (asking for the logarithm of a negative number, for example) should be caught by the program and warning messages sent to the user.

The previous description of generic programming languages indicates why finding bugs can be complicated. Programs can exhibit very complex behaviors, and tracing incorrect behaviors can be correspondingly difficult. One often hears the (true) statement, "Computers do what we say, not what we want." Users frequently want computers to be smart, fixing obvious design (mental) errors because they obviously conflict with what we want. However, this situation is much like what the novelist faces. Inexact meaning can confuse the reader; he or she does not have a direct pathway to the novelist's mind. As opposed to the novelist, extensive testing of your program can detect such errors and make your program approach perfection. Many operating systems supply interactive *debugger* programs that can trace the execution of a program in complete detail. They can display the values of any variable, stop at selected positions for evaluation, execute parts of the code in a statement-by-statement fashion, and so forth. These can be very helpful in finding difficult-to-locate bugs, but they still cannot read your mind.

Be that as it may, what can the programmer do when the program compiles (no syntactic errors) and does not cause system error messages (no dividing by zero) but the results are not correct? The simplest approach is to include extra statements in the program, referred to as debugging statements, that display (somewhat verbosely) values of internal variables.

For example, in a loop you would print the value of the loop index and all variables that the loop might be affecting. Because this output can be voluminous, the most fruitful approach is to debug smaller problems. With this debugging information, you can usually figure out the error, correct it, and change the comments accordingly. Without debugging, your program and internal documentation are unsynchronized.

Once the program is debugged, you could delete the added debugging statements. A better approach is just to hide them. You can do this two ways: comment them out or encase them in a conditional that is true when the program is in "debugging mode." The commenting approach completely removes the debugging statements from the program execution stream and allows you to put them back easily if further program elaborations result in errors. The use of conditionals does put an overhead on computational efficiency, but usually a small one.

1.6 Program Documentation

Comments inside a program are intended to help you and others understand program design and how it is organized. Frequently, comments describe what each variable means, how program execution is to proceed, and what each module's interface might be (what are the expected inputs and their formats and what outputs are produced). Program comments occur in the midst of the program's source and temporarily interrupt the highly restricted syntax of most programming languages. Comments are entirely ignored by the interpreter or compiler and are allowed to enhance program clarity for humans.

Documentation includes program comments but also external prose that describes what the program does, how the user interface controls program behavior, and what the output means. Making an executable program available to users does not help them understand how to use it. In UNIX, all provided commands are accompanied by what are referred to as *manual pages*: concise descriptions of what the program does, all user options, and descriptions of what error messages mean. Programs are useless without such documentation. Many programs provide such documentation whenever the user types something that clearly indicates a lack of knowledge about how to use the program. This kind of documentation must also be supplemented by prose a user can read. Professional programmers frequently write the documentation as the program is being designed. This simultaneous development of the program and documentation of how it is used often uncover user-interface design flaws.

1.7 Object-Oriented Formulations

The discussion above follows the older programming style in which the emphasis is placed on the procedures that a subprogram is to apply to the supplied data. Thus, it is referred to as *procedural programming*. The alternate approach focuses on the data and their supporting functions and is known as an *object-oriented* approach; it is the main emphasis of this work. It also generalizes the concept of data types and is usually heavily dependent on user-defined data types and their extension to abstract data types. These concepts are sketched in Figure 1.5.

The process of creating an object-oriented (OO) formulation involves at least three stages: object-oriented analysis (OOA), object-oriented design (OOD), and object-oriented programming (OOP). Many books and articles have been written on each of these three subjects. See, for example, the works of Coad and Yourdon [9], Filho and Devloo [15], Graham [19], Mossberg, Otto, and Thune [29], Meyer [28], Norton, Szymanski, and Decyk

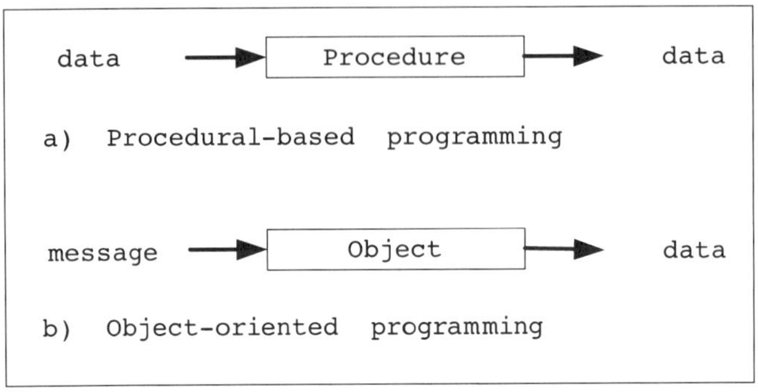

Figure 1.5: Two approaches to programming.

[32], and Rumbaugh et al. [36]. Formal graphical standards for representing the results of OOA and OOD have been established and are widely used in the literature [9]. Here the main emphasis will be placed on OOP on the assumption that the two earlier stages have been completed. In an effort to give some level of completeness, summaries

Table 1.3: OO Analysis Summary

Find objects and classes:

- Create an abstraction of the problem domain.
- Give attributes, behaviors, classes, and objects meaningful names.
- Identify structures pertinent to the system's complexity and responsibilities.
- Observe information needed to interact with the system as well as information to be stored.
- Look for information reuse: are there multiple structures; can subsystems be inherited?

Define the attributes:

- Select meaningful names.
- Describe the attribute and any constraints.
- What knowledge does it possess or communicate?
- Put it in the type or class that best describes it.
- Select accessibility as public or private.
- Identify the default and lower and upper bounds.
- Identify the different states it may hold.
- Note items that can either be stored or recomputed.

Define the behavior:

- Give the behaviors meaningful names.
- What questions should each be able to answer?
- What services should it provide?
- Which attribute components should it access?
- Define its accessibility (public or private).
- Define its interface prototype.
- Define any input–output interfaces.
- Identify a constructor with error checking to supplement the intrinsic constructor.
- Identify a default constructor.

Diagram the system:

- Employ an OO graphical representation such as the Coad–Yourdon method [9] or its extension by Graham [19].

Table 1.4: OO Design Summary

- Improve and add to the OOA results during OOD.
- Divide the member functions into constructors, accessors, agents, and servers.
- Design the human interaction components.
- Design the task management components.
- Design the data management components.
- Identify operators to be overloaded.
- Identify operators to be defined.
- Design the interface prototypes for member functions and for operators.
- Design code for reuse through "kind of" and "part of" hierarchies.
- Identify base classes from which other classes are derived.
- Establish the exception-handling procedures for all possible errors.

of OOA and OOD procedures are given in Tables 1.3 and 1.4, respectively. Having completed OOA and OOD studies one must select a language to actually implement the design. More than 100 objected-oriented languages are in existence and use today. They include such "pure" OO languages as Crisp, Eiffel [39], Rexx, Simula, Smalltalk and "hybrid" OO languages like C++, F90, Object Pascal, and so forth. In which of them should you invest your time? To get some insight into answers to this question, we should study the advice of some of the recognized leaders in the field. In his 1988 book on OO software construction B. Meyer [28] listed seven steps necessary to achieve object-orientedness in an implementation language. They are summarized in Table 1.5, and are all found to exist in F90 and F95. Thus, we proceed with F90 as our language

Table 1.5: Seven Steps to Object-Orientedness [28]

1. Object-based modular structure :
   - Systems are modularized on the basis of their data structure (in F90).
2. Data Abstraction :
   - Objects should be described as implementations of abstract data types (in F90).
3. Automatic memory management :
   - Unused objects should be deallocated by the language system (most in F90, in F95).
4. Classes :
   - Every nonsimple type is a module and every high-level module is a type (in F90).
5. Inheritance :
   - A class may be defined as an extension or restriction of another (in F90).
6. Polymorphism and dynamic binding :
   - Entities are permitted to refer to objects of more than one class, and operations can have different realizations in different classes (partially in F90/F95; expected in Fortran 200X).
7. Multiple and repeated inheritance :
   - A class can be delared as heir to more than one class and more than once to the same class (in F90).

of choice. The basic F90 procedures for OOP will be illustrated in some short examples in Chapter 3 after some preliminary material on abstract data types are covered in Chapter 2. Examples of employing F90 as an OOP language for mathematical and technical applications have been given by Akin and Singh [4], Akin [3], Cary et al. [8], Decyk Norton and Szymanski [10, 11], Gray and Roberts [20], George and Liu [18], Machiels and Deville [27], Norton et al. [31, 32], and Rumbaugh et al. [36] and Szymanski et al. [37, 38]. Additional OOP applications will also be covered in later chapters.

1.8 Exercises

1 Checking trigonometric identities

We know that the sine and cosine functions obey the trigonometric identity $\sin^2\theta + \cos^2\theta = 1$ no matter what value of θ is used. Write a pseudocode, or MATLAB, or F90 program that checks this identity. Let it consist of a loop that increments across N equally spaced angles between 0 and π and calculates the quantity in question, printing the angle and the result. Test your program for several values of N. (Later we will write a second version of this program that does not contain any analysis loops but uses instead MATLAB's or F90's ability to calculate functions of arrays.)

2 Newton–Raphson algorithm

A commonly used numerical method of solving the equation $f(x) = 0$ has its origins with the beginnings of calculus. Newton noted that the slope of a function tends to cross the x-axis near a function's position of zero value (called a *root*).

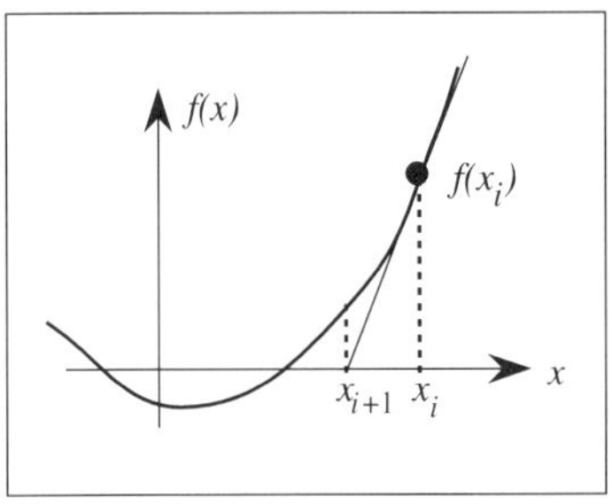

Because the function's slope at some point x_i equals its derivative $f'(x_i)$, the equation of the line passing through $f(x_i)$ is $f'(x_i)x + (f(x_i) - f'(x_i)x_i)$. Solving for the case when this expression equals the next trial root x_{i+1} is accomplished through the equation

$$x_{i+1} = x_i - \frac{f(x_i)}{f'(x_i)}$$

The algorithm proceeds by continuously applying this iterative equation until the error is "small." The definition of "small" is usually taken to mean that the absolute relative difference between successive iterations is less than some tolerance value ϵ. (Raphson extended these concepts to an array of functions.)

(a) In pseudocode, write a program that performs the Newton–Raphson algorithm. Assume that functions that evaluate the function and its derivative are available. What is the most convenient form of loop to use in your program?

(b) Translate your pseudocode into F90 or MATLAB and apply your program to the simple function $f(x) = e^{2x} - 5x - 1$. Use the functional expressions directly in your program or make use of functions.

3 Game of Life pseudocode

Develop a pseudocode outline for the main parts of the "Game of Life" discussed earlier and shown in Figure 1.3. Include pseudocode for a function to compute the next generation.

CHAPTER TWO

Data Types

Any computer program is going to have to operate on the available data. The valid data types that are available will vary from one language to another. Here we will examine the intrinsic or built-in data types and user-defined data types or structures and, finally, introduce the concept of the abstract data type, which is the basic foundation of object-oriented methods. We will also consider the precision associated with numerical data types. The Fortran data types are listed in Table 2.1. Such data can be used as constants, variables, pointers, and targets.

2.1 Intrinsic Types

The simplest data type is the `LOGICAL` type, which has the Boolean values of either `.true.` or `.false.` and is used for relational operations. The other nonnumeric data type is the `CHARACTER`. The sets of valid character values will be defined by the hardware system on which the compiler is installed. Character sets may be available in multiple languages such as English and Japanese. There are international standards for computer character sets. The two most common ones are the English character sets defined in the ASCII and EBCDIC standards that have been adapted by the International Standards Organization (ISO). Both of these standards for defining single characters include the digits (0 to 9), the 26 uppercase letters (A to Z), the 26 lowercase letters (a to z), common mathematical symbols, and many nonprintable codes known as control characters. We will see later that strings of characters are still referred to as being of the `CHARACTER` type, but they have a length that is greater than one. In other languages such a data type is often called a *string*. [Although not part of the F95 standard, the ISO Committee created a user-defined type known as the `ISO_VARIABLE_LENGTH_STRING`, which is available as a F95 source module.]

For numerical computations, numbers are represented as integers or decimal values known as *floating point numbers* or *floats*. The former is called an `INTEGER` type. The decimal values supported in Fortran are the `REAL` and `COMPLEX` types. The range and precision of these three types depend on the hardware being employed. At the present, 2002, most computers have 32-bit processors, but some offer 64-bit processors. This means that the precision of a calculated result from a single program could vary from one brand of computer to another. One would like to have a portable precision control so as to get the same answer from different hardware; whereas some languages, like C++, specify three ranges of precision (with specific bit widths), Fortran provides default precision types as well as two functions to allow the user to define the "kind" of precision desired.

Table 2.1: F90/95 Data types and pointer attributes

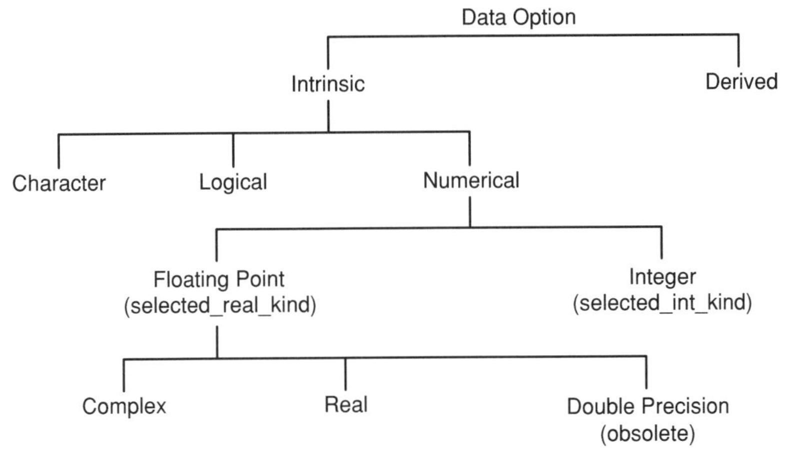

Still, it is good programming practice to employ a precision that is of the default, double, or quad precision level. Table 2.2 lists the default precisions for 32-bit processors. The first three entries correspond to types *int*, *float*, and *double*, respectively, of C++. Examples of F90 integer constants are

```
-32      0      4675123      24_short      24_long
```

and typical real constant examples are

```
-3.        0.123456        1.234567e+2      0.0       0.3_double
7.6543e+4_double        0.23567_quad      0.3d0
```

In both cases, we note that it is possible to impose a user-defined precision kind by appending an underscore (_) followed by the name of the integer variable that gives the precision kind number. For example, one could define

```
long = selected_int_kind(9)
```

to denote an integer in the range of -10^9 to 10^9, whereas

```
double = selected_real_kind(15,307)
```

Table 2.2: Numeric Types on 32-Bit Processors

Type	Bit Width	Significant Digits	Common Range
integer	16	10	−32,768 to 32,767
real	32	6	-10^{37} to 10^{37}
double precision[a]	64	15	-10^{307} to 10^{307}
complex	2@32	2@6	two reals

[a] Obsolete in F90; see `selected_real_kind`.

defines a real with 15 significant digits with an exponent range of ±307. Likewise, a higher precision real might be defined by the integer kind

```
quad = selected_real_kind(18,4932)
```

to denote 18 significant digits over the exponent range of ±4932. If these kinds of precision are available on your processors, then the F90 types of "integer (long)," "real (double)," and "real (quad)" would correspond to the C++ precision types of "long int," "double," and "long double," respectively. If the processor cannot produce the requested precision, then it returns a negative number as the integer kind number. Thus, one should always check that the kind (i.e., the preceding integer values of long, double, or quad) is not negative and report an exception if it is negative.

The old F77 intrinsic type of `DOUBLE PRECISION` has been declared obsolete since it is now easy to set any level of precision available on a processor. Another way to always define a double precision real on any processor is to use the "kind" function such as

```
double = kind(1.0d0)
```

where the symbol 'd' is used to denote the I/O of a double precision real. For completeness it should be noted that it is possible on some processors to define different kinds of character types, such as "greek" or "ascii," but in that case, the kind value comes before the underscore and the character string such as `ascii_`"a string."

To illustrate the concept of a defined precision intrinsic data type, consider a program segment to make available useful constants such as *pi* (3.1415...) or Avogadro's number ($6.02\ldots \times 10^{23}$). These are real constants that should not be changed during the use of the program. In F90, an item of that nature is known as a `PARAMETER`. In Figure 2.1, a selected group of such constants have been declared to be of double precision and stored in a `MODULE` named `Math_Constants`. The parameters in that module can be made available to any program one writes by including the statement "`use math_constants`" at the beginning of the program segment. The figure actually ends with a short sample program that converts the tabulated value of *pi* (line 23) to a default precision real (line 42) and prints both.

2.2 User-Defined Data Types

Although the intrinsic data types above have been successfully employed to solve a vast number of programming requirements, it is logical to want to combine these types in some structured combination that represents the way we think of a particular physical object or business process. For example, assume we wish to think of a chemical element in terms of the combination of its standard symbol, atomic number, and atomic mass. We could create such a data structure type and assign it a name, say `chemical_element`, so that we could refer to that type for other uses just like we might declare a real variable. In F90 we would define the structure with a `TYPE` construct as shown below (in lines 3–7):

```
[ 1]  program create_a_type
[ 2]  implicit none
[ 3]    type chemical_element                   ! a user defined data type
[ 4]      character (len=2) :: symbol
[ 5]      integer           :: atomic_number
[ 6]      real              :: atomic_mass
[ 7]    end type
```

```
Module Math_Constants     ! Define double precision math constants
 implicit none
 ! INTEGER, PARAMETER :: DP = SELECTED_REAL_KIND (15,307)
   INTEGER, PARAMETER :: DP = KIND (1.d0) ! Alternate form
real(DP), parameter:: Deg_Per_Rad  = 57.295779513082320876798155_DP
real(DP), parameter:: Rad_Per_Deg  = 0.017453292519943295769237_DP

real(DP), parameter:: e_Value      =  2.71828182845904523560287_DP
real(DP), parameter:: e_Recip      =  0.367879441171442321595523 8_DP
real(DP), parameter:: e_Squared    =  7.389056098930650227230427_DP
real(DP), parameter:: Log10_of_e   =  0.434294481903251827651128 9_DP

real(DP), parameter:: Euler        =  0.5772156649015328606_DP
real(DP), parameter:: Euler_Log    = -0.5495393129816448223_DP
real(DP), parameter:: Gamma        =  0.577215664901532860606512_DP
real(DP), parameter:: Gamma_Log    = -0.549539312981644822337662_DP
real(DP), parameter:: Golden_Ratio =  1.618033988749894848_DP

real(DP), parameter:: Ln_2         =  0.693147180559945309417232 1_DP
real(DP), parameter:: Ln_10        =  2.302585092994045684017991 5_DP
real(DP), parameter:: Log10_of_2   =  0.301029995663981195213738 9_DP

real(DP), parameter:: pi_Value     =  3.141592653589793238462643_DP
real(DP), parameter:: pi_Ln        =  1.144729885849400174143427_DP
real(DP), parameter:: pi_Log10     =  0.497149872694133854351268 3_DP
real(DP), parameter:: pi_Over_2    =  1.570796326794896619231322_DP
real(DP), parameter:: pi_Over_3    =  1.047197551196597746154214_DP
real(DP), parameter:: pi_Over_4    =  0.785398163397448309615660 8_DP
real(DP), parameter:: pi_Recip     =  0.318309886183790671537767 5_DP
real(DP), parameter:: pi_Squared   =  9.869604401089358618834491_DP
real(DP), parameter:: pi_Sq_Root   =  1.772453850905516027298167_DP

real(DP), parameter:: Sq_Root_of_2 =  1.4142135623730950488_DP
real(DP), parameter:: Sq_Root_of_3 =  1.7320508075688772935_DP

End Module Math_Constants

Program Test
  use Math_Constants                    ! Access all constants
  real :: pi                            ! Define local data type
  print *, 'pi_Value: ', pi_Value       ! Display a constant
  pi = pi_Value; print *, 'pi = ', pi   ! Convert to lower precision
End Program Test                        ! Running gives:
  ! pi_Value: 3.1415926535897931        ! pi = 3.14159274
```

Figure 2.1: Defining global double-precision constants.

Having created the new data type, we would need ways to define its values and to refer to any of its components. The latter is accomplished by using the component selection symbol "%." Continuing the program segment above we could write the following:

```
type (chemical_element) :: argon, carbon, neon       ! elements
type (chemical_element) :: Periodic_Table(109)       ! an array
real                    :: mass                      ! a scalar

carbon%atomic_mass   = 12.010            ! set a component value
carbon%atomic_number = 6                 ! set a component value
```

```
[14]     carbon%symbol         = "C"              ! set a component value
[15]
[16]     argon = chemical_element ("Ar", 18, 26.98) ! construct element
[17]
[18]     read *, neon                               ! get "Ne" 10 20.183
[19]
[20]     Periodic_Table( 5) = argon           ! insert element into array
[21]     Periodic_Table(17) = carbon          ! insert element into array
[22]     Periodic_Table(55) = neon            ! insert element into array
[23]
[24]     mass = Periodic_Table(5) % atomic_mass     ! extract component
[25]
[26]     print *, mass                         ! gives 26.9799995
[27]     print *, neon                         ! gives Ne 10 20.1830006
[28]     print *, Periodic_Table(17)           ! gives C  6  12.0100002
[29]   end program create_a_type
```

In the preceding program segment, we have introduced some new concepts:

- Defined argon, carbon, and neon to be of the `chemical_element` type (line 8).
- Defined a subscripted array to contain 109 `chemical_element` types (line 9).
- Used the selector symbol, %, to assign a value to each of the components of the carbon structure (line 15).
- Used the intrinsic "structure constructor" to define the argon values (line 16). The intrinsic construct or initializer function must have the same name as the user-defined type. It must be supplied with all of the components, and they must occur in the order that they were defined in the TYPE block.
- Read in all the neon components, in order (line 18). [The '*' means that the system is expected to find the next character automatically, integer and real, respectively, and to insert them into the components of neon.]
- Inserted argon, carbon, and neon into their specific locations in the periodic table array (lines 20–22).
- Extracted the `atomic_mass` of argon from the corresponding element in the `periodic_element` array (line 24).
- Printed the real variable, `mass` (line 26). [The '*' means to use a default number of digits.]
- Printed all components of neon (line 27). [Using a default number of digits.]
- Printed all the components of carbon by citing its reference in the periodic table array (line 28). [Note that the printed real value differs from the value assigned in line 12. This is due to the way reals are represented in a computer.]

A defined type can also be used to define other data structures. This is but one small example of the concept of code reuse. If we were developing a code that involved the history of chemistry, we might use the type above to create a type called *history* as shown below.

```
type (chemical_element)   :: oxygen

type history                       ! a second type using the first
  character (len=31)       :: element_name
  integer                  :: year_found
  type (chemical_element)  :: chemistry
end type history
```

```
type (history) :: Joseph_Priestley                    ! Discoverer

oxygen = chemical_element ("O", 76, 190.2)    ! construct element

Joseph_Priestley = history ("Oxygen", 1774, oxygen)   ! construct

print *, Joseph_Priestley ! gives Oxygen 1774 O 76 1.9020000E+02
```

Shortly we will learn about other important aspects of user-defined types such as how to define operators that use them as operands.

2.3 Abstract Data Types

Clearly, data alone are of little value. We must also have the means to input and output the data, subprograms to manipulate and query the data, and the ability to define operators for commonly used procedures. The coupling or encapsulation of the data with a select group of functions defining everything that can be done with the data type introduces the concept of an abstract data type (ADT). An ADT goes a step further in that it usually hides the details of how functions accomplish their tasks from the user. Only knowledge of input and output interfaces to the functions is described in detail. Even the components of the data types are kept private.

The word *abstract* in the term *abstract data type* is used to (1) indicate that we are interested only in the essential features of the data type, (2) to indicate that the features are defined in a manner that is independent of any specific programming language, and (3) to indicate that the instances of the ADT are being defined by their behavior and that the actual implementation is secondary. An ADT is an abstraction that describes a set of items in terms of a hidden or encapsulated data structure and a set of operations on that data structure.

Previously we created user-defined entity types such as the `chemical_element`. The primary difference between entity types and ADTs is that all ADTs include methods for operating on the type. Although entity types are defined by a name and a list of attributes, an ADT is described by its name, attributes, encapsulated methods, and possibly encapsulated rules.

Object-oriented programming is primarily a data abstraction technique. The purpose of abstraction and data hiding in programming is to separate behavior from implementation. For abstraction to work, the implementation must be encapsulated so that no other programming module can depend on its implementation details. Such encapsulation guarantees that modules can be implemented and revised independently. Hiding of the attributes and some or all of the methods of an ADT is also important in the process. In F90 the `PRIVATE` statement is used to hide an attribute or a method; otherwise, both will default to `PUBLIC`. Public methods can be used outside the program module that defines an ADT. We refer to the set of public methods or operations belonging to an ADT as the public interface of the type.

The user-defined data type, as given above, in F90 is not an ADT even though each is created with three intrinsic methods to construct a value, read a value, or print a value. Those methods cannot modify a type; they can only instantiate the type by assigning it a value and display that value. (Unlike F90, in C or C++, a user-defined type, or "struct," does not have an intrinsic constructor method or input/output methods.) Generally ADTs will have methods that modify or query a type's state or behavior.

From the preceding discussion we see that the intrinsic data types in any language (such as complex, integer and real in F90) are actually ADTs. The system has hidden methods

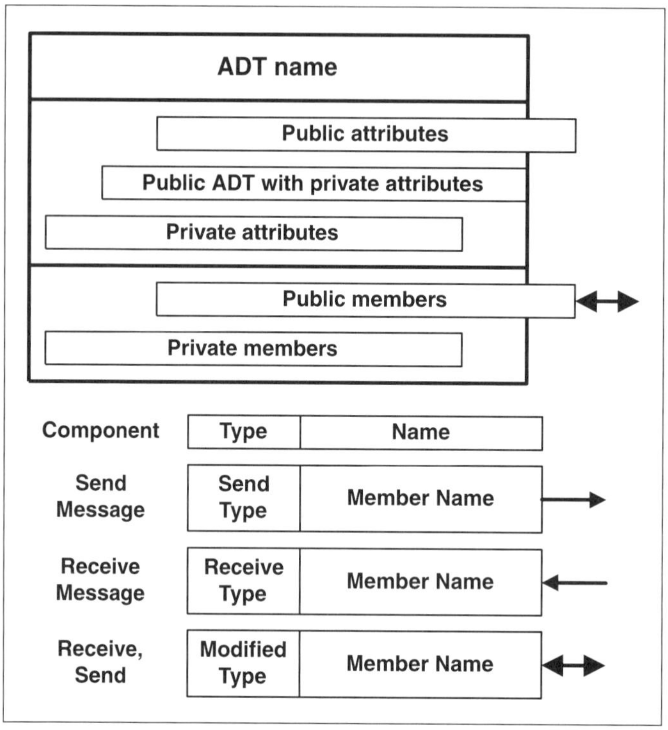

Figure 2.2: Graphical representation of ADTs.

(operators) to assign them values and to manipulate them. For example, we know that we can multiply any one of the numerical types by any other numerical type.

We do not know how the system does the multiplication, and we do not care. All computer languages provide functions to manipulate the intrinsic data types. For example, in F90 a square-root function, named *sqrt*, is provided to compute the square root of a real or complex number. From basic mathematics you probably know that two distinctly different algorithms must be used, and the choice depends on the type of the supplied argument. Thus, we call the *sqrt* function a generic function since its single name, *sqrt*, is used to select related functions in a manner hidden from the user. In F90 you can not take the square root of an integer; you must convert it to a real value and you receive a real answer. The preceding discussions of the methods (routines) that are coupled to a data type and describe what you can and can not do with the data type should give the programmer good insight into what must be done to plan and implement the functions needed to yield a relatively complete ADT.

It is common to have a graphical representation of the ADTs, and several different graphical formats are suggested in the literature. We will use the form shown in Figure 2.2, where a rectangular box begins with the ADT name and is followed by two partitions of that box that represent the lists of attribute data and associated member routines. Items that are available to the outside world are in subboxes that cross over the right border of the ADT box. They are the parts of the public interface to the ADT. Likewise, those items that are strictly internal, or private, are contained fully within their respective partitions of the ADT box. There is a common special case in which the name of the data type itself is available for external use but its individual attribute components are not. In that case the right edge of the private attributes lists lies on the right edge of the ADT box. In addition, we will often segment the smallest box for an item to give its type (or the most important type for members) and the name of the item. Public member boxes are also supplemented with an

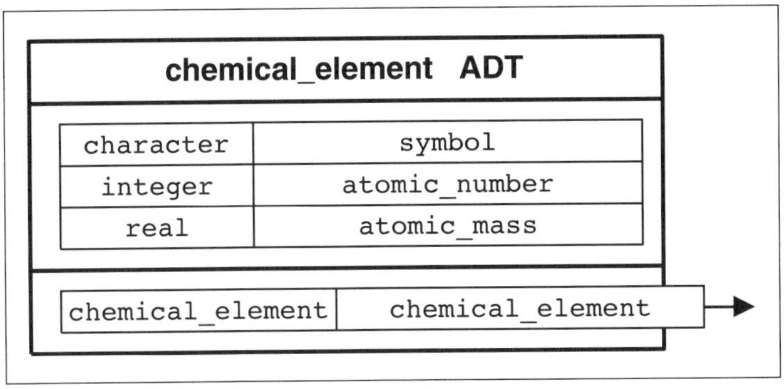

Figure 2.3: Representation of the public chemical_element ADT.

arrow to indicate which take in information (<--) or send out information (-->). Such a graphical representation of the previous `chemical_element` ADT, with all its items public, is shown in Figure 2.3.

The sequence of numbers known as Fibonacci numbers is the set that begins with 1 and 2 and where the next number in the set is the sum of the two previous numbers (1, 2, 3, 5, 8, 13, ...). A primarily private ADT to print a list of Fibonacci numbers up to some limit is represented graphically in Figure 2.4.

2.4 Classes

A class is basically the extension of an ADT by providing additional member routines to serve as *constructors*. Usually, those additional members should include a *default constructor* that has no arguments. Its purpose is to ensure that the class is created with acceptable default values assigned to all its data attributes. If the data attributes involve the storage of large amounts of data (memory), then one usually also provides a *destructor* member to free up the associated memory when it is no longer needed. The F95 language has an automatic deallocation feature not present in F90 and thus we will often formally deallocate memory associated with data attributes of classes.

As a short example we will consider an extension of the preceding Fibonacci_Number ADT. The ADT for Fibonacci numbers simply keeps up with three numbers (low, high, and

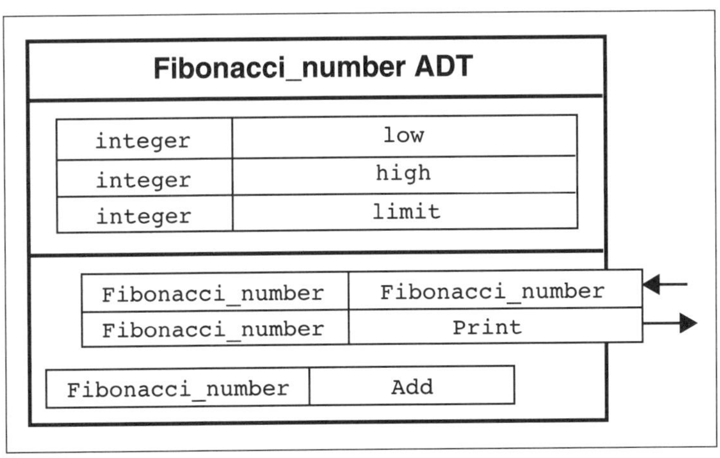

Figure 2.4: Representation of a Fibonacci_number ADT.

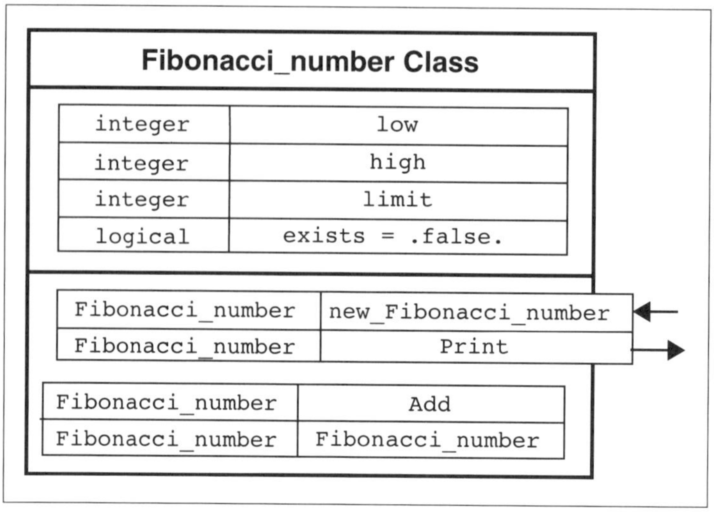

Figure 2.5: Representation of a Fibonacci_number Class.

limit). Its intrinsic initializer has the (default) name Fibonacci. We generalize that ADT to a class by adding a constructor named new_Fibonacci_number. The constructor accepts a single number that indicates how many values in the infinite list we wish to see. It is also a default constructor because, if we omit the one optional argument, it will list a minimum number of terms set in the constructor. The graphical representation of the Fibonacci_Number class extends Figure 2.4 for its ADT by at least adding one public constructor, called new_Fibonacci_number, as shown in Figure 2.5. Technically, it is generally accepted that a constructor should only be able to construct a specific object once. This differs from the intrinsic initializer that could be invoked multiple times to assign different values to a single user-defined type. Thus, an additional logical attribute has been added to the previous ADT to allow the constructor, new_Fibonacci_number, to verify that it is being invoked only once for each instance of the class. The coding for this simple class is illustrated in Figure 2.6. There the access restrictions are given on lines 4, 5, and 7, the attributes are declared on line 8, and the member functions are given in lines 13–38. The validation program is in lines 40–47, with the results shown as comments at the end (lines 49–53).

```
[ 1]  ! Fortran 90 OOP to print list of Fibonacci Numbers
[ 2]  Module class_Fibonacci_Number                ! file: Fibonacci_Number.f90
[ 3]   implicit none
[ 4]    public  :: Print                           ! member access
[ 5]    private :: Add                             ! member access
[ 6]    type Fibonacci_Number                      ! attributes
[ 7]      private
[ 8]      integer :: low, high, limit              ! state variables & access
[ 9]    end type Fibonacci_Number
[10]
[11]  Contains                                     ! member functionality
[12]
[13]    function new_Fibonacci_Number (max)  result (num) ! constructor
[14]    implicit none
[15]      integer, optional        :: max
[16]      type (Fibonacci_Number) :: num
```

```
      num = Fibonacci_Number (0, 1, 0)                   ! intrinsic
      if ( present(max) ) num = Fibonacci_Number (0, 1, max) ! intrinsic
      num%exists = .true.
  end function new_Fibonacci_Number

  function Add (this) result (sum)
  implicit none
    type (Fibonacci_Number), intent(in) :: this     ! cannot modify
    integer                             :: sum
      sum = this%low + this%high ; end function add  ! add components

  subroutine Print (num)
  implicit none
    type (Fibonacci_Number), intent(inout) :: num    ! will modify
    integer                          :: j, sum ! loops
      if ( num%limit < 0 ) return                   ! no data to print
      print *, 'M  Fibonacci(M)'                    ! header
      do j = 1, num%limit                           ! loop over range
        sum = Add(num)     ; print *, j, sum        ! sum and print
        num%low = num%high ; num%high = sum         ! update
      end do ; end subroutine Print
End Module class_Fibonacci_Number

program Fibonacci                          !** The main Fibonacci program
implicit none
  use class_Fibonacci_Number              ! inherit variables and members
  integer, parameter          :: end = 8    ! unchangeable
  type (Fibonacci_Number) :: num
    num = new_Fibonacci_Number(end)        ! manual constructor
    call Print (num)                       ! create and print list
end program Fibonacci                      ! Running gives:

! M  Fibonacci(M)     ; !  M  Fibonacci(M)
! 1 1                 ; !  5 8
! 2 2                 ; !  6 13
! 3 3                 ; !  7 21
! 4 5                 ; !  8 34
```

Figure 2.6: A simple Fibonacci class.

2.5 Exercises

1 Create a module of global constants of common (a) physical constants, (b) common units conversion factors.

2 Teams in a sports league compete in matches that result in a tie or a winning and losing team. When the result is not a tie, the status of the teams is updated. The winner is declared better that the loser and better than any team that was previously bettered by the loser. Specify this process by ADTs for the league, team, and match. Include a logical member function `is_better_than`, which expresses whether a team is better than another.

3 Several computing environments like Matlab and TK Solver provide a function, named pi (), to return the value of *pi*. Develop such a function as an enhancement of the Math_Constants module. Test it with a simple main program.

CHAPTER THREE

Object-Oriented Programming Concepts

3.1 Introduction

The use of object-oriented (OO) design and object-oriented programming (OOP) methods is becoming increasingly popular. Thus, it is useful to have an introductory understanding of OOP and some of the programming features of OO languages. You can develop OO software in any high-level language like C or Pascal. However, newer languages such as Ada, C++, and F90 have enhanced features that make OOP much more natural, practical, and maintainable. Appearing before F90, C++ currently is probably the most popular OOP language, yet F90 was clearly designed to have almost all of the abilities of C++. However, rather than study the new standards, many authors simply refer to the two-decade-old F77 standard and declare that Fortran can not be used for OOP. Here we will overcome that misinformed point of view.

Modern OO languages provide the programmer with three capabilities that improve and simplify the design of such programs: *encapsulation, inheritance,* and *polymorphism* (or generic functionality). Related topics involve *objects, classes,* and *data hiding*. An *object* combines various classical data types into a set that defines a new variable type or structure. A *class* unifies the new entity types and supporting data that represent its state with routines (functions and subroutines) that access or modify those data, or both. Every object created from a class, by providing the necessary data, is called an *instance* of the class. In older languages like C and F77, the data and functions are separate entities. An OO language provides a way to couple or encapsulate the data and its functions into a unified entity. This is a more natural way to model real-world entities that have both data and functionality. The encapsulation is done with a "module" block in F90 and with a "class" block in C++. This encapsulation also includes a mechanism whereby some or all of the data and supporting routines can be hidden from the user. The accessibility of the specifications and routines of a class is usually controlled by optional "public" and "private" qualifiers. *Data hiding* allows one the means to protect information in one part of a program from access and especially from being changed in other parts of the program. In C++ the default is that data and functions are "private" unless declared "public," whereas F90 makes the opposite choice for its default protection mode. In an F90 "module" it is the "contains" statement that, among other things, couples the data, specifications, and operators before it to the functions and subroutines that follow it.

Class hierarchies can be visualized when we realize that we can employ one or more previously defined classes (of data and functionality) to organize additional classes. Functionality programmed into the earlier classes may not need to be recoded to be usable in the later classes. This mechanism is called *inheritance*. For example, if we have defined an

Employee_class, then a Manager_class would inherit all of the data and functionality of an employee. We would then only be required to add only the totally new data and functions needed for a manager. We may also need a mechanism to redefine specific Employee_class functions that differ for a Manager_class. By using the concept of a class hierarchy, less programming effort is required to create the final enhanced program. In F90 the earlier class is brought into the later class hierarchy by the "use" statement followed by the name of the "module" statement block that defined the class.

Polymorphism allows different classes of objects that share some common functionality to be used in code that require only that common functionality. In other words, routines having the same generic name are interpreted differently depending on the class of the objects presented as arguments to the routines. This is useful in class hierarchies where a small number of meaningful function names can be used to manipulate different but related object classes. The concepts above are those essential to object-oriented design and OOP. In the later sections we will demonstrate by example additional F90 implementations of these concepts.

3.2 Encapsulation, Inheritance, and Polymorphism

We often need to use existing classes to define new classes. The two ways to do this are called *composition* and *inheritance*. We will use both methods in a series of examples. Consider a geometry program that uses two different classes: class_Circle and class_Rectangle, as represented graphically in Figures 3.1 and 3.2. and as partially implemented in F90, as shown in Figure 3.3. Each class shown has the data types and specifications to define the object and the functionality to compute its respective areas (lines 3–23). The operator % is employed to select specific components of a defined type. Within the geometry (main) program a single routine, compute_area, is invoked (lines 40 and 46) to return the area for *any* of the defined geometry classes. That is, a generic function name is used for all classes of its arguments and it, in turn, branches to the corresponding functionality supplied with the argument class. To accomplish this branching the geometry program first brings in the functionality of the desired classes via a "use" statement for each class module (lines 26 and 27). Those "modules" are coupled to the generic function by an "interface" block that has the generic function name compute_area (lines 30, 31). A "module procedure" list is included that gives one class routine name for each of the classes of argument(s) the generic

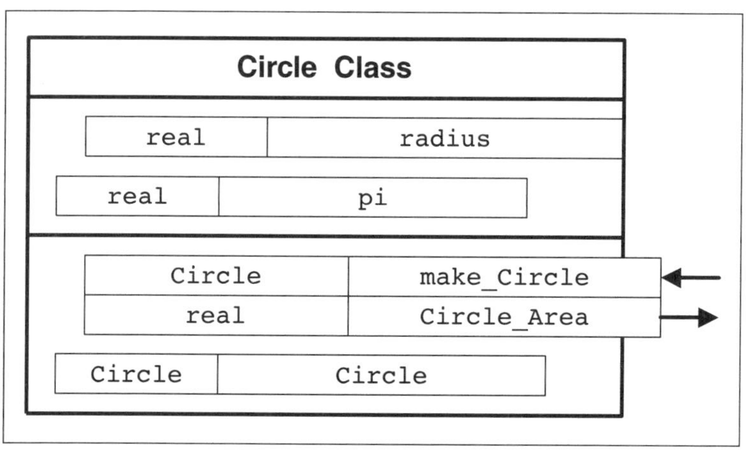

Figure 3.1: Representation of a circle class.

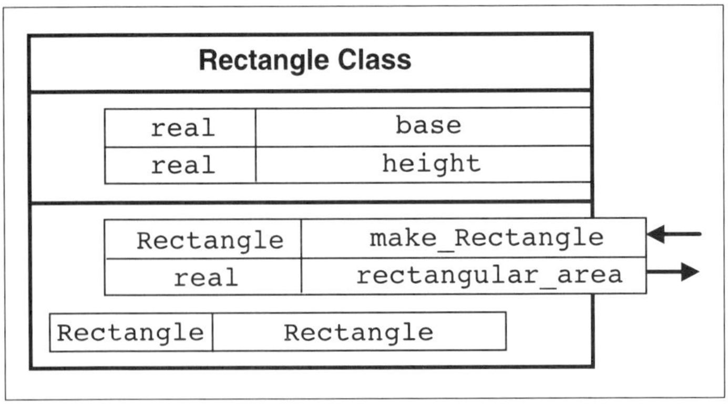

Figure 3.2: Representation of a rectangle class.

function is designed to accept. The ability of a function to respond differently when supplied with arguments that are objects of different types is called *polymorphism*. In this example we have employed different names, `rectangular_area` and `circle_area`, in their respective class modules, but that is not necessary. The "use" statement allows one to rename the class routines, to bring in only selected members of the functionality, or to do both.

Another terminology used in OOP is that of *constructors* and *destructors* for objects. An intrinsic constructor is a system function automatically invoked when an object is declared with all of its possible components in the defined order (see lines 39 and 45). In C++ and F90, the intrinsic constructor has the same name as the "type" of the object. One is illustrated in the statement

```
four_sides = Rectangle (2.1,4.3),
```

where previously we declared

```
type (Rectangle) :: four_sides,
```

which, in turn, was coupled to the `class_Rectangle`, which had two components, base and height, defined in that order, respectively. The intrinsic constructor in the sample statement sets component `base = 2.1` and component `height = 4.3` for that instance, `four_sides`, of the type `Rectangle`. This intrinsic construction is possible because all the expected components of the type were supplied. If all the components are not supplied, then the object cannot be constructed unless the functionality of the class is expanded by the programmer to accept a different number of arguments.

Assume that we want a special member of the `Rectangle` class, a square, to be constructed if the height is omitted. That is, we would use `height = base` in that case. Or, we may want to construct a unit square if height and base are omitted so that the constructor defaults to `base = height = 1`. Such a manual constructor, named `make_Rectangle`, is illustrated in Figure 3.4 (see lines 6–9). It illustrates some additional features of F90. Note that the last two arguments were declared to have the additional type attributes of "optional" (line 4) and that an associated logical function "present" is utilized (lines 7 and 9) to determine if the calling program supplied the argument in question. That figure also shows the results of the area computations for the corresponding variables "square" and "unit_sq" defined if the manual constructor is called with one or no optional arguments (line 6), respectively.

In the next section we will illustrate the concept of data hiding by using the `private` attribute. The reader is warned that the intrinsic constructor can not be employed if any of its arguments have been hidden. In that case a manual constructor must be provided to deal

```
!   Areas of shapes of different classes, using different
!             function names in each class
module class_Rectangle    ! define the first object class
implicit none
  type Rectangle
    real :: base, height ; end  type Rectangle
contains !  Computation of area for rectangles.
  function rectangle_area ( r ) result ( area )
    type ( Rectangle ), intent(in) :: r
    real                           :: area
      area = r%base * r%height ; end function rectangle_area
end module class_Rectangle
module class_Circle     ! define the second object class
implicit none
  real :: pi = 3.1415926535897931d0 ! a circle constant
  type Circle
    real :: radius ; end  type Circle
contains !      Computation of area for circles.
  function circle_area ( c ) result ( area )
    type ( Circle ), intent(in) :: c
    real                        :: area
      area = pi * c%radius**2 ; end function circle_area
end module class_Circle

program geometry  ! for both types in a single function
 use class_Circle
 use class_Rectangle
 implicit none
!     Interface to generic routine to compute area for any type
 interface compute_area
   module procedure rectangle_area, circle_area ; end interface

!     Declare a set geometric objects.
 type ( Rectangle ) :: four_sides
 type ( Circle    ) :: two_sides        ! inside, outside
 real               :: area = 0.0       ! the result

!     Initialize a rectangle and compute its area.
   four_sides = Rectangle ( 2.1, 4.3 )    ! implicit constructor
   area = compute_area ( four_sides )     ! generic function
   write ( 6,100 ) four_sides, area       ! implicit components list
   100 format ("Area of ",f3.1," by ",f3.1," rectangle is ",f5.2)

!     Initialize a circle and compute its area.
   two_sides = Circle ( 5.4 )             ! implicit constructor
   area = compute_area ( two_sides )      ! generic function
   write ( 6,200 ) two_sides, area
   200 format ("Area of circle with ",f3.1," radius is ",f9.5 )
end program geometry                      ! Running gives:
! Area of 2.1 by 4.3 rectangle is  9.03
! Area of circle with 5.4 radius is  91.60885
```

Figure 3.3: Multiple geometric shape classes.

```
  function  make_Rectangle (bottom, side) result (name)
!           Constructor for a Rectangle type
implicit none
   real, optional, intent(in) :: bottom, side
   type (Rectangle)           :: name
    name = Rectangle (1.,1.)       ! default to unit square
    if ( present(bottom) ) then    ! default to square
      name = Rectangle (bottom, bottom) ; end if
    if ( present(side) ) name = Rectangle (bottom, side) ! intrinsic
  end function  make_Rectangle
  . . .
  type ( Rectangle ) :: four_sides, square, unit_sq
!     Test manual constructors
  four_sides = make_Rectangle (2.1,4.3)  ! manual constructor, 1
  area = compute_area ( four_sides)      ! generic function
  write ( 6,100 ) four_sides, area
!     Make a square
  square = make_Rectangle (2.1)         ! manual constructor, 2
  area = compute_area ( square)         ! generic function
  write ( 6,100 ) square, area
!     "Default constructor", here a unit square
  unit_sq = make_Rectangle ()            ! manual constructor, 3
  area = compute_area (unit_sq)          ! generic function
  write ( 6,100 ) unit_sq, area
  . . .
! Running gives:
! Area of 2.1 by 4.3 rectangle is  9.03
! Area of 2.1 by 2.1 rectangle is  4.41
! Area of 1.0 by 1.0 rectangle is  1.00
```

Figure 3.4: A manual constructor for rectangles.

with any hidden components. Since data hiding is so common, it is probably best to plan on providing a manual constructor.

3.2.1 Sample Date, Person, and Student Classes

Before moving to some mathematical examples we will introduce the concept of data hiding and combine a series of classes to illustrate composition and inheritance.* First, consider a simple class to define dates and to print them in a pretty fashion, as shown in Figures 3.5 and 3.6. Although other modules will have access to the Date class they will not be given access to the number of components it contains (three), nor their names (month, day, year), nor their types (integers) because they are declared "private" in the defining module (lines 5 and 6). The compiler will not allow external access to data, routines, or both declared as private. The module, `class_Date`, is presented as a source "include" file in Figure 3.6 and in the future will be referenced by the file name `class_Date.f90`. Since we have chosen to hide all the user-defined components, we must decide what functionality we will provide to the users, who may have only executable access. The supporting documentation would have to name the public routines and describe their arguments and return results. The default intrinsic constructor would be available only to those who know full details about the components of the data type and if those components are "public." The intrinsic constructor, `Date` (lines 15 and 35), requires all the components be supplied, but it does no error or consistency checks.

* These examples mimic those given in Chapters 11 and 8 of the J.R. Hubbard book *Programming with C++*, McGraw-Hill, 1994, and usually use the same data for verification.

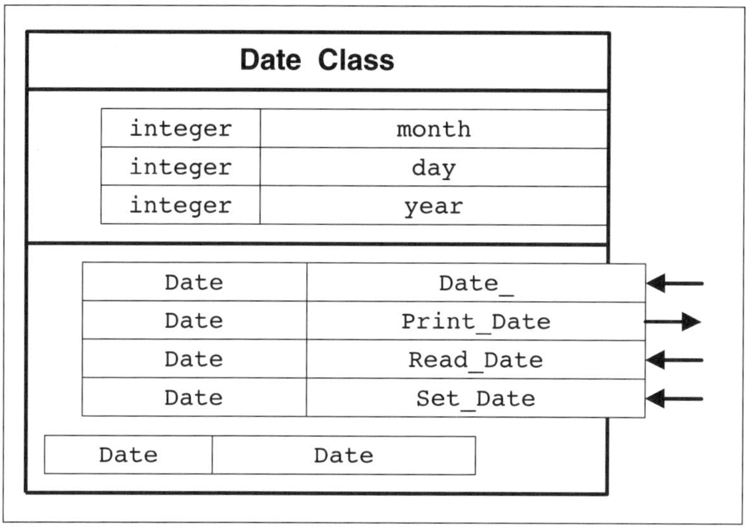

Figure 3.5: Graphical representation of a date class.

My practice is also to define a "public constructor" whose name is the same as the intrinsic constructor except for an appended underscore, that is, `Date_`. Its sole purpose is to do data checking and invoke the intrinsic constructor, `Date`. If the function `Date_` (line 11) is declared "public" it can be used outside the module `class_Date` to invoke the intrinsic constructor even if the components of the data type being constructed are all "private." In this example we have provided another manual constructor to set a date, `set_Date` (line 32) with a variable number of optional arguments. Also supplied are two subroutines to read and print dates, `read_Date` (line 28) and `print_Date` (line 17), respectively.

A sample main program that employs this class is given in Figure 3.7, which contains sample outputs as comments. This program uses the default constructor as well as all three programs in the public class functionality. Note that the definition of the class was copied in via an "include" (line 1) statement and activated with the "use" statement (line 4).

Now we will employ the `class_Date` within a `class_Person`, which will use it to set the date of birth (DOB) and date of death (DOD) in addition to the other `Person` components of name, nationality, and sex. As shown in Figure 3.8, we have made all the type components "private" but make all the supporting functionality public, as represented graphically in Figure 3.8. The functionality shown provides a manual constructor, `make_Person`, routines to set the DOB or DOD, and those for the printing of most components. The source code for the new `Person` class is given in Figure 3.9. Note that the manual constructor (line 13) utilizes "optional" arguments and initializes all components in case they are not supplied to the constructor. The `Date_` public function from the `class_Date` is "inherited" to initialize the DOB and DOD (lines 18, 56, and 61). That function member from the previous module was activated with the combination of the "include" and "use" statements. Of course, the "include" could have been omitted if the compile statement included the path name to that source. A sample main program for testing the `class_Person` is in Figure 3.10 along with comments containing its output. It utilizes the constructors `Date_` (line 8), `Person_` (line 11), and `make_Person` (line 25).

Next, we want to use the previous two classes to define a `class_Student` that adds something else special to the general `class_Person`. The student person will have additional "private" components for an identification number, the expected date of matriculation (DOM), the total course credit hours earned (credits), and the overall grade point average

```
module class_Date          ! filename: class_Date.f90
implicit none
 public  :: Date ! and everything not "private"

 type Date
   private
   integer :: month, day, year ; end type Date

contains ! encapsulated functionality

 function Date_ (m, d, y) result (x) ! public constructor
   integer, intent(in) :: m, d, y      ! month, day, year
   type (Date)         :: x            ! from intrinsic constructor
     if ( m < 1 .or. d < 1 ) stop 'Invalid components, Date_'
       x = Date (m, d, y) ; end function Date_

subroutine  print_Date (x)     ! check and pretty print a date
  type (Date), intent(in)      :: x
  character (len=*),parameter :: month_Name(12) = &
    (/ "January  ", "February ", "March    ", "April    ",&
       "May      ", "June     ", "July     ", "August   ",&
       "September", "October  ", "November ", "December "/)
    if ( x%month < 1 .or. x%month > 12 ) print *, "Invalid month"
    if ( x%day   < 1 .or. x%day   > 31 ) print *, "Invalid day  "
    print *, trim(month_Name(x%month)),' ', x%day, ", ", x%year;
end subroutine  print_Date

 subroutine  read_Date (x)          ! read month, day, and year
   type (Date), intent(out) :: x  ! into intrinsic constructor
     read *, x ; end subroutine  read_Date

 function set_Date (m, d, y) result (x)     ! manual constructor
   integer, optional, intent(in) :: m, d, y ! month, day, year
   type (Date)                   :: x
     x = Date (1,1,1997)              ! default, (or use current date)
     if ( present(m) ) x%month = m ; if ( present(d) ) x%day   = d
     if ( present(y) ) x%year  = y ; end function set_Date

end module class_Date
```

Figure 3.6: Defining a date class.

(GPA), as represented in Figure 3.11. The source lines for the type definition and selected public functionality are given in Figure 3.12. There the constructors are `make_Student` (line 20) and `Student_` (line 48). A testing main program with sample output is illustrated in Figure 3.13. Since there are various ways to utilize the various constructors, three alternate methods have been included as comments to indicate some of the programmer's options. The first two `include` statements (lines 1, 2) are actually redundant because the third `include` automatically brings in those first two classes.

3.3 Object-Oriented Numerical Calculations

Object-oriented programming is often used for numerical computation, especially when the standard storage mode for arrays is not practical or efficient. Often one will find specialized

```
include 'class_Date.f90'    ! see previous figure
program  Date_test
 use class_Date
 implicit none
   type (Date) :: today, peace

   ! peace = Date (11,11,1918) ! NOT allowed for private components
     peace = Date_ (11,11,1918)                ! public constructor
     print *, "World War I ended on "  ; call print_Date (peace)
     peace = set_Date (8, 14, 1945)            ! optional constructor
     print *, "World War II ended on " ; call print_Date (peace)
     print *, "Enter today as integer month, day, and year: "
     call read_Date(today)                     ! create today's date

     print *, "The date is ";  call print_Date (today)
end program  Date_test                 ! Running produces:
! World War I ended on November 11, 1918
! World War II ended on August 14, 1945
! Enter today as integer month, day, and year: 7 10 1997
! The date is July 10, 1997
```

Figure 3.7: Testing a date class.

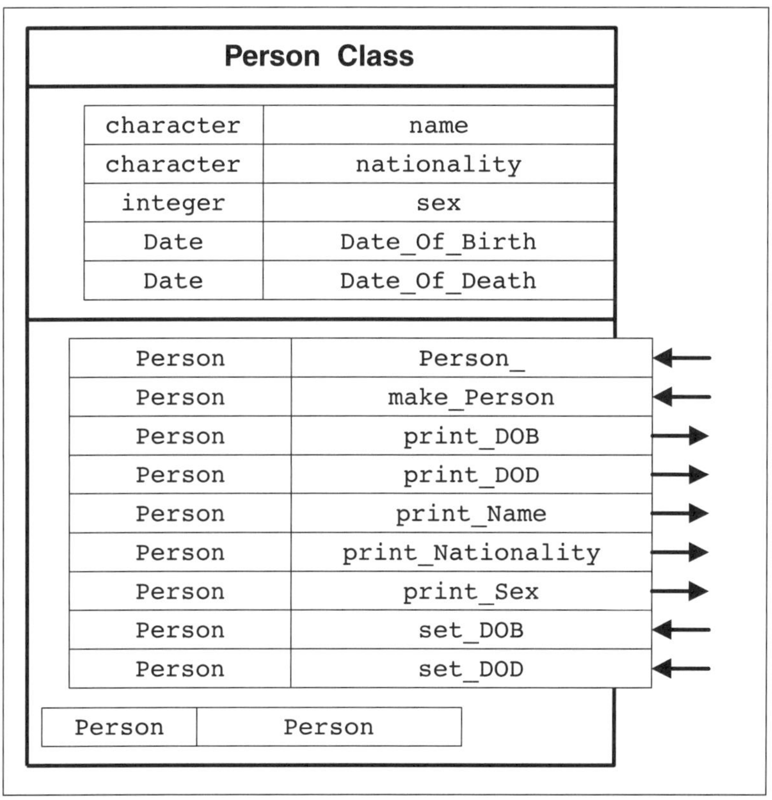

Figure 3.8: Graphical representation of a person class.

```
module class_Person          ! filename: class_Person.f90
use class_Date
implicit none
  public  :: Person
    type Person
      private
      character (len=20) :: name
      character (len=20) :: nationality
      integer            :: sex
      type (Date)        :: dob, dod    ! birth, death
    end type Person
contains
  function make_Person (nam, nation, s, b, d) result (who)
  !        Optional Constructor for a Person type
    character (len=*), optional, intent(in) :: nam, nation
    integer,           optional, intent(in) :: s      ! sex
    type (Date),       optional, intent(in) :: b, d   ! birth, death
    type (Person)                           :: who
      who = Person (" ","USA",1,Date_(1,1,0),Date_(1,1,0)) ! defaults
      if ( present(nam)    ) who % name        = nam
      if ( present(nation) ) who % nationality = nation
      if ( present(s)      ) who % sex         = s
      if ( present(b)      ) who % dob         = b
      if ( present(d)      ) who % dod         = d ; end function

  function Person_ (nam, nation, s, b, d) result (who)
  !        Public Constructor for a Person type
    character (len=*), intent(in) :: nam, nation
    integer,           intent(in) :: s      ! sex
    type (Date),       intent(in) :: b, d   ! birth, death
    type (Person)                 :: who
      who = Person (nam, nation, s, b, d) ; end function Person_

  subroutine print_DOB (who)
    type (Person), intent(in) :: who
      call  print_Date (who % dob) ; end subroutine  print_DOB

  subroutine print_DOD (who)
    type (Person), intent(in) :: who
      call print_Date (who % dod) ; end subroutine  print_DOD

  subroutine print_Name (who)
    type (Person), intent(in) :: who
      print *, who % name ; end subroutine print_Name

  subroutine print_Nationality (who)
    type (Person), intent(in) :: who
      print *, who % nationality ; end subroutine  print_Nationality

  subroutine print_Sex (who)
    type (Person), intent(in) :: who
      if ( who % sex == 1 ) then ; print *, "male"
      else ; print *, "female" ; end if ; end subroutine print_Sex

  subroutine set_DOB (who, m, d, y)
    type (Person), intent(inout) :: who
    integer, intent(in)          :: m, d, y ! month, day, year
      who % dob = Date_  (m, d, y) ;  end subroutine set_DOB

  subroutine set_DOD(who, m, d, y)
    type (Person), intent(inout) :: who
    integer, intent(in)          :: m, d, y ! month, day, year
      who % dod = Date_  (m, d, y) ;  end subroutine set_DOD
end module class_Person
```

Figure 3.9: Definition of a typical person class.

```
include 'class_Date.f90'
include 'class_Person.f90'                          ! see previous figure
program Person_inherit
 use class_Date ; use class_Person                  ! inherit class members
 implicit none
   type (Person) :: author, creator
   type (Date)   :: b, d                            ! birth, death
     b = Date_(4,13,1743) ; d = Date_(7, 4,1826) ! OPTIONAL
   !                       Method 1
   ! author =  Person ("Thomas Jefferson", "USA", 1, b, d) ! NOT if private
     author = Person_  ("Thomas Jefferson", "USA", 1, b, d) ! constructor
     print *, "The author of the Declaration of Independence was ";
     call  print_Name (author);
     print *, ". He was born on "; call print_DOB (author);
     print *, " and died on ";     call print_DOD (author); print *, ".";
   !                       Method 2
     author = make_Person ("Thomas Jefferson", "USA") ! alternate
     call  set_DOB (author, 4, 13, 1743)               ! add DOB
     call  set_DOD (author, 7,  4, 1826)               ! add DOD
     print *, "The author of the Declaration of Independence was ";
     call  print_Name (author)
     print *, ". He was born on "; call print_DOB (author);
     print *, " and died on ";     call print_DOD (author); print *, ".";
   !                       Another Person
     creator = make_Person ("John Backus", "USA")      ! alternate
     print *, "The creator of Fortran was "; call print_Name (creator);
     print *, " who was born in ";     call print_Nationality (creator);
     print *, ".";
end program Person_inherit                          ! Running gives:
! The author of the Declaration of Independence was Thomas Jefferson.
! He was born on April 13, 1743 and died on July 4, 1826.
! The author of the Declaration of Independence was Thomas Jefferson.
! He was born on April 13, 1743 and died on July 4, 1826.
! The creator of Fortran was John Backus who was born in the USA.
```

Figure 3.10: Testing the date and person classes.

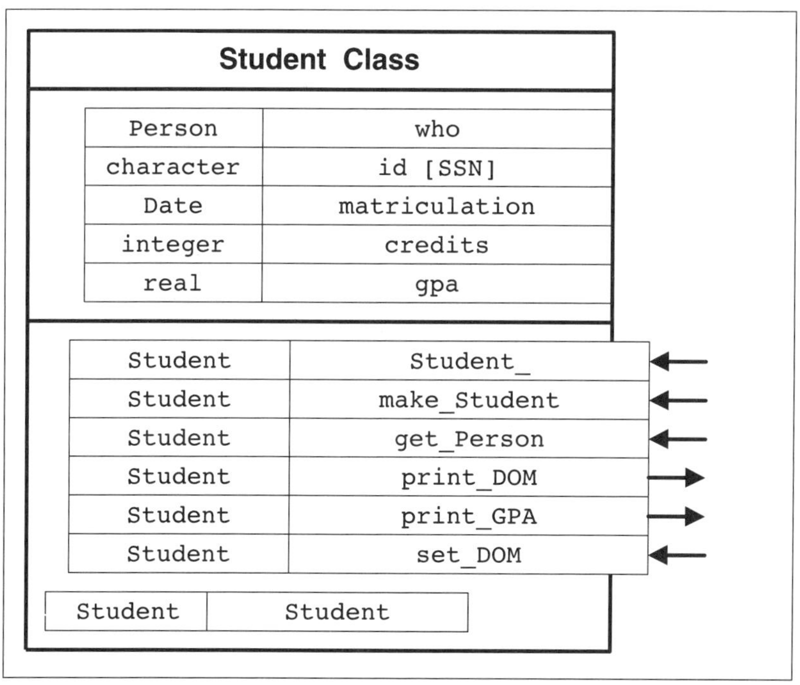

Figure 3.11: Graphical representation of a student class.

```
module class_Student                 ! filename class_Student.f90
use class_Person                     ! inherits class_Date
implicit none
 public :: Student, set_DOM, print_DOM
   type Student
     private
     type (Person)      :: who     ! name and sex
     character (len=9) :: id      ! ssn digits
     type (Date)        :: dom     ! matriculation
     integer            :: credits
     real               :: gpa     ! grade point average
   end type Student
contains   ! coupled functionality

  function get_person (s) result (p)
    type (Student), intent(in) :: s
    type (Person)                 :: p       ! name and sex
      p = s % who ; end function get_person

 function make_Student (w, n, d, c, g) result (x) ! constructor
 !         Optional Constructor for a Student type
   type (Person),                intent(in) :: w ! who
   character (len=*), optional, intent(in) :: n ! ssn
   type (Date),       optional, intent(in) :: d ! matriculation
   integer,           optional, intent(in) :: c ! credits
   real,              optional, intent(in) :: g ! grade point ave
   type (Student)                           :: x ! new student
     x = Student_(w, " ", Date_(1,1,1), 0, 0.)   ! defaults
     if ( present(n) ) x % id      = n            ! optional values
     if ( present(d) ) x % dom     = d
     if ( present(c) ) x % credits = c
     if ( present(g) ) x % gpa     = g ; end function make_Student

  subroutine print_DOM (who)
    type (Student), intent(in) :: who
      call print_Date(who%dom) ; end subroutine print_DOM

  subroutine print_GPA (x)
    type (Student), intent(in) :: x
      print *, "My name is "; call print_Name (x % who)
      print *, ", and my G.P.A. is ", x % gpa, "." ; end subroutine

  subroutine set_DOM (who, m, d, y)
    type (Student), intent(inout) :: who
    integer,         intent(in)    :: m, d, y
      who % dom = Date_( m, d, y) ; end subroutine set_DOM

  function Student_  (w, n, d, c, g) result (x)
  !          Public Constructor for a Student type
    type (Person),      intent(in) :: w ! who
    character (len=*), intent(in) :: n ! ssn
    type (Date),        intent(in) :: d ! matriculation
    integer,            intent(in) :: c ! credits
    real,               intent(in) :: g ! grade point ave
    type (Student)                 :: x ! new student
      x = Student (w, n, d, c, g) ; end function Student_
end module class_Student
```

Figure 3.12: Defining a typical student class.

```
include 'class_Date.f90'
include 'class_Person.f90'
include 'class_Student.f90' ! see previous figure
program create_Student                    ! create or correct a student
 use class_Student             ! inherits class_Person, class_Date also
 implicit none
  type (Person) :: p  ; type (Student) :: x
!                Method 1
    p = make_Person ("Ann Jones","",0)  ! optional person constructor
    call set_DOB (p, 5, 13, 1977)       ! add birth to person data
    x = Student_(p, "219360061", Date_(8,29,1955), 9, 3.1) ! public
    call print_Name (p)                              ! list name
    print *, "Born         :"; call print_DOB (p)      ! list dob
    print *, "Sex          :"; call print_Sex (p)      ! list sex
    print *, "Matriculated:"; call print_DOM (x)       ! list dom
    call print_GPA (x)                               ! list gpa
 !               Method 2
    x = make_Student (p, "219360061")    ! optional student constructor
    call set_DOM (x, 8, 29, 1995)        ! correct matriculation
    call print_Name (p)                              ! list name
    print *, "was born on :"; call print_DOB (p)       ! list dob
    print *, "Matriculated:"; call print_DOM (x)       ! list dom
 !               Method 3
    x = make_Student (make_Person("Ann Jones"), "219360061") !optional
    p = get_Person (x)                   ! get defaulted person data
    call set_DOM (x, 8, 29, 1995)        ! add matriculation
    call set_DOB (p, 5, 13, 1977)        ! add birth
    call print_Name (p)                              ! list name
    print *, "Matriculated:"; call print_DOM (x)       ! list dom
    print *, "was born on :"; call print_DOB (p)       ! list dob
end program create_Student                        ! Running gives:
! Ann Jones
! Born         : May 13, 1977
! Sex          : female
! Matriculated: August 29, 1955
! My name is Ann Jones, and my G.P.A. is 3.0999999.
! Ann Jones was born on: May 13, 1977 , Matriculated: August 29, 1995
! Ann Jones Matriculated: August 29, 1995 , was born on: May 13, 1977
```

Figure 3.13: Testing the student, person, and date classes.

storage modes like linked lists or tree structures used for dynamic data structures. Here we should note that many matrix operators are intrinsic to F90, and so one is more likely to define a `class_sparse_matrix` than a `class_matrix`. However, either class would allow us to encapsulate several matrix functions and subroutines into a module that could be reused easily in other software. Here, we will illustrate OOP applied to rational numbers and introduce the important topic of operator overloading. Additional numerical applications of OOP will be illustrated in later chapters.

3.3.1 A Rational Number Class and Operator Overloading

To illustrate an OOP approach to simple numerical operations we will introduce a fairly complete rational number class, called `class_Rational`, which is represented graphically in Figure 3.14. The defining F90 module is given in Figure 3.15. The type components have been made private (line 4), but not the type itself, and so we can illustrate the intrinsic constructor (lines 39 and 102); however, extra functionality has been provided to allow

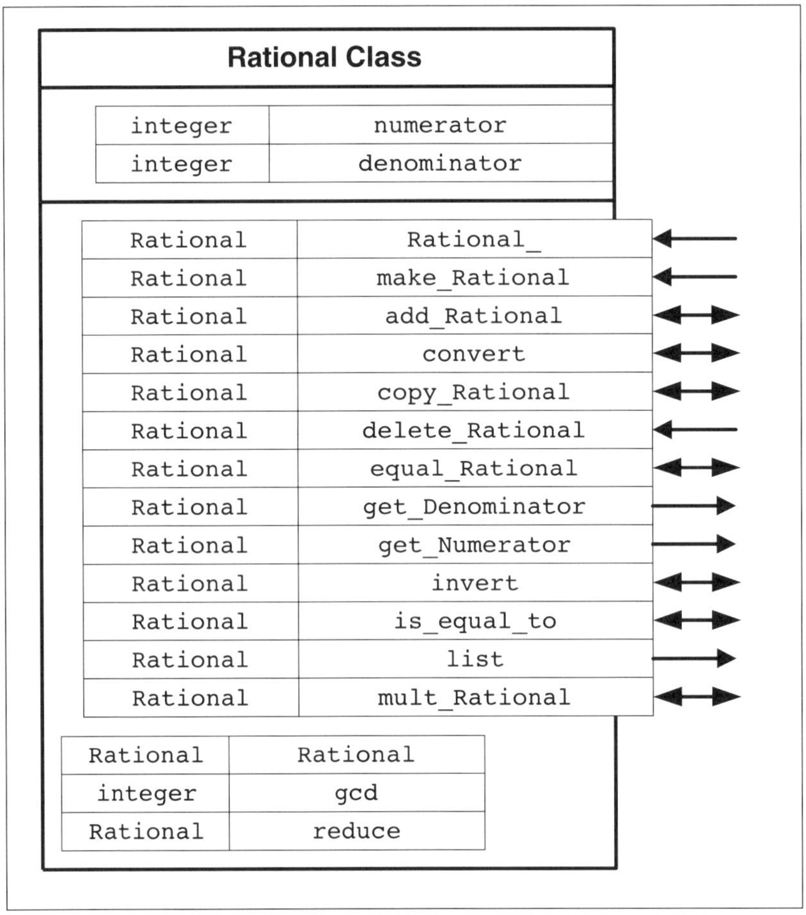

Figure 3.14: Representation of a rational number class.

users to get either of the two components (lines 53 and 57). The provided routines shown in that figure are

```
add_Rational     convert        copy_Rational     delete_Rational
equal_integer    gcd            get_Denominator   get_Numerator
invert           is_equal_to    ist               make_Rational
mult_Rational    Rational_      reduce
```

Procedures with only one return argument are usually implemented as functions instead of subroutines.

Note that we would form a new rational number, z, as the product of two other rational numbers, x and y, by invoking the `mult_Rational` function (line 91),

```
z = mult_Rational (x, y),
```

which returns z as its result. A natural tendency at this point would be simply to write this as $z = x * y$. However, before we could do that we would need to tell the operator, "*", how to act when provided with this new data type. This is known as *overloading* an intrinsic operator. We had the foresight to do this when we set up the module by declaring which of the "module procedures" were equivalent to this operator symbol. Thus, from the "interface operator (*)" statement block (line 14) the system now knows that the left and right operands of the "*" symbol correspond to the first and second arguments in the function

```
module class_Rational                  ! filename: class_Rational.f90
implicit none
 ! public, everything but following private routines
 private :: gcd, reduce
   type Rational
     private ! numerator and denominator
     integer :: num, den ; end type Rational

          ! overloaded operators interfaces
   interface assignment (=)
     module procedure equal_Integer ; end interface
   interface operator (+)           ! add unary versions & (-) later
     module procedure add_Rational ; end interface
   interface operator (*)           ! add integer_mult_Rational, etc
     module procedure mult_Rational ; end interface
   interface operator (==)
     module procedure is_equal_to ; end interface
contains                        ! inherited operational functionality
 function add_Rational (a, b) result (c)        ! to overload +
   type (Rational), intent(in) :: a, b          ! left + right
   type (Rational)             :: c
     c % num = a % num*b % den + a % den*b % num
     c % den = a % den*b % den
     call reduce (c) ; end function add_Rational

 function convert (name) result (value) ! rational to real
   type (Rational), intent(in) :: name
   real                        :: value  ! decimal form
     value = float(name % num)/name % den ; end function convert

 function copy_Rational (name) result (new)
   type (Rational), intent(in) :: name
   type (Rational)             :: new
     new % num = name % num
     new % den = name % den ; end function copy_Rational

 subroutine delete_Rational (name)      ! deallocate allocated items
   type (Rational), intent(inout) :: name       ! simply zero it here
     name = Rational (0, 1) ; end subroutine delete_Rational

 subroutine equal_Integer (new, I) ! overload =, with integer
   type (Rational), intent(out) :: new  ! left  side of operator
   integer,         intent(in)  :: I    ! right side of operator
     new % num = I ; new % den = 1 ; end subroutine equal_Integer

 recursive function gcd (j, k) result (g) ! Greatest Common Divisor
   integer, intent(in) :: j, k ! numerator, denominator
   integer             :: g
     if ( k == 0 ) then ; g = j
     else ; g = gcd ( k, modulo(j,k) )            ! recursive call
     end if ; end function gcd

 function  get_Denominator (name) result (n)    ! an access function
   type (Rational), intent(in) :: name
   integer                     :: n             ! denominator
     n = name % den ; end function  get_Denominator
```

```
  function  get_Numerator (name) result (n)     ! an access function
    type (Rational), intent(in) :: name
    integer                     :: n             ! numerator
      n = name % num ; end function  get_Numerator

  subroutine  invert (name)          ! rational to rational inversion
    type (Rational), intent(inout) :: name
    integer                        :: temp
      temp       = name % num
      name % num = name % den
      name % den = temp ; end subroutine invert

   function is_equal_to (a_given, b_given) result (t_f)
    type (Rational), intent(in) :: a_given, b_given  ! left == right
    type (Rational)             :: a, b              ! reduced copies
    logical                     :: t_f
      a = copy_Rational (a_given) ; b = copy_Rational (b_given)
      call reduce(a) ; call reduce(b)         ! reduced to lowest terms
      t_f = (a%num == b%num) .and. (a%den == b%den) ; end function

   subroutine list(name)                  ! as a pretty print fraction
    type (Rational), intent(in) :: name
      print *, name % num, "/", name % den ; end subroutine list

   function make_Rational (numerator, denominator) result (name)
   !        Optional Constructor for a rational type
    integer, optional, intent(in) :: numerator, denominator
    type (Rational)               :: name
      name = Rational(0, 1)                              ! set defaults
      if ( present(numerator)  ) name % num = numerator
      if ( present(denominator)) name % den = denominator
      if ( name % den == 0     ) name % den = 1          ! now simplify
      call reduce (name) ; end function make_Rational

  function  mult_Rational (a, b) result (c)           ! to overload *
    type (Rational), intent(in) :: a, b
    type (Rational)             :: c
      c % num = a % num * b % num
      c % den = a % den * b % den
      call reduce (c) ; end function mult_Rational

  function Rational_ (numerator, denominator) result (name)
  !        Public Constructor for a rational type
    integer, optional, intent(in) :: numerator, denominator
    type (Rational)               :: name
      if ( denominator == 0 ) then ; name = Rational (numerator, 1)
      else ; name = Rational (numerator, denominator) ; end if
  end function Rational_

  subroutine reduce (name)                ! to simplest rational form
    type (Rational), intent(inout) :: name
    integer                        :: g     ! greatest common divisor
      g          = gcd (name % num, name % den)
      name % num = name % num/g
      name % den = name % den/g ; end subroutine reduce
end module class_Rational
```

Figure 3.15: A fairly complete rational number class.

mult_Rational. Here it is not necessary to overload the assignment operator, "=", when both of its operands are of the same intrinsic or defined type. However, to convert an integer to a rational we could, and have, defined an overloaded assignment operator procedure (line 10). Here we have provided the procedure, equal_Integer, which is automatically invoked when we write type (Rational) y; y = 4. That would be simpler than invoking the constructor called make_rational. Before moving on, note that the system does not yet know how to multiply an integer times a rational number, or vice versa. To do that one would have to add more functionality such as a function, say int_mult_rn, and add it to the "module procedure" list associated with the "*" operator. A typical main program that exercises most of the rational number functionality is given in Figure 3.16, along with typical numerical output. It tests the constructors Rational_ (line 9), make_Rational (lines 15, 19, 26), and a simple destructor delete_Rational (line 39). The intrinsic constructor (line 7) could have been used only if all the attributes were public, and that is considered an undesirable practice in OOP. The simple destructor actually just sets the "deleted" number to have a set of default components. Later we will see that constructors and destructors often must dynamically allocate and deallocate, respectively, memory associated with a specific instance of some object.

When considering which operators to overload for a newly defined object one should consider those that are used in sorting operations, such as the greater-than, >, and less-than, <, operators. They are often useful because of the need to sort various types of objects. If those symbols have been correctly overloaded, then a generic object sorting routine might be used or would require only a few changes.

3.4 Discussion

The previous sections have only briefly touched on some important OOP concepts. More details will be covered later after a general overview of the features of the Fortran language. There are more than 100 OOP languages. Persons involved in software development need to be aware that F90 can meet almost all of their needs for an OOP language. At the same time F90 includes the F77 standard as a subset and thus allows efficient use of the many millions of Fortran functions and subroutines developed in the past. The newer F95 standard is designed to make efficient use of super computers and massively parallel machines. It includes most of the high-performance Fortran features that are in wide use. Thus, efficient use of OOP on parallel machines is available through F90 and F95.

None of the OOP languages have all the features one might desire. For example, the useful concept of a "template," which is standard in C++, is not in the F90 standard. Yet the author has found that a few dozen lines of F90 code will define a preprocessor that allows templates to be defined in F90 and expanded in line at compile time. The real challenge in OOP is the actual OOA and OOD that must be completed before programming can begin regardless of the language employed. For example, several authors have described widely different approaches for defining classes to be used in constructing OO finite element systems. Additional sample applications of OOP in F90 will be given in the following chapters.

3.5 Exercises

1 Use the class_Circle to create a class_Sphere that computes the volume of a sphere. Have a method that accepts an argument of a Circle. Use the radius of the Circle via a new member get_Circle_radius to be added to the class_Circle.

```
include 'class_Rational.f90'
program Rational_test
use class_Rational
implicit none
  type (Rational) :: x, y, z
  ! ------- only if Rational is NOT private ----------
  ! x = Rational(22,7)    ! intrinsic constructor if public components

    x = Rational_(22,7)   ! public constructor if private components
    write (*,'("public    x  = ")',advance='no'); call list(x)
    write (*,'("converted x  = ", g9.4)') convert(x)
    call invert(x)
    write (*,'("inverted 1/x = ")',advance='no');  call list(x)

    x = make_Rational ()                    ! default constructor
    write (*,'("made null x  = ")',advance='no'); call list(x)
    y = 4                                   ! rational = integer overload
    write (*,'("integer y    = ")',advance='no'); call list(y)
    z = make_Rational (22,7)                ! manual constructor
    write (*,'("made full z  = ")',advance='no'); call list(z)
  !                     Test Accessors
    write (*,'("top of z     = ", g4.0)') get_numerator(z)
    write (*,'("bottom of z  = ", g4.0)') get_denominator(z)
  !                     Misc. Function Tests
    write (*,'("making x = 100/360, ")',advance='no')
    x = make_Rational (100,360)
    write (*,'("reduced x = ")',advance='no'); call list(x)
    write (*,'("copying x to y gives ")',advance='no')
    y = copy_Rational (x)
    write (*,'("a new y = ")',advance='no'); call list(y)
  !                    Test Overloaded Operators
    write (*,'("z * x gives ")',advance='no'); call list(z*x) ! times
    write (*,'("z + x gives ")',advance='no'); call list(z+x) ! add
    y = z                                          ! overloaded assignment
    write (*,'("y = z gives y as ")',advance='no'); call list(y)
    write (*,'("logic y == x gives ")',advance='no'); print *, y==x
    write (*,'("logic y == z gives ")',advance='no'); print *, y==z
  !                     Destruct
    call delete_Rational (y)      ! actually only null it here
    write (*,'("deleting y gives y = ")',advance='no'); call list(y)
end program Rational_test                        ! Running gives:
!  public     x  =  22 / 7       !  converted x  = 3.143
!  inverted 1/x =   7 / 22       !  made null x  =  0 / 1
!  integer y     =  4 / 1        !  made full z  =  22 / 7
!  top of z      =   22          !  bottom of z  =    7
!  making x = 100/360, reduced x =  5 / 18
!  copying x to y gives a new y =  5 / 18
!  z * x gives  55 / 63          !  z + x gives  431 / 126
!  y = z gives y as  22 / 7      !  logic y == x gives  F
!  logic y == z gives  T         !  deleting y gives y =  0 / 1
```

Figure 3.16: Testing the rational number class.

2 Use the class_Circle and class_Rectangle to create a class_Cylinder that computes the volume of a right circular cylinder. Have a method that accepts arguments of a Circle and a height and a second method that accepts arguments of a Rectangle and a radius. In the latter member use the height of the Rectangle via a new member get_Rectangle_height to be added to the class_Rectangle.

3 Create a vector class to treat vectors with an arbitrary number of real coefficients. Assume that the class_Vector is defined as follows:

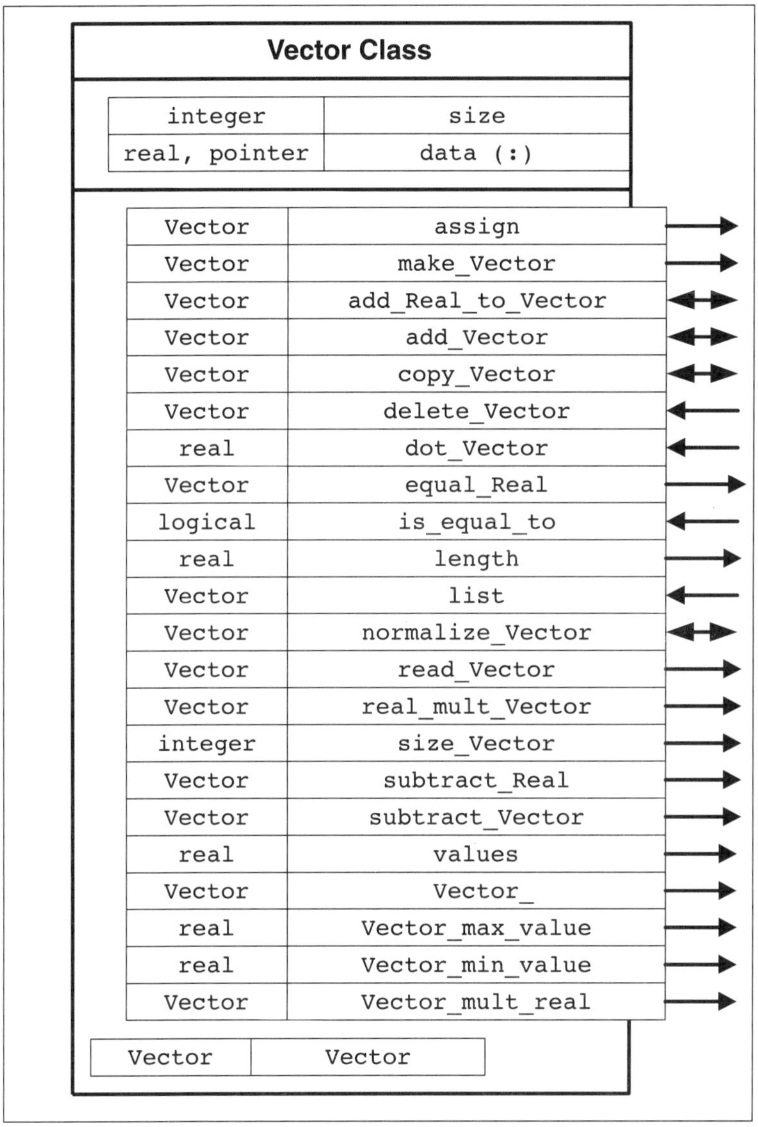

Overload the common operators of (+) with add_Vector and add_Real_to_Vector, (–) with subtract_Vector and subtract_Real, (*) with dot_Vector, real_mult_Vector and Vector_mult_real, (=) with equal_Real to set all coefficients to a single real number, and (==) with routine is_equal_to.

Include two constructors *assign* and make_Vector. Let *assign* convert a real array into an instance of a vector. Provide a destructor and means to read and write a vector, normalize a vector, and determine its extreme values.

4 Modify the preceding vector class to extend it to a Sparse_Vector_Class where the vast majority of the coefficients are zero. Store and operate only on the nonzero entries.

Sparse_Vector Class

integer	non_zeros
integer, pointer	rows (:)
real, pointer	values (:)

Sparse_Vector	make_Sparse_Vector
Sparse_Vector	add_Real_to_Sparse_Vector
Sparse_Vector	add_Sparse_Vector
Sparse_Vector	delete_Sparse_Vector
real	dot_Vector
Sparse_Vector	el_by_el_Mult
Sparse_Vector	equal_Vector
real	get_element
logical	is_equal_to
integer	largest_index
real	length
real	norm
Sparse_Vector	normalize_Vector
Sparse_Vector	pretty
Sparse_Vector	read_Vector
Sparse_Vector	real_mult_Sparse
integer	rows_of
Sparse_Vector	set_element
Sparse_Vector	show
Sparse_Vector	show_r_v
integer	size_of
Sparse_Vector	Sparse_mult_real
Sparse_vector	sub_Sparse_Vector
Sparse_Vector	sum_Sparse_Vector
real	Vector_max_value
real	Vector_min_value
Sparse_Vector	Vector_to_Sparse
Sparse_Vector	zero_Sparse

Sparse_Vector	Sparse_Vector

5 Consider an object for a simple inventory item as shown below:

```
module inventory_object
 implicit none
  public ! all member functions
  type inventory
   private ! all attributes
    character(len=50) :: name
    real              :: cost
    real              :: price
    integer           :: in_stock    ! number in stock
    integer           :: lead_time   ! work days to re-stock
  end type inventory

contains  ! functionality . . .
```

Plan the supporting methods needed to initialize an item, get or revise its attribute components, determine if it is empty, interactively input or output an item, save or restore to a binary file, and so forth. Consider if additional attributes, like the number of items, might be useful. Plan how such an object class could be used by an inventory system that keeps track of a large number of such items.

CHAPTER FOUR

Features of Programming Languages

The preceding chapter described the programming process as starting with a clearly specified task, expressing it mathematically as a set of algorithms, translating the algorithms into pseudocode, and finally, translating the pseudocode into a "real" programming language. The final stages of this prescription work because most (if not all) computational languages have remarkable similarities: they have statements, the sequencing of which is controlled by various loop and conditional constructs, and functions that foster program modularization. We indicated how similar MATLAB, C++, and Fortran are at this level, but these languages differ the more they are detailed. It is the purpose of this chapter to describe those details and bring you from a superficial acquaintance with a computational language to fluency. Today, the practicing engineer needs more than one programming language or environment. Once achieving familiarity with one, you will find that learning other languages is easy.

When selecting a programming tool for engineering calculations, one is often faced with two different levels of need. One level occurs when you need to solve a small problem quickly once, such as a homework assignment, and computational efficiency is not important. You may not care if your code takes 10 seconds or 100 seconds to execute; you want convenience. At that level it may make sense to use an engineering environment like MATLAB or Mathematica. At the other extreme you may be involved in wide-area weather prediction for which a 1-day run time instead of a 10-day run time defines a useful versus a nonuseful product. You might be developing a hospital laboratory system for reporting test results to an emergency room physician for whom an answer in 10 seconds versus an answer in 10 minutes can literally mean the difference between life or death for a patient. For programming at this level one wants an efficient language. Since such projects can involve programming teams in different countries, you want your language to be based on an international standard. Then you would choose to program a language such as C++ or F90. Because most students have experienced only the first-need level, they tend to overvalue the first approach and devalue the second. This chapter will illustrate that the skills needed for either approach are similar.

The structure of this chapter follows our usual progression in learning a language: what *variables* are, how variables can be combined into *expressions*, what constructs are available to control program *flow*, and how *functions* are defined so that we can employ modularity. The basics are described in Chapter 1; we assume you are familiar with the language basics described there. Initially, this chapter will parallel the program composition section of Chapter 1 as applied in the C++, F90, and MATLAB languages and then it will bring in more advanced topics.

The features of F90 to be discussed here have been combined in a series of tables and placed in Appendix A. It is expected that we will want to refer to those tables as we read

Table 4.1: Comment Syntax

Language	Syntax	Location
MATLAB	`% comment (to end of line)`	anywhere
C++	`// comment (to end of line)`	anywhere
F90	`! comment (to end of line)`	anywhere
F77	`* comment (to end of line)`	column 1

this section as well as later when we program. At times, references to C++ and MATLAB have been given to show the similarities between most languages and to provide an aid for when having to interface in reading codes in those languages.

4.1 Comments

In MATLAB and Fortran, a single character – '%' in MATLAB, '!' in F90 – located anywhere in a line of text means that the *remainder* of the text on that line constitutes the comment. In C, an entirely different structure for comments occurs. Comments begin with the two-character sequence '/*' and end with the next occurrence of the two-character sequence '*/'. In C, comments can occur anywhere in a program; they can consume a portion of a line, temporarily interrupting a statement, or they can span multiple lines of text. Although C++ allows the use of the C comment syntax, it has added a more popular two-character sequence '//' to precede a comment to the end of a line. Table 4.1 gives a summary of these comments syntax. It is also in the "Fortran 90 Overview" for quick reference. Samples of comment statements are shown in Figure 1.3, which gives the corresponding versions of the classic "hello world" program included in most introductory programming texts.

4.2 Statements and Expressions

Before introducing statements and expressions, we offer a word about documenting what you program. We encourage the heavy use of comments. The three languages of concern here all allow comment lines and comments appended to the end of statements. Their form is given in Figure 1.3 and Table 4.1.

The preceding languages currently allow variable names to contain up to 31 characters and allow the use of the underscore, '_', to aid in clarity by serving as a virtual space character, as in my_name. Another useful convention is to use uppercase first letters for words composing part of a variable's name: MyName. Fortran and MATLAB allow a program line to contain up to 132 characters, whereas C++ has no limit on line length. Since the old F77 standard was physically limited to holes punched in a card, it allowed only a line length of 72 characters and a maximum name length of 6 characters but did not allow the use of the underscore in a name. In this text, we will usually keep line lengths to less than 65 characters in order to make the programs more readable.

A statement in these three languages has a structure common to them all:

```
variable = expression
```

The built-in, or intrinsic, data types allowed for variables are summarized in Table 4.2. Additional user-defined types will be considered later. The expressions usually involve the use of arithmetic operators (Table 4.3) relational operators (Table 4.4), or both. The order

Table 4.2: Intrinsic Data Types of Variables

Storage	MATLAB[a]	C++	F90	F77
byte		char	character::	character
integer		int	integer::	integer
single precision		float	real::	real
double precision		double	real*8::	double precision
complex		[b]	complex::	complex
Boolean		bool	logical::	logical
argument			parameter::	parameter
pointer		*	pointer::	
structure		struct	type::	

[a] MATLAB4 requires no variable type declaration; the only two distinct types in MATLAB are strings and reals (which include complex). Booleans are just 0's and 1's treated as reals. MATLAB5 allows the user to select more types.

[b] There is no specific data type for a complex variable in C++; they must be created by the programmer.

in which the language applies these operators is called their precedence, which is shown in Table 4.5. The precedence is also given in the "Fortran 90 Overview" for quick reference.

In moving from MATLAB to high-level languages one finds that it is necessary to define the type of each variable. Fortran has a default-naming convention for its variables, and it allows an easy overriding of that built-in "implicit" convention. Since most engineering and mathematical publications used the letters from "i" through "n" as subscripts, summation ranges, loop counters, and so forth, Fortran first was released with implicit variable typing such that all variables whose name began with the letters "i" through "n," inclusive, defaulted to integers unless declared otherwise. All other variables defaulted to be real unless declared otherwise. In other words, you can think of the default code as if it contained the statements

```
IMPLICIT INTEGER (I-N)       ! F77 and F90 Default
IMPLICIT REAL    (A-H, O-Z) ! F77 and F90 Default
```

Table 4.3: Arithmetic Operators

Description	MATLAB[a]	C++	Fortran[b]
addition	+	+	+
subtraction[c]	-	-	-
multiplication	* and .*	*	*
division	/ and ./	/	/
exponentiation	^ and .^	pow[d]	**
remainder		%	
increment		++	
decrement		--	
parentheses (expression grouping)	()	()	()

[a] When performing arithmetic operations on matrices in MATLAB, a period ('.') must be placed before the operator if scalar arithmetic is desired. Otherwise, MATLAB assumes matrix operations; figure out the difference between '*' and '.*'. Note that since matrix and scalar addition coincide, no '.+' operator exists (same holds for subtraction).

[b] Fortran 90 allows the user to change operators and to define new operator symbols.

[c] In all languages the minus sign is used for negation (i.e., changing sign).

[d] In C++ the exponentiation is calculated by function $pow(x, y)$.

Table 4.4: Relational Operators (Arithmetic and Logical)

Description	MATLAB	C++	F90	F77
Equal to	==	==	==	.EQ.
Not equal to	~=	!=	/=	.NE.
Less than	<	<	<	.LT.
Less or equal	<=	<=	<=	.LE.
Greater than	>	>	>	.GT.
Greater or equal	>=	>=	>=	.GE.
Logical NOT	~	!	.NOT.	.NOT.
Logical AND	&	&&	.AND.	.AND.
Logical inclusive OR	!	||	.OR.	.OR.
Logical exclusive OR	xor		.XOR.	.XOR.
Logical equivalent	==	==	.EQV.	.EQV.
Logical not equivalent	~=	!=	.NEQV.	.NEQV.

The effect is automatic even if the statements are omitted.

Explicit-type declarations override any given IMPLICIT types. For example, if the code had the implicit defaults above, one could also explicitly identify the exceptions to those default rules such as the statements

```
INTEGER :: Temp_row
REAL :: Interest = 0.04 ! declare and initialize
CHARACTER (Len=8) :: Months_of_year(12)
```

Table 4.5: Precedence Pecking Order

MATLAB Operators	C++ Operators	F90 Operators[a]	F77 Operators
()	() [] -> .	()	()
+ -	! ++ -- + - * & (type) sizeof	**	**
* /	* / %	* /	* /
+ -[b]	+ -[b]	+ -[b]	+ -[b]
< <= > >=	<< >>	//	//
== ~=	< <= > >=	== /= < <= > >=	.EQ. .NE. .LT. .LE. .GT. .GE.
~	== !=	.NOT.	.NOT.
&	&&	.AND.	.AND.
|	||	.OR.	.OR.
=	|	.EQV. .NEQV.	.EQV. .NEQV.
	?:		
	= += -= *= /= %= &= ^= |= <<= >>=		
	,		

[a] User-defined unary (binary) operators have the highest (lowest) precedence in F90.

[b] These are binary operators representing addition and subtraction. Unary operators + and − have higher precedence.

We will also see that the programmer can define new data types and explicitly declare their type as well.

The F90 standard discourages the use of any IMPLICIT variables such as

```
IMPLICIT COMPLEX (X-Z)           ! Complex variables
IMPLICIT DOUBLE PRECISION (A-H)  ! Double Precision reals
```

and encourages the use of

```
IMPLICIT NONE,
```

which forces the programmer to specifically declare the type of each and every variable used and is referred to as *strong typing*. However, you need to know that such default variable types exist because they are used in many millions of lines of older Fortran code, and at some point you will need to use or change such an existing program.

A sample program that employs the typical math operators in F90 is shown in Figure 4.1. It presents examples of addition (line 12), subtraction (line 15), multiplication (line 18), division (line 21), as well as the use of the remainder or modulo function (line 24), exponentiation (line 27), and square root operators (line 30). In addition it shows a way of inputting data from the default input device (line 10). The results are appended as comments (lines 33–41). Observe that a program must include one and only one segment that begins with the word `program` (line 1) and ends with the line `end program` (line 33). If a name is assigned to the program, then it must be appended to both of these lines. Often the name of `main` is used, as here, but it is not required as it is in C++ . A C++ formulation of this example is included for comparison in the appendix C as are several other examples from this chapter.

A special expression available in MATLAB and F90 uses the colon operator (`:`) to indicate forming a vector (row matrix) of numbers according to an arithmetic progression. In MATLAB, the expression `b:i:e` means the vector $[b\ (b+i)\ (b+2i)\ \cdots\ (b+Ni)]$, where $(b+Ni)$ is the largest number less than or equal to (greater than or equal to if i is negative) the value of the variable `e`. Thus, `b` means "beginning value," `i` means the increment, and `e` the end value. The expression `b:e` means that the increment equals 1. You can use this construct to excise a portion of a vector or matrix. For example, `x(2:5)` equals the vector comprising the second through fifth elements of `x`, and `A(3:5,i:j)` creates a matrix from the third, fourth, and fifth rows, ith through jth columns of the matrix `A`. The language F90 uses the convention of `b:e:i` and has the same defaults when `:i` is omitted. This operator, also known as the *subscript triplet*, is described in Table 4.6.

Of course, expressions often involve the use of functions. A tabulation of the built-in functions in our languages is given in Table 4.7 and the F90 overview as are all the remaining tables of this chapter.

The arguments of functions and subprograms have some important properties that vary with the language used. Primarily, we are interested in how actual arguments are passed to the dummy arguments in the subprogram. This data passing happens by either of two fundamentally different ways: by reference or by value. One should understand the difference between these two mechanisms.

"Passing by reference" means that the address in memory of the actual argument is passed to the subprogram instead of the value stored at that address. The corresponding dummy argument in the subprogram has the same address. That is, both arguments refer to the same memory location, and thus any change to that argument within the subprogram is passed back to the calling code. A variable is passed by reference to a subroutine whenever it is expected that it should be changed by the subprogram. A related term is "dereferencing." When you

```
program simple_arithmetic
! Examples of simple arithmetic in F90
implicit none
  integer :: Integer_Var_1, Integer_Var_2      ! user inputs
  integer :: Mult_Result, Div_Result, Add_Result
  integer :: Sub_Result, Mod_Result
  real    :: Pow_Result, Sqrt_Result

   print *, 'Enter two integers:'
   read  *, Integer_Var_1, Integer_Var_2

   Add_Result = Integer_Var_1 + Integer_Var_2
   print *, Integer_Var_1,' + ', Integer_Var_2,' = ', Add_Result

   Sub_Result = Integer_Var_1 - Integer_Var_2
   print *, Integer_Var_1,' - ', Integer_Var_2,' = ', Sub_Result

   Mult_Result = Integer_Var_1 * Integer_Var_2
   print *, Integer_Var_1,' * ', Integer_Var_2,' = ', Mult_Result

   Div_Result = Integer_Var_1 / Integer_Var_2
   print *, Integer_Var_1,' / ', Integer_Var_2,' = ', Div_Result

   Mod_Result = mod (Integer_Var_1, Integer_Var_2) ! remainder
   print *, Integer_Var_1,' mod ', Integer_Var_2,' = ', Mod_Result

   Pow_Result = Integer_Var_1 ** Integer_Var_2   ! raise to power
   print *, Integer_Var_1,' ^ ', Integer_Var_2,' = ', Pow_Result

   Sqrt_Result = sqrt( real(Integer_Var_1))
   print *,'Square root of ', Integer_Var_1,' = ', Sqrt_Result

end program simple_arithmetic    ! Running produces:
  ! Enter two integers:     25    4
  ! 25  +  4  =  29
  ! 25  -  4  =  21
  ! 25  *  4  =  100
  ! 25  /  4  =  6, note integer
  ! 25  mod  4  =  1
  ! 25  ^  4  =  3.9062500E+05
  ! Square root of  25  =  5.0000000
```

Figure 4.1: Typical math and functions in F90.

Table 4.6: Colon Operator Syntax and Its Applications

Syntax	F90	MATLAB	Use	F90	MATLAB
Default	B:E:I[a]	B:I:E	Array subscript ranges	yes	yes
≥ B	B:	B:	Character positions in a string	yes	yes
≤ E	:E	:E	Loop control	no	yes
Full range	:	:	Array element generation	no	yes

[a] B = Beginning, E = Ending, I = Increment

Table 4.7: Mathematical functions

Description	MATLAB	C++	F90	F77
exponential	exp(x)	exp(x)	exp(x)	exp(x)
natural log	log(x)	log(x)	log(x)	log(x)
base 10 log	log10(x)	log10(x)	log10(x)	log10(x)
square root	sqrt(x)	sqrt(x)	sqrt(x)	sqrt(x)
raise to power (x^r)	x.^r	pow(x,r)	x**r	x**r
absolute value	abs(x)	fabs(x)	abs(x)	abs(x)
smallest integer>x	ceil(x)	ceil(x)	ceiling(x)	
largest integer<x	floor(x)	floor(x)	floor(x)	
division remainder	rem(x,y)	fmod(x,y)	mod(x,y)[a]	mod(x,y)
modulo			modulo(x,y)[a]	
complex conjugate	conj(z)		conjg(z)	conjg(z)
imaginary part	imag(z)		imag(z)	aimag(z)
drop fraction	fix(x)		aint(x)	aint(x)
round number	round(x)		nint(x)	nint(x)
cosine	cos(x)	cos(x)	cos(x)	cos(x)
sine	sin(x)	sin(x)	sin(x)	sin(x)
tangent	tan(x)	tan(x)	tan(x)	tan(x)
arccosine	acos(x)	acos(x)	acos(x)	acos(x)
arcsine	asin(x)	asin(x)	asin(x)	asin(x)
arctangent	atan(x)	atan(x)	atan(x)	atan(x)
arctangent[b]	atan2(x,y)	atan2(x,y)	atan2(x,y)	atan2(x,y)
hyperbolic cosine	cosh(x)	cosh(x)	cosh(x)	cosh(x)
hyperbolic sine	sinh(x)	sinh(x)	sinh(x)	sinh(x)
hyperbolic tangent	tanh(x)	tanh(x)	tanh(x)	tanh(x)
hyperbolic arccosine	acosh(x)			
hyperbolic arcsine	asinh(x)			
hyperbolic arctan	atanh(x)			

[a] Differ for $x < 0$.

[b] atan2(x,y) is used to calculate the arctangent of x/y in the range $[-\pi, +\pi]$. The one-argument function atan(x) computes the arctangent of x in the range $[-\pi/2, +\pi/2]$.

dereference a memory address, you are telling the computer to get the information located at the address. Typically, one indirectly gives the address by citing the name of a pointer variable or a reference variable.

"Passing by value" means that the value of the actual argument stored at its address in memory is copied and the copy is passed to the dummy argument in the subprogram. Thus, any change to the argument within the subprogram is not passed back to the calling code. The two passing methods do not clearly show the intended use of the argument within the subprogram. Is it to be passed in for use only, passed in for changing and returned, or is it to be created in the subprogram and passed out for use in the calling code? For additional safety and clarity modern languages provide some way to allow the programmer to optionally specify such intent explicitly.

Both C++ and MATLAB use the pass-by-value method as their default mode. This means the value associated with the argument name, say arg_name, is copied and passed to the function. That copying could be very inefficient if the argument is a huge array. To denote that you want to have the C++ argument passed by reference you must precede the argument name with an ampersand (&), such as &arg_name, in the calling code. Then within the subprogram

Table 4.8: Flow Control Statements

Description	C++	F90	F77	MATLAB
Conditionally execute statements	`if` `{ }`	`if` `end if`	`if` `end if`	`if` `end`
Loop a specific number of times	`for k=1:n` `{ }`	`do k=1,n` `end do`	`do # k=1,n` `# continue`	`for k=1:n` `end`
Loop an indefinite number of times	`while` `{ }`	`do while` `end do`	— —	`while` `end`
Terminate and exit loop	`break`	`exit`	`go to`	`break`
Skip a cycle of loop	`continue`	`cycle`	`go to`	—
Display message and abort	`error()`	`stop`	`stop`	`error`
Return to invoking function	`return`	`return`	`return`	`return`
Conditional array action	—	`where`	—	`if`
Conditional alternate statements	`else` `else if`	`else` `elseif`	`else` `elseif`	`else` `elseif`
Conditional array alternatives	— —	`elsewhere` —	— —	`else` `elseif`
Conditional case selections	`switch { }`	`select case` `end select`	`if` `end if`	`if` `end`

the corresponding dummy variable must be dereferenced by preceding the name with an asterisk (*) such as `*arg_name`. Conversely, Fortran uses the passing-by-reference method as its default mode. On the rare occasions when one wants to pass by value simply surround the argument name with parentheses, for example (`arg_name`), in the calling code. In either case it is recommended that you cite each argument with the optional "intent" statement within the subprogram. Examples of the two passing options are covered in Section 4.5.

4.3 Flow Control

The basic flow control constructs present in our selected engineering languages are *loops* – repetitive execution of a block of statements – and *conditionals* – diversions around blocks of statements. A typical set of flow-control statement types are summarized in Table 4.8. Most of these will be illustrated in detail in the following sections.

4.3.1 Explicit Loops

The following discussion will introduce the important concept of loops. These are required in most programs. However, the reader is warned that today the writing of explicit loops is generally not the most efficient way to execute a loop operation in Fortran90 and MATLAB. Of course, older languages like F77 and C do require them; thus, the time spent here not only covers the explicit loop concepts but aids one in reading older languages. Our pseudocode for the common loops is

Loop	Pseudocode

Indexed loop	`for index=b,i,e`
	  statements
	  `end for`

Pretest loop	`while (test)`
	  statements
	  `end while`

Posttest loop	`do`
	  statements
	  `if (test) exit`
	  `end do`

In engineering programming one often needs to perform a group of operations repeatedly. Most computer languages have a statement to execute this powerful and widely used feature. In Fortran this is the DO statement, and in C++ and MATLAB it is the FOR statement. This one statement provides for the initialization, incrementing, and testing of the loop variable plus repeated execution of a group of statements contained within the loop. In Fortran77, the loop always cites a label number that indicates the extent of the statements enclosed in the loop. This is allowed in F90, but not recommended, and is considered obsolete. Instead, the END DO indicates the extent of the loop, and the number label is omitted in both places. However, F90 does allow a name to be assigned to a loop. Then the structure is denoted as NAME:DO followed by END DO NAME. Examples of the syntax for these statements for the languages of interest are given in Table 4.9.

A simple example of combining loops and array indexing is illustrated in Figures. 4.2 and 4.3. Note in Figure 4.2 that the final value of a loop counter (called *Integer_Var* here) upon exiting the loop (line 10) can be language- or compiler-dependent despite their being same here. In Figure 4.3, we introduce for the first time a variable with a single subscript (line 5) containing five numbers (integers) to be initialized manually (lines 8–10) and then to be

Table 4.9: Basic Loop Constructs

Loop	MATLAB	C++	Fortran

Indexed loop	`for index=matrix`
	  statements
	  `end`
		`for (init;test;inc)`
		  {
		  statements
		  }
			`do index=b,e,i`
			  statements
			  `end do`

Pretest loop	`while (test)`
	  statements
	  `end`
		`while (test) {`
		  statements
		  }
			`do while (test)`
			  statements
			  `end do`

Posttest loop		`do {`
		  statements
		  `} while (test)`
			`do`
			  statements
			  `if (test) exit`
			  `end do`

```
program  simple_loop
! Examples of a simple loop in F90
implicit none
   integer  Integer_Var

     do Integer_Var = 0,4,1
         print *, 'The loop variable is:', Integer_Var
     end do ! over Integer_Var

     print *, 'The final loop variable is:', Integer_Var

end program simple_loop !  Running produces:
!  The loop variable is: 0
!  The loop variable is: 1
!  The loop variable is: 2
!  The loop variable is: 3
!  The loop variable is: 4
!  The final loop variable is: 5 <- NOTE
```

Figure 4.2: Typical looping concepts in F90.

listed in a loop (lines 12–15) over all their values. Note that C++ stores the first entry in an array at position zero (see appendix C listing), MATLAB uses position one, and F90 defaults to position one.

In C++ and Fortran 90, a special option is allowed to create loops that run "forever." These could be used, for example, to read an unknown amount of data until terminated,

```
[ 1]  program  array_indexing
[ 2]  !  Examples of simple array indexing in F90
[ 3]  implicit none
[ 4]    integer, parameter :: max = 5
[ 5]    integer  Integer_Array(max) ! =(/ 10 20 30 40 50 /), or set below
[ 6]    integer  loopcount
[ 7]
[ 8]      Integer_Array(1) = 10    ! F90 index starts at 1, usually
[ 9]      Integer_Array(2) = 20 ; Integer_Array(3) = 30
[10]      Integer_Array(4) = 40 ; Integer_Array(5) = 50
[11]
[12]      do loopcount = 1, max                         ! & means continued
[13]          print *, 'The loop counter is: ', loopcount, &
[14]          ' with an array value of: ',Integer_Array(loopcount)
[15]      end do ! over loopcount
[16]
[17]      print *, 'The final loop counter is: ', loopcount
[18]
[19]  end program array_indexing
[20]  !  Running produces:
[21]  ! The loop counter is: 1 with an array value of: 10
[22]  ! The loop counter is: 2 with an array value of: 20
[23]  ! The loop counter is: 3 with an array value of: 30
[24]  ! The loop counter is: 4 with an array value of: 40
[25]  ! The loop counter is: 5 with an array value of: 50
[26]  ! The final loop counter is: 6
```

Figure 4.3: Simple array indexing in F90.

in a nonfatal way, by the input statement. In C++, one omits the three loop controls, such as

```
for (;;) {// forever loop
    loop_block
    } // end forever loop,
```

whereas in F90, one simply omits the loop control and gives only the DO command:

```
do ! forever
   loop_block
end do ! forever
```

Most of the time, an infinite loop is used as a *loop_while_true* or a *loop_until_true* construct. These will be considered shortly.

4.3.2 Implied Loops

Fortran and MATLAB have shorthand methods for constructing "implied loops." Both languages offer the colon operator to imply an incremental range of integer values. Its syntax and types of applications are given in Table 4.6 (page 61). The allowed usages of the operator differ slightly between the two languages. Note that this means that the loop controls are slightly different in that the do control employs commas instead of colons. For example, two equivalent loops are

Fortran	MATLAB
do k=B,E,I	for k=B:I:E
A(k) = k**2	A(k) = k∧2
end do	end

Fortran offers an additional formal implied do loop that replaces the do and end do with a closed pair of parentheses in the syntax

```
(object, k = B,E,I),
```

where again the increment, `I`, defaults to unity if not supplied. The implied do above is equivalent to the formal loop

```
do k=B,E,I
  define the object ...
end do.
```

However, the object defined in the implied loop can only be utilized for four specific Fortran operations: *(1)* `read` actions, *(2)* `print` and `write` actions, *(3)* `data` variables (not value) definitions, and *(4)* definition of array elements. For example,

```
print *, (4*k-1, k=1,10,3) ! 3, 15, 27, 39
read *, (A(j,:), j=1,rows) ! read A by rows, sequentially.
```

The implied do loops can be nested to any level like the standard do statement. One simply makes the inner loop the object of the outer loop so that

```
((object_j_k, j=min, max), k=k1,k2,inc)
```

implies the nested loop

```
do k=k1,k2,inc
  do j=min, max
    utilize the object_j_k
  end do ! over j
end do ! over k.
```

For example,

```
print *, (((A(k)*B(j)+3), j=1,5), k=1,max)
! read array by rows in each plane
read *, (((A(i,j,k), j=1,cols), i=1,rows), k=1,max).
```

Actually, there is even a simpler default form of implied dos for reading and writing arrays. That default is to access arrays by columns. That is, process the leftmost subscript first. Thus, for an array with three subscripts,

```
read *, A    ⟺    read *, (((A(i,j,k), i=1,rows), j=1,cols), k=1,planes).
```

Both languages allow the implied loops to be employed to create an array vector simply by placing the implied loop inside the standard array delimit symbols. For example, we may want an array to distribute $N + 1$ points equally over the distance from zero to D.

```
F90:     X = (/(k,k=0,N)/)* D/(N+1)
MATLAB : X = [0:N] * D / (N+1),
```

which illustrates that MATLAB allows the use of the colon operator to define arrays, but F90 does not.

In addition to locating elements in an array by the regular incrementing of loop variables, both Fortran90 and MATLAB support even more specific selections of elements: by random location via vector subscripts, or by value via logical masks such as `where` and `if` in F90 and MATLAB, respectively.

4.3.3 Conditionals

Logic tests are frequently needed to control the execution of a block of statements. The most basic operation occurs when we want to do something when a logic test gives a true answer. We call that a simple `IF` statement. When the test is true, the program executes the block of statements following the `IF`. Often only one statement is needed, and so C++ and Fortran allow that one statement to end the line that begins with the `IF` logic. Frequently we will *nest* another `IF` within the statements from a higher level `IF`. The common language syntax forms for the simple `IF` are given in Table 4.10 along with the examples of where a second true group is nested inside the first, as shown in Table 4.11.

The next simplest case occurs where we need to do one thing when the answer is true and a different thing when the logic test is false. Then the syntax changes simply to an `IF` {***true group***} `ELSE` {***false group***} mode of execution. The typical `IF-ELSE` syntaxes of the various languages are given in Table 4.12. Of course, the statement groups above can contain other `IF` or `IF-ELSE` statements nested within them. They can also contain any valid statements, including `DO` or `FOR` loops.

The most complicated logic tests occur when the number of cases for the answer goes beyond the two (true-false) of the `IF-ELSE` control structure. These multiple case decisions can be handled with the `IF-ELSEIF-ELSE` control structures whose syntax is given in Table 4.13. They involve a sequence of logic tests, each of which is followed by a group of statements to be

Table 4.10: `IF` Constructs. The quantity `_Expression` means a logical expression having a value that is either `TRUE` of `FALSE`. The term *`true statement`* or *`true group`* means that the statement or group of statements, respectively, are executed if the conditional in the `if` Statement evaluates to `TRUE`

MATLAB	Fortran	C++

`if l_expression`
  `true group`
`end`
	`IF (l_expression) THEN`
	  `true group`
	`END IF`
		`if (l_expression)`
		  `{`
		   `true group;`
		  `}`

	`IF (l_expression)` *`true statement`*	`if (l_expression)` *`true statement;`*

executed if, and only if, the test answer is true. There can be any number of such tests. They are terminated with an ELSE group of default statements to be executed if *none* of the logic tests are true. Actually, the ELSE action is optional. For program clarity or debugging, it should be included even if it only prints a warning message or contains a comment statement. Typical "if" and "if-else" coding is given in Figures 4.4, 4.5, and 4.6. Figure 4.4 simply uses the three logical comparisons of "greater than" (line 9), "less than" (line 12), or "equal to" (line 15), respectively. Figure 4.5 goes a step further by combining two tests with a logical "and" test (line 9) and includes a second else branch (line 11) to handle the case where the `if` is false. Although the input to these programs was numbers (line 7), the third sample program in Figure 4.6 accepts logical input (lines 6,8) that represents either true or false values and carries out Boolean operations to negate an input (via NOT in line 9) or to compare two inputs (with an AND in line 11, or OR in line 17, etc.) to produce a third logical value.

Since following the logic of many `IF-ELSEIF-ELSE` statements can be very confusing, both the C++ and Fortran languages allow a CASE selection or "switching" operation based on the value (numerical or character) of some expression. For any allowed specified CASE value, a group of statements is executed. If the value does not match any of the specified allowed CASE values, then a default group of statements are executed. These are illustrated in Table 4.14.

Table 4.11: Nested `IF` Constructs

MATLAB	Fortran	C++

`if l_expression1`
  `true group A`
 `if l_expression2`
   `true group B`
 `end`
  `true group C`
`end`
`statement group D`
	`IF (l_expression1) THEN`
	  `true group A`
	 `IF (l_expression2) THEN`
	   `true group B`
	 `END IF`
	  `true group C`
	`END IF`
	`statement group D`
		`if (l_expression1)`
		 `{`
		 `true group A`
		 `if (l_expression2)`
		  `{`
		   `true group B`
		  `}`
		  `true group C`
		 `}`
		`statement group D`

Table 4.12: Logical IF-ELSE Constructs

MATLAB	Fortran	C++

if l_expression
  true group A
else
  false group B
end
	IF (l_expression) THEN
	  true group A
	ELSE
	  false group B
	END IF
		if (l_expression)
		  {
		  true group A
		  }
		else
		  {
		  false group B
		  }

Fortran90 offers an additional optional feature called *construct names* that can be employed with the IF and SELECT CASE constructs above to improve the readability of the program. The optional name, followed by a colon, precedes the key words IF and SELECT CASE. To be consistent, the name should also follow the key words END IF or END SELECT, which always close the constructs. The construct name option is also available for loops where it offers an additional pair of control actions that will be explained later. Examples of these optional F90 features are given in Table 4.15.

Although C++ and MATLAB do not formally offer this option, the same enhancement of readability can be achieved by using the trailing comment feature to append a name or description at the beginning and end of these logic construct blocks.

Both C++ and Fortran allow statement labels and provide controls to branch to specific labels. Today you are generally advised **not** to use a GO TO and its associated label! However, they are common in many F77 codes. There are a few cases in which a GO TO is still considered acceptable. For example, the pseudo-WHILE construct of F77 requires a GO TO

Table 4.13: Logical IF-ELSE-IF constructs

MATLAB	Fortran	C++

if l_expression1
  true group A
elseif l_expression2
  true group B
elseif l_expression3
  true group C
else
  default group D
end
	IF (l_expression1) THEN
	  true group A
	ELSE IF (l_expression2) THEN
	  true group B
	ELSE IF (l_expression3) THEN
	  true group C
	ELSE
	  default group D
	END IF
		if (l_expression1)
		  {
		  true group A
		  }
		else if (l_expression2)
		  {
		  true group B
		  }
		else if (l_expression3)
		  {
		  true group C
		  }
		else
		  {
		  default group D
		  }

```
program relational_operators
! Examples of relational "if" operator in F90
implicit none
   integer :: Integer_Var_1, Integer_Var_2      ! user inputs

     print *, 'Enter two integers:'
     read  *, Integer_Var_1, Integer_Var_2

     if ( Integer_Var_1 > Integer_Var_2 ) &
       print *, Integer_Var_1,' is greater than ', Integer_Var_2

     if ( Integer_Var_1 < Integer_Var_2 ) &
       print *, Integer_Var_1,' is less than ', Integer_Var_2

     if ( Integer_Var_1 == Integer_Var_2 ) &
       print *, Integer_Var_1,' is equal to ', Integer_Var_2

end program relational_operators

!  Running with 25 and 4 produces:
! Enter two integers:
! 25  is greater than 4
```

Figure 4.4: Typical relational operators in F90.

as follows:

```
initialize test
IF (l_expression) THEN
    true statement group
    modify logical value
    GO TO #
END IF.
```

The GO TO can also be utilized effectively in both Fortran and C++ to break out of several nested loops. This is illustrated in Table 4.16. The "break-out" construct can be used in the situation when, as a part of a subroutine, you want the program to exit the loop and also the subroutine, returning control to the calling program. To do that, one would simply

```
program if_else_logic
!  Illustrate a simple if-else logic in F90
implicit none
   integer Integer_Var

     print *,'Enter an integer: '
     read  *, Integer_Var

     if ( Integer_Var > 5 .and. Integer_Var < 10 ) then
        print *, Integer_Var, ' is greater than 5 and less than 10'
     else
        print *, Integer_Var, ' is not greater than 5 and less than 10'
     end if ! range of input

end program if_else_logic
!
! Running with 3 gives: 3  is not greater than 5 and less than 10
! Running with 8 gives: 8  is greater than 5 and less than 10
```

Figure 4.5: Typical If-Else uses in F90.

```
program Logical_operators
! Examples of Logical operators in F90
implicit none
  logical :: Logic_Var_1, Logic_Var_2
    print *,'Print logical value of A (T or F):'
    read  *, Logic_Var_1
    print *,'Print logical value of B (T or F):'
    read  *, Logic_Var_2
    print *,'NOT A is ', (.NOT. Logic_Var_1)

    if ( Logic_Var_1 .AND. Logic_Var_2 ) then
      print *, 'A ANDed with B is true'
    else
      print *, 'A ANDed with B is false'
    end if ! for AND

    if ( Logic_Var_1 .OR. Logic_Var_2 ) then
      print *, 'A ORed with B is true'
    else
      print *, 'A ORed with B is false'
    end if ! for OR

    if ( Logic_Var_1 .EQV. Logic_Var_2 ) then
      print *, 'A EQiValent with B is true'
    else
      print *, 'A EQiValent with B is false'
    end if ! for EQV

    if ( Logic_Var_1 .NEQV. Logic_Var_2 ) then
      print *, 'A Not EQiValent with B is true'
    else
      print *, 'A Not EQiValent with B is false'
    end if ! for NEQV

end program Logical_operators
! Running with T and F produces:
! Print logical value of A (T or F): T
! Print logical value of B (T or F): F
! NOT A is F
! A ANDed with B is false
! A ORed with B is true
! A EQiValent with B is false
! A Not EQiValent with B is true
```

Figure 4.6: Typical logical operators in F90.

replace the GO TO statement with the RETURN statement. In F90, one should also append the comment "! to calling program" to assist in making the subroutine more readable.

You may find it necessary to skip a cycle in loop execution, exit from a single loop, or do both. Both Fortran and C++ provide these control options without requiring the use of a GO TO. To skip a loop cycle, Fortran90 and C++ use the statements CYCLE and continue, respectively, and EXIT and break to abort a loop. These constructs are shown in Tables 4.17 and 4.18. Other forms of the GO TO in F77 were declared obsolete in F90 and should not be used. The Fortran abort examples could also use the RETURN option described above in the rare cases when it proves to be more desirable or efficient.

As mentioned earlier, F90 allows the programmer to use "named" DO constructs. In addition to improving readability, this feature also offers additional control over nested loops

Table 4.14: Case Selection Constructs

F90	C++
SELECT CASE (expression)	switch (expression)
CASE (value 1)	{
group 1	case value 1 :
CASE (value 2)	*group 1*
group 2	break;
⋮	case value 2 :
CASE (value n)	*group 2*
group n	break;
CASE DEFAULT	⋮
default group	case value n :
END SELECT	*group n*
	break;
	default:
	default group
	break;
	}

because we can associate the CYCLE and EXIT commands with a specific loop (Table 4.19). Without the optional name, the CYCLE and EXIT commands act only on the innermost loop in which they lie. We will see later that Fortran90 allows another type of loop called WHERE that is designed to operate on arrays.

4.3.3.1 Looping While True or Until True. It is very common to need to perform a loop so long as a condition is true or to run the loop until a condition becomes `true`. The two are very similar, and both represent loops that would run forever unless specifically terminated. We will refer to these two approaches as WHILE loops and UNTIL loops. The WHILE logic test is made first to determine if the loop will be entered. Clearly, this means that if the logic test is `false` the first time it is tested, the statement blocks controlled by the WHILE are never executed. If the WHILE loop is entered, something in the loop must eventually change the value of a variable in the logic test or the loop would run forever. Once a change causes the WHILE logic test to be `false`, control is transferred to the first statement following the WHILE structure. By way of comparison, an UNTIL loop is always entered at least once. When the

Table 4.15: F90 Optional Logic Block Names

F90 Named IF	F90Named SELECT
name: IF (logical_1) THEN	name: SELECT CASE (expression)
true group A	CASE (value 1)
ELSEIF (logical_2) THEN	*group 1*
true group B	CASE (value 2)
ELSE	*group 2*
default group C	CASE DEFAULT
ENDIF name	*default group*
	END SELECT name

Table 4.16: GO TO Break-out of nested loops. This situation can be an exception to the general recommendation to avoid GO TO statements.

Fortran 77	C++
`DO 1 ...`	`for (...) {`
`  DO 2 ...`	`  for (...) {`
`    ...`	`    ...`
`    IF (disaster) THEN`	`    if (disaster)`
`      GO TO 3`	`      go to error`
`    END IF`	`    ...`
`    ...`	`  }`
`2 END DO`	`}`
`1 END DO`	`error:`
`3 *next statement*`	

loop is entered, a beginning statement group is executed. Then the logic test is evaluated. If the test result is `true`, the loop is exited and control is passed to the next statement after the group. If the test is `false`, then an optional second statement group is executed before the loop returns to the beginning statement group. The pseudocode for these two similar structures are given as follows:

while true	until true
`logic_variable = true`	`logic_variable = false`
`begin:`	`begin:`
`if (logic_variable) then % true`	*`statements`*
`  true_group`	`if (logic_variable) then`
`  re-evaluate logic_variable`	`  exit the loop`
`go to begin`	`else % false`
`else % false`	`  false_group`
`  exit loop`	`  re-evaluate logic_variable`
`end if`	`go to begin`
	`end if`

Table 4.17: Skip a Single Loop Cycle

F77	F90	C++
`DO 1 I = 1,N`	`DO I = 1,N`	`for (i=1; i<n; i++)`
`  ...`	`  ...`	`  {`
`  IF (skip condition) THEN`	`  IF (skip condition) THEN`	`  if (skip condition)`
`    GO TO 1`	`    CYCLE ! to next I`	`    continue; // to next`
`  ELSE`	`  ELSE`	`  else if`
`    *false group*`	`    *false group*`	`    *false group*`
`  END IF`	`  END IF`	`  end`
`1 continue`	`END DO`	`  }`

Table 4.18: Abort a Single Loop

F77

```
DO 1 I = 1,N
  IF (exit condition) THEN
    GO TO 2
  ELSE
    false group
  END IF
1 CONTINUE
2 next statement
```

F90

```
DO I = 1,N
  IF (exit condition) THEN
    EXIT ! this do
  ELSE
    false group
  END IF
END DO
next statement
```

C++

```
for (i=1; i<n; i++)
  {
  if (exit condition)
    break;// out of loop
  else if
    false group
  end
  }
next statement
```

Since these constructs are commonly needed, several programming languages offer some support for them. For example, Pascal has a REPEAT UNTIL command, and C++ has the DO-WHILE pair for the until-true construct. For the more common while-true loops, C++ and MATLAB offer a WHILE command, and Fortran 90 includes the DO WHILE. However, F77 only has the obsolete IF-GO TO pairs, as illustrated in Tables 4.17, 4.18. Many current programmers consider the WHILE construct obsolete because it is less clear than a DO-EXIT pair or a "for-break" pair. Indeed, the F90 standard has declared the DO WHILE as obsolete and eligible for future deletion from the language. We can see how the loop-abort feature of C++ and F90 includes both the WHILE and UNTIL concepts. For example, the F90 construct

```
initialize logical_variable
DO WHILE (logical_variable) ! is true
  true_group
  re-evaluate logical_variable
END DO ! while true
     :
```

Table 4.19: F90 DO's named for control

```
main: DO ! forever
  test: DO k=1,k_max
    third: DO m=m_max,m_min,-1
      IF (test condition) THEN
        CYCLE test ! loop on k
      END IF
    END DO third ! loop on m
    fourth: DO n=n_min,n_max,2
      IF (main condition) THEN
        EXIT main ! forever loop
    END DO fourth ! on n
  END DO test ! over k
END DO main
next statement
```

is entirely equivalent to the aborted endless loop

```
initialize logical_variable
DO ! forever while true
  IF (.NOT. logical_variable) EXIT ! as false
  true_group
  re-evaluate logical_variable
END DO ! while true
      ⋮
```

Likewise, a minor change includes the following UNTIL construct:

```
DO ! forever until true
  beginning statements and initialization
  IF (logical_expression) EXIT ! as true
    false group
    re-evaluate logical_variable
END DO ! until true.
```

When approached in the C++ language, we have the following `WHILE` loop:

```
initialize logical_variable
while (logical_variable)
  { // is true
  true_group
  re-evaluate logical_variable
  } // end while true.
```

Recalling the standard `for` syntax, one could view

```
for (expr_1; expr_2; expr_3)
  {
  true_group
  } // end for
```

as equivalent to the preceding `WHILE` in `for` form as follows:

```
expr_1;
while (expr_2)
  { // is true
  true_group
  expr_3;
  } // end while true.
```

If we omit all three `for` expressions, then it becomes an "infinite loop" or a "do forever" that can represent a `WHILE` or `UNTIL` construct by proper placement of the `break` command. Furthermore, C has the `do-while` construct that is equivalent to Pascal's `REPEAT-UNTIL` as follows:

```
do // forever until true
  statements
  evaluate logical_variable
while (logical_variable) // is true.
```

Table 4.20: Looping While a Condition is True

MATLAB	C++

initialize test
while l_expression
  true group
  change test
end
	initialize test
	while (l_expression)
	  {
	  true group
	  change test
	  }

F77	**F90**

initialize test
# continue 	
  IF (l_expression) THEN
    true group
    change test
    go to #
  END IF
	initialize test
	do while (l_expression)
	  true group
	  change test
	end do

The syntax for the classical WHILE statements in C++, Fortran, and MATLAB are given in Table 4.20. Fortran90 has declared the DO WHILE obsolete and recommends the DO-EXIT pair instead. Using infinite loops with clearly aborted stages is a less error-prone approach to programming.

4.4 Subprograms

The concept of modular programming requires the use of numerous subprograms or procedures to execute independent segments of the calculations or operations. Typically, these procedures fall into classes such as functions, subroutines, and modules. We will consider examples of the procedures for each of our target languages. These are shown in Table 4.21.

Recall that Table 4.7 compared several intrinsic functions that are common to both F90 and MATLAB. For completeness, all of the Fortran90 functions are listed both alphabetically and by subject in Appendix A. Similar listings for MATLAB can be found in the MATLAB *Primer*.

4.4.1 Functions and Subroutines

Historically, a function was a subprogram employing one or more input arguments and returning a single result value. For example, a square root or logarithm function would accept a single input value and return a single result. All of the languages of interest allow the user to define such a function, and they all provide numerous intrinsic or built-in functions of this type. As you might expect, such a procedure is called a *function* in C++, Fortran, and MATLAB. As an example of such a procedure, consider the calculation of the mean value of a sequence of numbers defined as

$$\text{mean} = \frac{1}{n}\sum_{k=1}^{n} x_k \ .$$

Table 4.21: Function definitions. In each case, the function being defined is named `f` and is called with `m` arguments `a1, . . . , am`

Function Type	MATLAB[a]	C++	Fortran

program	*statements*
	[y1 ...yn]=f(a1,...,am)
	[end of file]
		main(argc,char **argv)
		{
		statements
		y = f(a1,I,am);
		}
			program main
			type y
			type a1, ...,type am
			statements
			y = f(a1, ...,am)
			call s(a1, ...,am)
			end program

subroutine		void f
		(type a1, ...,type am)
		{
		statements
		}
			subroutine s(a1, ...,am)
			type a1, ...,type am
			statements
			end

function	function [r1 ...rn] =f(a1, ...,am) *statements*	type f (type a1, ...,type am) { *statements* }	function f(a1, ...,am) type f type a1, ...,type am *statements* end

[a] Every function or program in MATLAB must be in separate files.

In Fortran 90, a subprogram to return the mean (average) could be

```
function mean(x)
! mean = sum of vector x, divided by its size
  real ::  mean, x(:)
    mean = sum(x)/size(x)
end function mean.
```

Note that our function has employed two other intrinsic functions: `size` to determine the number of elements in the array `x` and `sum` to carry out the summation of all elements in `x`. Originally in Fortran, the result value was required to be assigned to the name of the function. That is still a valid option in F90, but today it is considered better practice to specify a result value name to be returned by the function. The `mean` function is a MATLAB intrinsic and can be used directly.

To illustrate the use of a result value, consider the related "median" value in F90:

```
function mid_value(x) result(median)
! return the middle value of vector x
  real :: median, x(:)
     median = x(size(x)/2) ! what if size = 1 ??
end function mid_value.
```

To apply these two functions to an array, say `y`, we would simply write `y_ave = mean(y)`, and `y_mid = mid_value(y)`, respectively. Although Fortran allows a "function" to return only a single object, both C++ and MATLAB use that subprogram name to return any number of result objects. Fortran employs the name "subroutine" for such a procedure. Such

Table 4.22: Arguments and Return Values of Subprograms

	One-Input, One-Result Procedures
MATLAB	`function out = name (in)`
F90	`function name (in) ! name = out`
	`function name (in) result (out)`
C++	`name (in, out)`[a]
	Multiple-Input, Multiple-Result Procedures
MATLAB	`function [inout, out2] = name (in1, in2, inout)`
F90	`subroutine name (in1, in2, inout, out2)`[a]
C++	`name(in1, in2, inout, out2)`[a]

[a] Other arrangements acceptable

procedures are allowed to have multiple inputs and multiple outputs (including none). The syntax of the first line of these two subprogram classes is shown in Table 4.22. Note that a typical subprogram may have no arguments, multiple input arguments (`in1, in2, inout`), multiple result arguments (`inout, out2`), and arguments that are used for both input and result usage (`inout`). These representative names have been selected to reflect that a programmer usually intends for arguments to be used for input only, or for result values only, or for input, modification, and output. It is considered good programming practice to declare such intentions to aid the compiler in detecting unintended uses; F90 provides the `INTENT` statement for this purpose but does not require its use.

Having outlined the concepts of subprograms, we will review some presented earlier and then give some new examples. Figure 1.3 presented a clipping function earlier expressed in pseudocode. A corresponding Fortran implementation of such a clipping function is given in Figure 4.7. Note that it is very similar to the pseudocode version.

For the purpose of illustration, an alternate F90 version of the Game of Life, shown earlier in Chapter 1 as pseudocode, is given in the assignment solutions section. Clearly we have not introduced all the features utilized in these sample codes, and thus you should continue to refer back to them as your programming understanding grows.

A simple program that illustrates program composition is `maximum.f90`, which asks the user to specify several integers from which the program finds the largest. It is given in Figure 4.8. Note how the main program accepts the user input (lines 15,20), and the `maxint` function (line 22) finds the maximum (lines 25–34). Perhaps modularity would have been better served by expressing the input portion by a separate function. Of course, this routine is not really needed since F90 provides intrinsic functions to find maximum and minimum values (`maxval, minval`) and their locations in any array (`maxloc, minloc`). A similar C++ program composition is shown for comparison in the appendix C.

4.4.2 Global Variables

We have seen that variables used inside a procedure can be thought of as dummy variable names that exist only in the procedure unless they are members of the argument list. Even if they are arguments to the procedure, they can still have names different from the names employed in the calling program. This approach can have disadvantages. For example, it might lead to a long list of arguments, say 20 lines, in a complicated procedure. For this and other reasons, we sometimes desire to have variables that are accessible by any and all procedures at any time. These are called *global variables* regardless of their type.

```
program clip_an_array
!     clip the elements of an array
  implicit none
    real, parameter    :: limit = 3
    integer, parameter :: n = 5
    real               :: y(n), x(n)
!    Define x values that will be clipped
      x = (/ (-8. + 3.*k, k = 1,n) /)   ! an implied loop
      do i = 1, n
        y(i) = clip (x(i), limit)
      end do
      print *, x
      print *, y

contains   ! methods

function clip (x, L) result (c)
!   c = clip(x, L) - clip the variable x, output
!   x = scalar variable,                   input
!   L = limit of the clipper,              input
!
    real, intent(in) :: x, L    ! variable types
    real             :: c       ! variable types
    intent (in) x, L            ! argument uses
      if  ( abs(x) <= L ) then    ! abs of x less than or equal L
        c = x;                    ! then use x
      else                        ! absolute of x greater than L ?
        c = sign(L,x)             ! sign of x times L
      end if ! of value of x
    end function ! clip
end program clip_an_array
!
! produces:
! -5.0000000  -2.0000000   1.0000000   4.0000000   7.0000000
! -3.0000000  -2.0000000   1.0000000   3.0000000   3.0000000
```

Figure 4.7: Clipping a set of array values in F90.

Generally, we explicitly declare them to be global and provide some means by which they can be accessed, and thus modified, by selected procedures. When a selected procedure needs, or benefits from, access to a global variable, one may wish to control which subset of global variables is accessible by the procedure. The typical initial identification of global variables and the ways to access them are shown in Table 4.23.

An advanced aspect of the concept of global variables is the topics of inheritance and object-oriented programming. Fortran 90, and other languages like C++, offer these advanced concepts. In F90, inheritance is available to a `module`, a main `program`, or both, and their "internal subprograms" defined as those procedures following a `contains` statement but occurring before an `end module` or the `end program` statement. Everything that appears before the `contains` statement is available to, and can be changed by, the internal subprograms. Those inherited variables are more than local but not quite global; thus, they may be thought of as *territorial* variables. The structure of these internal subprograms with inheritance is shown in Figure 4.9.

Perhaps the most commonly used global variables are those necessary to calculate the amount of central processor unit (cpu) time, in seconds, that a particular code segment used during its execution. All systems provide utilities for that purpose, but some are more friendly

```
program maximum ! of a set of integers (see intrinsic maxval)
 implicit none
  interface ! declare function interface prototype
    function maxint (input, input_length) result(max)
    integer, intent(in) :: input_length, input(:)
    integer              :: max
    end function ! maxint
  end interface

  integer, parameter :: ARRAYLENGTH=100
  integer            :: integers(ARRAYLENGTH);
  integer            :: i, n;

  ! Read in the number of integers
     print *,'Find maximum; type n: '; read *, n
     if ( n > ARRAYLENGTH .or. n < 0 ) &
         stop 'Value you typed is too large or negative.'

     do i = 1, n            ! Read in the user's integers
        print *, 'Integer ', i, '?'; read  *, integers(i)
     end do ! over n values
     print *, 'Maximum: ', maxint (integers, n)
end program maximum

function maxint (input, input_length) result(max)
! Find the maximum of an array of integers
  integer, intent(in) :: input_length, input(:)
  integer             :: i, max

    max = input(1);   ! initialize
     do i = 1, input_length ! note could be only 1
       if ( input(i) > max ) max = input(i);
     end do ! over values
end function maxint                    ! produces this result:
! Find maximum; type n:  4
! Integer  1?  9
! Integer  2?  6
! Integer  3?  4
! Integer  4?  -99
! Maximum:  9
```

Figure 4.8: Search for largest value in F90.

than others. MATLAB provides a pair of functions, called `tic` and `toc`, that act together to provide the desired information. To illustrate the use of global variables we will develop an F90 module called `tic_toc` to hold the necessary variables along with the routines `tic` and `toc`. It is illustrated in Figure 4.10, where the module constants (lines 4–7) are set (lines 18, 27) and computed (line 28) in the two `internal` functions.

4.4.3 Bit Functions

We have discussed the fact that the digital computer is based on the use of individual bits. The subject of bit manipulation is one that we do not wish to pursue here. However, advanced applications do sometimes require these abilities, and the most common uses have been declared in the so-called military standards USDOD-MIL-STD-1753 and made part of the

Table 4.23: Defining and Referring to Global Variables

	Global Variable Declaration
MATLAB	`global` list of variables
F77	`common` /set_name/ list of variables
F90	`module` set_name `save` `type` (type_tag) :: list of variables `end module` set_name
C++	`extern` list of variables
	Access to Global Variables
MATLAB	`global` list of variables
F77	`common` /set_name/ list of variables
F90	`use` set_name, `only` subset of variables `use` set_name2 list of variables
C++	`extern` list of variables

Fortran 90 standard. Several of these features are also a part of C++. Table 4.24 gives a list of those functions.

4.4.4 Exception Controls

An exception handler is a block of code invoked to process specific error conditions. Standard exception control keywords in a language are usually associated with the allocation of resources, such as files or memory space, or input–output operations. For many applications we simply want to catch an unexpected result and output a message so that the programmer can correct the situation. In that case we may not care if the exception aborts the execution. However, if one is using a commercial execute-only program, then it is very disturbing to have a code abort. We would at least expect the code to respond to a fatal error by closing

```
module or program  name_inherit
     Optional territorial variable, type specification, and calls
     contains

            subroutine  Internal_1
            territorial specifications and calls
            contains

                  subroutine  Internal_2
                  local computations
                  end subroutine  Internal_2

                  subroutine  Internal_3
                  local computations
                  end subroutine  Internal_3

            end subroutine  Internal_1

end  name_inherit
```

Figure 4.9: F90 internal subprogram structure.

```
module tic_toc
! Define global constants for timing increments
 implicit none
   integer  :: start  ! current value of system clock
   integer  :: rate   ! system clock counts/sec
   integer  :: finish ! ending value of system clock
   real     :: sec    ! increment in sec, (finish-start)/rate
  ! Useage:   use tic_toc       ! global constant access
  !           call tic          ! start clock
  !           . . .             ! use some cpu time
  !           cputime = toc () ! for increment
contains ! access to start, rate, finish, sec
  subroutine  tic
! -----------------------------------------------
! Model the matlab tic function, for use with toc
! -----------------------------------------------
    implicit none
      call system_clock ( start, rate ) ! Get start value and rate
  end subroutine tic

  function  toc ( ) result(sec)
! -----------------------------------------------
! Model the matlab toc function, for use with tic
! -----------------------------------------------
    implicit none
    real    :: sec
      call system_clock ( finish )          ! Stop the execution timer
      sec = 0.0
      if ( finish >= start ) sec = float(finish - start) / float(rate)
  end function toc
end module tic_toc
```

Figure 4.10: A module for computing CPU times.

Table 4.24: Bit Function Intrinsics

<table>
<tr><th>Action</th><th>C++</th><th>F90</th></tr>
<tr><td>Bitwise AND</td><td>&</td><td>iand</td></tr>
<tr><td>Bitwise exclusive OR</td><td>^</td><td>ieor</td></tr>
<tr><td>Bitwise exclusive OR</td><td>|</td><td>ior</td></tr>
<tr><td>Circular bit shift</td><td></td><td>ishftc</td></tr>
<tr><td>Clear bit</td><td></td><td>ibclr</td></tr>
<tr><td>Combination of bits</td><td></td><td>mvbits</td></tr>
<tr><td>Extract bit</td><td></td><td>ibits</td></tr>
<tr><td>Logical complement</td><td>~</td><td>not</td></tr>
<tr><td>Number of bits in integer</td><td>sizeof</td><td>bit_size</td></tr>
<tr><td>Set bit</td><td></td><td>ibset</td></tr>
<tr><td>Shift bit left</td><td>≪</td><td>ishft</td></tr>
<tr><td>Shift bit right</td><td>≫</td><td>ishft</td></tr>
<tr><td>Test on or off</td><td></td><td>btest</td></tr>
<tr><td>Transfer bits to integer</td><td></td><td>transfer</td></tr>
</table>

```
module exceptions
 implicit none
  integer, parameter :: INFO = 1, WARN = 2, FATAL = 3
  integer            :: error_count = 0
  integer            :: max_level   = 0
contains

 subroutine exception (program, message, flag)
   character(len=*)     :: program
   character(len=*)     :: message
   integer,    optional :: flag

     error_count = error_count + 1

     print *, 'Exception Status Thrown'
     print *, '  Program :', program
     print *, '  Message :', message
     if ( present(flag) ) then
       print *, '  Level   :', flag
       if ( flag > max_level ) max_level = flag
     end if ! flag given
 end subroutine exception

 subroutine exception_status ()
   print *
   print *, "Exception Summary:"
   print *, "  Exception count = ", error_count
   print *, "  Highest level   = ", max_level
 end subroutine exception_status
end module exceptions
```

Figure 4.11: A minimal exception handling module.

down the program in some gentle fashion that saves what was completed before the error and maybe even offers us a restart option. Here we provide only the minimum form of an exceptions module that can be used by other modules to pass warnings of fatal messages to the user. It includes an integer flag that can be utilized to rank the severity of possible messages. It is shown in Figure 4.11. In the following list we will summarize the F90 optional error flags that should always be checked and are likely to lead to a call to the exception handler.

Dynamic Memory: The ALLOCATE and DEALLOCATE statements both use the optional flag STAT= to return an integer flag that can be tested to invoke an exception handler. The integer value is zero after a successful (de)allocation and a positive value otherwise. If STAT= is absent, an unsuccessful result stops execution.

File Open/Close: The OPEN, CLOSE, and ENDFILE statements allow the use of the optional keyword IOSTAT= to return an integer flag which is zero if the statement executes successfully, and a positive value otherwise. They also allow the older standard exception keyword ERR= to be assigned a positive integer constant label number of the statement to which control is passed if an error occurs. An exception handler could be called by that statement.

File Input/Output: The READ, WRITE, BACKSPACE, and REWIND statements allow the IOSTAT= keyword to return a negative integer if an end-of-record (EOR) or end-of-file (EOF) is encountered, a zero if there is no error, and a positive integer if an error occurs (such as reading a character during an integer input). They also allow the ERR= error label branching described in the last entry for the file open/close operations.

In addition, the READ statement also retains the old standard keyword END= to identify a label number to which control transfers when an end-of-file (EOF) is detected.

Status Inquiry: Whether in UNIT mode or FILE mode, the INQUIRE statement for file operations allows the IOSTAT= and ERR= keywords like the OPEN statement. In addition, either mode supports two logical keywords: EXISTS= to determine if the UNIT (or FILE) exists, and OPENED= to determine if a (the) file is connected to this (an) unit.

Optional Arguments: The PRESENT function returns a logical value to indicate whether an optional argument was provided in the invocation of the procedure in which the function appears.

Pointers and Targets: The ASSOCIATED function returns a logical value to indicate whether a pointer is associated with a specific target or with any target.

4.5 Interface Prototype

Compiler languages are more efficient than interpreted languages. If the compiler is going to generate calls to functions or subprograms correctly, it needs to know certain things about the arguments and returned values. The number of arguments, their type, their rank, their order, and so forth, must be the same. This collection of information is called the "interface" to the function or subprogram. In most of our sample codes the functions and subprograms have been included in a single file. In practice they are usually stored in separate external files and often written by others. Thus, the program that is going to use these external files must be given a "prototype" description of them. In other words, a segment of prototype, or interface, code is a definition used by the compiler to determine what parameters are required by the subprogram as it is called by your program. The interface prototype code for any subprogram can usually be created by simply copying the first few lines of the subprogram (and maybe the last one) and placing them in an interface directory.

To compile a subprogram successfully modern computer science methods sometimes require the programmer to specifically declare the interface to be used in invoking a subprogram even if that subprogram is included in the same file. This information is called a "prototype" in C and C++ and an "interface" in F90. If the subprogram already exists, one can easily create the needed interface details by making a copy of the program and deleting from the copy all information except that which describes the arguments and subprogram type. If the program does not exist, you write the interface first to define what will be expected of the subprogram regardless of who writes it. It is considered good programming style to include explicit interfaces, or prototype code, even if they are not required.

If in doubt about the need for an explicit interface, see if the compiler gives an error because it is not present. In F90 the common reasons for needing an explicit interface are *(1)* passing an array that has only its rank declared (e.g., A(:,:), B(:); these are known as "assumed-shape" arrays) and *(2)* using a function to return a result that is *(a)* an array of unknown size, or *(b)* a pointer, or *(c)* a character string with a dynamically determined length. Advanced features like optional argument lists, user-defined operators, or generic subprogram names (to allow differing argument types) also require explicit operators.

In C++ before calling an external function, it must be declared with a prototype of its parameters. The general form for a function is

```
function_type function_name ( argument_type_list);
```

where the `argument_type_list` is the comma separated list of pairs of type and name for each argument of the function. These names are effectively treated as comments and may be different from the names in the calling program or even omitted. The use of a prototype was shown in Figure 4.8 and is used again in Figure 4.12, which also illustrates passing arguments by reference or by value.

An interface block for external subprograms is not required by F77 (thereby leading to hard-to-find errors) but is strongly recommended in F90 and is explicitly required in several situations. The general form for an F90 interface is

```
interface interface_name
    function_interface_body
    subroutine_interface_body
    module_procedure_interface_body
end interface interface_name,
```

where a typical function_interface_body would be

```
function_type function_name (argument_name_list) result ( name )
  implicit none
  argument_type, intent_class :: name_list
end function function_name,
```

where the argument_name_list is the comma separated list of names. Of course, the function_type refers to the result argument name. These names may be different from the names in the calling program. A typical subroutine_interface_body would be

```
subroutine subroutine_name (argument_name_list)
 implicit none
  argument_type, intent_class :: name_list
end subroutine subroutine_name,
```

where the argument_name_list is the comma separated list of names. The topic of a module procedure is covered elsewhere. The use of an interface block was shown in Figure 4.8 and used in two new codes, shown in Figure 4.12 and the corresponding C++ code in the appendix C, which also illustrate passing arguments by reference (line 23) and by value (line 19) in both F90 and C++. The important, and often confusing, topic of passing by reference or value was discussed in Section 4.2 and is related to other topics to be considered later such as the use of "pointers" in C++ and F90 and the "intent" attribute of F90 arguments. Passing by reference is default in F90, and passing by value is default in C++ .

4.6 Characters and Strings

All of our languages offer convenient ways to manipulate and compare strings of characters. The characters are defined by one of the international standards such as ASCII, which is usually used on UNIX, or the EBCDIC set. These contain both printable and nonprintable

```
program declare_interface
implicit none
! declare the interface prototypes
interface
  subroutine  Change (Refer)
    integer :: Refer; end subroutine Change
  subroutine No_Change (Value)
    integer :: Value; end subroutine No_Change
end interface

! illustrate passing by reference and by value in F90

  integer :: Input_Val, Dummy_Val

    print *, "Enter an integer: "
    read *, Input_Val; print *, "Input value was ", Input_Val

  ! pass by value
    call No_Change ( (Input_Val) )  !  Use but do not change
    print *, "After No_Change it is ", Input_Val

  ! pass by reference
    call Change ( Input_Val )       !  Use and change
    print *, "After Change it is ", Input_Val
end program declare_interface

  subroutine  Change (Refer)
  ! changes Refer in calling code IF passed by reference
    integer :: Refer
      Refer = 100;
      print *, "Inside Change it is set to ", Refer
  end subroutine Change

  subroutine No_Change (Value)
  ! does not change Value in calling code IF passed by value
    integer :: Value
      Value  = 100;
      print *, "Inside No_Change it is set to ", Value
  end subroutine No_Change

! Running gives:
! Enter an integer: 12
! Input value was  12
! Inside No_Change it is set to  100
! After No_Change it is  12
! Inside Change it is set to  100
! After Change it is  100
```

Figure 4.12: Passing arguments by reference and by value in F90.

(control) characters. On a UNIX system, the full set can be seen with the command man ascii. In the 256-character ASCII set, the uppercase letters begin at character number 65, 'A', and the corresponding lowercase values are 32 positions higher (character 97 is 'a'). These printable characters begin at character 32, as shown in Table 4.25 for the ASCII standard. The first 33 characters are "nonprinting" special control characters. For example, NUL = null, EOT = end of transmission, BEL = bell, BS = backspace, and HT = horizontal tab. To enter a control character, one must simultaneously hold down the CONTROL key and hit

Table 4.25: The ASCII Character Set

0	NUL	1	SOH	2	STX	3	ETX	4	EOT	5	ENQ	6	ACK	7	BEL
8	BS	9	HT	10	NL	11	VT	12	NP	13	CR	14	SO	15	SI
16	DLE	17	DC1	18	DC2	19	DC3	20	DC4	21	NAK	22	SYN	23	ETB
24	CAN	25	EM	26	SUB	27	ESC	28	FS	29	GS	30	RS	31	US
32	SP	33	!	34	"	35	#	36	$	37	%	38	&	39	'
40	(	41	)	42	*	43	+	44	,	45	-	46	.	47	/
48	0	49	1	50	2	51	3	52	4	53	5	54	6	55	7
56	8	57	9	58	:	59	;	60	<	61	=	62	>	63	?
64	@	65	A	66	B	67	C	68	D	69	E	70	F	71	G
72	H	73	I	74	J	75	K	76	L	77	M	78	N	79	O
80	P	81	Q	82	R	83	S	84	T	85	U	86	V	87	W
88	X	89	Y	90	Z	91	[	92	\	93	]	94	^	95	--
96	‘	97	a	98	b	99	c	100	d	101	e	102	f	103	g
104	h	105	i	106	j	107	k	108	l	109	m	110	n	111	o
112	p	113	q	114	r	115	s	116	t	117	u	118	v	119	w
120	x	121	y	122	z	123	{	124	|	125	}	126	~	127	DEL

the letter that is 64 positions higher in the list. That is, an end of transmission EOT is typed as CONTROL-D. The code SP denotes the space character, and we will use the underscore "_" to represent a blank in strings.

We can employ the standard relational operators (e.g., less than) to compare strings and would find that 'bad' < 'dog' < 'same' == 'same__', that 'word' > 'WORD', and that 'four' < 'one' < 'two,' whereas '1' < '2' < '4'. Note that the preceding equality occurred because trailing blanks are not considered in relational operations, *but* leading blanks are considered: 'same' ≠ '__same'. The F90 function adjustL removes leading blanks and appends them to the right end. Thus, it adjusts the string to the left so that 'same' == adjustL('__same'). This and other F90 intrinsic character functions are summarized in Table 4.26.

All blanks are considered when determining the length of a character string. In F90 the intrinsic function LEN provides these data so that LEN('same') = 4, LEN('__same') = 6, and LEN('same__') = 7. There is another intrinsic function, LEN_TRIM, that provides the string length but ignores trailing blanks. By way of comparison: LEN_TRIM('same') = 4, LEN_TRIM('__same') = 6, and LEN_TRIM('same__') = 4. Each character in a string or any internal substrings may be referenced by the colon operator. Given a character variable we can define a substring, say sub, as

```
sub = variable(K:L) for 0 < K,L <= LEN(variable)
    = null          for K > L
    = error         for K or L  >  LEN(variable).
```

For example, given the string 'howl', we can define bird = string(2:4) = 'owl', and prep = string(1:3) = 'how'.

The F90 and F77 operator used to concatenate strings into larger strings is "//." Continuing the last example, we see that the concatenation string(1:3)//'_'//string(2:4)//'?' is 'how_owl?', whereas the concatenation 'same__'//'word' becomes 'same__word', and 'bad'//'_'//'dog' becomes 'bad_dog'. Programs illustrating the reading and concatenating two strings are given in Figure 4.13 and in the companion C++ code in the appendix C.

Table 4.26: F90 Character Functions

ACHAR (I)	Character number I in ASCII collating set
ADJUSTL (STRING)	Adjust left
ADJUSTR (STRING)	Adjust right
CHAR (I) *	Character I in processor collating set
IACHAR (C)	Position of C in ASCII collating set
ICHAR (C)	Position of C in processor collating set
INDEX (STRING, SUBSTRING)[a]	Starting position of a substring
LEN (STRING)	Length of a character entity
LEN_TRIM (STRING)	Length without trailing blanks
LGE (STRING_A, STRING_B)	Lexically greater than or equal
LGT (STRING_A, STRING_B)	Lexically greater than
LLE (STRING_A, STRING_B)	Lexically less than or equal
LLT (STRING_A, STRING_B)	Lexically less than
REPEAT (STRING, NCOPIES)	Repeated concatenation
SCAN (STRING, SET)[a]	Scan a string for a character in a set
TRIM (STRING)	Remove trailing blank characters
VERIFY (STRING, SET)[a]	Verify the set of characters in a string
STRING_A//STRING_B	Concatenate two strings

[a] Optional arguments not shown.

Sometimes one needs to type in a nonprinting character such as a tab or a newline. To allow this, special transmissions have been allowed for, as summarized in Table 4.27.

Remember the ASCII character features: the uppercase letters correspond to numbers 65 through 90 in the list, and the lowercase letters are numbers 97 through 122; thus, if we wanted to convert "G" to "g" we could use commands such as

```
character (len = 1) :: lower_g, UPPER_G
lower_g = achar(iachar('G') + 32)
```

or vice versa,

```
UPPER_G = achar(iachar('g') - 32),
```

since they differ by 32 locations. Likewise, because the zero character "0" occurs in position 48 of the ASCII set we could convert a single digit to the same numerical value with

```
integer :: number_5
number_5 = iachar('5') - 48
```

and so forth for all 10 digits. To convert a string of digits, such as '5623', to the corresponding number 5623, we could use a looping operation such as

```
 character (len = 132) :: digits
 integer               :: d_to_n, power, number
!       Now build the number from its digits
 if (digits == ' ') then
   print *, 'warning, no number found'
   number = 0
```

```
program operate_on_strings
!  Compare two strings
!  Concatenate two character strings together
!  Get the combined length
  implicit none
  character(len=20) :: String1, String2
  character(len=40) :: String3
  integer           :: length

    print *,'Enter first string (20 char max):'
    read  '(a)', String1    ! formatted

    print *,'Enter second string (20 char max):'
    read  '(a)', String2    ! formatted

  ! compare (also see LGE LGT functions)
    if ( String1 == String2 ) then
      print *, "They are the same."
    else
      print *, "They are different."
    end if

  ! concatenate
    String3 = trim (String1) // trim (String2)

    print *,'The combined string is:', String3
    length = len_trim (String3)
    print *,'The combined length is:', length

end program operate_on_strings
!  Running with "red" and "bird" produces:
!  Enter first string (20 char max): red
!  Enter second string (20 char max): bird
!  They are different.
!  The combined string is: redbird
!  The combined length is: 7
!  Also "the red" and "bird" works
```

Figure 4.13: Using two strings in F90.

Table 4.27: How to Type Nonprinting Characters

Action	ASCII Character	F90 Input[a]	C++ Input
Alert (Bell)	7	Ctrl-G	\a
Backspace	8	Ctrl-H	\b
Carriage Return	13	Ctrl-M	\r
End of Transmission	4	Ctrl-D	Ctrl-D
Form Feed	12	Ctrl-L	\f
Horizontal Tab	9	Ctrl-I	\t
New Line	10	Ctrl-J	\n
Vertical Tab	11	Ctrl-K	\v

[a] "Ctrl-" denotes control action; that is, simultaneous pressing of the CONTROL key and the letter following.

```
[ 1]  program  string_to_numbers
[ 2]  !  Convert a character string to an integer in F90
[ 3]    implicit none
[ 4]    character(len=5)  :: Age_Char
[ 5]    integer           :: age
[ 6]
[ 7]      print *, "Enter your age: "
[ 8]      read *, Age_Char                        ! a character string
[ 9]
[10]    ! convert using an internal file read
[11]      read (Age_Char, fmt = '(i5)') age  ! convert to integer
[12]
[13]      print *, "Your integer age is      ", age
[14]      print '(" Your binary age is       ", b8)', age
[15]      print '(" Your hexadecimal age is ", z8)', age
[16]      print '(" Your octal age is        ", o8)', age
[17]
[18]  end program string_to_numbers
[19]  !
[20]  ! Running gives:
[21]  ! Enter your age: 45
[22]  ! Your integer age is       45
[23]  ! Your binary age is        101101
[24]  ! Your hexadecimal age is       2D
[25]  ! Your octal age is              55
```

Figure 4.14: Converting a string to an integer with F90.

```
else
  number = 0
  k      = len_trim(digits)
  do m = k, 1, -1 ! right to left
    d_to_n = iachar(digits(m:m)) - 48
    power  = 10**(k-m)
    number = number + d_to_n*power
  end do ! over digits
  print *, 'number = ', number.
```

However, since loops can be inefficient, it is better to learn that, in F90, an "internal file" can be (and should be) employed to convert one data type to another. Here we could simply code

```
! internal file called convert
  write(convert, ''(A)'')  digit
  read(convert, ''(I4)'')  number
```

to convert a character to an integer (or real) number. Converting strings to integers is shown in the codes given in Figure 4.14 (line 11) and the corresponding C++ appendix routine. Similar procedures would be used to convert strings to reals. The C++ version (see appendix C) uses the intrinsic function "atoi," whereas the F90 version uses an internal file for the conversion.

One often finds it useful to change the case of a string of characters. Some languages provide intrinsic functions for that purpose. In C++ and MATLAB, the functions to convert a

```
[ 1]  function  to_lower (string)  result (new_string) ! like C
[ 2]  ! -----------------------------------------------------------
[ 3]  !         Convert a string or character to lower case
[ 4]  !          (valid for ASCII or EBCDIC processors)
[ 5]  ! -----------------------------------------------------------
[ 6]    implicit none
[ 7]    character (len = *), intent(in) :: string      ! unknown length
[ 8]    character (len = len(string))    :: new_string  ! same length
[ 9]    character (len = 26), parameter ::                &
[10]              UPPER = 'ABCDEFGHIJKLMNOPQRSTUVWXYZ',   &
[11]              lower = 'abcdefghijklmnopqrstuvwxyz'
[12]    integer :: k     ! loop counter
[13]    integer :: loc   ! position in alphabet
[14]      new_string = string         ! copy everything
[15]      do k = 1, len(string)      ! to change letters
[16]        loc = index ( UPPER, string(k:k))               ! first upper
[17]        if (loc /= 0 ) new_string(k:k) = lower(loc:loc) ! convert it
[18]      end do ! over string characters
[19]  end function to_lower
```

Figure 4.15: Converting a string to lowercase with F90.

string to all lowercase letters are called `tolower` and `lower`, respectively. Here we define a similar F90 function called `to_lower`, which is shown in Figure 4.15 along with a testing program in Figure 4.16. Note that the testing program uses an interface to `to_lower` (lines 5–14) that presupposes the routine was compiled and stored externally to the testing program. The `to_lower` function employs the intrinsic function `index` (line 16) to see if the kth

```
[ 1]  program up_down ! test character case inversion functions
[ 2]    implicit none
[ 3]    character (len = 24) :: test='ABCDefgh1234abcdZYXWzyxw'
[ 4]
[ 5]      interface
[ 6]        function to_lower (string) result (new_string)
[ 7]          character (len = *), intent(in) :: string
[ 8]          character (len = len(string))    :: new_string
[ 9]        end function to_lower
[10]        function to_upper (string) result (new_string)
[11]          character (len = *), intent(in) :: string
[12]          character (len = len(string))    :: new_string
[13]        end function to_upper
[14]      end interface
[15]
[16]        print *,            test
[17]        print *, to_lower (test)
[18]        print *, to_upper (test)
[19]  end program      ! running gives
[20]  ! ABCDefgh1234abcdZYXWzyxw
[21]  ! abcdefgh1234abcdzyxwzyxw
[22]  ! ABCDEFGH1234ABCDZYXWZYXW
```

Figure 4.16: Testing string conversions with F90.

Table 4.28: Referencing Defined Data-Type Structure Components

C, C++	`Variable.component.sub_component`
F90	`Variable%component%sub_component`

character of the input string is an uppercase letter. The intrinsic function `len` is also used (line 8) to force the `new_string` to be the same length as the original string.

4.7 User-Defined Data Types

Variables, as in mathematics, represent some quantity; unlike mathematics, many languages force the programmer to define what *type* the variable is. Generic kinds of type are integer, floating point (single, double, and quadruple precision), and complex-valued floating point. Table 4.2 (page 58) presents the data types inherent in the various languages. The majority of beginning programmers find the requirement most languages impose of defining explicitly each variable's type to be tedious, unnecessary, and a source of bugs. It is tedious because the programmer must think not only about what the variable represents but also how the computations calculate its value, unnecessary because mathematics does not work that way (the variable x represents a quantity regardless of whether it turns out to be an integer or a complex value), and bug-creating because computations involving different types and assigned to a typed variable can yield nonmathematical results (for example, dividing the integers 1 with 3 and assigning the results to an integer yields a zero value).

MATLAB is one language in which variables are not explicitly typed. (Beginning programmers cheer!) Internally, MATLAB represents numbers in double-precision floating point. If a variable's value corresponds to an integer, MATLAB will gleefully print it that way, effectively hiding its floating point representation. A surprise occurs when a calculation accidentally becomes complex: MATLAB will (silently) change what the variable represents from being real to being complex. For example, MATLAB will, without complaint, calculate `x=log(-1)` and assign the value $3.14159i$ to x. In many applications, the expression yielded the value of -1 because of an error, and MATLAB will let the error propagate. (Beginning programmers sigh!) Most, if not all typed languages will immediately announce the evaluation of the logarithm

Table 4.29: Defining New Types of Data Structure

C, C++
```
struct data_tag {
    intrinsic_type_1 component_names;
    intrinsic_type_2 component_names;
};
```

F90
```
type data_tag
    intrinsic_type_1 :: component_names;
    intrinsic_type_2 :: component_names;
end type data_tag
```

Table 4.30: Nested Data Structure Definitions

C, C++	`struct data_tag {`
	`    intrinsic_type_1 component_names;`
	`    struct tag_2 component_names;`
	`} ;`

F90	`type data_tag`
	`    intrinsic_type :: component_names;`
	`    type (tag_2) :: component_names;`
	`end type data_tag`

of a negative number and halt execution. Explicitly defining the kinds of values a variable will assume helps programming clarity and run-time debugging to some degree.

In C++ there are four intrinsic (i.e., built-in) types of data – integer, single- and double-precision reals, and character – and F90 has the similar set: integer, real, complex, logical, and character; F90 also allows the user to create a specific precision level for integer and real data. The C++ language has specified byte sizes for 3 character, 6 integer, 1 single-precision real, and 2 double-precision real data types for a total of 12 intrinsic data types.

In addition to intrinsic types, C, C++, and F90 allow the formation of new types of data – *structures* – that are collections of values of not necessarily the same type. These procedures are named `struct` or `type` in C and F90, respectively.

To go along with this freedom, F90 allows you to define new operations to act on the derived types. Although C++ retains the *struct* keyword, it is viewed as a *class* with only public data members and no functions. In other words, in C++ *class* is a generalization of *struct* and, thus, *class* is the preferred keyword to use. As an example of a task made easier by derived data, consider creating parts of a data structure to be used in an address book. We will need a variable that can have components and sub-components. They are referenced by a special syntax and defined as illustrated in Tables 4.28 and 4.29. This procedure for defining a new type of data structure can be "nested" by referring to other derived type entities defined earlier in the program. These concepts are shown in Table 4.30. One should declare the data type of all variables used in a program module. This is also true for user-defined data structures. Table 4.31 outlines the forms of these statements, how structures are initialized, and how component values are assigned.

There are times when either the derived type variable or its components, or both, could be subscripted objects (i.e., arrays). Then care must be taken in the interpretation of which variable or component is being addressed. Table 4.32 illustrates the typical combinations with the F90 syntax.

Table 4.31: Declaring, Initializing, and Assigning Components of User-Defined Data Types

C, C++	`struct data_tag variable_list; /* Definition */`
	`struct data_tag variable = {component_values}; /* Initialization */`
	`variable.component.sub_component = value; /* Assignment */`

F90	`type (data_tag) :: variable_list ! Definition`
	`variable = data_tag (component_values) ! Initialization`
	`variable%component%sub_component = value ! Assignment`

Table 4.32: F90-derived type component interpretation

```
INTEGER, PARAMETER :: j_max = 6
TYPE meaning_demo
  INTEGER, PARAMETER :: k_max = 9, word = 15
  CHARACTER (LEN = word) :: name(k_max)
END TYPE meaning_demo
TYPE (meaning_demo) derived(j_max)
```

Construct	Interpretation
derived	All components of all derived's elements
derived(j)	All components of jth element of derived
derived(j)%name	All k_max components of name within j^{th} element of derived
derived%name(k)	Component k of the name array for all elements of derived
derived(j)%name(k)	Component k of the name array of jth element of derived

As a concrete example, consider a phone_type and address_type definition.

F90

```
type phone_type
  integer :: area_code, number, extension
end type phone_type
type address_type
  integer :: number
  character (len = 35) :: street, city
  character (len =  2) :: state
  integer :: zip_code
end type address_type
```

C++

```
struct phone_type {
  int area_code, number, extension;
  };
struct address_type {
  int number;
  char street[35], city[35];
  char state[2];
  int zip_code;
  } ;
```

These could be used to define part of a person_type

F90

```
type person_type
  character (len = 50) :: name
  type (phone_type) :: phone
  type (address_type) :: address
  integer :: born_year
end type person_type
```

C++

```
struct person_type {
  char name[50];
  struct phone_type phone;
  struct address_type address;
  int born_year;
  };
```

We define two people with

F90

```
type (person_type) :: sammy, barney
```

C++

```
struct person_type sammy, barney;
```

or build an address-book array filled with the data structures above by defining

F90

```
integer, parameter :: number = 99
type (person_type), dimension (number) :: address_book
```

C++

```
#define NUMBER 99
struct person_type address_book[NUMBER];
```

and then initialize, or "construct" Sammy's phone and zip code as

F90

```
sammy%phone = phone_type (713, 5278100, 0)
sammy%zip_code = 770051892
```

C++

```
sammy.phone = {713, 5278100, 0};
sammy.zip_code = 770051892;
```

and print them with

F90

```
print *, sammy%phone
print *, sammy%address%zip_code
```

C++

```
printf("(%d)%d, extension %d",
  sammy.area_code,
  sammy.number,
  sammy.extension);
printf("%d", sammy.zip_code);
```

and then define specific members for Barney with the "constructor"

F90

```
barney = person_type("Barn Owl", &
  phone_type(0,0,0), &
  sammy%address, 1892, "Sammy's cousin")
```

C++

```
barney = {"Barn Owl", {0,0,0},
  sammy.address, 1892,
  "Sammy's cousin"};
```

Note the difference in the defined type constructors. Two are actually used here because the second component must be defined as a phone_type. In C++ brackets are used to enclose the supplied components of each user-defined type. In contrast F90 has an intrinsic function that is created automatically by the type definition, and this function accepts all of the components required by the type. That is why the function name "phone_type" appears in the intrinsic constructor routine "person_type." Finally, put them in the book.

F90

```
address_book(1) = sammy
address_book(2) = barney
```

C++

```
address_book[1] = sammy;
address_book[2] = barney;
```

Figure 4.17 presents a sample code for utilizing user-defined structure types using F90 (there is a C++ version in the appendix C). First a "person" structure is created (lines 4–7)

```
[ 1]  program  structure_components
[ 2]  !  Define structures and components, via F90
[ 3]    implicit none
[ 4]    type  Person     ! define a person structure type
[ 5]       character (len=20) ::  Name
[ 6]       integer            ::  Age
[ 7]    end type  Person
[ 8]
[ 9]    type  Who_Where  ! use person type in a new structure
[10]       type (Person)      ::  Guest
[11]       character (len=40) ::  Address
[12]    end type  Who_Where
[13]
[14]    !  Fill a record of the Who_Where type components
[15]       type  (Who_Where)  Record;
[16]
[17]         print *,"Enter your name: "
[18]         read  *, Record % Guest % Name
[19]
[20]         print *,"Enter your city: "
[21]         read  *, Record % Address
[22]
[23]         print *,"enter your age: "
[24]         read  *, Record % Guest % Age
[25]
[26]         print *,"Hello ", Record % Guest % Age, " year old ", &
[27]            Record % Guest % Name, " in ", Record % Address
[28]
[29]  end program structure_components
[30]
[31]  !  Running with input: Sammy, Houston, 104 gives
[32]  !  Hello 104 year old Sammy in Houston
[33]  !
[34]  !  But try: Sammy Owl, Houston, 104 for a bug
```

Figure 4.17: Using multiple structures in F90.

by using only the intrinsic types of integers and characters. It then is used in turn within an additional data structure (line 10). The components of the structures are read (lines 18, 21, 24) and outputted (lines 26, 27). For more general data suggested in the comments, formatted input–output controls would be necessary.

4.7.1 Overloading Operators

As a complete short example of utilizing many of the new programming features that come with user-defined data structures we will consider the use of a familiar old mathematics system: fractions. Recall that a fraction is the ratio of two integers. We will therefore define a new data type called *Fraction*. It will simply consist of two integer types named *num* and *denom*. New data types can be defined in any program unit. For maximum usefulness we will place the definition in a module named *Fractions*. To use this new data type we will want to have subprograms to define a fraction, list its components, and multiply two fractions together, and to equate one fraction to another. In addition to the intrinsic constructor function `fraction` we will create a manual constructor function called `assign` having two arguments – the numerator value and denominator value – and will use them to return a fraction type. The listing subroutine, called `list_Fraction`, simply needs the name of the fraction to be printed. The function `mult_Fraction` accepts two fraction names and returns the third fraction as their product. Finally, we provide a function that equates the components of one fraction to those in a new fraction.

This data structure is presented in Figure 4.18. There we note that the module starts with the definition of the new data type (lines 2–4) and is followed with the "contains" statement (line 13). The subprograms that provide the functionality of the fraction data

```
[ 1]  module Fractions   ! F90 "Fraction" data structure and functionality
[ 2]     implicit none
[ 3]     type Fraction             ! define a data structure
[ 4]        integer :: num, den ! with two "components"
[ 5]     end type Fraction
[ 6]
[ 7]     interface operator (*)  ! extend meaning to fraction
[ 8]       module procedure mult_Fraction ; end interface
[ 9]
[10]     interface assignment (=) ! extend meaning to fraction
[11]       module procedure equal_Fraction ; end interface
[12]
[13]  contains ! functionality
[14]    subroutine assign (name, numerator, denominator)
[15]      type (Fraction), intent(inout) :: name
[16]      integer, intent(in)            :: numerator, denominator
[17]
[18]      name % num = numerator   ! % denotes which "component"
[19]      if ( denominator == 0 ) then
[20]            print *, "0 denominator not allowed, set to 1"
[21]            name % den = 1
[22]      else; name % den = denominator
[23]      end if ; end subroutine assign
[24]
[25]    subroutine list(name)
[26]      type (Fraction), intent(in) :: name
[27]
[28]      print *, name % num, "/", name % den ; end subroutine list
[29]
[30]    function  mult_Fraction (a, b) result (c)
[31]      type (Fraction), intent(in) :: a, b
[32]      type (Fraction)             :: c
[33]
[34]      c%num = a%num * b%num  ! standard = and * here
[35]      c%den = a%den * b%den  ; end function  mult_Fraction
[36]
[37]    subroutine equal_Fraction (new, name)
[38]      type (Fraction), intent(out) :: new
[39]      type (Fraction), intent(in)  :: name
[40]
[41]      new % num = name % num  ! standard = here
[42]      new % den = name % den  ; end subroutine equal_Fraction
[43]  end module Fractions
```

Figure 4.18: Overloading operations for new data types.

```
[ 1]  program test_Fractions
[ 2]   use Fractions
[ 3]    implicit none
[ 4]    type (Fraction) :: x, y, z
[ 5]
[ 6]    x = Fraction (22,7)       ! default constructor
[ 7]    write (*,'("default   x   = ")', advance='no') ; call list(x)
[ 8]    call assign(y,1,3)        ! manual constructor
[ 9]    write (*,'("assigned  y   = ")', advance='no') ; call list(y)
[10]    z = mult_Fraction (x,y)   ! function use
[11]    write (*,'("x mult y = ")', advance='no') ; call list(z);
[12]    print *, "Trying overloaded * and = for fractions:"
[13]    write (*,'("y * x gives ")', advance='no') ; call list(y*x) ! multi
[14]    z = x*y                   ! new operator uses
[15]    write (*,'("z = x*y gives ")', advance='no') ; call list(z) ! add
[16]  end program test_Fractions                          ! Running gives:
[17]  ! default   x   = 22/7      ! assigned  y   = 1/3   ! x mult y = 22/21
[18]  ! Trying overloaded * and = for fractions:
[19]  ! y * x gives 22/21         ! z = x*y gives 22/21
```

Figure 4.19: Testing overloading for new data types.

type follow the "contains" statement and are thus coupled to the definition of the new type. When we have completed defining the functionality to go with the new data type we end the module.

In this example the program to invoke the fraction type follows in Figure 4.19. To access the module, which defines the new data type and its supporting functions, we simply employ a "use" statement at the beginning of the program (line 2). The program declares three `Fraction` type variables (line 4): x, y, and z. The variable x is defined to be 22/7 with the intrinsic type constructor (line 6), and y is assigned a value of 1/3 by using the function `assign` (line 8). Both values are listed for confirmation. Then we form the new fraction, $z = 22/21$, by invoking the `mult_Fraction` function (line 10),

```
z = mult_Fraction (x, y),
```

which returns z as its result. A natural tendency at this point would be simply to write this as $z = x * y$. However, before we could do that we would have to tell the operators "*" and "=" how to act when provided with this new data type. This is known as *overloading* an intrinsic operator. We had the foresight to do this when we set up the module by declaring which of the "module procedures" were equivalent to each operator symbol. Thus, from the "interface operator (*)" statement block the system now knows that the left and right operands of the "*" symbol correspond to the first and second arguments in the function `mult_Fraction`. Likewise, the left and right operands of "=" are coupled to the first and second arguments, respectively, of subroutine `equal_Fraction`. The testing `test_Fractions` and verification results are in Figure 4.19. Before moving on, note that the system does not yet know how to multiply an integer times a fraction, or vice versa. To do that one would have to add more functionality such as a function, say `int_mult_frac`, and add it to the "module procedure" list associated with the "*" operator.

When considering which operators to overload for a newly defined data type, one should consider those that are used in `sorting` operations such as the greater-than, >, and less-than, <, operators. They are often useful because of the need to sort various types of data. If those symbols have been correctly overloaded, then a generic sorting routine might be used and would require few changes.

4.7.2 User-Defined Operators

In addition to the many intrinsic operators and functions we have seen so far, the F90 user can also define new operators or extend existing ones. User-defined operators can employ intrinsic data types, user-defined data types, or both. The user-defined operators, or extensions, can be unary or binary (i.e., have one or two arguments). The operator symbol must be included between two periods such as '`.op.`'. Specific examples will be given in the next chapter.

4.8 Pointers and Targets

The beginning of every data item must be stored in a computer memory at a specific address. The address of that data item is called a *pointer* to the data item, and a variable that can hold such an address is called a *pointer variable*. Often it is convenient to have a pointer to a variable, an array, or a subarray. MATLAB, F90, and C++ provide this sophisticated feature. The major benefits of pointers are that they allow dynamic data structures, such as "linked lists" and "tree structures," as well as recursive algorithms. Note that rather than containing data themselves, pointer variables simply exist to point to where some data are stored. Unlike C and MATLAB the F90 pointers are more like the "reference variables" of the C++ language in that they are mainly an alias or synonym for another variable, or part of another variable. They do not allow one to get the literal address easily in memory as does C. This is why programmers who write computer operating systems usually prefer C over F90. But F90 pointers allow easy access to array partitions for computational efficiency, which C++ does not. Pointers are often used to pass arguments by reference.

The item to which a pointer points is known as a *target* variable. Thus, every pointer has a logical status associated with it that indicates whether or not it is currently pointing to a target. The initial value of the association is `.false.`, or undefined.

4.8.1 Pointer-Type Declaration

For every type of data object that can be declared in the language, including derived types, a corresponding type of pointer and target can be declared (Table 4.33).

Table 4.33: Definition of Pointers and Accessing Their Targets

	C++	F90
Declaration	`type_tag *pointer_name;`	`type (type_tag), pointer :: pointer_name`
Target	`&target_name`	`type (type_tag), target :: target_name`
Examples	`char *cp, c;`	`character, pointer :: cp`
	`int *ip, i;`	`integer, pointer :: ip`
	`float *fp, f;`	`real, pointer :: fp`
	`cp = & c;`	`cp => c`
	`ip = & i;`	`ip => i`
	`fp = & f;`	`fp => f`

Table 4.34: Nullifying a Pointer to Break Target Association

C, C++	`pointer_name = NULL`
F90	`nullify (list_of_pointer_names)`
F95	`pointer_name = NULL()`

Although the use of pointers gives programmers more options for constructing algorithms, they also have a potentially severely detrimental effect on program execution efficiency. To ensure that compilers can produce code that executes efficiently, F90 restricts the variables to which a pointer can point to those specifically declared to have the attribute `target`. This, in part, makes the use of pointers in F90 and C++ somewhat different. Another major difference is that C++ allows arithmetic to be performed on the pointer address, but F90 does not.

So far, we have seen that F90 requires specific declarations of a `pointer` and a potential `target`. However, C++ employs two unary operators, & and *, to deal with pointers and targets, respectively. Thus, in C++ the operator `&variable_name` means "the address of" `variable_name`, and the C++ operator `*pointer_name` means "the value at the address of" `pointer_name`.

4.8.2 Pointer Assignment

In F90, a pointer is required to be associated with a target by a single pointer assignment statement; however, C allows, but does not require, a similar statement (see Table 4.33). After such a statement, the pointer has a new association status, and one could employ the F90 intrinsic inquiry function `associated(pointer_name, target_name)` to return `.true.` as the logical return value. If a programmer wishes to break or nullify a pointer's association with a target but not assign it another target, he or she can nullify the pointer, as shown in Table 4.34.

4.8.3 Using Pointers in Expressions

The most important rule about using pointers in F90 expressions is that, wherever a pointer occurs, it is treated as its associated target. That is, the target is automatically substituted for the pointer when the pointer occurs in an expression. For example, consider the actions in Figure 4.20 (where the results are stated as comments).

4.8.4 Pointers and Linked Lists

Pointers are the simplest available mechanism for dynamic memory management of arrays such as stacks, queues, trees, and linked lists. These are extraordinarily flexible data structures because their size can grow or shrink during the execution of a program. For linked lists the basic technique is to create a derived type that consists of one or more data elements and at least one pointer. Memory is allocated to contain the data, and a pointer is set to reference the next occurrence of data. If one pointer is present, the list is a singly linked list and can only be traversed in one direction: head to tail, or vice versa. If two pointers are present, the list is doubly linked and can be traversed in either direction. Linked lists allow the data of interest to be scattered all over memory and use pointers to weave through memory, gathering data as required. Detailed examples of the use of linked lists are covered in Chapter 8.

```
program  pt_expression
!
!       F90 example of using pointers in expressions
   implicit none
   integer, POINTER :: p, q, r
   integer, TARGET  :: i = 1, j = 2, k = 3

   q => j                      ! q points to integer j
   p => i                      ! p points to integer i
!
!       An expression that "looks like" pointer arithmetic
!       automatically substitutes the target value:
!
   q = p + 2                   ! means: j = i + 2 = 1 + 2 = 3
   print *, i, j, k            ! print target values
   p => k                      ! p now points to k
   print *, (q-p)              ! means print j - k = 3 - 3 = 0
!
!       Check associations of pointers
   print *, associated (r)     ! false
   r => k                      ! now r points to k, also
   print *, associated (p,i)   ! false
   print *, associated (p,k)   ! true
   print *, associated (r,k)   ! true
end program pt_expression
```

Figure 4.20: Using F90 pointers in expressions.

As a conceptual example of when one might need to use linked lists, think of applications where one never knows in advance how many data entries will be needed. For example, when a surveyor determines the exact perimeter of a building or plot of land, critical measurements are taken at each angle. If the perimeter has N sides, the surveyor measures the length of each side and the interior angle each side forms with the next. Often the perimeter has visual obstructions, and offsets around them must be made, recorded, and corrected for later use. Regardless of how careful the surveyor is, errors are invariably introduced during the measurement process. However, the error in angle measurements can be bounded.

The program for implementing the recording and correcting of the angles in a survey could be written using a singly linked list. A linked list is chosen because the programmer has no idea how many sides the perimeter has, and linked lists can grow arbitrarily. Because of the linked list's ability to absorb a short or long data stream, the user does not have to be asked to count the number of legs in the traverse. The program begins by declaring a derived type that contains one angle measurement and a pointer to the next measurement. A count is kept of the number of legs in this loop, and the forward pointer for the last angle read is cleared (set to null) to signal the end of list. After all the data are read, the entire list of angles is reviewed to get the total of the measurements. This starts by revisiting the head of the list and adding together all the angle measurements until a null pointer is encountered, signaling the end of list. Then the error can be computed and distributed equally among the legs of the traverse.

4.9 Accessing External Source Files and Functions

At times one finds it necessary or efficient to utilize other software from libraries, other users, or different paths in directories. Of course, you could always resort to the brute force approach by using a text editor to copy the desired source code into your program. However, this is unwise not only because it wastes storage but more important because it gives multiple copies of a module that must all be found and changed if future revisions are needed or desired. Better methods of accessing such codes can be defined either inside your program, or external to it in the "linking" phase after compiling has been completed.

High-level languages like C, C++, and F90 allow one or more approaches for accessing such software from within your code. One feature common to all these languages is the availability of an "include" statement that gives the system path to the desired code file. At compile time, and only then, a temporary copy of the indicated code from that file is literally copied and inserted into your program at the location of the corresponding "include" statement.

It is common practice, but not required, to denote such code fragments with name extensions of ".h" and ".inc," in C++ and F90, respectively. For example, to use a program called "class_Person" the following statement could be inserted in your program:

```
C, C++: include <class_Person.h>
F90   : include 'class_Person.inc'
```

if the files, class_Person.h or class_Person.inc, were in the same directory as your program. Otherwise, it is necessary to give the complete system path to the file such as

```
include '/home/caam211/Include/inv.f90'
include '/home/caam211/Include/SolveVector.f90',
```

which gives source links to the `caam211` course files for the function `inv(A)` for returning the inverse of a matrix A and the function `SolveVector(A,B)`, which returns the solution vector X for the matrix system A*X = B.

In F90 one can also provide a "module" that defines constants, user-defined types, supporting subprograms, operators, and so forth. Any of those features can be accessed by first including such an F90 module before the main program and later invoking it with a "use" statement that cites the "module" name. For example, the F90 program segments

```
include '/home/caam211/Include/caam211_operators.f90'
Program  Lab2_A_2
...
  call  test_matrix ( A, B, X )  ! form and invert test matrix
...
subroutine  test_matrix ( A, B, X )
 use caam211_operators                ! included above
  implicit none
  real :: A(:,:), B(:), X(:)
  real :: A_inv(size(A,1),size(A,1)) ! automatic array allocation
    A_inv = inv(A)
    X     = A .solve. B               ! like X = A \ B in Matlab
    ...
```

gives a source link to the `caam211` course "module" source file named `caam211_operators.f90`, which contains subprograms, such as the function `inv()`, and operator definitions like `.solve.`, which is equivalent to the "\" operator in MATLAB.

In the last example the omission of the "include" statement would require a compiler-dependent statement to allow the system to locate the module cited in the "use" statement. For the National Algorithms Group (NAG) F90 compiler that link would be given as

```
f90 -o go /home/caam211/Include/caam211_operators.f90 my.f90
```

if the segment above were stored in the file named `my.f90`, whereas for the Cray F90 compiler a path flag, `-p`, to the compiled version is required such as

```
f90 -o go -p /home/caam211/Include/caam211_op_CRAY.o my.f90.
```

Either would produce an executable file, which is named "go" in this example.

4.10 Procedural Applications

In this section we will consider two common examples of procedural algorithms: fitting curves to experimental data and sorting numbers, strings, and derived types. Sorting concepts will be discussed again in Chapter 7.

4.10.1 Fitting Curves to Data

We must often deal with measurements and what they result in: data. Measurements are never exact because they are limited by instrument sensitivity and are contaminated by noise. To determine trends (how measurements are related to each other), confirm theoretical predictions, and the like, engineers must frequently *fit* functions to data. The "curve" fit is intended to be smoother than a raw plot of the data and will, it is hoped, reveal more about the underlying relation between the variables than would otherwise be apparent.

Often, these functions take *parametric* form: The functional form is specified but has unknown coefficients. Suppose you want to fit a straight line to a dataset. With y denoting the measurement and x the independent variable, we wish to fit the function $y = f(x) = mx + b$ to the data. The fitting process amounts to determining a few quantities of the assumed linear functional form – the parameters m and b – from the data. You know that two points define a straight line; consequently, only two of the (x, y) pairs need be used. But which two should be used? In virtually all real-world circumstances, the measurements do not precisely conform to the assumed functional form. Thus, fitting a curve by selecting a few values (two in the linear case) and solving for the function's parameters produce a circumspect "fit," to say the least. Instead, the most common approach is to use all the data in the curve-fitting process. Because you frequently have much more data than parameters, you have what is known as an *overdetermined* problem. In most cases, no parameter values produce a function that will fit all the data exactly. Overdetermined problems can be solved by specifying an *error criterion* (what is an error and how large is the deviation of data from the assumed curve) and finding the set of parameter values that minimizes the error criterion. With this approach, we can justifiably claim to have found the best parameter choices.

4.10.1.1 The "Least-Squares" Approach. Far and away the most common error criterion is the *mean-squared error*: Given measurement pairs (x_i, y_i), $i = 1, \ldots, N$, the mean squared error ϵ^2 equals the average across the dataset of $\left(y_i - f(x_i)\right)^2$, the squared error between the ith measurement and the assumed parametric function $f(x_i)$:

$$\epsilon^2 = \frac{1}{N}\sum_{i=1}^{N}\left[y_i - f(x_i)\right]^2.$$

Least-squares fitting of functions to data amounts to minimizing the dataset's mean-squared error with respect to the parameters.

To illustrate the least-squares approach, we will fit a linear function to a dataset. Substituting the assumed functional form $f(x) = mx + b$ into the expression for the mean-squared error, we have

$$\epsilon^2 = \frac{1}{N}\sum_{i=1}^{N}\left[y_i - (mx_i + b)\right]^2.$$

We can find a set of equations for the parameters m and b that minimize this quantity by evaluating the derivative of ϵ^2 with respect to each parameter and setting each to zero as follows:

$$\frac{d\epsilon^2}{dm} = \frac{1}{N}\sum_{i=1}^{N} -2x_i\left[y_i - (mx_i + b)\right] = 0$$

$$\frac{d\epsilon^2}{db} = \frac{1}{N}\sum_{i=1}^{N} -2\left[y_i - (mx_i + b)\right] = 0.$$

After some simplification, we find that we have two *linear* equations to solve for the fitting parameters:

$$m \cdot \left(\frac{1}{N}\sum_{i=1}^{N} x_i^2\right) + b \cdot \left(\frac{1}{N}\sum_{i=1}^{N} x_i\right) = \frac{1}{N}\sum_{i=1}^{N} x_i y_i$$

$$m \cdot \left(\frac{1}{N}\sum_{i=1}^{N} x_i\right) + b = \frac{1}{N}\sum_{i=1}^{N} y_i.$$

Thus, finding the least-squares fit of a straight line to a set of data amounts to solving a set of two linear equations, the coefficients of which are computed from the data. Note that the four summations in the last equation have the same range count (N) and could be evaluated in a single explicit loop.

An Aside

Because fitting data with a linear equation yields a set of two easily solved equations for the parameters, one approach to fitting *nonlinear* curves to data is to convert the nonlinear problem into a linear one. For example, suppose we want to fit a *power law* to the data: $f(x) = ax^b$. Instead of minimizing the mean-squared error directly, we transform the data so that we are fitting it with a linear curve. In the power-law case, the logarithm of the fitting curve is linear in the parameters: $\log f(x) = \log a + b \log x$. This equation is not linear in the parameter a. For purposes of least-squares fits, we instead treat $a' = \log a$ as the linear fit parameter, solve the resulting set of linear equations for a', and calculate $a = \exp a'$ to determine the power-law fitting parameter. By evaluating the logarithm of x_i and y_i and applying the least-squares equations governing the fitting of a linear curve to data, we can fit a power-law function to data. Thus, calculating a linear least-squares fit to data underlies general approximation of measurements by smooth curves. For an insight to the types of relationships that can be determined, see the following summary.

x-axis	y-axis		Relationship
Linear	Linear	$y = mx + b$	linear
Linear	Logarithmic	$\log y = mx + b$	exponential: $y = e^b \cdot e^{mx}$
Logarithmic	Linear	$y = m \log x + b$	logarithmic
Logarithmic	Logarithmic	$\log y = m \log x + b$	power-law: $y = e^b \cdot x^m$

We can now specify the computations required by the least-squares fitting algorithm mathematically.

Algorithm: Least-Squares Fitting of Straight Lines to Data

1. Given N pairs of data points (x_i, y_i)
2. Calculate* $a_{11} = \frac{1}{N}\sum_{i=1}^{N} x_i^2$, $a_{12} = \frac{1}{N}\sum_{i=1}^{N} x_i$, $a_{21} = \frac{1}{N}\sum_{i=1}^{N} x_i$, $a_{22} = 1$, $c_1 = \frac{1}{N}\sum_{i=1}^{N} x_i y_i$, and $c_2 = \frac{1}{N}\sum_{i=1}^{N} y_i$.
3. Solve the set of linear equations

$$\begin{bmatrix} a_{11} & a_{12} \\ a_{21} & a_{22} \end{bmatrix} \begin{bmatrix} m \\ b \end{bmatrix} = \begin{bmatrix} c_1 \\ c_2 \end{bmatrix},$$

which for two equations can be done by hand to yield

$$m = (a_{12} \cdot c_2 - N \cdot c_1)/(a_{12} \cdot a_{21} - N \cdot a_{11})$$
$$b = (c_2 - m \cdot a_{12})/N.$$

4. Calculate the mean-squared error $\epsilon^2 = \frac{1}{N}\sum_{i=1}^{N}[y_i - (mx_i + b)]^2$.

4.10.1.2 Implementing the Least-Squares Algorithm. In F90, such calculations can be performed two different ways: one expresses the looping construct directly; the other uses more efficient intrinsic array routines inside F90. On the assumption that the $\{x_i\}$ are stored in the vector `x`, the coefficient `a12` can be calculated (at least) two ways:

1.
```
sum_x = 0
N = size(x)
do i = 1,N
   sum_x = sum_x + x(i)
end do
a12 = sum_x/N
```

2. `a12 = sum(x)/size(x).`

Clearly, the second method produces a somewhat simpler expression than the first and is vastly superior to the first. In the sample code that follows in Figure 4.21 we use the intrinsic array functions but encourage the reader to check the results with a single loop that computes all six terms needed to find `m` and `b`.

* Note that these calculations can be performed in one loop rather than four.

```
program linear_fit
! -----------------------------------------------------
!      F90 linear least-squares fit on data in file
!              specified by the user.
! -----------------------------------------------------
implicit none
integer, parameter    :: filenumber = 1 ! RISKY
real, allocatable     :: x(:), y(:)     ! data arrays
character (len = 64) :: filename        ! name of file to read
integer               :: lines          ! number of input lines
real                  :: fit(3)         ! final results

interface
  function inputCount(unit) result(linesOfInput)
    integer, intent(in) :: unit         ! file unit number
    integer             :: linesOfInput ! result
  end function inputCount
  subroutine readData (inFile, lines, x, y)
    integer, intent(in)  :: inFile,   lines     ! file unit, size
    real,    intent(out) :: x(lines), y(lines) ! data read
  end subroutine readData
end interface

!   Get the name of the file containing the data.
  write (*,*) 'Enter the filename to read data from:'
  read  (*,'(A64)') filename

!   Open that file for reading.
  open (unit = filenumber, file = filename)

!   Find the number of lines in the file
  lines = inputCount (filenumber)
  write (*,*) 'There were ',lines,' records read.'

!   Allocate that many entries in the x and y array
  allocate (x(lines), y(lines))

  call readData (filenumber, lines, x, y)   ! Read data
  close (filenumber)

  call lsq_fit (x, y, fit)                  ! least-squares fit
  print *, "the slope is     ", fit(1) ! display the results
  print *, "the intercept is ", fit(2)
  print *, "the error is     ", fit(3)
  deallocate (y, x)
contains

  subroutine lsq_fit (x, y, fit)
! -----------------------------------------------------
!         Linear least-squares fit, A u = c
! -----------------------------------------------------
!  fit   = slope, intercept, and mean squared error of fit.
!  lines = the length of the arrays x and y.
!  x     = array containing the independent variable.
!  y     = array containing the dependent variable data.
  implicit none
```

```
[57]     real,     intent(in)  :: x(:), y(size(x))
[58]     real,     intent(out) :: fit(3)
[59]     integer               :: lines
[60]     real                  :: m,     b,      mse
[61]     real                  :: sumx, sumx2, sumy, sumxy
[62]
[63]  !    Summations
[64]       sumx   = sum ( x )      ; sumx2 = sum ( x**2 )
[65]       sumy   = sum ( y )      ; sumxy = sum ( x*y )
[66]
[67]  !    Calculate slope intercept
[68]       lines = size(x)
[69]       m = (sumx*sumy - lines*sumxy)/(sumx**2 - lines*sumx2)
[70]       b = (sumy - m*sumx)/lines
[71]
[72]  !    Predicted y points and the sum of squared errors.
[73]       mse = sum ( (y - m*x - b)**2 )/lines
[74]       fit(1) = m ; fit(2) = b ; fit(3) = mse      ! returned
[75]     end subroutine lsq_fit
[76]
[77]     end program linear_fit
[78]
[79]  ! Given test set 1 in file lsq_1.dat:
[80]  ! -5.000000 -2.004481
[81]  ! -4.000000 -1.817331
[82]  ! -3.000000 -1.376481
[83]  ! -2.000000 -0.508725
[84]  ! -1.000000 -0.138670
[85]  !  0.000000  0.376678
[86]  !  1.000000  0.825759
[87]  !  2.000000  1.036343
[88]  !  3.000000  1.815817
[89]  !  4.000000  2.442354
[90]  !  5.000000  2.636355
[91]  ! Running the program yields:
[92]  !
[93]  ! Enter the filename to read data from: lsq_1.dat
[94]  ! There were  11  records read.
[95]  ! the slope is       0.4897670746
[96]  ! the intercept is   0.2988743484
[97]  ! the error is       0.2139159478E-01
```

Figure 4.21: A typical least-squares linear fit program.

There are a few new features demonstrated in this sample code. In line 7 we have specified a fixed unit number to associate with the data file to be specified by the user. But we did not do an INQUIRE to see if that unit was already in use. We will accept a user input filename (lines 9, 26 and 29) that contains the data to be fitted. An interface (lines 12–21) is provided to external routines that will determine the number of lines of data in the file and read those data into the two arrays. Those two routines are given elsewhere. Of course, the memory for the data arrays must be dynamically allocated (line 36) before they can be read (line 38). After the least-squares fit is computed (line 41) and printed, the memory space for the data is freed (line 45).

In the `lsq_fit` subroutine (line 48) the three items of interest are passed in the array `fit`. (Routine `lsq_fit` could have been written as a function; try it.) Observe that `y` must

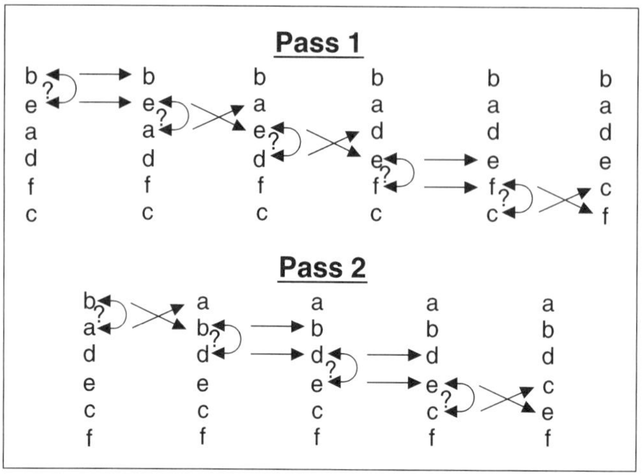

Figure 4.22: Example passes of the bubble-sort algorithm through data.

be the same length as array x, and so the `size` intrinsic was used to ensure that (line 57). The data summations are evaluated with the `sum` intrinsic (lines 63–65) and it is used again to evaluate the mean-squared error `mse` (line 72), as described in step 4 of the algorithm. The test data (lines 80–90) and results (lines 93–97) are given as comments, as usual. Since no explicit loops have been used, this form would be more efficient on vector computers and some parallel computers.

4.10.2 Sorting

One of the most useful computational routines is sorting: ordering a sequence of data according to some rule. For example, the alphabetized list of filenames producted by a system directory command is far easier to read than an unsorted list would be. Furthermore, data can be fruitfully sorted in more than one way. As an example, you can sort system files by their creation date.

Sorting algorithms have been well studied by computer scientists in a quest to find the most efficient. We use here the *bubble sort algorithm*, which is perhaps the oldest but not most efficient. This algorithm makes multiple passes over a list, going down the list and interchanging adjacent elements in the list if necessary to put them in order. For example, consider the list `[b, e, a, d, f, c]`, shown in Figure 4.22, that we wish to sort to alphabetical order. In the first pass, the algorithm begins by examining the first two list elements `(b, e)`. Since they are in order, these two are left alone. The next two elements `(e, a)` are not in order; these two elements of the list are interchanged. In this way, we "bubble" the element `a` toward the top and `e` toward the bottom. The algorithm proceeds through the list, interchanging elements if need be until the last element is reached. Note that the bottom of the list at the end of the first pass contains the correct entry. This effect occurs because of the algorithm's structure: the "greatest" element will always propagate to the list's end. Once through the pass, we see that the list is in better, but not perfect, order. We must perform another pass just like the first to improve the ordering. Thus, the second pass need consider only the first $n - 1$ elements, the third $n - 2$, and so forth. The second pass does make the list better formed. After more passes, the list eventually becomes sorted. To produce a completely sorted list, the bubble-sort algorithm requires no more passes than the number of elements in the list minus one.

The following F90 routines illustrate some of the initial features of a simple procedural approach to a simple process like the bubble-sort algorithm. We begin by considering the sorting of a list of real numbers as shown in subroutine Sort_Reals in Figure 4.23.

In line 1 we have passed in the size of the array and the actual array (called database). Note that the database has (intent) inout because we plan to overwrite the original database with the newly sorted order, which is done in lines 18–20. For efficiency's sake we have included an integer counter, swaps_Made, so that we can determine if the sort has terminated early. If we wished to apply the same bubble-sort algorithm to an integer array, all we would have to do is change the procedure name and lines 6 and 10 that describe the type of data being sorted (try it).

That is true because the compiler knows how to apply the > operator to all the standard numerical types in the language. But what if we want to sort character strings, or other types of objects? Fortran has lexical operators (like LGE) to deal with strings, but user-defined objects would require that we overload the > operator if the expected users would not find the overloading to be confusing. In other words, you could develop a fairly general sort routine if we changed lines 6 and 10 to be

```
[ 6]   type (Object), intent(inout) :: database (lines)
[10]   type (Object)                :: temp
```

and provided an overloading of > so that line 17 made sense for the defined object (or for selected component of it).

```
[ 1]  subroutine Sort_Reals (lines, database)
[ 2]  ! Bubble Sort of (changed) Real Database
[ 3]
[ 4]   implicit none
[ 5]   integer, intent(in)    :: lines              ! number of records
[ 6]   real,    intent(inout) :: database (lines)   ! records in database
[ 7]
[ 8]   integer :: swaps_Made          ! number of swaps made in one pass
[ 9]   integer :: count              ! loop variable
[10]   real    :: temp               ! temporary holder for making swap
[11]
[12]     do ! Repeat this loop forever... (until we break out of it)
[13]       swaps_Made = 0                    ! Initially, we've made no swaps
[14]       ! Make one pass of the bubble sort algorithm
[15]       do count = 1, (lines - 1)
[16]         ! If item is greater than the one after it, swap them
[17]         if ( database (count) > database (count + 1) ) then
[18]                temp                 = database (count)
[19]                database (count)     = database (count + 1)
[20]                database (count + 1) = temp
[21]                swaps_Made            = swaps_Made + 1
[22]          end if
[23]        end do
[24]        ! If we made no swaps, break out of the loop.
[25]        if ( swaps_Made == 0 ) exit ! do count swaps
[26]      end do
[27]  end subroutine Sort_Reals
```

Figure 4.23: Bubble sort of a real array.

```
[ 1]   subroutine Sort_String (lines, database)
[ 2]   ! Bubble Sort of (Changed) String Database
[ 3]    implicit none
[ 4]
[ 5]    integer,           intent(in)     :: lines            ! input size
[ 6]    character(len=*), intent(inout)  :: database (lines) ! records
[ 7]
[ 8]    character (len = len(database (1))) :: temp ! swap holder
[ 9]    integer :: swaps_Made       ! number of swaps in a pass
[10]    integer :: count            ! loop variable
[11]
[12]      interface ! to_lower
[13]        function  to_lower (string)  result (new_String)
[14]          character (len = *), intent(in) :: string
[15]          character (len = len(string))   :: new_String
[16]        end function to_lower
[17]      end interface ! to_lower
[18]
[19]      do ! Repeat this loop forever... (until we break out of it)
[20]        swaps_Made = 0                ! Initially, we've made no swaps
[21]        ! Make one pass of the bubble sort algorithm
[22]        do count = 1, (lines - 1)
[23]          ! If the element is greater than the one after it, swap them
[24]          if ( LGT (to_lower (database (count    )),
[25]                    to_lower (database (count + 1))) ) then
[26]              temp                  = database (count     )
[27]              database (count     ) = database (count + 1)
[28]              database (count + 1) = temp
[29]              swaps_Made            = swaps_Made + 1
[30]          end if
[31]        end do
[32]        ! If we made no swaps, berak out of the loop.
[33]        if ( swaps_Made == 0) exit ! do count swaps
[34]      end do
[35]    end subroutine Sort_String
```

Figure 4.24: Bubble sort of an array of character strings.

To illustrate the sort of change that is necessary to sort character strings, consider subroutine Sort_String (Figure 4.24):

To keep the same style as the previous algorithm and overload the > operator we would have to have a procedure that utilizes the lexical operators in lines 24 and 25, along with the interface definition on lines 12 through 17, to define the meaning of > in the context of a string. Although the concept of a "template" for a code to carry out a bubble-sort on any list of objects may maximize code reuse it may not always be obvious what > means when it is overloaded by you or some other programmer.

Note that in the two sorting examples above we have assumed that we had the authority to change the original database and that it was efficient to do so. Often that is not the case. Imagine the case in which the database represents millions of credit card users, each with large number of components of numbers, character strings, or general objects. If many workers are accessing those data for various sorting needs, you probably would not allow the original dataset to be changed for reasons of safety or security. Then we consider an alternative to moving around the actual database components. That is, we should consider

```
[ 1]  subroutine Integer_Sort (lines, database, order)
[ 2]  ! Ordered Bubble Sort of (Unchanged) Integer Database
[ 3]
[ 4]   implicit none
[ 5]   integer, intent(in)  :: lines              ! number of records
[ 6]   integer, intent(in)  :: database (lines)   ! records in database
[ 7]   integer, intent(out) :: order    (lines)   ! the order array
[ 8]
[ 9]   integer :: swaps_Made        ! number of swaps made in one pass
[10]   integer :: count             ! loop variable
[11]   integer :: temp              ! temporary holder for making swap
[12]
[13]     order = (/ (count, count = 1, lines) /) ! default order
[14]     do ! Repeat this loop forever... (until we break out of it)
[15]       swaps_Made = 0               ! Initially, we've made no swaps
[16]       ! Make one pass of the bubble sort algorithm
[17]       do count = 1, (lines - 1)
[18]         ! If item is greater than the one after it, swap them
[19]         if ( database (order (count)) >      &
[20]              database (order (count + 1)) ) then
[21]                temp            = order (count)
[22]                order (count)     = order (count + 1)
[23]                order (count + 1) = temp
[24]                swaps_Made        = swaps_Made + 1
[25]          end if
[26]        end do
[27]        ! If we made no swaps, break out of the loop.
[28]        if ( swaps_Made == 0 ) exit ! do count swaps
[29]      end do
[30]  end subroutine Integer_Sort
```

Figure 4.25: An ordered bubble sort of an integer array.

using moving pointers to large data components, or pseudopointers such as an ordering array. The use of an ordering array is shown in Figure 4.25 where subroutine Integer_Sort now includes an additional argument.

The third argument has intent (out), as shown in line 7, and is an integer array of the same length as the original database, which has now been changed to intent (in) so the compiler will not allow us to change the original data. If the data are properly sorted as supplied, then it should not be changed and the new order should be the same as the original sequential input. That is why line 13 initializes the return order to a sequential list. Then we slightly change the previous sort logic so that lines 19 through 23 now check what is in an ordered location and change the order number when necessary but never the original data. After exiting this routine you could list the information, in sorted order, without changing the original data simply by using vector subscripts in a print statement like

```
print *, database (order).
```

Clearly you could write a very similar program using a true "pointer" array since they are now standard in Fortran.

Next we will start to generalize the idea of sorting to include the sorting of objects that may have numerous components. Assume the each record object to be read is defined as in Figure 4.26. There may be thousands, or millions, of such records to be read from a file,

```
module record_Module
!-----------------------------------------------------------
! record_Module holds the "record" type
!-----------------------------------------------------------
  ! record is a data structure with two names and an id number.
  type record
    character (len=24) :: last_Name   ! last name
    character (len=24) :: first_Name  ! first name
    integer            :: id          ! id number
  end type record
end module record_Module
```

Figure 4.26: A typical record in a list to be sorted.

sorted by name, or both, number, and then displayed in sorted order. Program test_bubble in Figure 4.27 illustrates one approach to such a problem. Here, since the database of records is to read from a file we do not yet know how many there are to be stored. Therefore, the database is declared allocatable in line 13 and allocated later in line 35 after we have evaluated the file size of a file named by the user. Although not generally necessary, we have selected to have an order array for names and a different one for numbers. They are sort_by_Name and sort_by_Number, respectively and are treated in a similar fashion to the database memory allocation, as noted in lines 13–14, and line 35.

In line 21 we have arbitrarily set a unit number to be used for the file. That is okay for a very small code but an unnecessary and unwise practice in general. The Fortran intrinsic "inquire" allows one to determine which units are inactive, and we could create a function, say Get_Next_Unit, to select a safe unit number for our input operation. After accepting a file name we open the unit and count the number of lines present in the file (see line 30). Had the database been on the standard input device and not contained any nonprinting control characters, we could have easily read it with the statement

```
read *, database
```

However, it does contain tabs (ASCII character number 9) and is in a user-defined file instead of the standard input device; thus, line 38 invokes subroutine read_Data to get the database. Of course, once the tabs and commas have been accounted for and the names and identification number extracted, it uses an intrinsic constructor on each line to form its database entry such as

```
database (line_Count) = Record (last, first, id)
```

After all the records have been read into the database, note that line 42 extracts all the last names with the syntax

```
database (:) last_Name
```

so they are copied into subroutine String_Sort, as its second argument, and the ordered list sort_by_Name) is returned to allow operations that need a last name sort. Likewise, subroutine Integer_Sort, shown above, is used in line 50 to sort the identification numbers and save the data in order list sort_by_Number. The ordered lists are used in show_Data, in lines 46 and 53, to display the sorted information without changing the original data.

```
program test_bubble
!-----------------------------------------------------------
! test_bubble asks for a filename for a file of names and id
! numbers, loads in the data from a file into the database,
! finds sorting orders, and prints sorted data
!-----------------------------------------------------------
 use record_Module      ! need this to use the 'record' type
  implicit none
! We define the database as an allocatable array of records.
  type (record), allocatable :: database (:)

! These arrays hold the sorted order of the database entries.
  integer, allocatable :: sort_by_Name   (:)
  integer, allocatable :: sort_by_Number (:)

  character (len = 64) :: file_Name   ! file to read data from
  integer              :: lines      ! number of lines of input
  integer              :: file_Number ! the input file number
  integer              :: loop_Count  ! loop counter

    file_Number = 1       ! arbitrarily set file_Number to 1

    write (*,*) 'Enter the filename to read data from:'
    read  (*,'(A64)') file_Name

  ! Open our file and assign the number to 'file_Number'
    open (unit = file_Number, file = file_Name)

  ! Find the number of lines in the input file with input_Count.
    lines = input_Count (file_Number)
    write (*,*) 'There are ', lines,' records.'

  ! Allocate that many entries in the database and order arrays
    allocate ( database (lines) )
    allocate ( sort_by_Name (lines), sort_by_Number (lines) )

  ! Read the data from file into the database and close the file.
    call read_Data (file_Number, lines, database)
    close (file_Number)

  ! Sort the database by name; the order will be in sort_by_Name.
    call String_Sort (lines, database (:)%last_Name, sort_by_Name)
    write (*,*); write (*,*) 'Data sorted by name: '; write (*,*)

  ! Print out the data in the database sorted by name
    call show_Data (lines, database, sort_by_Name)
    write (*,*); write (*,*) 'Data sorted by number:'; write (*,*)

  ! Sort the database by id numbers; new order is sort_by_Number.
    call Integer_Sort (lines, database (:)%id, sort_by_Number)

  ! Print out the data in the database sorted by number.
    call show_Data (lines, database, sort_by_Number)
end program test_bubble
```

Figure 4.27: Testing of ordered bubble sorts.

If the supplied file, say namelist, contained data in the format of (String comma String tab Number) with the entries

```
Indurain, Miguel 5623
van der Aarden, Eric 1245
Rominger, Tony 3411
Sorensen, Rolf 341
Yates, Sean 8998
Vandiver, Frank 45
Smith, Sally 3821
Johnston, David 3421
Gillis, Malcolm 3785
Johns, William     7234
Johnston, Jonathan 7234
Johnson, Alexa 5190
Kruger, Charlotte 2345
Butera, Robert 7253
Armstrong, Lance 2374
Hegg, Steve 9231
LeBlanc, Lucien 23
Peiper, Alan 5674
Smith-Jones, Nancy 9082
```

the output would be

```
! Enter the filename to read data from: namelist
! There are  19  records.
!
! Data sorted by name:
!
! Armstrong                 Lance                   2374
! Butera                    Robert                  7253
! Gillis                    Malcolm                 3785
! Hegg                      Steve                   9231
! Indurain                  Miguel                  5623
! Johns                     William                 7234
! Johnson                   Alexa                   5190
! Johnston                  David                   3421
! Johnston                  Jonathan                7234
! Kruger                    Charlotte               2345
! LeBlanc                   Lucien                    23
! Peiper                    Alan                    5674
! Rominger                  Tony                    3411
! Smith                     Sally                   3821
! Smith-Jones               Nancy                   9082
! Sorensen                  Rolf                     341
! van der Aarden            Eric                    1245
! Vandiver                  Frank                     45
! Yates                     Sean                    8998
!
```

and

```
! Data sorted by number:
!
! LeBlanc                   Lucien                    23
! Vandiver                  Frank                     45
! Sorensen                  Rolf                     341
```

Pass 1						Pass 2					Pass 3	
Level						Level					Level	
1	2	3	4	5	6	1	2	3	4	5	1	2
Sorted						Sorted					Sorted	
b	b	b	b	b	b	b	a	a	a	a	a	a
e	e	a	a	a	a	a	b	b	b	b	b	b
a	a	e	d	d	d	d	d	d	d	d	c	c
d	d	d	e	e	e	e	e	e	e	c	d	d
f	f	f	f	f	c	c	c	c	c	e	e	e
c	c	c	c	c	f	f	f	f	f	f	f	f
Is_Was[a]						Is_Was					Is_Was	
	1	1		1	1			1	3	3	3	3
	2	3		3	3			3	1	1	1	1
	3	2		4	4			4	4	4	4	6
	4	4		2	2			2	2	6	6	4
	5	5		5	6			6	6	2	2	2
	6	6		6	5			5	5	5	5	5

[a] Is_Was (j) = k. What is position j <u>was</u> position k.

Figure 4.28: Sorting via an order vector, array (Is_Was) → a b c d e f.

```
! van der Aarden       Eric           1245
! Kruger               Charlotte      2345
! Armstrong            Lance          2374
! Rominger             Tony           3411
! Johnston             David          3421
! Gillis               Malcolm        3785
! Smith                Sally          3821
! Johnson              Alexa          5190
! Indurain             Miguel         5623
! Peiper               Alan           5674
! Johns                William        7234
! Johnston             Jonathan       7234
! Butera               Robert         7253
! Yates                Sean           8998
! Smith-Jones          Nancy          9082
! Hegg                 Steve          9231
```

4.11 Exercises

1 Frequently we need to know how many lines exist in an external file that is to be used by our program. Usually we need that information to `dynamically allocate` memory for the arrays that will be constructed from the file data to be read. Write an F90 program or routine that will accept a unit number as input, open that unit, loop over the lines of data in the file connected to the unit, and return the number of lines found in the file. (An external file ends when the `iostat` from a read is less than zero.)

2 A related problem is to read a table of data from an external file. In addition to knowing the number of lines in the file it is necessary to know the number of entities (columns) per line and to verify that all lines of the file have the same number of columns. Develop

an F90 program for that purpose. (This is the sort of checking that the Matlab `load` function must do before loading an array of data.)

3 Write a program that displays the current date and time and uses the module `tic_toc`, in Figure 4.10, to display the CPU time required for a calculation.

4 Develop a companion function called `to_upper` that converts a string to all uppercase letters. Test it with the program above.

5 Develop a function that will take an external file unit number and count the number of lines in the file connected to that unit. This assumes that the file has been "opened" on that unit. The interface to the function is to be

```
interface
  function inputCount(unit) result(linesOfInput)
    integer, intent(in) :: unit          ! file unit number
    integer             :: linesOfInput ! result
  end function inputCount
end interface
```

6 Assume the file in the previous problem contains two real values per line. Develop a subroutine that will read the file and return two vectors holding the first and second values, respectively. The interface to the subroutine is to be

```
interface
  subroutine readData (inFile, lines, x, y)
    integer, intent(in)  :: inFile,    lines     ! file unit, size
    real,    intent(out) :: x(lines), y(lines) ! data read
  end subroutine readData
end interface
```

7 Written replies to the questions given below will be required. All of the named files are provided in source form as well as being listed in the text. The cited figure number indicates where some or all of the code is discussed in the text.

(a) *Figure 1.3* — `hello.f90`
What is it necessary to split the printing statement so that "Hello" and "world" occur on different program lines, that is, to continue it over two lines?

(b) *Figure 4.1* — `arithmetic.f90`
What is the meaning of the symbol (`mod`) used to get the Mod_Result?
What is the meaning of the symbol (**) used to get the Pow_Result?

(c) *Figure 4.3* — `array_index.f90`
Is it good practice to use a loop index outside the loop? Why?

(d) *Figure 4.4* — `more_or_less.f90`
What does the symbol (>) mean here?
What does the symbol (==) mean here?

(e) *Figure 4.5* — `if_else.f90`
What does the symbol (`.and.`) mean here? Can its preceding and following arguments be interchanged (is it commutative)?

(f) *Figure 4.6* — `and_or_not.f90`
What does the symbol (`.not.`) mean here?
What does the symbol (`.or.`) mean here? Can its preceding and following arguments be interchanged (is it commutative)?

(g) *Figure 4.7* — `clip.f90`
What does the symbol (<=) mean here?

(h) *Figure 4.8* — `maximum.f90`
What are the input and output arguments for the maxint function?

8 The vertical motion of a projectile at any time t has a position given by $y = y_0 + V_0 * t - 1/2 * g * t^2$ and a velocity of $V = V_0 - g * t$ when upward is taken as positive and where the initial conditions on the starting position and velocity at $t = 0$ are y_0 and V_0, respectively. Here the gravitational acceleration term g has been taken downward. Recall that the numerical value of g depends on the units employed. Use metric units with $g = 9.81$ m/s^2 for distances measured in meters and time in seconds.
Write a C++ or F90 program that will accept initial values of y_0 and V_0 and then compute and print y and V for each single input value of time t. Print the results for $y_0 = 1.5$ meters and $V_0 = 5.0$ m/s for times $t = 0.5$, 2.0, and 4.0 seconds.

9 Modify the projectile program written in Problem 2 to have it print the time, position, and velocity for times ranging from 0.0 to 2.0 seconds in increments of 0.05 seconds. If you use a direct loop, do not use real loop variables. Conclude the program by having it list the approximate maximum (positive) height reached and the time when that occurred. The initial data will be the same but should be printed for completeness. The three columns of numbers should be neat and right justified. In that case the default print format (print * in F90) will usually not be neat, and one must employ a "formatted" print or write statement.

10 The greatest common divisor of two positive integers can be computed by at least two different approaches. There is a looping approach known as the Euclidean algorithm that has the following pseudocode:

```
Rank two positive integers as max and min.
do while min > 0
  Find remainder of max divided by min.
  Replace max by min.
  Replace min by the remainder
end do
Display max as the greatest common divisor.
```

Implement this approach and test with $max = 532 = 28 * 19$ and $min = 112 = 28 * 8$. The names of the remainder functions are given in Table 4.7.

Another approach to some algorithms is to use a "recursive" method that employs a subprogram, which calls itself. This may have an advantage in clarifying the algorithm, reducing the roundoff error associated with the computations, or both. For example, in computer graphics Bernstein polynomials are often used to display curves and surfaces efficiently by using a recursive definition in calculating their value at a point.

The greatest common divisor evaluation can also be stated in terms of a recursive function, say gcd, having max and min as its initial two arguments. The following pseudocode defines the function:

```
gcd(max, min) is
    a) max if min = 0, otherwise
    b) gcd(min, remainder of max divided by min) if min > 0.
```

Also implement this version and verify that it gives the same result as the Eulerian algorithm. Note that F90 requires the use of the word "recursive" when defining the subprogram statement block. For example,

```
recursive function gcd(...) result(g)
    ....
end function gcd.
```

11 It is not uncommon for data files to be prepared with embedded tabs. Since a tab is a nonprinting control character, you can not see it in a listing. However, if you read the file expecting an integer, real, or complex variable, the tab will cause a fatal read error. So one needs a tool to clean up such a file.
Write a program to read a file and output a duplicate copy with the exception that all tabs are replaced with a single space. One could read a complete line and check its characters or read the file character by character. Remember that C++ and F90 have opposite defaults when advancing to a new line. That is, F90 advances to the next line, after any read or write, unless you include the format control, `advance = 'no'`, whereas C++ does not advance unless you include the new line control, "<< endl," and C does not advance unless you include the new line control, "\n."

12 Engineering data files consisting of discrete groups of variable types often begin with a control line that lists the number of rows and columns of data of the first variable type that follow beginning with the next line. At the end of the data block, the format repeats: control line, variable type, data block, and so forth, until all the variable types are read (or an error occurs where the end of file is encountered). Write a program that reads such a file and contains an integer set, a real set, and a second real set.

13 Neither C++ or F90 provides an inverse hyperbolic tangent function. Write such a function, called `arctanh`. Test it with three different arguments against the values given by MATLAB.

14 Often if one is utilizing a large number of input–output file units it may be difficult to keep up with which one you need. One approach to dealing with that problem may be to define a unit_Class or to create an units_Module to provide functionality and global access to file information. In the latter case assume that we want to provide a function simply to find a unit number that is not currently in use and utilize it for our input–output action:

```
interface
function get_next_io_unit () result (next)
    integer :: next    ! the next available unit number
  end function get_next_io_unit
end interface.
```

Use the Fortran INQUIRE statement to build such a utility. If you are familiar with MATLAB you will see this is similar to its *fopen* feature.

CHAPTER FIVE

Object-Oriented Methods

5.1 Introduction

In Section 1.7 we outlined procedures that should be considered while conducting the object-oriented analysis and object-oriented design phases that are necessary before the OOP can begin. Here we will expand on those concepts, but the reader is encouraged to read some of the books on those subjects. Many of the references on OOA and OOD rely heavily on detailed graphical diagrams to describe the classes, their attributes and states, and how they interact with other classes. Often those OO methods do not go into any programming language–specific approaches. Our interest is on OOP, and so we usually will assume that the OOA and OOD have been completed and supplied to us as a set of tables that describe the application and possibly a software interface contract. Sometimes we will use a subset of the common OO methods diagrams to represent the attributes and members of our classes graphically. Since they are being used for OOP, the graphical representations will contain, in part, the intrinsic-data type descriptions of the language being employed as well as the derived types created with them.

5.2 The Drill Class

Our first illustration of typical OO methods will be to apply them to a common electric drill. It feeds a rotating cutting bit through a workpiece, thereby removing a volume of material. The effort (power or torque) required to make the hole clearly depends on the material of the workpiece as well as the attributes of the drill.

Table 5.1 contains a summary of the result of an OO analysis for the drill object. They are further processed in Table 5.2, which gives the results of the OO design phase. When the OOD phase is complete, we can create the graphical representation of our `Drill` class, as shown in Figure 5.1. At this point one can begin the actual OOP in the target language. The coding required for this object is so small we could directly put it all together in one programming session. However, that is usually not the case. Often segments of the coding will be assigned to different programming groups that must interface with each other to produce a working final code. Frequently this means that the OOP design starts with defining the interfaces to each member function. That is, all of the given and return arguments must be defined with respect to their type, whether they are changed by the member, and so forth. Such an interface can be viewed as a contract between a software supplier and a client user

Table 5.1: Electric Drill OO Analysis

Attributes
What knowledge does it possess or require?

- Rotational speed (revolutions per minute)
- Feed rate per revolution (mm/rev)
- Diameter of the bit (mm)
- Power consumed (W)

Behavior
What questions should it be able to answer?

- What is the volumetric material removal rate? (mm^3/s)
- What is the cutting torque? (N·m)
- What is the material being removed?

Interfaces
What entities need to be inputted or outputted?

- Material data
- Torque produced
- Power

Formulas

Area :	$A = \pi\, d^2/4$	(mm^2)
Angular velocity :	ω, 1 rev/min $= \frac{2\pi}{60}$ rad/s	(rad/s)
Material removal rate :	$M = A \cdot \text{feed} \cdot \omega$	(mm^3/s)
Power :	$P = m \cdot u = T \cdot \omega$	(W)
Torque :	$T = P/\omega$, 1 m = 1000 mm	(N·mm)
Diameter :	d	(mm)
Feed rate :	feed	(mm/rev)
Material dissipation :	u	(W·s/mm^3)

of the software. Once the interface has been finalized, it can be written and given to the programmer to flesh out the full routine, but the interface itself cannot be changed.

The interface prototype for our drill object members is given in Figure 5.2. In this case the remaining coding is defined by a set of equations that relate the object attributes, selected member results, material data, and a few conversion constants to obtain the proper units. Those relationships are given in Table 5.1.

The full implementation of the drill class is given in Figure 5.3, and a `main` program to test the drill class is given in Figure 5.4. When we wrote the manual constructor, `Drill_`, in this example we chose to utilize the intrinsic constructor `Drill` (in lines 18 and 21) rather than to include lines assigning values to each of the components of our data type. If at some later time we add or delete a component in the type declaration, then the number of required arguments for the intrinsic constructor would also change. That would require the revision of all members that used the intrinsic constructor. An advantage of the object-oriented approach to programming is that we know that all such routines (that can access the intrinsic constructor) are encapsulated within this class-declaration module, and we can be sure that no other code segments need to be changed to remain consistent with the new version. That is, OOP helps with code maintenance.

Table 5.2: Electric Drill OO Design

Attributes

Name	*Type*	*Private*	*Description*
diameter	real	Y	Bit diameter (mm)
feed	real	Y	Bit feed rate (mm/rev)
speed	real	Y	Bit rotational speed (rpm)

Behavior

Name	*Private*	*Description*
drill_	N	Default constructor using all attributes, or none
get_mr_rate	N	Material removal rate (mm^3/sec)
get_torque	N	Required torque (N·m)
power	N	Required power (W)

Data

Name	*Description*
u	Material power description per unit volume (W s/mm^3)

Interfaces

Name	*Description*
read	Input drill and material data
print	Output object results

5.3 Global Positioning Satellite Distances

Consider the problem of traveling by ship or airplane between two points on the earth. Here we assume that there are no physical obstructions that prevent the vehicle from following the shortest path, which is an arc of a "great circle" on the earth's surface. We will neglect the

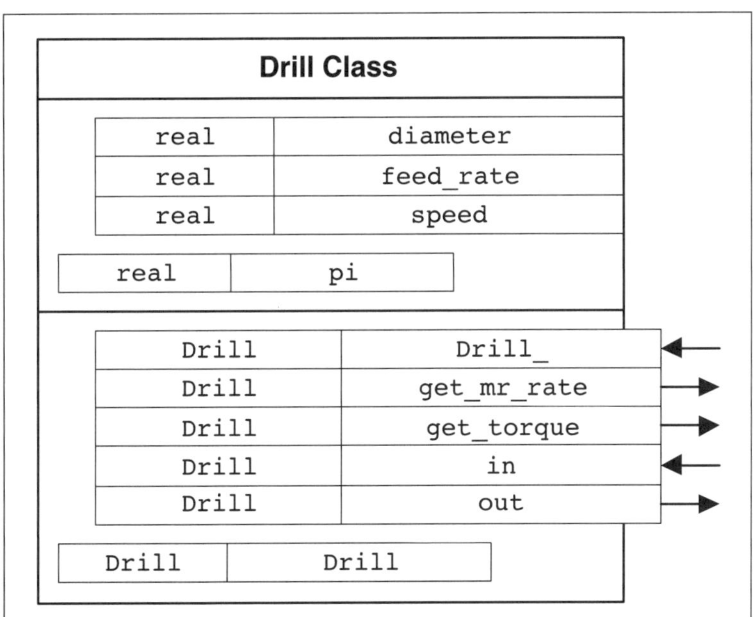

Figure 5.1: Graphical representation of an electric drill class.

```
interface
! type (Drill) :: x ; x = Drill (d, f, s)  ! intrinsic constructor

  function Drill_ (d, f, s) result (x) ! default constructor
    real, optional :: d, f, s          ! given diameter, feed, speed
    type (Drill)   :: x                ! the Drill instance
  end function Drill_

  function get_mr_rate (x) result (r) ! material removal rate
    type (Drill), intent(in) :: x     ! a given drill instance
    real                     :: r     ! volume cut rate
  end function get_mr_rate

  function get_torque (x, unit_Power) result (t) ! torque from power
    type (Drill), intent(in) :: x           ! given drill instance
    real,         intent(in) :: unit_Power  ! dissipated in cutting
    real                     :: t           ! resulting torque
  end function get_torque

  subroutine in (x)                         ! read a Drill instance
    type (Drill), intent(out) :: x          ; end subroutine in

  subroutine out (x)                        ! output a Drill instance
    type (Drill), intent(in) :: x           ! given drill instance
  end subroutine out
end interface
```

Figure 5.2: Drill object contract interface prototype.

altitude of the airplane in comparison with the earth's radius. The original and final positions are to be defined in terms of their angles of latitude (measured N or S from the equator) and longitude (measured E or W from Greenwich, England). These two attributes define an angular position from a defined reference point on the spherical surface of the earth. They are measured in terms of whole degrees, whole minutes (1 degree = 60 minutes), and seconds (1 minute = 60 seconds). Historically, whole seconds are usually used, but they give positions that are only accurate to about 300 meters. Thus, we will use a real variable for the seconds to allow for potential reuse of the software for applications that require more accuracy, such as those using Global Positioning Satellite (GPS) data. Recall that latitude and longitude have associated directional information of north or south, and east or west, respectively. Also, in defining a global position point it seems logical to include a name for each position. Depending on the application, the name may identify a city or port, or a "station number" in a land survey, or a "path point number" for a directed robot motion.

Eventually, we want to compute the great arc distance between given pairs of latitude and longitude. That solid geometry calculation requires that one use angles that are real numbers measured in radians ($2pi = 360$ degrees). Thus, our problem description begins with an `Angle` class as its basic class. Both latitude and longitude will be defined to be of the `Position_Angle` class, and we observe that a `Position_Angle` is a "Kind-Of" `Angle`, or a `Position_Angle` has an "Is-A" relationship to an `Angle`. The positions we seek are on a surface, and so only two measures (latitude and longitude) are needed to define the location uniquely, which we will refer

```
module class_Drill                              ! class name
  implicit none                                 ! enforce strong typing
  real, parameter :: pi = 3.141592654           ! or use math_constants
  public          :: Drill, Drill_, get_mr_rate, get_torque
  real, private   :: diameter, feed, speed

  type Drill                                    ! defined type, private data
    real :: diameter, feed, speed ; end type

contains ! member functions, overloaded & new operators

! type (Drill) :: x ; x = Drill (d, f, s)  ! intrinsic constructor

  function Drill_ (d, f, s) result (x) ! default constructor
    real, optional :: d, f, s             ! given diameter, feed, speed
    type (Drill)   :: x                   ! the Drill instance
     if ( present(d) .and. present(f) .and. present(s) ) then
       x = Drill (d, f, s)                ! intrinsic constructor
     else                                 ! check various input options
       if ( .not. ( present(d) ) ) then ! no diameter given
          x = Drill (10., 0., 0.)         ! default 10mm, at rest zero
       end if ! default form
     end if ! full form
  end function Drill_

  function get_mr_rate (x) result (r) ! material removal rate, mm3/sec
    type (Drill), intent(in) :: x  ! a given drill instance
    real                     :: r  ! volume cut rate
     r = 0.25 * pi * x%diameter * x%diameter * x%feed * x%speed/60.
  end function get_mr_rate

  function get_torque (x, unit_Power) result (t) ! torque from power
    type (Drill), intent(in) :: x              ! given drill instance
    real, intent(in)         :: unit_Power     ! dissipated in cutting
    real                     :: t              ! resulting torque
    real                     :: rad_per_sec ! radians per second
     rad_per_sec = 2 * pi * x%speed / 60.
     t = get_mr_rate(x) * unit_Power / rad_per_sec     ! torque
  end function get_torque

  subroutine in (x)                            ! input a Drill instance
    type (Drill), intent(out) :: x             ! given drill instance
     read *, x                                 ! get intrinsic data
  end subroutine in

  subroutine out (x)                           ! output a Drill instance
    type (Drill), intent(in) :: x              ! given drill instance
     print *,"Drill"; print *, " Diameter: ",x % diameter
     print *," Feed     : ",x % feed; print *," Speed    : ",x % speed
  end subroutine out
end module class_Drill                         ! close class definition
```

Figure 5.3: An electrical drill class.

```
program test_Drill  ! test the Drill class
 use class_Drill          ! i.e., all public members and public data
 implicit none
 type (Drill) :: drill_A, drill_B, drill_C
 real          :: unit_Power
  print *, "Enter diameter (mm), feed (mm/rev), speed (rpm):"
  call in (drill_A)
  print *, "Enter average power unit for material ( W.s/mm**3):"
  read *, unit_Power ; call out (drill_A)               ! user input
  print *, "Material removal rate is: ", get_mr_rate(drill_A), &
           " mm**3/sec"
  print *, "Torque in this material is: ",  &
           & get_torque (drill_A, unit_Power), " W.s"
  drill_B = Drill_ (5., 4., 3.); call out (drill_B) ! manual
  drill_C = Drill_ ();           call out (drill_C) ! default
end program test_Drill                          ! Running gives
! Enter diameter (mm), feed (mm/rev), speed (rpm): 10 0.2 800
! Enter average power unit for material ( W.s/mm**3): 0.5
! Drill
!  Diameter: 10.
!  Feed    : 0.200000003
!  Speed   : 800.
! Material removal rate is: 209.439514 mm**3/sec
! Torque in this material is: 1.25 W.s
! Drill
!  Diameter: 5.
!  Feed    : 4.
!  Speed   : 3.
! Drill
!  Diameter: 10.
!  Feed    : 0.E+0
!  Speed   : 0.E+0
```

Figure 5.4: Testing an electrical drill class.

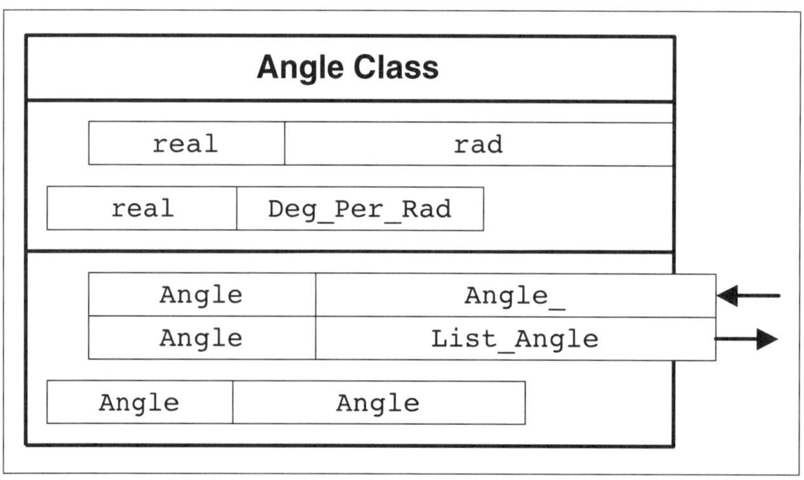

Figure 5.5: Graphical representation of an angle class.

Table 5.3: Great Arc OO Analysis

Attributes
What knowledge does it possess or require?

- Global position 1 (latitude, longitude)
- Global position 2 (latitude, longitude)
- Smallest arc (km)
- Radius of the earth (km)

Behavior
What questions should it be able to answer?

- What is the (smallest) great arc between the points?

What services should it provide?

- Default value (Greenwich, Greenwich, 0.0)
- Initialize for two positions
- Convert kilometers to miles

Relationships
What are its related classes?

- Has-A pair of Global_Positions

Interfaces
What entities need to be input or output?

- The distance between two positions.

Table 5.4: Global Position OO Analysis

Attributes
What knowledge does it possess or require?

- Latitude (degrees, minutes, seconds, and direction)
- Longitude (degrees, minutes, seconds, and direction)

Behavior
What questions should it be able to answer?

- What is the latitude of the location?
- What is the longitude of the location?

What services should it provide?

- Default position (Greenwich)
- Initialize a position (latitude and longitude)

Relationships
What are its related classes?

- Part-Of GreatArc
- Has-A pair of Position_Angles

Interfaces
What entities need to be inputted or outputted?

- The latitude and longitude and a position name.

Table 5.5: Position Angle OO Analysis

Attributes
What knowledge does it possess or require?

- Magnitude (degrees, minutes, seconds)
- Direction (N or S or E or W)

Behavior
What questions should it be able to answer?

- What is its magnitude and direction?

What services should it provide?

- Default value (0, 0, 0.0, N)
- Initialization to input value

Relationships
What are its related classes?

- Part-Of Global_Positions
- Is-A Angle

Interfaces
What entities need to be inputted or outputted?

- None

Table 5.6: Angle OO Analysis

Attributes
What knowledge does it possess or require?

- Signed value (radians)

Behavior
What questions should it be able to answer?

- What is the current value?

What services should it provide?

- Default values (0.0)
- Conversion to signed decimal degrees
- Conversion to signed degree, minutes, and decimal seconds
- Conversion from signed decimal degrees
- Conversion from signed degree, minutes, and decimal seconds

Relationships
What are its related classes?

- Base Class for Position_Angle

Interfaces
What entities need to be inputted or outputted?

- None

Table 5.7: Class Great_Arc OO Design

Attributes

Name	*Type*	*Private*	*Description*
point_1	Global_Position	Y	Lat-Long-Name of point 1
point_2	Global_Position	Y	Lat-Long-Name of point 2
arc	real	Y	Arc distance between points

Behavior

Name	*Private*	*Description*
Great_Arc_	N	Constructor for two position points
get_Arc	N	Compute great arc between two points

Data

Name	*Description*
Earth_Radius_Mean	Conversion factor
m_Per_Mile	Conversion factor

Interfaces

Name	*Description*
List_Great_Arc	Print arc values (two positions and distance)
List_Pt_to_Pt	Print distance and two points

Table 5.8: Class Global_Position OO Design

Attributes

Name	*Type*	*Private*	*Description*
latitude	Position_Angle	Y	Latitude
longitude	Position_Angle	Y	Longtitude
name	characters	Y	Point name

Behavior

Name	*Private*	*Description*
Global_Position_	N	Constructor for d-m-s pairs and point name
set_Lat_and_Long_at	N	Constructor for lat-long-name set
get_Latitude	N	Return latitude of a point
get_Longitude	N	Return longitude of a point
set_Latitude	N	Insert latitude of a point
set_Longitude	N	Insert longitude of a point

Data

Name	*Description*
None	

Interfaces

Name	*Description*
List_Position	Print name and latitude, longitude of a position

Table 5.9: Class Position_Angle OO Design

Attributes

Name	*Type*	*Private*	*Description*
deg	integer	Y	Degrees of angle
min	integer	Y	Minutes of angle
sec	real	Y	Seconds of angle
dir	character	Y	Compass direction

Behavior

Name	*Private*	*Description*
Default_Angle	N	Default constructor
Decimal_min	N	Constructor for decimal minutes
Decimal_sec	N	Constructor for decimal seconds
Int_deg	N	Constructor for whole deg
Int_deg_min	N	Constructor for whole deg, min
Int_deg_min_sec	N	Constructor for whole deg, min, sec
to_Decimal_Degrees	N	Convert position angle values to decimal degree
to_Radians	N	Convert position angle values to decimal radian

Data

Name	*Description*
None	

Interfaces

Name	*Description*
List_Position_Angle	Print values for position angle
Read_Position_Angle	Read values for position angle

to as the `Global_Position`. Here we see that the two `Position_Angle` object values are a "Part-Of" the `Global_Position` class, or we can say that a `Global_Position` "Has-A" `Position_Angle`.

The sort of relationships between classes that we have noted above are quite common and relate to the concept of inheritance as a means of reusing code. In an "Is-A" relationship, the derived class is a variation of the base class. Here the derived class `Position_Angle` forms an "Is-A" relation to the base class, `Angle`. In a "Has-A" relationship, the derived class has

Table 5.10: Class Angle OO Design

Attributes

Name	*Type*	*Private*	*Description*
rad	real	Y	Radian measure of the angle (rad)

Behavior

Name	*Private*	*Description*
Angle_	N	A generic constructor
List_Angle	N	List angle value in radians and degrees

Data

Name	*Description*
Deg_per_Rad	Unit conversion parameter

```
module class_Angle        ! file: class_Angle.f90
 implicit none
  type Angle              ! angle in (signed) radians
    private
    real :: rad           ! radians
  end type
  real, parameter:: Deg_Per_Rad = 57.2957795130823209d0
contains

 function Angle_ (r) result (ang) ! public constructor
   real, optional :: r             ! radians
   type (Angle)   :: ang
     if ( present(r) ) then
            ang = Angle (r)    ! intrinsic constructor
     else ; ang = Angle (0.0)  ! intrinsic constructor
     end if ; end function Angle_

  subroutine List_Angle (ang)
    type (Angle), intent(in) :: ang
      print *, 'Angle = ', ang % rad, ' radians (', &
                 Deg_Per_Rad * ang % rad, ' degrees)'
  end subroutine List_Angle
end module class_Angle
```

Figure 5.6: A definition of the class angle.

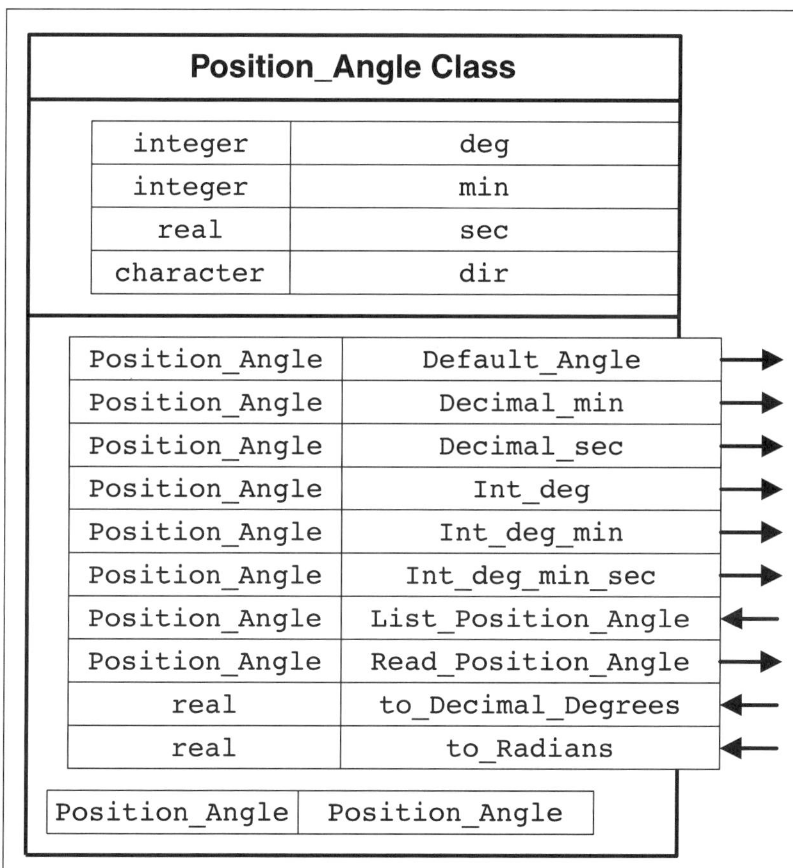

Figure 5.7: Graphical representation of a position angle class.

```
module class_Position_Angle ! file: class_Position_Angle.f90
  use class_Angle
  implicit none
  type Position_Angle        ! angle in deg, min, sec
    private
    integer   :: deg, min    ! degrees, minutes
    real      :: sec         ! seconds
    character :: dir         ! N | S, E | W
  end type
contains

 function Default_Angle () result (ang) ! default constructor
   type (Position_Angle) :: ang
     ang = Position_Angle (0, 0, 0., 'N')  ! intrinsic
 end function Default_Angle

 function Decimal_min (d, m, news) result (ang) ! public
   integer,   intent(in)  :: d               ! degrees
   real,      intent(in)  :: m               ! minutes
   character, intent(in)  :: news            ! N | S, E | W
   type (Position_Angle)  :: ang             ! angle out
   integer                :: min             ! minutes
   real                   :: s               ! seconds
     min = floor ( m ) ; s = (m - min)*60.   ! convert
     ang = Position_Angle (d, m, s, news)    ! intrinsic
 end function Decimal_min

 function Decimal_sec (d, m, s, news) result (ang) ! public
   integer,   intent(in)  :: d, m            ! degrees, minutes
   real,      intent(in)  :: s               ! seconds
   character, intent(in)  :: news            ! N | S, E | W
   type (Position_Angle) :: ang              ! angle out
     ang = Position_Angle (d, m, s, news)    ! intrinsic
 end function Decimal_sec

 function Int_deg (d, news) result (ang)   ! public
   integer,   intent(in)  :: d             ! degrees, minutes
   character, intent(in)  :: news          ! N | S, E | W
   type (Position_Angle) :: ang            ! angle out
     ang = Position_Angle (d, 0, 0.0, news)  ! intrinsic
 end function Int_deg

 function Int_deg_min (d, m, news) result (ang) ! public
   integer,   intent(in)  :: d, m            ! degrees, minutes
   character, intent(in)  :: news            ! N | S, E | W
   type (Position_Angle) :: ang              ! angle out
     ang = Position_Angle (d, m, 0.0, news)  ! intrinsic
 end function Int_deg_min

 function Int_deg_min_sec (d, m, s, news) result (ang) ! public
   integer,   intent(in)  :: d, m, s         ! deg, min, seconds
   character, intent(in)  :: news            ! N | S, E | W
   type (Position_Angle) :: ang              ! angle out
     ang = Position_Angle (d, m, real(s), news)  ! intrinsic
 end function Int_deg_min_sec

```

```
subroutine List_Position_Angle (a)
 type (Position_Angle) :: a   ! angle
   print 5, a ; 5 format (i3, " ", i2,"' ", f8.5, '" ', a1)
end subroutine

subroutine Read_Position_Angle (a)
 type (Position_Angle) :: a   ! angle
   read *, a%deg, a%min, a%sec, a%dir ; end subroutine

function to_Decimal_Degrees (ang) result (degrees)
  type (Position_Angle), intent(in) :: ang
  real                              :: degrees
    degrees = ang%deg + ang%min/60. + ang%sec/60.
    if (ang%dir == "S" .or. ang%dir == "s" .or. &
        ang%dir == "W" .or. ang%dir == "w") degrees = -degrees
end function to_Decimal_Degrees

function to_Radians (ang) result (radians)
  type (Position_Angle), intent(in) :: ang
  real                              :: radians
    radians = (ang%deg + ang%min/60. + ang%sec/60.)/Deg_Per_Rad
    if (ang%dir == "S" .or. ang%dir == "s" .or. &
        ang%dir == "W" .or. ang%dir == "w") radians = -radians
end function to_Radians
end module class_Position_Angle
```

Figure 5.8: A Definition of the class position angle.

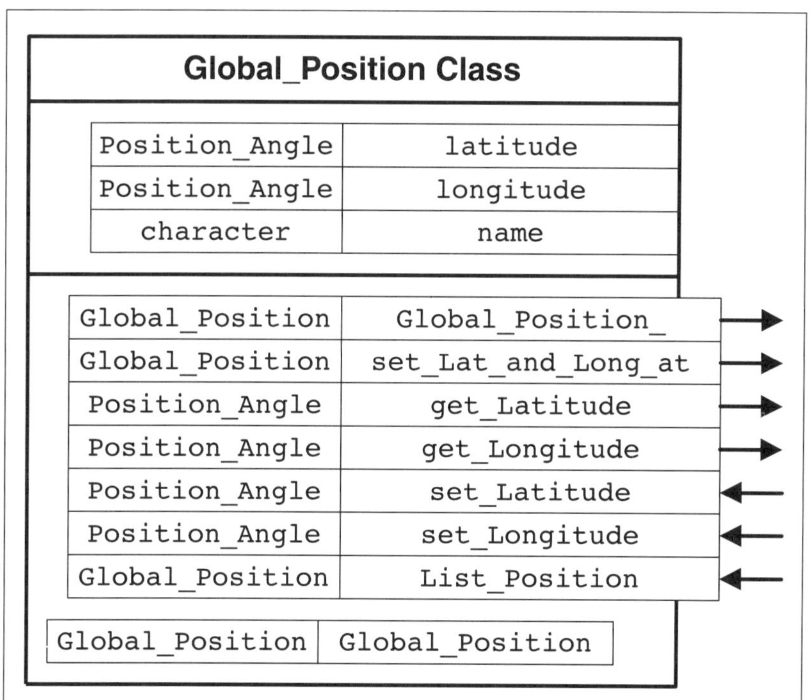

Figure 5.9: Graphical representation of a global position class.

```
module class_Global_Position
  use class_Position_Angle
  implicit none
  type Global_Position
    private
    type (Position_Angle) :: latitude, longitude
    character (len=31)    :: name
  end type Global_Position
contains

  function Global_Position_ (d1, m1, s1, c1,  &  ! constructor
                             d2, m2, s2, c2, n) result (GP)
   integer,    intent(in)  :: d1, m1, s1     ! deg, min, sec
   integer,    intent(in)  :: d2, m2, s2     ! deg, min, sec
   character,  intent(in)  :: c1, c2         ! compass
   character (len=*)       :: n              ! name
   type (Global_Position) :: GP              ! returned position
     GP % latitude  =  Int_deg_min_sec (d1, m1, s1, c1)
     GP % longitude =  Int_deg_min_sec (d2, m2, s2, c2)
     GP % name      = n  ; end function Global_Position_

  function set_Lat_and_Long_at (lat, long, n) result (GP) ! cons
    type (Position_Angle), intent(in) :: lat, long         ! angles
    character (len=*),     intent(in) :: n                 ! name
    type (Global_Position)            : GP                 ! position
      GP % latitude = lat   ; GP % longitude = long
      GP % name     = n     ; end function set_Lat_and_Long_at

  function get_Latitude (GP) result (lat)
    type (Global_Position), intent(in) :: GP
    type (Position_Angle)              :: lat
      lat = GP % latitude ; end function get_Latitude

  function get_Longitude (GP) result (long)
    type (Global_Position), intent(in) :: GP
    type (Position_Angle)              :: long
      long = GP % longitude ; end function get_Longitude

  subroutine set_Latitude (GP, lat)
    type (Global_Position), intent(inout) :: GP
    type (Position_Angle), intent(in)     :: lat
      GP % latitude = lat ; end subroutine set_Latitude

  subroutine set_Longitude (GP, long)
    type (Global_Position), intent(inout) :: GP
    type (Position_Angle), intent(in)     :: long
      GP % longitude = long ; end subroutine set_Longitude

  subroutine List_Position (GP)
    type (Global_Position), intent(in) :: GP
      print *, 'Position at ', GP % name
      write (*,'(" Latitude:  ")', advance = "no")
      call List_Position_Angle (GP % latitude)
      write (*,'(" Longitude: ")', advance = "no")
      call List_Position_Angle (GP % longitude)
  end subroutine List_Position
end module class_Global_Position
```

Figure 5.10: A definition of the class global position.

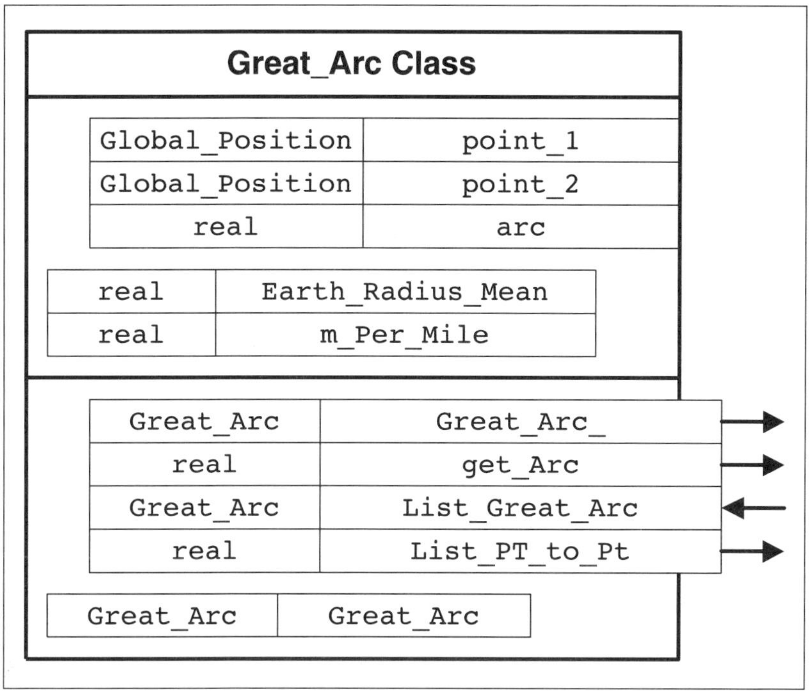

Figure 5.11: Graphical representation of a great arc class.

an attribute or property of the base class. Here the derived class of Global_Position forms a "Has-A" relation to its base class of Position_Angle. Also, the Great_Arc class forms a "Has-A" relation to the Global_Position class.

Looking back at previous classes in Chapter 3, we observe that the class Student "Is-A" variation of the class Person and the class Person forms at least one "Has-A" relationship with the class Date. In general we know that a graduate student is a "Kind-Of" student, but not every student is a graduate student. This subtyping, or "Is-A" relationship, is also called interface inheritance. Likewise, complicated classes can be designed from simpler or composition inheritance.

The OO analysis tables for the classes of Great_Arc, Global_Position, Position_Angle, and Angle are given in Tables 5.3 through 5.6, respectively. Historically people have specified latitude and longitude mainly in terms of whole (integer) degrees, minutes, and seconds. Sometimes you find navigation charts that give positions in whole degrees and decimal minutes. Today GPS data are being used for various types of high-accuracy positioning such as land surveys, or the control of robots as they move over distances of a few meters. The latter will clearly need decimal-second values in their constructor. Thus, we will create several constructors for the position angles. In the next chapter we will review how to access any of them, based on the signature of their arguments, through the use of a single polymorphic routine name. These considerations and the OOA tables lead to the construction of the corresponding set of OO Design tables given in Tables 5.7 through 5.10. Those OOD tables can lead to software interface contracts to be distributed to the programming groups. When combined and tested, they yield the corresponding class modules, which are shown for the classes Angle, Position_Angle, Global_Position, and Great_Arc in Figures 5.6 to 5.12, respectively. They, in turn, are verified by the main program given in Figure 5.13 along with its output.

```
module class_Great_Arc
 use class_Global_Position
  implicit none
  real, parameter :: Earth_Radius_Mean = 6.371d6 ! meters
  real, parameter :: m_Per_Mile        = 1609.344
  type Great_Arc
    type (Global_Position) :: point_1, point_2
    real                   :: arc
  end type Great_Arc
contains

  function Great_Arc_ (GP1, GP2) result (G_A)        ! constructor
    type (Global_Position), intent(in) :: GP1, GP2   ! points
    type (Great_Arc)                   :: G_A        ! earth arc
      G_A = Great_Arc (GP1, GP2, get_Arc (GP1, GP2)) ! intrinsic
  end function Great_Arc_

  function get_Arc (GP1, GP2) result (dist)
    type (Global_Position), intent(in) :: GP1, GP2
    real                               :: dist
    real :: lat1, lat2, long1, long2
    !  convert latitude, longitude to radians
      lat1  = to_Radians (get_Latitude (GP1))
      lat2  = to_Radians (get_Latitude (GP2))
      long1 = to_Radians (get_Longitude (GP1))
      long2 = to_Radians (get_Longitude (GP2))
    !  compute great circle arc of earth
      dist = 2 * Earth_Radius_Mean                            &
           * asin( sqrt ( (sin((lat1 - lat2)/2.))**2          &
           + cos(lat1)*cos(lat2)*(sin((long1-long2)/2.))**2 ) )
  end function get_Arc

  subroutine List_Great_Arc (A_to_B)
    type (Great_Arc), intent(in) :: A_to_B
    real                         :: dist      ! in meters
      print * ; print *, "The great circle arc between"
      call List_Position (A_to_B % point_1)
      call List_Position (A_to_B % point_2)
      dist = A_to_B % arc                      ! convert to km and miles
      print *, "is ", dist/1000, " km  (", dist/m_Per_Mile, "miles)."
  end subroutine List_Great_Arc

  subroutine List_Pt_to_Pt (GP1, GP2)                          ! alternate
    type (Global_Position), intent(in) :: GP1, GP2            ! points
    real                               :: arc                 ! distance
      print * ; print *, "The great circle arc between"
      call List_Position (GP1) ; call List_Position (GP2)
      arc = get_Arc (GP1, GP2)                                 ! in meters
      print *, "is ", arc/1000, " km  (", arc/m_Per_Mile, "miles)"
  end subroutine List_Pt_to_Pt
end module class_Great_Arc
```

Figure 5.12: Definition of the class great arc.

```
program test_Great_Arc
 use class_Great_Arc
 implicit none
 type (Great_Arc)       :: arc
 type (Global_Position) :: g1, g2
 type (Position_Angle)  :: a1, a2
 type (Angle)           :: ang
 real                   :: deg, rad
   a1 = Decimal_sec     (10, 30, 0., "N"); call List_Position_Angle(a1)
   a1 = Int_deg_min_sec(10, 30, 0, "N"); call List_Position_Angle(a1)
   a1 = Int_deg_min     (10, 30, "N"); call List_Position_Angle(a1)
   a1 = Int_deg         (20, "N"); call List_Position_Angle(a1)
!   call Read_Position_Angle (a2)
   a2 = Decimal_sec     (30, 48, 0., "E"); call List_Position_Angle(a2)
   ang = Angle_ (1.0)              ; call List_Angle (ang)
   deg = to_Decimal_Degrees (a1) ; print *, deg, deg/Deg_Per_Rad
   rad = to_Radians (a1)          ; print *, rad
!
   g1 = set_Lat_and_Long_at (a1, a2, 'g1')
   call List_Position (g1)
   g2 = Global_Position_ (20, 5, 40, "S", 75, 0, 20, "E", 'g2')
   call List_Position (g2)
   print *, "Arc = ", get_Arc (g1, g2), " (meters)"
   g1 = Global_Position_ ( 0, 0, 0, "N", 0, 0, 0, "E", 'equator')
   g2 = Global_Position_ (90, 0, 0, "N", 0, 0, 0, "E", 'N-pole')
   call List_Pt_to_Pt (g1, g2)
   arc = Great_Arc_ (g1, g2) ; call List_Great_Arc (arc)
end program test_Great_Arc           ! running gives:
! 10 30'  0.00000" N  ; ! 10 30'  0.00000" N ; ! 10 30'  0.00000" N
! 20  0'  0.00000" N  ; ! 30 48'  0.00000" N
! Angle =  1.000000000  radians ( 57.29578018  degrees)
! 20.00000000 0.3490658402          ; ! 0.3490658402
! Position at g1                    ; ! Position at g2
! Latitude:   20  0'  0.00000" N  ; ! Latitude:   20  5' 40.00000" S
! Longitude:  30 48'  0.00000" E  ; ! Longitude:  75  0' 20.00000" E
! Arc =  6633165.000  (meters)
!
! The great circle arc between
! Position at equator               ; ! Position at N-pole
! Latitude:    0  0'  0.00000" N  ; ! Latitude:   90  0'  0.00000" N
! Longitude:   0  0'  0.00000" E  ; ! Longitude:   0  0'  0.00000" E
! is  10007.54297  km  ( 6218.398926 miles)
!
! The great circle arc between
! Position at equator               ; ! Position at N-pole
! Latitude:    0  0'  0.00000" N  ; ! Latitude:   90  0'  0.00000" N
! Longitude:   0  0'  0.00000" E  ; ! Longitude:   0  0'  0.00000" E
! is  10007.54297  km  ( 6218.398926 miles)
```

Figure 5.13: Testing the great arc class interactions.

5.4 Exercises

1 Referring to Chapter 3, develop OOA and OOD tables for the (a) `Geometric` class, (b) `Date` class, (c) `Person` class, and (d) `Student` class.

2 Develop the graphical representations for the classes in the (a) drill study and (b) global position study.

3 Use the classes in the GPS study to develop a main program that will read a list (vector) of `Global_Position` types and use them to output a square table of great arc distances from one site to each of the others. That is, the table entry in row `j`, column `k` gives the arc from site `j` to site `k`. Such a table would be symmetric (with zeros along one diagonal), and so you may want to give only half of it.

4 Modify the given `Class_Position_Angle` to provide a polymorphic interface for a constructor `Position_Angle_` that will accept decimal, integer, or no data for the seconds value. Also allow for the omission of the minutes value.

CHAPTER SIX

Inheritance and Polymorphism

6.1 Introduction

As we saw earlier in our introduction to OOP, *inheritance* is a mechanism for deriving a new class from an older *base class*. That is, the base class, sometimes called the *super class*, is supplemented or selectively altered to create the new *derived class*. Inheritance provides a powerful code reuse mechanism since a hierarchy of related classes can be created that share the same code. A class can be derived from an existing base class using the module construct illustrated in Figure 6.1.

We note that the inheritance is invoked by the USE statement. Sometimes an inherited entity (attribute or member) needs to be slightly amended for the purposes of the new classes. Thus, at times one may want to bring into the new class selectively only certain entities from the base class. The modifier ONLY in a USE statement allows one to select the desired entities from the base class as illustrated in Figure 6.2. It is also common to develop name conflicts when combining entities from one or more related classes. Thus, a rename modifier, =>, is also provided for a USE statement to allow the programmer to pick a new *local* name for an entity inherited from the base class. The form for that modifier is given in Figure 6.3.

It is logical to extend any or all of the aforementioned inheritance mechanisms to produce multiple inheritance. *Multiple Inheritance* allows a derived class to be created by using inheritance from more than a single base class. Although multiple inheritance may at first seem like a panacea for efficient code reuse, experience has shown that a heavy use of multiple inheritance can result in entity conflicts and be otherwise counterproductive. Nevertheless it is a useful tool in OOP. In F90 the module form for selective multiple inheritance would combine the USE options above in a single module, as illustrated in Figure 6.4.

6.2 Sample Applications of Inheritance

6.2.1 The Professor Class

In the introductory examples of OOP in Chapter 3 we introduced the concepts of inheritance and multiple inheritance by the use of the `Date` class, `Person` class, and `Student` class. To reinforce those concepts we will reuse those three classes and will have them be inherited by a Professor class. Given the common "publish or perish" aspect of academic life, the Professor class must keep up with the number of publications of the professor. The new class is given in Figure 6.5 along with a small validation program in Figure 6.6.

```
module derived_class_name
        use base_class_name
! new attribute declarations, if any
                    ...
contains


      ! new member definitions
                    ...
end module derived_class_name
```

Figure 6.1: F90 single inheritance form.

```
module derived_class_name
        use base_class_name, only: list_of_entities
! new attribute declarations, if any
                    ...
contains


      ! new member definitions
                    ...
end module derived_class_name
```

Figure 6.2: F90 selective single inheritance form.

```
module derived_class_name
        use base_class_name, local_name => base_entity_name
! new attribute declarations, if any
                    ...
contains


      ! new member definitions
                    ...
end module derived_class_name
```

Figure 6.3: F90 single inheritance form with local renaming.

```
module derived_class_name
        use base1_class_name
        use base2_class_name
        use base3_class_name, only: list_of_entities
        use base4_class_name, local_name => base_entity_name
! new attribute declarations, if any
                    ...
contains


        ! new member definitions
                    ...
end module derived_class_name
```

Figure 6.4: F90 multiple selective inheritance with renaming.

```
module class_Professor    ! file: class_Professor.f90
  implicit none
  public  :: print, name
  private :: publs
    type Professor
       character (len=20) :: name
       integer            :: publs   ! publications
    end type Professor
contains
    function  make_Professor (n, p) result (who)
      character (len=*), optional, intent(in) :: n
      integer,           optional, intent(in) :: p
      type (Professor)                        :: who ! out
        who%name        = " "                ! set defaults
        who%publs       = 0.0
        if ( present(n) ) who%name  = n  ! construct
        if ( present(p) ) who%publs = p
    end function  make_Professor

    function  print (who)
      type (Professor), intent(in) :: who
        print *, "My name is ", who%name,  &
         ", and I have ", who%publs, " publications."
    end function  print
end module class_Professor
```

Figure 6.5: A professor class.

Note that the validation program brings in three different versions of the "print" member (lines 7–9) and renames two of them to allow a polymorphic print statement (lines 12–14) that selects the proper member based solely on the class of its argument. Observe that the previous `Date` class is brought into the `main` through the use of the `Person` class (in line 7). Of course, it is necessary to have an interface defined for the overloaded member name so that the compiler knows which candidate routines to search at run time. This example also serves to remind the reader that Fortran does not have keywords that are not allowed to be used by the programmer. In this case the print function (lines 20, 23, 26) has automatically replaced the intrinsic print function of Fortran. Most languages, including C++, do not allow one to do that.

6.2.2 The Employee and Manager Classes

Next we will begin the popular employee–manager classes as examples of common related classes demonstrating the use of inheritance. Once again the idea behind encapsulating these data and their associated functionality is to model a pair of real-world entities – an employee and a manager. As we go through possible relations between these two simple classes it becomes clear that there is no unique way to establish the classes and how they should interact. We begin with a minimal approach and then work through two alternate versions to reach the point where an experienced OO programmer might have begun. The first `Employee` class, shown in Figure 6.7, has a name and pay rate as its attributes. Only the intrinsic constructor is used within the member `setDataE` to concatenate a first name and last name to form the complete name attribute and to accept the pay rate. To query members, `getNameE` and `getRate` are provided to extract either of the desired attributes. Finally, member `payE` is provided to compute the pay earned by an employee. It assumes

```
! Multiple Inheritance and Polymorphism of the "print" function
include 'class_Person.inc'          ! also brings in class_Date
include 'class_Student.inc'
include 'class_Professor.inc'

program test_four_classes
  use class_Person                            ! no changes
  use class_Student,   print_S => print ! renamed to print_S
  use class_Professor, print_F => print ! renamed to print_F
  implicit none

!  Interface to generic routine, print, for any type argument
   interface  print  ! using renamed type dependent functions
     module procedure print_Name, print_S, print_F
   end interface

   type (Person) :: x; type (Student) :: y; type (Professor) :: z

      x = Person ("Bob"); ! default constructor
      call print(x);      ! print person type

      y = Student ("Tom", 3.47); ! default constructor
      call print(y);      ! print student type

      z = Professor ("Ann", 7); ! default constructor
      call print(z);      ! print professor type
      ! alternate constructors not used
end program test_four_classes         ! Running gives:
! Bob
! My name is Tom, and my G.P.A. is 3.4700000.
! My name is Ann, and I have 7 publications.
```

Figure 6.6: Bringing four classes and three functions together.

that an employee is paid by the hour. A simple testing main program is shown in Figure 6.8 It simply defines two employees (`l1` and `l2`), assigns their names and pay rates, and then computes and displays their pay based on the respective number of hours worked. Note that both `l1` and `l2` are each an instance of a class, and therefore they are objects and thus distinctly different from a class.

Next we deal with a manager, which Is-A "kind of" employee. One difference is that some managers may be paid a salary rather than an hourly rate. Thus we have the `Manager` class inherit the attributes of the `Employee` class and add a new logical attribute `isSalaried`, which is true when the manager is salary based. To support such a case we must add a new member `setSalaried`, which can turn the new attribute on or off, and a corresponding member `payM` that uses the `isSalaried` flag when computing the pay. The `class_Manager_1` module is shown in Figure 6.9. Note that the constructor `Manager_` defaults to an hourly worker (line 34), and it uses the inherited employee constructor (line 32). Figure 6.10 shows a test program to validate the manager class (and indirectly the employee class). It defines a salaried manager, `mgr1`, an hourly manager `mgr2`, and prints the name and weekly pay for both. (Verify these weekly pay amounts.)

With these two classes we have mainly used different program names for members that do similar things in each class (the author's preference). However, many programmers prefer to use a single member name for a typical operation regardless of the class of the operand.

```
module class_Employee_1
! The module class_Employee_1 contains both the
! data and functionality of an employee.
!
  implicit none
  public :: setDataE, getNameE, payE  ! the Functionality

  type Employee                      ! the Data
    private
    character(30) :: name
    real          :: payRate ; end type Employee

contains ! inherited internal variables and subprograms

  function setDataE (lastName, firstName, newPayRate) result (E)
    character(*), intent(in) :: lastName
    character(*), intent(in) :: firstName
    real,         intent(in) :: newPayRate
    type (Employee)          :: E             ! employee
                   ! use intrinsic constructor
      E = Employee((trim(firstName)//" "//trim(lastName)),newPayRate)
  end function setDataE

  function getNameE ( Person ) result (n)
    type (Employee), intent(in) :: Person
    character(30)               :: n         ! name
      n = Person % name ; end function getNameE

  function getRate ( Person ) result ( r )
    type (Employee), intent(in) :: Person
    real                        :: r         ! rate
      r = Person % payRate ; end function getRate

  function payE ( Person, hoursWorked ) result ( amount )
    type (Employee), intent(in) :: Person
    real,            intent(in) :: hoursWorked
    real                        :: amount
      amount = Person % payRate * hoursWorked ; end function payE
end module class_Employee_1
```

Figure 6.7: First definition of an employee class.

We also restricted all the attributes to `private` and allowed all the members to be `public`. We could use several alternate approaches to building our `Employee` and `Manager` classes. For example, assume we want a single member name called pay to be invoked for an employee or manager (or executive). Furthermore we will allow the attributes to be `public` instead of `private`. Lowering the access restrictions to the attributes makes it easier to write an alternate program, but it is not a recommended procedure since it breaks the data-hiding concept that has been shown to be important to OO software maintenance and reliability. The alternate `Employee` and `Manager` classes are shown in Figures 6.11 and 6.12, respectively. Note that they both have a `pay` member, but their arguments are of different classes and their internal calculations are different. Now we want a validation program that will create both classes of individuals and use a single member name, `PrintPay`, to print the proper pay amount from the single member name `pay`. This can be done in different ways. One problem that arises in our plan to reuse the code in the two alternate class modules is

```
program test_Employee_1
! Example use of employees
  use class_Employee_1
  type (Employee)  empl1, empl2

! Set up 1st employee and print out his name and pay
    empl1 = setDataE ( "Jones", "Bill", 25.0 )
    print *, "Name: ", getNameE ( empl1 )
    print *, "Pay: ", payE ( empl1, 40.0 )

! Set up 2nd employee and print out her name and pay
    empl2 = setDataE ( "Doe", "Jane", 27.5 )
    print *, "Name: ", getNameE ( empl2 )
    print *, "Pay: ", payE ( empl2, 38.0 )
end program test_Employee_1     ! Running produces;
!  Name: Bill Jones    !  Pay:    1000.
!  Name: Jane Doe      !  Pay:    1045.
```

Figure 6.8: First test of an employee class.

that neither contains a pay-printing member. We will need two new routines, `PrintPayEmployee` and `PrintPayManager`, and a generic or polymorphic interface to them. We have at least three ways to do this. One way is to place the two routines in an external file (or external to the main program if in the same file), leave the two class modules unchanged, and have the main program begin with (or INCLUDE) an external interface prototype. This first approach to `main` is shown in Figure 6.13. Note that the two new external routines must each use their respective class module.

A second approach would be to have the two new routines become internal to the `main`, after line 32, and occur before `end program`. Another change would be that each routine would have to omit its use statement (such as lines 35 and 42). Why? Because they are now internal to `main` and it has already made use of the two classes (in line 2). That approach is shown in Figure 6.13.

A third approach would be the most logical and consistent with OOP principles. It is to make all the class attributes `private`, place the print members in each respective class, insert a single generic name interface in each class, and modify the `test_Manager_2` program to use the polymorphic name regardless of the class of the argument it acts upon. The improved version of the classes is given in Figures 6.14, 6.15, and 6.16. Observe that generic interfaces for `PrintPay` and `getName` have been added, but that we could not do that for a corresponding `setData`. Do you know why? A final improvement will be given as an assignment.

6.3 Polymorphism

Fortran 90 and 95 do not include the full range of polymorphism abilities that one would like to have in an object-oriented language. It is expected that the Fortran 2000 standard will add those abilities.

Some of the code "reuse" features can be constructed through the concept of subprogram "templates," which will be discussed below. The lack of a standard "Is-A" polymorphism can be overcome in F90/95 by the use of the `SELECT CASE` feature to define "subtypes" of objects. This approach of subtyping programming provides the desired additional functionality, but

```
module class_Manager_1
! Gets class_Employee_1 and adds additional functionality
  use class_Employee_1
  implicit none
  public :: setSalaried, payM

  type Manager                ! the Data
    private
    type (Employee) :: Person
    integer        :: isSalaried    ! ( or logical )
  end type Manager

contains ! inherited internal variables and subprograms

  function getEmployee ( M ) result (E)
    type (Manager ), intent(in) :: M
    type (Employee)             :: E
      E = M % Person ; end function getEmployee

  function  getNameM ( M ) result (n)
    type (Manager ), intent(in) :: M
    type (Employee)             :: E
    character(30)               :: n         ! name
      n = getNameE(M % Person); end function getNameM

  function Manager_ (lastName, firstName, newPayRate) result (M)
    character(*), intent(in) :: lastName
    character(*), intent(in) :: firstName
    real,         intent(in) :: newPayRate
    type (Employee)          :: E          ! employee
    type (Manager )          :: M          ! manager constructor
      E = setDataE (lastName, firstName, newPayRate)
                 ! use intrinsic constructor
      M = Manager(E, 0) ! default to no salary
  end function Manager_

  function setDataM (lastName, firstName, newPayRate) result (M)
    character(*), intent(in) :: lastName
    character(*), intent(in) :: firstName
    real,         intent(in) :: newPayRate
    type (Employee)          :: E              ! employee
    type (Manager )          :: M              ! manager
      E = setDataE (lastName, firstName, newPayRate)
      M % Person = E
  end function setDataM

  subroutine setSalaried ( Who, salariedFlag )
    type (Manager), intent(inout) :: Who
    integer,        intent(in)    :: salariedFlag
      Who % isSalaried = salariedFlag ; end subroutine setSalaried

  function payM ( Human, hoursWorked ) result ( amount )
    type (Manager), intent(in) :: Human
    real,           intent(in) :: hoursWorked
    real                       :: amount, value
      value = getRate( getEmployee(Human) )
      if ( Human % isSalaried == 1 ) then  ! (or use logical)
```

```
            amount = value
          else
            amount = value * hoursWorked
          end if ; end function payM
    end module class_Manager_1
```

Figure 6.9: A first declaration of a manager class.

it is clearly not as easy to change or extend as an inheritance feature built into the language standard. A short example will be provided.

6.3.1 Templates

One of our goals has been to develop software that can be reused for other applications. There are some algorithms that are effectively independent of the object type on which they operate. For example, in a sorting algorithm one often needs to interchange, or swap, two objects. A short routine for that purpose follows:

```
subroutine swap_integers (x, y)
  implicit none
  integer, intent(inout) :: x, y
  integer                :: temp
    temp = x
    x    = y
    y    = temp
end subroutine swap_integers.
```

```
program test_Manager_1      ! Example use of managers
  use class_Manager_1
  implicit none
  type (Manager)  mgr1, mgr2

  ! Set up 1st manager and print out her name and pay

    mgr1 = setDataM ( "Smith", "Kimberly", 1900.0 )
    call setSalaried ( mgr1, 1 )  ! Has a salary

    print *, "Name: ", getNameM ( mgr1)
    print *, "Pay: ", payM ( mgr1, 40.0 )

  ! Set up 2nd manager and print out his name and pay

    ! mgr2 = setDataM ( "Danish", "Tom", 46.5 )
    ! call setSalaried ( mgr2, 0 )  ! Doesn't have a salary
    !                         or
    mgr2 = Manager_  ( "Danish", "Tom", 46.5 )

    print *, "Name: ", getNameM ( mgr2)
    print *, "Pay: ", payM ( mgr2, 40.0 )
end program test_Manager_1     ! Running produces;
!  Name: Kimberly Smith                   !  Pay: 1900.
!  Name: Tom Danish                       !  Pay: 1860.
```

Figure 6.10: First test of a manager class.

```
module class_Employee_2  ! Alternate
  implicit none
  public :: setData, getName, pay  ! the Functionality

  type  Employee                   ! the Data
    character(30) :: name
    real          :: payRate
  end type  Employee

contains ! inherited internal variables and subprograms

  subroutine setData ( Person, lastName, firstName, newPayRate )
    type (Employee) :: Person
    character(*)    :: lastName
    character(*)    :: firstName
    real            :: newPayRate
      Person % name    = trim (firstName) // " " // trim (lastName)
      Person % payRate = newPayRate
  end subroutine setData

  function  getName ( Person )
    character(30)   :: getName
    type (Employee) :: Person
      getName = Person % name
  end function getName

  function  pay ( Person, hoursWorked )
    real            :: pay
    type (Employee) :: Person
    real            :: hoursWorked
      pay = Person % payRate * hoursWorked
  end function pay
end module class_Employee_2
```

Figure 6.11: Alternate public access form of an employee class.

Observe that in this form it appears necessary to have one version for integer arguments and another for real arguments. Indeed we might need a different version of the routine for each type of argument that you may need to swap. A slightly different approach would be to write our swap algorithm as

```
subroutine swap_objects (x, y)
  implicit none
  type (Object), intent(inout) :: x, y
  type (Object)                :: temp
    temp = x
    x    = y
    y    = temp
end subroutine swap_objects,
```

which would be a single routine that would work for any `Object`, but it has the disadvantage that one needs to find a way to redefine the `Object` type for each application of the routine. That would not be an easy task. (Although we will continue with this example using the algorithm in the preceding forms, it should be noted that the approaches above would not be efficient if x and y were very large arrays or derived-type objects. In that case we would

```
module class_Manager_2  ! Alternate
  use class_Employee_2, payEmployee => pay ! renamed
  implicit none
  public :: setSalaried, payManager

  type  Manager                  ! the Data
    type (Employee) :: Person
    integer         :: isSalaried      ! ( or logical )
  end type  Manager

contains ! inherited internal variables and subprograms

  subroutine setSalaried ( Who, salariedFlag )
    type (Manager) :: Who
    integer        :: salariedFlag
      Who % isSalaried = salariedFlag
  end subroutine setSalaried

  function  pay ( Human, hoursWorked )
    real           :: pay
    type (Manager) :: Human
    real           :: hoursWorked

      if ( Human % isSalaried == 1 ) then  ! (or use logical)
        pay = Human % Person % payRate
      else
        pay = Human % Person % payRate * hoursWorked
      end if
  end function pay
end module class_Manager_2
```

Figure 6.12: Alternate public access form of a manager class.

modify the algorithm slightly to employ pointers to the large data items and simply swap the pointers for a significant increase in efficiency.)

Consider ways that we might be able to generalize these routines so that they could accept and swap any specific type of arguments. For example, the first two versions could be rewritten in a so-called `template` form as

```
subroutine swap_Template$ (x, y)
  implicit none
  Template$, intent(inout) :: x, y
  Template$                :: temp
    temp = x
    x    = y
    y    = temp
end subroutine swap_Template$.
```

In this template, the dollar sign ($) was included in the "wildcard" because, although it is a valid member of the F90 character set, it is not a valid character for inclusion in the name of a variable, derived type, function, module, or subroutine. In other words, a template in the illustrated form would not compile, but such a name could serve as a reminder that its purpose is to produce a code that can be compiled after the "wildcard" substitutions have been made.

```
program test_Manager_2  ! Alternate employee and manager classes
  use class_Manager_2   ! and thus Employee_2
  implicit none
 !    supply interface for external code not in classes
  interface PrintPay ! For TYPE dependent arguments
    subroutine PrintPayManager ( Human, hoursWorked )
      use class_Manager_2
      type (Manager) :: Human
      real           :: hoursWorked
    end subroutine
    subroutine PrintPayEmployee ( Person, hoursWorked )
      use class_Employee_2
      type (Employee) :: Person
      real            :: hoursWorked
    end subroutine
  end interface

  type (Employee) empl   ;  type (Manager)  mgr

  ! Set up an employee and print out his name and pay
    call setData ( empl, "Burke", "John", 25.0 )

    print *, "Name: ", getName ( empl )
    call PrintPay ( empl, 40.0 )

  ! Set up a manager and print out her name and pay
    call setData ( mgr % Person, "Kovacs", "Jan", 1200.0 )
    call setSalaried ( mgr, 1 )  ! Has a salary

    print *, "Name: ", getName ( mgr % Person )
    call PrintPay ( mgr, 40.0 )
end program test_Manager_2

  subroutine PrintPayEmployee ( Person, hoursWorked )
   use class_Employee_2
    type (Employee) :: Person
    real            :: hoursWorked
      print *, "Pay: ", pay ( Person, hoursworked )
  end subroutine

  subroutine PrintPayManager ( Human, hoursWorked )
   use class_Manager_2
    type (Manager) :: Human
    real           :: hoursWorked
      print *, "Pay: ", pay ( Human , hoursworked )
  end subroutine
! Running produces;
! Name: John Burke
! Pay:    1000.
! Name: Jan Kovacs
! Pay:    1200.
```

Figure 6.13: Testing the alternate employee and manager classes.

```
module class_Employee_3                  ! the base class
 implicit none                          ! strong typing
 private :: PrintPayEmployee, payE      ! private members
  type Employee                         ! the Data
    private                             ! all attributes private
    character(30) :: name
    real          :: payRate ; end type Employee

  interface PrintPay                     ! a polymorphic member
    module procedure PrintPayEmployee ; end interface
  interface getName                      ! a polymorphic member
    module procedure getNameE            ; end interface
! NOTE: can not have polymorphic setData. Why ?

contains ! inherited internal variables and subprograms

  function setDataE (lastName, firstName, newPayRate) result (E)
    character(*), intent(in) :: lastName
    character(*), intent(in) :: firstName
    real,         intent(in) :: newPayRate    ! amount per period
    type (Employee)          :: E             ! employee
                  ! use intrinsic constructor
      E = Employee((trim(firstName)//" "//trim(lastName)),newPayRate)
  end function setDataE

  function getNameE ( Person ) result (n)
    type (Employee), intent(in) :: Person
    character(30)               :: n          ! name
      n = Person % name ; end function getNameE

  function getRate ( Person ) result ( r )
    type (Employee), intent(in) :: Person
    real                        :: r          ! rate of pay
      r = Person % payRate ; end function getRate

  function payE ( Person, hoursWorked ) result ( amount )
    type (Employee), intent(in) :: Person
    real,            intent(in) :: hoursWorked
    real                        :: amount
      amount = Person % payRate * hoursWorked ; end function payE

  subroutine PrintPayEmployee ( Person, hoursWorked )
    type (Employee) :: Person
    real            :: hoursWorked
       print *, "Pay: ", payE ( Person, hoursworked )
  end subroutine
end module class_Employee_3
```

Figure 6.14: A better private access form of an employee class.

With this type of template it would be very easy to use a modern text editor to do a global substitution of any one of the intrinsic types `character`, `complex`, `double precision`, `integer`, `logical`, or `real` for the "wildcard" keyword `Template$` to produce a source code to swap any or all of the intrinsic data types. There would be no need to keep up with all the different routine names if we placed all of them in a single module and also created a generic `interface` to them such as

```
module class_Manager_3              ! the derived class
!   Get class_Employee_3, add additional attribute & members
 use class_Employee_3              ! inherited base class
 implicit none                    ! strong typing
 private :: PrintPayManager, payM, getNameM  ! private members

  type Manager                          ! the Data
    private                             ! all attributes private
    type (Employee) :: Person
    integer         :: isSalaried       ! 1 if true (or use logical)
  end type Manager

  interface PrintPay                    ! a polymorphic member
    module procedure PrintPayManager ; end interface
  interface getName                     ! a polymorphic member
    module procedure getNameM           ; end interface

contains ! inherited internal variables and subprograms

  function getEmployee ( M ) result (E)
    type (Manager ), intent(in) :: M
    type (Employee)             :: E
      E = M % Person ; end function getEmployee

  function  getNameM ( M ) result (n)
    type (Manager ), intent(in) :: M
    type (Employee)             :: E
    character(30)               :: n          ! name
      n = getNameE(M % Person); end function getNameM

  function Manager_ (lastName, firstName, newPayRate) result (M)
    character(*), intent(in) :: lastName
    character(*), intent(in) :: firstName
    real,         intent(in) :: newPayRate
    type (Employee)          :: E    ! employee
    type (Manager )          :: M    ! manager constructed
      E = setDataE (lastName, firstName, newPayRate)
                                      ! use intrinsic constructor
      M = Manager(E, 0)               ! default to hourly
  end function Manager_

  function setDataM (lastName, firstName, newPayRate) result (M)
    character(*), intent(in) :: lastName
    character(*), intent(in) :: firstName
    real,         intent(in) :: newPayRate    ! hourly OR weekly
    type (Employee)          :: E             ! employee
    type (Manager )          :: M             ! manager constructed
      E = setDataE (lastName, firstName, newPayRate)
      M % Person = E ; M % isSalaried = 0      ! default to hourly
  end function setDataM

  subroutine setSalaried ( Who, salariedFlag ) ! 0=hourly, 1=weekly
    type (Manager), intent(inout) :: Who
    integer,        intent(in)    :: salariedFlag  ! 0 OR 1
      Who % isSalaried = salariedFlag ; end subroutine setSalaried
```

```

    function payM ( Human, hoursWorked ) result ( amount )
      type (Manager), intent(in) :: Human
      real,           intent(in) :: hoursWorked
      real                       :: amount, value
        value = getRate( getEmployee(Human) )
        if ( Human % isSalaried == 1 ) then
          amount = value                   ! for weekly person
        else
          amount = value * hoursWorked ! for hourly person
        end if ; end function payM

    subroutine PrintPayManager ( Human, hoursWorked )
      type (Manager) :: Human
      real           :: hoursWorked
        print *, "Pay: ", payM ( Human , hoursworked )
    end subroutine
  end module class_Manager_3
```

Figure 6.15: A better private access form of a manager class.

```
module swap_library
  implicit none
  interface swap    ! the generic name
    module procedure swap_character, swap_complex
    module procedure swap_double precision, swap_integer
    module procedure swap_logical, swap_real
  end interface
contains
  subroutine swap_characters (x, y)
   . . .
```

```
program test_Manager_3    ! Final employee and manager classes
  use class_Manager_3 ! and thus class_Employee_3
  implicit none

  type (Employee) empl   ;  type (Manager)  mgr

  ! Set up a hourly employee and print out his name and pay
    empl = setDataE ( "Burke", "John", 25.0 )

    print *, "Name: ", getName ( empl )
    call PrintPay ( empl, 40.0 )          ! polymorphic

  ! Set up a weekly manager and print out her name and pay
    mgr = setDataM ( "Kovacs", "Jan", 1200.0 )
    call setSalaried ( mgr, 1 )           ! rate is weekly

    print *, "Name: ", getName ( mgr )
    call PrintPay ( mgr, 40.0 )           ! polymorphic
end program test_Manager_3                  ! Running produces;
! Name: John Burke
! Pay:    1000.
! Name: Jan Kovacs
! Pay:    1200.
```

Figure 6.16: Testing the better employee–manager forms.

```
  end subroutine swap_characters
  subroutine swap_ . . .
   . . .
end module swap_library.
```

The use of a text editor to make such substitutions is not very elegant, and we expect that there may be a better way to pursue the concept of developing a reusable software template. The concept of a text editor substitution also fails when we go to the next logical step and try to use a derived-type argument instead of any of the intrinsic data types. For example, if we were to replace the "wildcard" with our previous `type (chemical_element)` that would create

```
subroutine swap_type (chemical_element) (x,y)
  implicit none
  type (chemical_element), intent (inout)::x,y
  type (chemical_element)                ::temp
        temp = x
        x    = y
        y    = temp
end subroutine swap_type (chemical_element).
```

This would fail to compile because it violates the syntax for a valid function or subroutine name as well as the end function or end subroutine syntax. Except for the first- and last-line syntax errors, this would be a valid code. To correct the problem we simply need to add a little logic and omit the characters `type ( )` when we create a function, module, or subroutine name that is based on a derived-type data entity. Then we obtain

```
subroutine swap_chemical_element (x,y)
  implicit none
  type (chemical_element), intent (inout)::x,y
  type (chemical_element)                ::temp
        temp = x
        x    = y
        y    = temp
end subroutine swap_chemical_element,
```

which yields a completely valid routine.

Unfortunately, text editors do not offer us such logic capabilities. However, as we have seen, high-level programming languages like C++ and F90 do have those abilities. At this point you should be able to envision writing a `pre-processor` program that would accept a file of template routines and replace the template "wildcard" words with the desired generic forms to produce a module or `header file` containing the expanded source files that can then be brought into the desired program with an `include` or `use` statement. The C++ language includes a template preprocessor to expand template files as needed. Some programmers criticize F90/95 for not offering this ability as part of the standard. A few C++ programmers criticize templates and advise against their use. Regardless of the merits of including template preprocessors in a language standard, it should be clear that it is desirable to plan software for its efficient reuse.

With F90, if one wants to take advantage of the concepts of templates, then the only choices are to carry out a little text editing or develop a preprocessor with the outlined capabilities. The former is clearly the simplest and for many projects may take less time than developing such a template preprocessor. However, if one makes the time investment to produce a template preprocessor, a tool would be obtained that could be applied to basically any coding project.

6.4 Subtyping Objects (Dynamic Dispatching)

One polymorphic feature missing from the Fortran 90 standard that is common to most object-oriented languages is called run-time polymorphism or *dynamic dispatching*. (This feature is expected in Fortran 200X as an "extensible" function.) In the C++ language this ability is introduced in the so-called virtual function. To emulate this ability is quite straightforward in F90 but is not elegant since it usually requires a group of if-elseif statements or other selection processes. It is only tedious if the inheritance hierarchy contains many unmodified subroutines and functions. The importance of the lack of standardized dynamic dispatching depends on the problem domain to which it must be applied. For several applications demonstrated in the literature the alternate use of subtyping has worked quite well and resulted in programs that have been shown to run several times faster than equivalent C++ versions.

We implement dynamic dispatching in F90 by a process often called subtyping. Two features must be constructed to do this. First, a pointer object, which can point to any subtype member in an inheritance hierarchy, must be developed. Remember that F90 uses the operator '=>' to assign pointers to objects, and any object to be pointed at must have the TARGET attribute. Second, we must construct a (dynamic) dispatching mechanism to select the single appropriate procedure to execute at any time during the dynamic execution of the program. This step is done by checking which of the pointers actually points to an object and then passing that (unique) pointer to the corresponding appropriate procedure. In F90 the necessary checking can be carried out by using the ASSOCIATED intrinsic. Here, an if-elseif or other selection method is developed to serve as a dispatch mechanism to select the unique appropriate procedure to be executed based on the actual class referenced in the controlling pointer object. This subtyping process is also referred to as implementing a *polymorphic class*. Of course, the details of the actual dispatching process can be hidden from the procedures that utilize the polymorphic class. The polymorphic class knows only about the interfaces and data types defined in the hierarchy and nothing about how those procedures are implemented.

This process will be illustrated by creating a specific polymorphic class, in this case called `Is_A_Member_Class`, which has polymorphic procedures named `new`, `assign`, and `display`. They will construct a new instance of the object, assign it a value, and list its components. The minimum example of such a process requires two members and is easily extended to any number of member classes. We begin by illustrating a short dynamic dispatching program and then defining each of the subtype classes of interest. The validation of this dynamic dispatching through a polymorphic class is shown in Figure 6.17. There a target is declared for reach possible subtype, and then each of them is constructed and sent on to the other polymorphic functions. The results clearly show that different display procedures were used depending on the class of object supplied as an argument. It is expected that the new Fortran 200X standard will allow such dynamic dispatching in a much simpler fashion.

The first subtype is a class, `Member_1_Class`, which has two real components and the encapsulated functionality to construct a new instance and another to accept a pointer to such a subtype and display related information. It is shown in Figure 6.18. The next subtype class, `Member_2_Class`, has three components: two reals and one of type `Member_1`. It has

```
program Dynamic_Dispatching
use Is_A_Member_Class
implicit none

  type (Is_A_Member)      :: generic_member
  type (member_1), target :: pt_to_memb_1
  type (member_2), target :: pt_to_memb_2
  character(len=1) :: c

    c = 'A'
    call new (pt_to_memb_1, 1.0, 2.0)
    call assign (generic_member, pt_to_memb_1)
    call display_members (generic_member, c)

    c = 'B'
    call new (pt_to_memb_2, 1.0, 2.0, 3.0, 4.0)
    call assign (generic_member, pt_to_memb_2)
    call display_members (generic_member, c)

end program Dynamic_Dispatching
! running gives
! display_memb_1 A
! display_memb_2 B
```

Figure 6.17: Test of dynamic dispatching.

```
Module Member_1_Class
 implicit none
  type member_1
    real :: real_1, real_2
  end type member_1

contains

  subroutine new_member_1 (member, a, b)
    real, intent(in) :: a, b
    type (member_1)  :: member
      member%real_1 = a ; member%real_2 = b
  end subroutine new_member_1

  subroutine display_memb_1  (pt_to_memb_1, c)
    type (member_1), pointer :: pt_to_memb_1
    character(len=1),   intent(in) :: c
     print *, 'display_memb_1 ', c
  end subroutine display_memb_1

End Module Member_1_Class
```

Figure 6.18: The first subtype class member.

```
Module Member_2_Class
 Use Member_1_class
  implicit none
  type member_2
    type (member_1)  :: r_1_2
    real :: real_3, real_4
  end type member_2

contains

  subroutine new_member_2 (member, a, b, c, d)
    real, intent(in) :: a, b, c, d
    type (member_2)  :: member
      call new_member_1 (member%r_1_2, a, b)
      member%real_3 = c ; member%real_4 = d
  end subroutine new_member_2

  subroutine display_memb_2  (pt_to_memb_2, c)
    type (member_2), pointer :: pt_to_memb_2
    character(len=1),   intent(in) :: c
      print *, 'display_memb_2 ', c
  end subroutine display_memb_2

End Module Member_2_Class
```

Figure 6.19: The second subtype class member.

the same sort of functionality but clearly must act on more components. It has also inherited the functionally from the `Member_1_Class`; as displayed in Figure 6.19.

The polymorphic class, `Is_A_Member_Class`, is shown in Figure 6.20. It includes all of the encapsulated data and functions of the two subtypes above by including their use statements. The necessary pointer object is defined as an `Is_A_Member` type that has a unique pointer for each subtype member (two in this case). That is, at any given time during execution it will associate only one of the pointers in this list with an actual pointer object, and the other pointers are nullified. That is why this dispatching is referred to as "dynamic." Dispatching also defines a polymorphic interface to each of the common procedures to be applied to the various subtype objects. In the polymorphic function assignment of the dispatching is done very simply. First, all pointers to the family of subtypes are nullified, and then the unique pointer component to the subtype of interest is set to point to the desired member. The dispatching process for the display procedure is different. It requires an if-elseif construct that contains calls to all of the possible subtype members (two here) and a fail-safe default state to abort the process or undertake the necessary exception handling. Since all but one of the subtype pointer objects have been nullified, the dispatching process employs the ASSOCIATED intrinsic function to select the one, and only, procedure to call and passes the pointer object on to that procedure. In F90 a pointer can be nullified by using the NULLIFY statement, whereas F95 allows the alternative of pointing at the intrinsic NULL function, which returns a disassociated pointer. The NULL function can also be used to define the initial association status of a pointer at the point it is declared. That is a better programming style.

There are other approaches for implementing the dynamic dispatching concepts. Several examples are give in the publications by the group Decyk, Norton, and Szymanski [10, 11, 37, 38] and on Professor Szymanski's Website [47].

```
Module Is_A_Member_Class
Use Member_1_Class ; Use Member_2_Class
 implicit none

  type Is_A_Member
    private
    type (member_1), pointer :: pt_to_memb_1
    type (member_2), pointer :: pt_to_memb_2 ! etc for others
  end type Is_A_Member

  interface new
    module procedure new_member_1
    module procedure new_member_2 ! etc for others
  end interface

  interface assign
    module procedure assign_memb_1
    module procedure assign_memb_2 ! etc for others
  end interface

  interface display
    module procedure display_memb_1
    module procedure display_memb_2 ! etc for others
  end interface

contains

  subroutine assign_memb_1 (Family, member)
   type (member_1), target, intent(in)  :: member
   type (Is_A_Member),      intent(out) :: Family
     call nullify_Is_A_Member (Family) ! nullify all
     Family%pt_to_memb_1 => member
  end subroutine assign_memb_1

  subroutine assign_memb_2 (Family, member)
   type (member_2), target, intent(in)  :: member
   type (Is_A_Member),      intent(out) :: Family
     call nullify_Is_A_Member (Family) ! nullify all
     Family%pt_to_memb_2 => member
  end subroutine assign_memb_2 ! etc for others

  subroutine nullify_Is_A_Member (Family)
    type (Is_A_Member), intent(inout) :: Family
      nullify (Family%pt_to_memb_1)
      nullify (Family%pt_to_memb_2) ! etc for others
  end subroutine nullify_Is_A_Member

  subroutine display_members (A_Member, c)
    type (Is_A_Member), intent(in) :: A_Member
    character(len=1),   intent(in) :: c

  ! select the one proper member
      if      ( associated (A_Member%pt_to_memb_1) ) then
              call display (A_Member%pt_to_memb_1, c)
      else if ( associated (A_Member%pt_to_memb_2) ) then
              call display (A_Member%pt_to_memb_2, c) ! etc for others
      else ! default case
        stop 'Error, no member defined in Is_A_Member_Class'
      end if
  end subroutine display_members
End Module Is_A_Member_Class
```

Figure 6.20: The polymorphic class for subtypes.

6.5 Exercises

1 Write a main program that will use the Class_X and Class_Y given below to invoke each of the f(v) routines and assign a value of 66 to the integer component in X and 44 to the integer component in Y. (Solution given.)

```
module class_X
  public :: f
  type X_; integer a; end type X_
contains ! functionality
  subroutine f(v); type (X_), intent(in) :: v
    print *,"X_ f() executing"; end subroutine
end module class_X

module class_Y
  use class_X, X_f => f  ! renamed
  public :: f
  type Y_; integer a; end type Y_  ! dominates X_ a
contains          ! functionality, overrides X_ f()
  subroutine f(v);  type (Y_), intent(in) :: v
    print *,"Y_ f() executing"; end subroutine
end module class_Y
```

2 Create the generic interface that would allow a single constructor name, `Position_Angle_`, to be used for all the constructors given in the previous chapter for the class `Position_Angle`. Note that this is possible because they all had unique argument signatures. Also provide a new `main` program to test this polymorphic version.

3 Modify the last `Manager` class by deleting the member `setDataM` and replace its appearance in the last `test_Manager_3` with an existing constructor (but not used) in that class. Also provide a generic `setData` interface in the class `Employee` as a nicer name and to allow for other employees, like executives, who may have different kinds of attributes that may need to be set in the future. Explain why we could not use `setDataM` in the generic `setData`.

4 The final member `setDataE` in `Employee` is actually a constructor, and the name is misleading since it does not just set data values but also builds the name. Rename `setDataE` to the constructor notation `Employee_` and provide a new member in `Employee` called `setRateE` that only sets the employee pay rate.

5 Design and build an inventory system that will utilize and support the inventory object developed earlier. It should be able to initialize an allocatable array of such objects, add to it, revise the objects, and save the inventory array to a binary file that could be used as backup or to restart the system. It is desirable to be able to reallocate the inventory array when it gets full. Develop a program to test the inventory system and the objects it contains. Remember that most of the attributes are private.

CHAPTER SEVEN

OO Data Structures

7.1 Data Structures

We have seen that F90 has a very strong intrinsic base for supporting the use of subscripted arrays. Fortran arrays can contain intrinsic data types as well as user-defined types (i.e., ADTs). One cannot directly have an array of pointers, but an array containing defined types that are pointers or that have components that are pointers is allowable. Arrays offer an efficient way to contain information and to insert and extract information. However, there are many times when creating an efficient algorithm dictates that we use some specialized storage method, or *container*, and a set of operations to act with that storage mode. The storage representation and the set of operations that are allowed for it are known as a *data structure*. How you store and retrieve an item from a container is often independent of the nature of the item itself. Thus, different instances of a data structure may produce containers for different types of objects. Data structures have the potential for a large amount of code reuse, which is a basic goal of OOP methods. In the following sections we will consider some of the more commonly used containers. We will begin with stacks and queues, which are illustrated in Figure 7.1.

7.2 Stacks

A stack is a data structure in which access is restricted to the last inserted object. It is referred to as a *last-in first-out* (LIFO) container. In other words, a stack is a container to which elements may only be inserted or removed at one end of the container called the *top* of the stack. It behaves much like a pile of dinner plates. You can place a new element on the pile (widely known as a *push*), remove the top element from the pile (widely known as a *pop*), and identify the element on the top of the pile. You can also have the general concept of an empty pile, and possibly a full pile if it is associated with some type of restrictive container. Since at this point we only know about using arrays as containers, we will construct a stack container by using an array.

Assume that we have defined the attributes of the "object" that is to use our container by building a module called object_type. Then we could declare the array implementation of a stack type to be

```
module stack_type
  use object_type ! to define objects in the stack
  implicit none
```

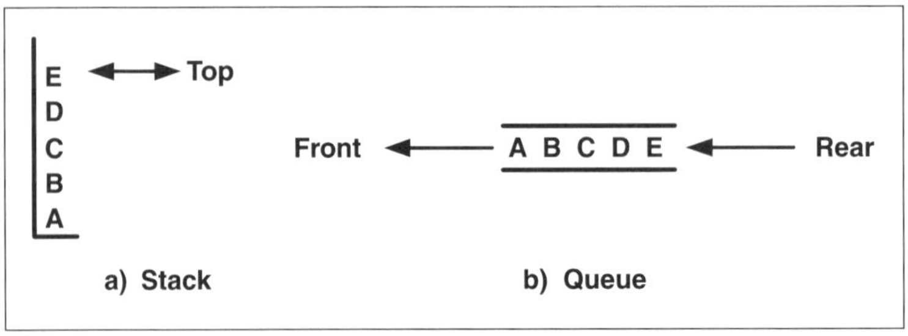

Figure 7.1: Simple containers.

```
   integer, parameter :: limit = 999 ! stack size limit

   type stack
     private
       integer        :: size         ! size of array
       integer        :: top          ! top of stack
       type (Object) :: a(limit)      ! stack items array
   end type stack
end module stack_type.
```

The interface contract to develop one such stack support system (or ADT) is given as

```
module stack_of_objects
implicit none
  public :: stack, push_on_Stack, pop_from_Stack, &
            is_Stack_Empty, is_Stack_Full

interface  ! for a class_Stack contract

  function make_Stack (n) result (s)   ! constructor
    use stack_type                     ! to define stack structure
    integer, optional :: n             ! size of stack
    type (stack)      :: s             ! the new stack
  end function make_Stack

  subroutine push_on_Stack (s, item)    ! push item on top of stack
    use stack_type                      ! for stack structure
    type (stack),  intent(inout) :: s
    type (Object), intent(in)    :: item
  end subroutine push_on_Stack

  function pop_from_Stack (s) result (item) ! pop item from top
    use stack_type                          ! for stack structure
    type (stack), intent(inout) :: s
    type (Object)               :: item
  end function pop_from_Stack

  function is_Stack_Empty (s) result (b)  ! test stack
    use stack_type                        ! for stack structure
    type (stack), intent(in) :: s
    logical                  :: b
  end function is_Stack_Empty

  function is_Stack_Full (s) result (b)  ! test stack
    use stack_type                       ! for stack structure
```

```
    type (stack), intent(in) :: s
    logical                  :: b
  end function is_Stack_Full

end interface
end module stack_of_objects.
```

In the interface we see that some of the member services (is_Stack_Empty and is_Stack_Full) are independent of the contained objects. Others (pop_from_Stack and push_on_Stack) explicitly depend on the object utilizing the container. Of course, the constructor (here make_Stack) always indirectly relates to the object being contained in the array. The full details of a Stack class are given in Figure 7.2.

For a specific implementation test we will simply utilize objects that have a single integer attribute. That is, we define the object of interest by a code segment like

```
module object_type
  type Object
    integer :: data  ; end type  ! one integer attribute
end module object_type.
```

Obviously, there are many other types of objects one may want to create and place in a container like a stack. At present one would have to edit the segment above to define all the attributes of the object. (Begin to think about how you might seek to automate such a process.) The new Stack class is tested in Figure 7.3, and a history of a typical stack is sketched in Figure 7.4. The only part of that code that depends on a specific object is in line 7, where the (public) intrinsic constructor, Object, was utilized rather that some more general constructor, say Object_.

In Figure 7.2 note that we have used an alternate syntax and specified the type of function result (logical, object, or stack) as a prefix to the function name (lines 17, 29, 37, 40). The author thinks that the form used in the interface contract is easier to read and understand since it requires an extra line of code; however, some programmers prefer the condensed style of Figure 7.2. Later we will examine an alternate implementation of a stack by using a linked list.

The stack implementation shown here is not complete. For example, some programmers like to include a member, say show_Stack_top, to display the top element on the container without removing it from the stack. Also we need to be concerned about *preconditions* that need to be satisfied for a member and may require that we throw an exception message. You cannot pop an item off of an empty stack, nor can you push an item onto the top of a full stack. Only the member pop_from_Stack does such pre-condition checking in the sample code. Note that members is_Stack_Empty and is_Stack_Full are called *accessors*, as is show_Stack_top, since they query the container but do not change it.

7.3 Queues

A comparison of a stack and another simple container, a *queue*, is given in Figure 7.1. The name queue comes from the British word that means waiting in a line for service. A queue is a container into which elements may be inserted at one end, called the *rear*, and leave only from the other end, called the *front*. The first element in the queue expects to be the first serviced and, thus, be the first out of line. A queue is a *first-in first-out* (FIFO) container system. In planning our first queue container we will again make use of an array of objects. In doing so it is quickly found that you are much less likely to encounter a full queue if it

```
module class_Stack
implicit none
  use exceptions  ! to warn of errors
  use object_type
  public :: stack, push_on_Stack, pop_from_Stack, &
            is_Stack_Empty, is_Stack_Full
  integer, parameter :: limit = 999 ! stack size limit

type stack
  private
    integer        :: size          ! size of array
    integer        :: top           ! top of stack
    type (Object) :: a(limit)      ! stack items array
 end type
contains ! encapsulated functionality

type (stack) function make_Stack (n) result (s)     ! constructor
  integer, optional :: n ! size of stack
    s%size = limit ; if ( present (n) ) s%size = n
    s%top = 0       ! object array not initialized
end function make_Stack

subroutine push_on_Stack (s, item) ! push item on top of stack
  type (stack),  intent(inout) :: s
  type (Object), intent(in)    :: item
    s%top = s%top + 1 ; s%a(s%top) = item
end subroutine push_on_Stack

type (Object) function pop_from_Stack (s) result (item) ! off top
  type (stack), intent(inout) :: s
    if ( s%top < 1 ) then
      call exception ("pop_from_Stack","stack is empty")
    else
      item = s%a(s%top) ; s%top = s%top - 1
    end if ; end function pop_from_Stack

logical function is_Stack_Empty (s) result (b)
  type (stack), intent(in) :: s
    b = ( s%top == 0 ) ; end function is_Stack_Empty

logical function is_Stack_Full (s) result (b)
  type (stack), intent(in) :: s
    b = ( s%top == s%size ) ; end function is_Stack_Full

end module class_Stack
```

Figure 7.2: A typical stack class.

is stored as a so-called fixed circular array with a total of `Q_Size_Limit` storage slots. At this point we define the structure of our queue to be

```
module Queue_type
!  A queue stored as a so-called fixed circular array with a total
!  of Q_Size_Limit storage slots; requires remainder function, mod.
!     (version 1, i.e., without allocatable arrays and pointers)
  use object_type  ! to define objects in the Container
  implicit none
```

```
include 'class_Stack.f'       ! previous figure
program Testing_a_Stack
use class_Stack
implicit none
 type (stack)  :: b
 type (object) :: value, four, five, six

   four = Object(4) ; five = Object(5) ; six = Object(6)  ! initialize

   b = make_Stack(3)                                   ! private constructor
   print *, is_Stack_Empty(b), is_Stack_Full(b) ! b = [], empty

   call  push_on_Stack (b, four)                ! b = [4]
   call  push_on_Stack (b, five)                ! b = [5,4]
   call  push_on_Stack (b, six )                ! b = [6,5,4], full
   print *, is_Stack_Empty(b), is_Stack_Full(b) ! F T

   value = pop_from_Stack (b) ; print *, value    ! b = [5,4]
   print *, is_Stack_Empty(b), is_Stack_Full(b) ! F F

   value = pop_from_Stack (b) ; print *, value    ! b = [4]
   print *, is_Stack_Empty(b), is_Stack_Full(b) ! F F

   value = pop_from_Stack (b) ; print *, value    ! b = [], empty
   print *, is_Stack_Empty(b), is_Stack_Full(b) ! T F

   value = pop_from_Stack (b)                   ! nothing to pop
 end program Testing_a_Stack   ! running gives:
 ! T F  ! F T
 ! 6    ! F F
 ! 5    ! F F
 ! 4    ! T F
 ! Exception occurred in subprogram pop_from_Stack
 ! With message: stack is empty
```

Figure 7.3: Testing a stack of objects.

```
 integer, parameter :: Q_Size_Limit = 999

 type Queue
   private
     integer       :: head                    ! index of first element
     integer       :: tail                    ! index of last element
     integer       :: length                  ! size of used storage
     type (Object) :: store (Q_Size_Limit) ! a circular array
 end type Queue
end module Queue_type.
```

An interface contract that will allow us to build a typical queue is

```
module Queue_of_Objects
implicit none
  public :: Queue, Add_to_Q, Create_Q, Get_Front_of_Q, Is_Q_Empty,&
            Is_Q_Full, Get_Length_of_Q, Remove_from_Q

interface  ! for a class_Queue contract

 subroutine Add_to_Q (Q, item)          ! add to tail of queue
   use Queue_type                       ! for Queue structure
```

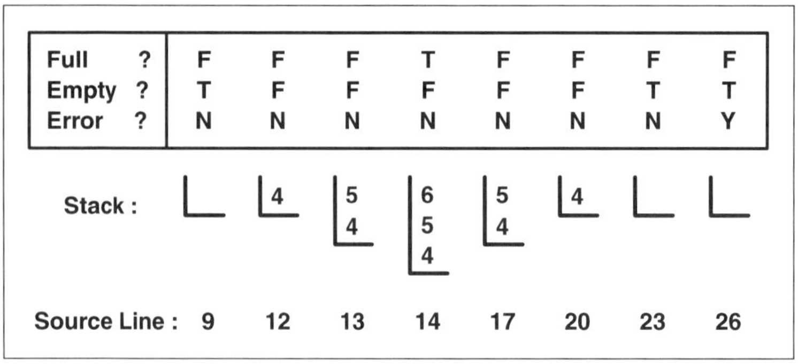

Figure 7.4: Steps in the stack testing.

```
    type (Queue),  intent(inout) :: Q
    type (Object), intent(in)    :: item ; end Subroutine Add_to_Q

  function Create_Q (N) result (Q)     ! manual constructor
    use Queue_type                     ! for Queue structure
    integer, intent(in) :: N          ! size of the new array
    type (Queue)        :: Q ;        end function Create_Q

  function Get_Capacity_of_Q (Q) result (item)
    use Queue_type                       ! for Queue structure
    type (Queue), intent(in) :: Q
    type (Object)            :: item ; end function Get_Capacity_of_Q

  function Get_Front_of_Q (Q) result (item)
    use Queue_type                     ! for Queue structure
   type (Queue), intent(in) :: Q
   type (Object)            :: item ; end function Get_Front_of_Q

  function Is_Q_Empty (Q) result(B)
    use Queue_type                     ! for Queue structure
    type (Queue), intent(in) :: Q
    logical                  :: B ; end function Is_Q_Empty

  function Is_Q_Full (Q) result(B)
    use Queue_type                     ! for Queue structure
    type (Queue), intent(in) :: Q
    logical                  :: B ; end function Is_Q_Full

  function Get_Length_of_Q (Q) result (N)
    use Queue_type                     ! for Queue structure
    type (Queue), intent(in) :: Q
          integer                  :: N ; end function Get_Length_of_Q

  subroutine Remove_from_Q (Q)         ! remove from head of queue
    use Queue_type                     ! for Queue structure
    type (Queue), intent(inout) :: Q; end subroutine Remove_from_Q

  end interface
end module Queue_of_Objects.
```

For a specific version we provide full details for objects containing an integer in Figure 7.5 and test and display the validity of the implementation in Figure 7.6, where again the objects are taken to be integers (lines 15, 19, 20).

```
module class_Queue                         ! file: class_Queue.f90

! A queue stored as a so-called fixed circular array with a total of
! Q_Size_Limit storage slots; requires remainder function, mod.
!     (i.e., without allocatable arrays and pointers)

 use exceptions                           ! inherit exception handler
 implicit none

 public :: Queue, Add_to_Q, Create_Q, Get_Front_of_Q
           Is_Q_Full, Get_Length_of_Q, Remove_from

  integer, parameter :: Q_Size_Limit = 3

  type Queue
    private
      integer :: head                   ! index of first element
      integer :: tail                   ! index of last element
      integer :: length                 ! size of used storage
      integer :: store (Q_Size_Limit) ! a circular array of elements
  end type Queue

contains                                ! member functionality

 Subroutine Add_to_Q (Q, item)          ! add to tail of queue
   type (Queue), intent(inout) :: Q
   integer,      intent(in)    :: item

     if ( Is_Q_Full(Q) ) call exception ("Add_to_Q","full Q")
     Q%store (Q%tail) = item
     Q%tail          = 1 + mod (Q%tail, Q_Size_Limit)
     Q%length        = Q%length + 1 ; end Subroutine Add_to_Q

 type (Queue) function Create_Q (N) result (Q)    ! manual constructor
   integer, intent(in) :: N  ! size of the new array
   integer             :: k  ! implied loop

     if (N > Q_Size_Limit) call exception("Create_Q","increase size")
     Q = Queue (1, 1, 0, (/ (0, k=1,N) /))     ! intrinsic constructor
 end function Create_Q

 integer function Get_Capacity_of_Q (Q) result (item)
   type (Queue), intent(in) :: Q

     item = Q_size_Limit - Q%length ; end function Get_Capacity_

 integer function Get_Front_of_Q (Q) result (item)
  type (Queue), intent(in) :: Q

    if (Is_Q_Empty(Q)) call exception("Get_Front_of_Q","em
    item = Q%store (Q%head) ; end function Get_Front_of_Q

 logical function Is_Q_Empty (Q) result(B)
  type (Queue), intent(in) :: Q

    B = (Q%length == 0) ; end function Is_Q_Empty

```

```
  logical function Is_Q_Full (Q) result(B)
    type (Queue), intent(in) :: Q

      B = (Q%length == Q_Size_Limit) ; end function Is_Q_Full

  integer function Get_Length_of_Q (Q) result (N)
    type (Queue), intent(in) :: Q
      N = Q%length ; end function Get_Length_of_Q

  subroutine Remove_from_Q (Q)            ! remove from head of queue
    type (Queue), intent(inout) :: Q

      if (Is_Q_Empty(Q)) call exception("Remove_from_Q","empty Q"
      Q%head    = 1 + mod (Q%head, Q_Size_Limit)
      Q%length = Q%length - 1 ; end subroutine Remove_from_Q

end module class_Queue               ! file: class_Queue.f
```

Figure 7.5: A typical queue class.

7.4 Linked Lists

From our limited discussion of stacks and queues it should be easy to see that to try to insert or remove an object at the middle of a stack or queue is not an efficient process. *Linked lists* are containers that make it easy to perform the operations of insertion and deletion. A linked list of objects can be thought of as a group of boxes, usually called *nodes*, each containing an object to be stored and a *pointer*, or reference, to the box containing the next object in the list. In most of our applications a list is referenced by a special box, called the *header* or *root* node, which does not store an object but serves mainly to point to the first linkable box and thereby produces a condition in which the list is never truly empty. This simplifies the insertion scheme by removing an algorithmic special case. We will begin our introduction of these topics with a *singly linked list*, also known as a simple list. It is capable of being traversed in only one direction, from the beginning of the list to the end, or vice versa.

As we have seen, arrays of data objects work well so long as we know, or can compute in advance, the amount of data to be stored. The data structures (linked lists and trees) to be considered here employ *pointers* to store and change data objects when we do not know the required amount of storage in advance. During program execution linked lists and trees allow separate memory allocations for each individual data object. However, they do not permit direct access to an arbitrary object in the container. Instead some searching must be performed, and thus linked lists and trees incur an execution time penalty for such an access operation. That penalty is smaller in tree structures than in linked lists (but is smallest of all in arrays).

Linked lists and trees must use pointer (reference) variables. Fortran pointers can simply be thought of as an alias for other variables of the same type. We are beginning to see that pointers give a programmer more power. However, that includes more power to "shoot yourself in the foot"; they make it hard to find some errors and can lead to new types of errors such as the so-called memory leaks. Recall that each pointer must be in one of three states: undefined, null, or associated. As dummy arguments within routines, pointer variables cannot be assigned the INTENT attribute. That means they have a greater potential for undesired *side effects*. To avoid accidentally changing a pointer it is good programming practice to state clearly in comments the INTENT of all dummy pointer arguments and to copy those immediately with an INTENT IN attribute. Thereafter, working with the

```
program Testing_a_Queue
 use class_Queue  ! inherit its methods & class global constants
 implicit none

 type (Queue) :: C, B              ! not used, used
 integer :: value, limit = 3       ! work items

   C = Create_Q (limit)           ! private constructor
   print *, "Length of C = ",   Get_Length_of_Q (C)
   print *, "Capacity of C = ", Get_Capacity_of_Q (C)
   print *, "C empty? full? ",  is_Q_Empty (C), is_Q_Full (C)  !

   B = Create_Q (3)               ! private constructor
   print *, "B empty? full? ",  is_Q_Empty (B), is_Q_Full (B)  !

   call Add_to_Q (B, 4);         print *, "B = [4]"
   print *, "Length of B = ",   Get_Length_of_Q (B)
   print *, "B empty? full? ",  is_Q_Empty (B), is_Q_Full (B)  !

   call Add_to_Q (B, 5);         print *, " B = [4,5]"
   call Add_to_Q (B, 6);         print *, " B = [4,5,6], full"
   print *, "Length of B = ",   Get_Length_of_Q (B)
   print *, "B empty? full? ",  is_Q_Empty (B), is_Q_Full (B)  !
   print *, "Capacity of B = ", Get_Capacity_of_Q (B)

   value = Get_Front_of_Q (B);  print *, "Front Q value = ", value

   call Remove_from_Q (B);       print *, "Removing from B"
   print *, "Length of B = ",   Get_Length_of_Q (B)
   print *, "B empty? full? ",  is_Q_Empty (B), is_Q_Full (B) !
   value = Get_Front_of_Q (B);  print *, "Front Q value = ", value

   call Remove_from_Q (B);       print *, "Removing from B"
   print *, "Length of B = ",   Get_Length_of_Q (B)
   print *, "B empty? full? ",  is_Q_Empty (B), is_Q_Full (B) !

   call Remove_from_Q (B);       print *, "Removing from B"
   print *, "Length of B = ",   Get_Length_of_Q (B)
   print *, "B empty? full? ",  is_Q_Empty (B), is_Q_Full (B) !

   print *, "Removing from B";  call Remove_from_Q (B)
   call exception_status
end program Testing_a_Queue          ! running gives:
! Length of C = 0        ! Capacity of C = 3    ! C empty? full? T,  F
! B empty? full? T,  F
! B = [4]                ! Length of B = 1      ! B empty? full? F,  F
! B = [4,5]
! B = [4,5,6], full      ! Length of B = 3      ! B empty? full? F,  T
! Capacity of B = 0      ! Front Q value = 4    ! Removing from B
! Length of B = 2        ! B empty? full? F,  F ! Front Q value = 5
! Removing from B        ! Length of B = 1      ! B empty? full? F,  F
! Removing from B        ! Length of B = 0      ! B empty? full? T,  F
! Removing from B
! Exception Status Thrown
!   Program :Remove_from_Q
!   Message :empty Q
!   Level   : 5
!
! Exception Summary:
!   Exception count =  1
!   Highest level   =  5
```

Figure 7.6: Testing of the queue class.

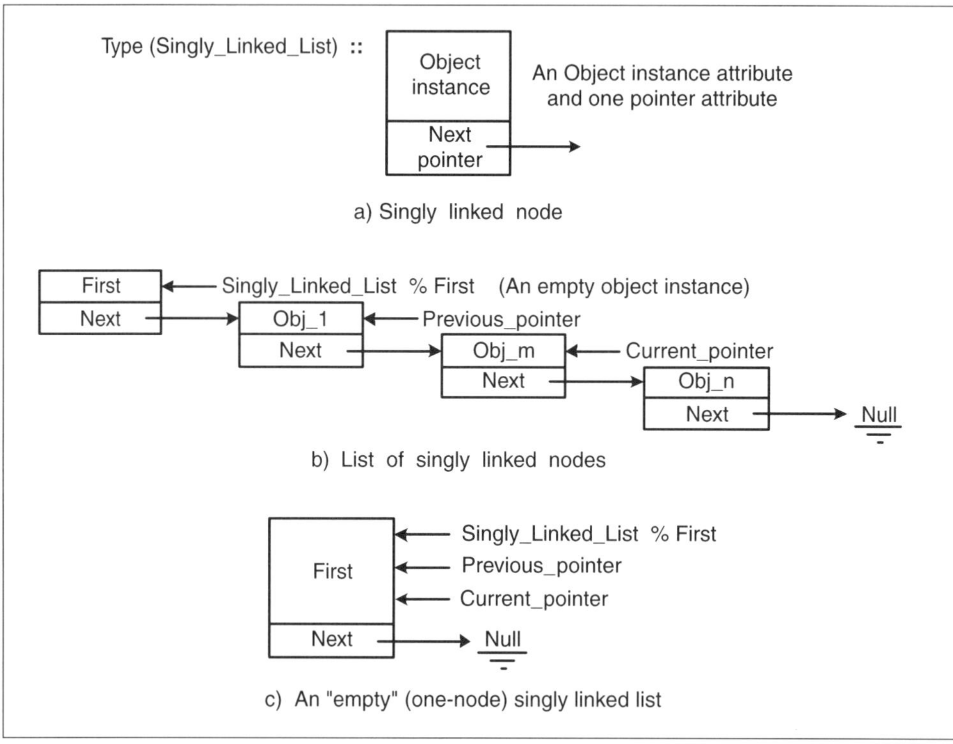

Figure 7.7: Singly linked list terminology.

copied pointer guarantees that an error or later modification of the routine cannot produce a side effect on the pointer. We also want to avoid a *dangling pointer*, which is caused by a deallocation that leaves its target object forever inaccessible. A related problem is a memory leak or *unreferenced storage* such as the program segment

```
real, pointer :: X_ptr (:)
  allocate ( X_ptr (Big_number) )
  ... ! use X_ptr
  nullify ( X_ptr ) ! dangling pointer
```

because now there is no way to release memory for X_ptr. To avoid this we need to free the memory before the pointer is nullified, and so the segment becomes

```
real, pointer :: X_ptr (:)
  allocate ( X_ptr(Big_number) )
  ... ! use X_ptr
  deallocate ( X_ptr ) ! memory released
  nullify ( X_ptr ).
```

Remember that in F95 the memory is automatically deallocated at the end of the scope of the variable unless one retains the variable with a SAVE statement (and formally deallocates it elsewhere).

7.4.1 Singly Linked Lists

We begin the study of the singly linked list by showing the notations employed in Figure 7.7. From experience we have chosen to have a dummy first node, called `first`, to simplify our algorithms so that a list is never truly empty. Also, as we scan through a list we will

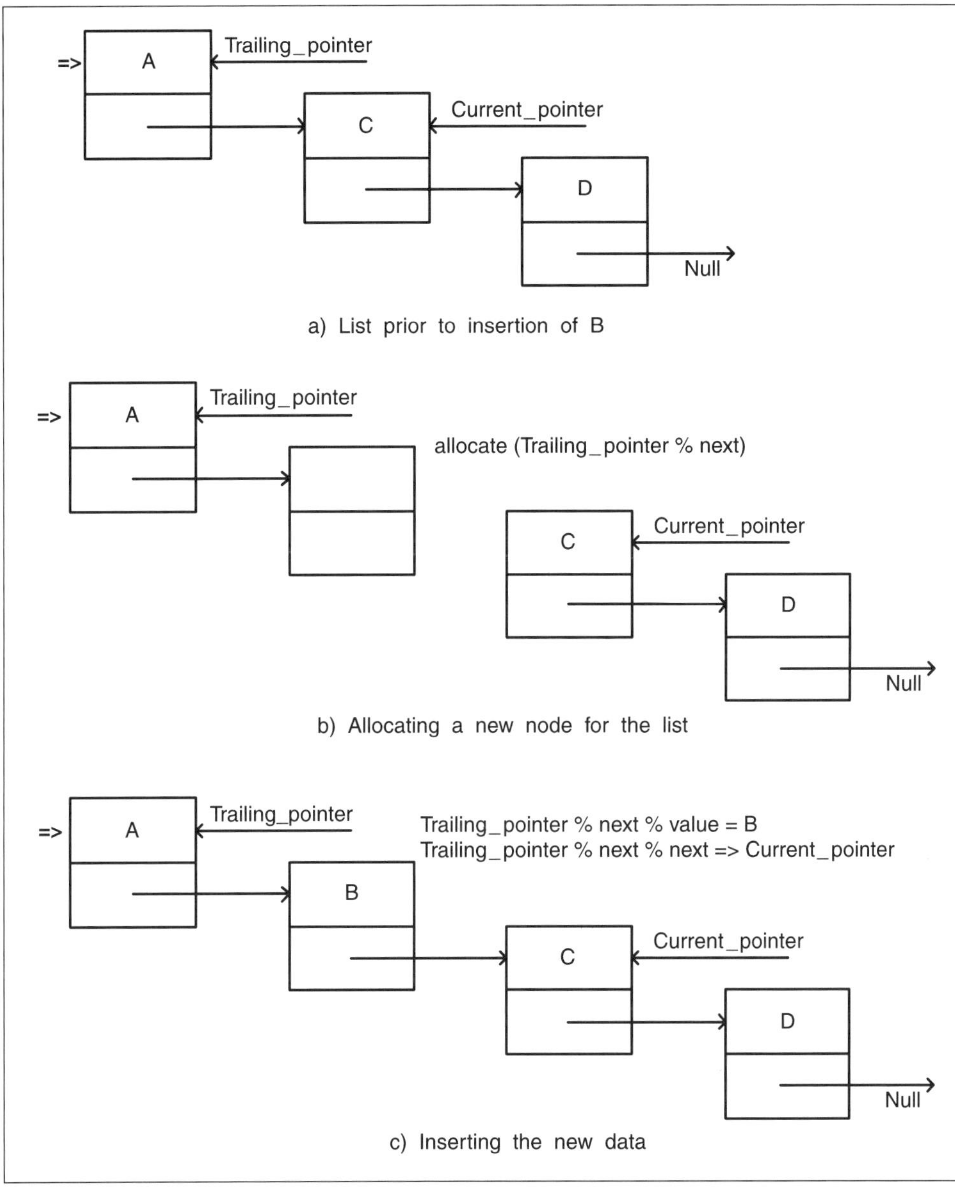

Figure 7.8: Inserting an object in a singly linked list.

use one pointer, called `current`, to point to the current object in the list and a companion, called `previous`, to point to the directly preceding object (if any). If no objects have been placed in the list, then both of these simply point to the `first` node. The end of the list is denoted by the `next` pointer attribute taking on the `null` value. To insert or delete objects one must be able to rank two objects. This means that to have a generic linked list one must overload the relational operators (< and ==) when the object to be placed in the container is defined. Since most objects have different types of attributes, the overloading process is clearly application dependent. The process for inserting an object is sketched in Figure 7.8, and that for deleting an object is in Figure 7.9.

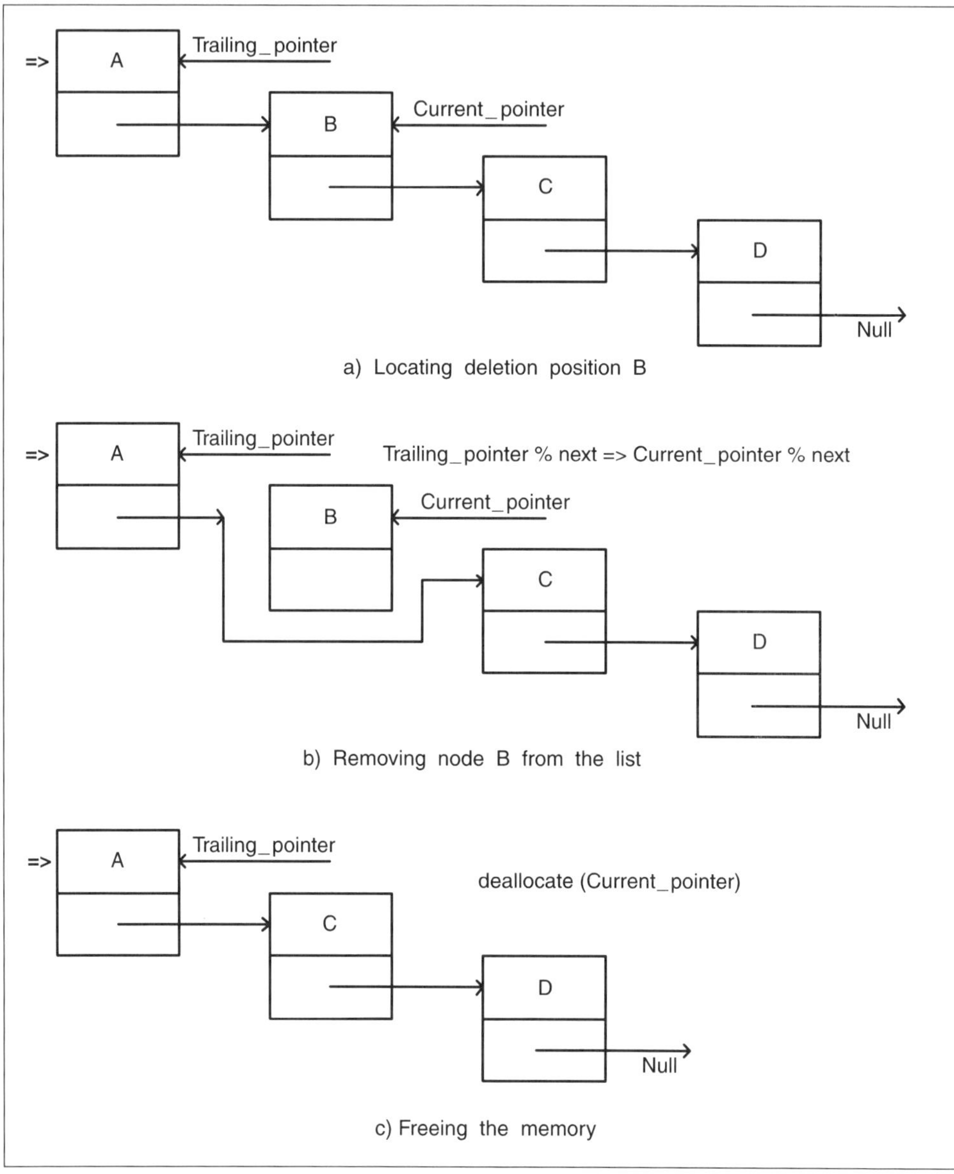

Figure 7.9: Deleting an object from a singly linked list.

The `Singly_Linked_List` class is given in Figure 7.10. It starts with the definition of a singly linked node (lines 5–9) that has an object attribute and a pointer attribute to locate the next node. Then a list is begun (lines 11–14) by creating the dummy first node that is considered to represent an empty list. The object deletion member must employ an overloaded operator (line 29), as must the insertion member (line 53). Observe that a list never gets "full," unless the system runs out of memory. The empty list test member (line 63) depends on the pointer status but is independent of the objects stored. The constructor for a list (line 69) simply creates the first node and nullifies it. The printing member (line 75) is called an `iterator` since it runs through all objects in the list. The testing program for this container type and its output results are given in Figure 7.11. To test such a container it

```
module singly_linked_list
 use class_Object
 implicit none

  type S_L_node                              ! Singly Linked Node
    private
    type (Object)              :: value      ! Object attribute
    type (S_L_node), pointer :: next         ! Pointer to next node
  end type S_L_node

  type S_L_list                        ! Singly Linked List of Nodes
    private
    type (S_L_node), pointer :: first ! Dummy first object in list
  end type S_L_list

contains
  subroutine S_L_delete (links, Obj, found)
    type (S_L_list), intent (inout) :: links
    type (Object),    intent (in)     :: Obj
    logical,          intent (out)    :: found
    type (S_L_node), pointer          :: previous, current

    ! find location of Obj
      previous => links%first          ! begin at top of list
      current  => previous%next        ! begin at top of list
      found = .false.                   ! initialize
      do
        if ( found .or. (.not. associated (current)) return ! list end
          if ( Obj == current%value ) then ! *** OVERLOADED ***
            found = .true. ; exit ! this location search
          else ! move the next node in list
            previous => previous%next
            current  => current%next
          end if
      end do ! to find location of node with Obj
    ! delete if found
      if ( found )  then
        previous%next => current%next ! redirect pointer
        deallocate ( current )         ! free space for node
      end if
  end subroutine S_L_delete

  subroutine S_L_insert (links, Obj )
    type (S_L_list), intent (inout) :: links
    type (Object),    intent(in)      :: Obj
    type (S_L_node), pointer          :: previous, current

  !  Find location to insert a new object
      previous => links%first                  ! initialize
      current  => previous%next                ! initialize
      do
        if ( .not. associated (current) ) exit ! insert at end
          if ( Obj < current%value ) exit      ! *** OVERLOADED ***
            previous => current                ! inserbefor current
            current  => current%next           ! move to next node
      end do ! to locate insert node
  !  Insert before current (duplicates allowed)
```

```
          allocate ( previous%next )       ! get new node space
          previous%next%value = Obj        ! new object inserted
          previous%next%next => current    ! new next pointer
       end subroutine S_L_insert

       function is_S_L_empty (links) result (t_or_f)
         type (S_L_list), intent (in) :: links
         logical                      :: t_or_f
           t_or_f = .not. associated ( links%first%next )
        end function is_S_L_empty

        function S_L_new () result (new_list)
          type (S_L_list) :: new_list
            allocate ( new_list%first )          ! get memory for the object
            nullify  ( new_list%first%next )     ! begin with empty list
        end function S_L_new

        subroutine print_S_L_list (links)
          type (S_L_list), intent (in) :: links
          type ( S_L_node), pointer    :: current
          integer                      :: counter
            current => links%first%next
            counter = 0 ; print *,'Link    Object Value'
            do
              if ( .not. associated (current) ) exit ! list end
                counter = counter + 1
                print *, counter, '      ', current%value
                current => current%next
            end do
        end subroutine print_S_L_list
     end module singly_linked_list
```

Figure 7.10: A typical singly linked list class of objects.

is necessary to have an object type defined. Here an object with a single integer value was selected, and thus it was easy to overload the relational operators with a clear meaning, as shown in Figure 7.12.

7.4.1.1 Example: A List of Sparse Vectors. In this example we want to create a linked list to hold sparse vectors (singly subscripted arrays) where the length of each vector is specified. We will perform simple operations on all the vectors such as input them, normalize them, add them (if their sizes are the same), and so. In doing this we will make use of some of the efficiencies that F90 provides for arrays such as using the subscript array triplet to avoid serial loops forth, and operating on arrays by name alone. This is an example in which a similar C++ implementation would be much longer because of the need to provide all the serial loops.

7.4.2 Doubly Linked Lists

The notations of the doubly linked list are shown in Figure 7.13. Again we have chosen to have a dummy first node, called `header`, to simplify our algorithms so that a list is never truly empty. Also, as we scan through a list we will use one pointer, called `current`, to point to the current object in the list and a companion, called `previous`, to point to the directly preceding object (if any). If no objects have been placed in the list, then both of these simply point to the `header` node. The end of the list is denoted by the `next` pointer attribute taking on the `null` value. To insert or delete objects one must be able to rank two objects.

```
program test_singly_linked   ! test a singly linked object list
use singly_linked_list
implicit none
  type (S_L_list) :: container
  type (Object)   :: Obj_1, Obj_2, Obj_3, Obj_4
  logical         :: delete_ok

    Obj_1 = Object(15) ; Obj_2 = Object(25) ! constructor
    Obj_3 = Object(35) ; Obj_4 = Object(45) ! constructor
    container = S_L_new()
    print *, 'Empty status is ', is_S_L_empty (container)
    call S_L_insert (container, Obj_4) ! insert object
    call S_L_insert (container, Obj_2) ! insert object
    call S_L_insert (container, Obj_1) ! insert object
    call print_S_L_list (container)

    call S_L_delete (container, obj_2, delete_ok)
    print *, 'Object: ', Obj_2, '  deleted status is ', delete_ok
    call print_S_L_list (container)
    print *, 'Empty status is ', is_S_L_empty (container)

    call S_L_insert (container, Obj_3) ! insert object
    call print_S_L_list (container)
    call S_L_delete (container, obj_1, delete_ok)
    print *, 'Object: ', Obj_1, '  deleted status is ', delete_ok
    call S_L_delete (container, obj_4, delete_ok)
    print *, 'Object: ', Obj_4, '  deleted status is ', delete_ok
    call print_S_L_list (container)
    print *, 'Empty status is ', is_S_L_empty (container)

    call S_L_delete (container, obj_3, delete_ok)
    print *, 'Object: ', Obj_3, '  deleted status is ', delete_ok
    print *, 'Empty status is ', is_S_L_empty (container)
    call print_S_L_list (container)
end program test_singly_linked          ! running yields
! Empty status is  T
! Link    Object Value
! 1       15
! 2       25
! 3       45
! Object:  25  deleted status is  T
! Link    Object Value
! 1       15
! 2       45
! Empty status is  F
! Link    Object Value
! 1       15
! 2       35
! 3       45
! Object:  15  deleted status is  T
! Object:  45  deleted status is  T
! Link    Object Value
! 1       35
! Empty status is  F
! Object:  35  deleted status is  T
! Empty status is  T
! Link    Object Value
```

Figure 7.11: Testing the singly linked list with integers.

```
module class_Object
implicit none
  type Object              ! An integer object for testing lists
    integer :: data ; end type Object

  interface operator (<)            ! for sorting or insert
    module procedure less_than_Object ; end interface
  interface operator (==)            ! for sorting or delete
    module procedure equal_to_Object ; end interface

contains                            ! overload definitions only
  function less_than_Object (Obj_1, Obj_2) result (Boolean)
    type (Object), intent(in) :: Obj_1, Obj_2
    logical                   :: Boolean
      Boolean = Obj_1%data < Obj_2%data    ! standard (<) here
  end function less_than_Object
  function equal_to_Object (Obj_1, Obj_2) result (Boolean)
    type (Object), intent(in) :: Obj_1, Obj_2
    logical                   :: Boolean
      Boolean = Obj_1%data == Obj_2%data   ! standard (==) here
  end function equal_to_Object
end module class_Object
```

Figure 7.12: Typical object definition to test a singly linked list.

This means that in order to have a generic linked list one must again overload the relational operators (< and ==) when the object to be placed in the container is defined.

An incomplete but illustrative Doubly_Linked_List class is given in Figure 7.14. It starts with the definition of a doubly linked node (lines 4–8) that has an object attribute and a pair of pointer attributes to locate the nodes on either side of the object. Then a list is begun (lines 11–14) by creating the dummy first node that is consider to represent an empty

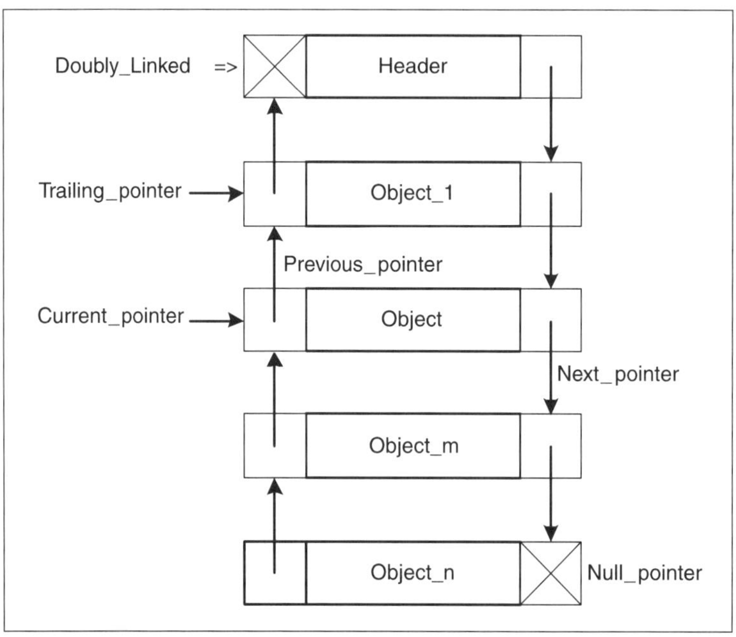

Figure 7.13: Notations for a doubly linked list.

```
module doubly_linked_list
use class_Object
implicit none
  type D_L_node
    private
       type (Object)              :: Obj
       type (D_L_node), pointer :: previous
       type (D_L_node), pointer :: next
  end type D_L_node

  type D_L_list
    private
       type (D_L_node), pointer :: header
  end type D_L_list

contains

function D_L_new () result (new_list)        ! constructor
  type (D_L_list) :: new_list
    allocate (new_list % header)
    nullify  (new_list % header % previous)
    nullify  (new_list % header % next)
end function D_L_new

subroutine destroy_D_L_List (links)           ! destructor
  type (D_L_list), intent (in) :: links
  type (D_L_node), pointer     :: current
    do
      current => links % header % next
      if ( .not. associated ( current ) ) exit
        current % previous % next => current % next
        if ( associated ( current % next ) ) then
           current % next % previous => current % previous
        end if
        nullify ( current % previous )
        nullify ( current % next )
        print *, 'Destroying object ', current % Obj
        deallocate ( current )
    end do
    deallocate ( links % header )
    print *,'D_L_List destroyed'
end subroutine destroy_D_L_List
subroutine D_L_insert_before (links, values)
  type (D_L_list), intent (in) :: links
  type (Object),   intent (in)  :: values
  type (D_L_node), pointer     :: current     ! Temp traversal pointer
  type (D_L_node), pointer     :: trailing    ! Preceding node pointer
!  Find location to insert new node, in ascending order
    trailing => links % header                ! initialize
    current  => trailing % next               ! initialize
    do
      if (.not. associated (current)) exit    ! insert at end
        if (values < current % Obj ) exit     ! insert before current
          trailing => current                 ! move to next node
          current  => current % next          ! move to next node
    end do
```

```
[ 57]  !  Insert before current (duplicates allowed)
[ 58]      allocate (trailing % next)                ! get new node space
[ 59]      trailing % next % Obj  = values           ! new object inserted
[ 60]  !  Insert the new pointers
[ 61]      if (.not. associated (current)) then      ! End of list (special)
[ 62]        nullify (trailing % next % next)
[ 63]        trailing % next % previous => trailing
[ 64]      else                                     ! Not the end of the list
[ 65]        trailing % next % next => current
[ 66]        trailing % next % previous => trailing
[ 67]        current % previous => trailing % next
[ 68]      end if
[ 69]  end subroutine D_L_insert_before
[ 70]
[ 71]  function Get_Obj_at_Ptr  (ptr_to_Obj)  result ( values)
[ 72]    type (D_L_node), intent (in)  :: ptr_to_Obj
[ 73]    type (Object)                 :: values   ! intent out
[ 74]      values = ptr_to_Obj % Obj
[ 75]  end function Get_Obj_at_Ptr
[ 76]
[ 77]  function Get_Ptr_to_Obj (links, values) result (ptr_to_Obj)
[ 78]    type (D_L_list), intent (in) :: links       ! D_L_list header
[ 79]    type (Object),   intent (in)  :: values     ! Node identifier Object
[ 80]    type (D_L_node), pointer      :: ptr_to_Obj ! Pointer to the Object
[ 81]    type (D_L_node), pointer      :: current    ! list traversal pointer
[ 82]      current => links % header % next
[ 83]      do ! Search list, WARNING: runs forever if values not in list
[ 84]        if (current % Obj ==  values) exit     ! *** OVERLOADED ***
[ 85]          current => current % next
[ 86]      end do
[ 87]      ptr_to_Obj => current                     ! Return pointer to node
[ 88]  end function Get_Ptr_to_Obj
[ 89]
[ 90]  subroutine print_D_L_list ( links )
[ 91]    type (D_L_list), intent (in) :: links
[ 92]    type (D_L_node), pointer      :: current ! Node traversal pointer
[ 93]    integer                       :: counter ! Link position
[ 94]  !  Traverse the list and print its contents to standard output
[ 95]      current => links % header % next
[ 96]      counter = 0 ; print *,'Link    Object Value'
[ 97]      do
[ 98]        if (.not. associated (current)) exit
[ 99]          counter = counter + 1
[100]          print *, counter, '      ', current % Obj
[101]          current => current % next
[102]      end do
[103]  end subroutine print_D_L_list
[104]  end module doubly_linked_list
```

Figure 7.14: A typical doubly linked list class of objects.

list. The object insertion member must employ an overloaded operator (line 53) as before. Observe that a list never gets "full" unless the system runs out of memory. The constructor for a list (line 18) simply creates the first node and nullifies its pointers. A corresponding destructor (line 25) has been provided to delete everything associated with the list when we are done with it. The printing member (line 90) is called an `iterator` since it runs through all objects in the list. The testing program for this container type and its output results are

```
program Test_doubly_linked
use doubly_linked_list
implicit none
  type (D_L_list)              :: container
  type (Object)                :: Obj_1, Obj_2, Obj_3, Obj_4
  type (Object)                :: value_at_pointer
  type (D_L_node), pointer :: point_to_Obj_3

  Obj_1 = Object (15) ; Obj_2 = Object (25)
  Obj_3 = Object (35) ; Obj_4 = Object (45)
  container = D_L_new ()
  ! print *, 'Empty status is ', is_D_L_empty (container)
  call D_L_insert_before (container, Obj_4)
  call D_L_insert_before (container, Obj_2)
  call D_L_insert_before (container, Obj_1)
  call D_L_insert_before (container, Obj_3)
  call print_D_L_list (container)

  ! find and get Obj_3
  point_to_Obj_3 = Get_Ptr_to_Obj (container, ObjL
  value_at_pointer = Get_Obj_at_Ptr (point_to_
  print *, 'Object: ', Obj_3, '  has a value of ', value_at_pointer
  call destroy_D_L_List (container)
end program Test_doubly_linked                    ! Running gives:
! Link    Object Value
! 1       15
! 2       25
! 3       35
! 4       45
! Object:  35   has a value of  35
! Destroying object  15
! Destroying object  25
! Destroying object  35
! Destroying object  45
! D_L_List destroyed
```

Figure 7.15: Testing a partial doubly linked list.

given in Figure 7.15. Here an object with a single integer value was selected, and thus it was easy to overload the relational operators with a clear meaning, as shown in Figure 7.12.

7.5 Direct (Random) Access Files

Often it may not be necessary to create special-object data structures such as those outlined above. From its beginning Fortran has had the ability to create a sophisticated random access data structure in which the implementation details are hidden from its user. This was necessary originally since the language was utilized on computers with memory sizes that are considered tiny by today's standard (e.g., 16 Kb), but it was still necessary to create and modify large amounts of data efficiently. The standard left the actual implementation details to the compiler writers. That data structure is known as a "direct access file." It behaves like a single subscript array in that the object at any position can be read, modified, or written at random so long as the user keeps up with the position of interest. The user simply supplies

```
program random_access_file
! create a file and access or modify it randomly
implicit none
  character(len=10) :: name
  integer :: j, rec_len, no_name, no_open
  integer :: names = 0, unit = 1

! find the hardware dependent record length of the object
! to be stored and modified. Then open a binary file.
    inquire (iolength = rec_len) name
    open (unit, file = "random_list", status = "replace",
          access = "direct", recl = rec_len,
          form = "unformatted", iostat = no_open)
    if ( no_open > 0 ) stop 'open failed for random_list'

! read and store the names sequentially
    print *, ' '; print *, 'Original order'
    do ! forever from standard input
      read (*, '(a)', iostat = no_name)  name
      if ( no_name < 0 ) exit ! the read loop
        names = names + 1                 ! record number
        write (unit, rec = names) name    ! save record
        print *, name                     ! echo
    end do
    if ( names == 0 ) stop 'no records read'

! list names in reverse order
    print *, ' '; print *, 'Reverse order'
    do j = names, 1, -1
      read (unit, rec = j) name
      print *, name
    end do ! of random read

! change the middle name in random file
    write (unit, rec = (names + 1)/2) 'New_Name'

! list names in original order
    print *, ' '; print *, 'Modified data'
    do j = 1, names
      read (unit, rec = j) name
      print *, name
    end do ! of random read

    close (unit) ! replace previous records and save
end program random_access_file
! Running with input of:    Name_1
!                           B_name
!                           3_name
!                           name_4
!                           Fifth
! Yields:
! Original order  Reverse order  Modified data
!  Name_1           Fifth          Name_1
!  B_name           name_4          B_name
!  3_name           3_name          New_Name
!  name_4           B_name          name_4
!  Fifth           Name_1          Fifth
```

Figure 7.16: Utilizing a random access file as a data structure.

the position, known as the record number, as additional information in the read and write statements. With today's hardware, if the file is stored on a virtual disk (stored in random access memory) there is practically no difference in access times for arrays and direct files.

It should be noted here that, since pointers are addresses in memory, they can not be written to any type of file. That, of course, means that no object having a pointer as an attribute can be written either. Thus, in some cases one must employ the other types of data structures illustrated earlier in the chapter.

To illustrate the basic concepts of a random access file consider the program called random_access_file, which is given in Figure 7.16. In this case the object is simply a character string, as defined in line 4. The hardware transportability of this code is assured by establishing the required constant record with the inquire function given in line 10. It is then used in opening the file, which is designated as a direct file in line 12. Lines 16–24 create the object record numbers in a sequential fashion. They also define the new object to be stored with each record. In lines 27–32 the records are accessed in a backwards order but could have been accessed in any random or partial order. In line 35 a random object is given a new value. Finally, the changes are outputed in a sequential order in lines 37–42. Sample input data and program outputs are included as comments at the end of the program.

7.6 Exercises

1 Write a subprogram that traverses a singly linked list, removing each node and freeing the memory, thus leaving it empty.

2 Write a subprogram that traverses a doubly linked list, removing each node and freeing the memory, thus leaving it empty.

3 Write a subprogram that traverses a circular linked list, removing each node and freeing the memory, thus leaving it empty.

4 Write a subprogram for inserting an item after some other given element in a doubly linked list.

CHAPTER EIGHT

Arrays and Matrices

8.1 Subscripted Variables: Arrays

It is common in engineering and mathematics to employ a notation in which one or more subscripts are appended to a variable that is a member of some larger set. Such a variable may be a member of a list of scalars, or it may represent an element in a vector, matrix, or Cartesian tensor.* In engineering computation, we usually refer to subscripted variables as *arrays*. Since programming languages do not have a convenient way to append the subscripts, we actually denote them by placing them in parentheses or square brackets. Thus, an element usually written as A_{jk} becomes `A(j,k)` in Fortran and MATLAB, and `A[j][k]` in C++.

Arrays have properties that need to be understood in order to utilize them correctly in any programming language. The primary feature of an array is that it must have at least one subscript. The "rank" of an array is the number of subscripts, or dimensions, it has. Fortran allows an array to have up to seven subscripts, C++ allows four, and MATLAB allows only two since it deals only with matrices. An array with two subscripts is called a rank-two array, and one with a single subscript is called a rank-one array, or a vector. Matrices are rank-two arrays that obey special mathematical operations. A scalar variable has no subscripts and is sometimes called a rank-zero array. Rank-one arrays with an extent of one are also viewed as a scalar.

The "extent" of a subscript or dimension is the number of elements allowed for that subscript. That is, the extent is an integer that ranges from the lower bound of the subscript to its upper bound. The lower bound of a subscript is zero in C++, and it defaults to unity in Fortran. However, Fortran allows the programmer to assign any integer value to the lower and upper bounds of a subscript.

The "size" of an array is the number of elements in it. That is, the size is the product of the extents of all of its subscripts. Most languages require the extent of each subscript be provided in order to allocate memory storage for the array.

The "shape" of an array is defined by its rank and extents. The shape is a rank-one array in which each of its elements is the extent of the corresponding subscript of the array whose shape is being determined. Both Fortran and MATLAB have statements that return the shape and size of an array as well as statements for defining a new array by reshaping an existing array.

* An nth order tensor has n subscripts and transforms to different coordinate systems by a special law. The most common uses are scalars ($n = 0$) and vectors ($n = 1$).

Table 8.1: Typical Vector Initialization

Action	C++[a]	F90	F77	MATLAB
Preallocate	`integer A[100]`	`INTEGER A(100)`	`INTEGER A(100)`	`A(100)=0`

Initialize	`for j=0,99`
	`  A[j]=12`
	`end`
		`A=12`	`do 5 J=1,100`
			`  A(J)=12`
			`5 continue`
				`for j=1:100`
				`  A(j)=12`
				`end`

[a] Arrays in C++ have a starting index of zero.

It is also important to know which of two "storage mode" options a language employs to store and access array elements. This knowledge is especially useful when reading or writing full arrays. Arrays are stored either by varying their leftmost subscript first or by varying the rightmost subscript first. These are referred to as "column-wise" and "row-wise" access, respectively. Clearly, they are the same for rank-one arrays and differ for arrays of higher rank. Column-wise storage is used by Fortran and C++, whereas MATLAB uses row-wise storage.

Matrices are arrays that usually have only two subscripts: the first represents the row number, and the second the column number where the element is located. Matrix algebra places certain restrictions on the subscripts of two matrices when they are added or multiplied, and so forth. The fundamentals of matrices are covered in detail in this chapter.

Both Fortran and C++ require you to specify the maximum range of each subscript of an array before the array or its elements are used. MATLAB does not have this as a requirement, but preallocating the array space can drastically improve the speed of MATLAB as well as make much more efficient use of the available memory. If you do not preallocate MATLAB arrays, then the interpreter must check at each step to see if a position larger than the current maximum has been reached. If so, the maximum value is increased, and memory is found to store the new element. Thus, failure to preallocate MATLAB arrays is permissible but inefficient.

For example, assume we want to set a vector A having 100 elements to an initial value of 12. The procedures are compared in Table 8.1. This example could also have been done efficiently in F90 and MATLAB by using the colon operator: `A(1:100) = 12`. The programmer should be alert for the chance to replace loops with the colon operator (:) because it is more concise, but retains readability, and executes more quickly. The joys of the colon operator are described more fully in Section 8.1.3 (page 186).

Array operations often use special characters and operators. Fortran has "implied" DO loops associated with its array operations (see Section 4.3.2, page 66). Similar features in MATLAB and F90 are listed in Table 8.2.

Table 8.2: Special Array Characters

Purpose	F90	MATLAB
Form subscripts	( )	( )
Separate subscripts and elements	,	,
Generate elements and subscripts	:	:
Separate commands	;	;
Form arrays	(/ /)	[ ]
Continue to new line	&	...
Indicate comment	!	%
Suppress printing	default	;

Fortran has always had efficient array-handling features, but until the release of F90 it was not easy to dynamically create and release the memory space needed to store arrays. That is a useful feature for arrays that require large amounts of space but are not needed for the entire life of the program. Several types of arrays are available in F90, and the most recent types have been added to allow the use of array operations and intrinsic functions similar to those in MATLAB. Without getting into the details of the F90 standards and terminology, we will introduce the most common array usages in historical order:

```
F77: Constant Arrays, Dummy Dimension Arrays, Variable Rank Arrays
F90: Automatic Arrays, Allocatable Arrays.
```

These different approaches all have the common feature that memory space needed for an array must be set aside (allocated) before any element in the array is utilized.

The new F90 array features include the so-called automatic arrays. An automatic array is one that appears in a subroutine or function and has its size, but not its name, provided in the argument list of the subprogram. For example,

```
subroutine auto_A_B (M, N, Other_arguments)
  implicit none
  integer :: M, N
  real    :: A(M, N), B(M)    ! Automatic arrays
  ! Create arrays A & B and use them for some purpose
    ...
end subroutine auto_A_B.
```

would automatically allocate space for the M rows and N columns of the array A and for the M rows of array B. When the purpose of the subroutine is finished and it "returns" to the calling program – the array space is automatically released and the arrays A and B cease to exist. This is a useful feature – especially in object-oriented programs. If the system does not have enough space available to allocate for the array, the program stops and gives an error message to that effect. With today's large memory computers, that is unlikely to occur except for the common user error in which the dimension argument is undefined.

An extension of this concept that allows more flexibility and control is the allocatable array. An allocatable array is one that has a known rank (number of subscripts) but an initially unknown extent (range over each subscript). It can appear in any program, function, or subroutine. For example,

```
program  make_A_B       ! Allocatable arrays
 implicit none
 real, allocatable :: A(:,:), B(:)    ! Declares rank of each
 integer           :: M, N            ! Row and column sizes
 integer           :: A_B_Status       ! Optional status check
   print *,"Enter the number of rows and columns: "
   read  *, M, N  ! Now know the (default) extent of each subscript
     allocate ( A(M, N), B(M), stat = A_B_Status ) ! dynamic storage
!  Verify that the dynamic memory was available
     if ( A_B_Status /= 0 ) stop "Memory not available in make_A_B"
! Create arrays A & B and use them for some purpose
     ...
     deallocate (A, B) ! free the memory space
! Do other things
     ...
end program  make_A_B
```

would specifically allocate space for the M rows and N columns of the array A and for the M rows of array B and optionally verify space availability. When the purpose of the arrays is finished, the space is specifically released and the arrays A and B cease to exist. The optional status-checking feature is useful in the unlikely event that the array is so large that the system does not have that much dynamic space available. Then the user has the option of closing down the program in some desirable way or simply stopping on the spot.

The old F77 standard often encouraged the use of dummy dimension arrays. The dummy dimension array is one that appears in a subroutine, or function, and has its size and its name provided in the argument list of the subprogram. For example,

```
subroutine dummy_A_B (M, N, A, B, Other_things)
  implicit none
  integer :: M, N
  real    :: A(M, N), B(M)    ! dummy arrays
 !  Create arrays A & B and use them for some purpose
    ...
end subroutine dummy_A_B
```

would imply that *existing* space for the M rows and N columns of the array A and for the M rows of array B (*or more*) had been declared or allocated in the calling program. When the purpose of the subroutine is finished and it "returns" to the calling program, the space in the calling program for the arrays A and B continues to exist until the declaring program unit terminates.

Of course the use of constant-dimensioned arrays is always allowed. The constant-dimension array is one that appears in any program unit and has integer constants, or integer *parameter* variables (preferred) as given extents for each subscript of an array. For example,

```
program  main
 implicit none
 integer, parameter :: M_max=20, N_max=40 ! Maximum expected
 integer            :: Days_per_Month(12) ! Constant array
 integer            :: M, N               ! User sizes
 real :: A(M_max, N_max), B(M_max)         ! Constant arrays
   print *,"Enter the number of rows and columns: "
   read  *, M, N                  ! The user extent of each subscript

!  Verify that the constant memory is available
   if ( M > M_max ) stop "Row size exceeded in main"
   if ( N > N_max ) stop "Column size exceeded in main"
! Create arrays A & B and use them for some purpose
   call  dummy_A_B (M, N, A, B, Other_things)  ! dummy arrays
   ...
end program main

 subroutine dummy_A_B (M, N, A, B, Other_things)  ! dummy arrays
   implicit none
   integer :: M, N
   real    :: A(M, N), B(M)
  !  Create arrays A & B and use them for some purpose
    ...
 end subroutine dummy_A_B.
```

In general it is considered very bad style to use integer constants like 12 in a dimension or in a DO loop control except for the unusual case in which its meaning is obvious and you never expect to have to change the number. In the sample declaration,

```
integer :: Days_per_Month(12) ! Constant array.
```

Table 8.3: Typical Array Definitions

Action	F90	MATLAB
Define size[a]	`integer :: A (2, 3)`	`A(2,3)=0;`
Enter rows	`A(1,:)=(/1,7,-2/)`	`A=[1,7,-2;`
	`A(2,:)=(/3,4,6/)`	`3,4,6];`

[a] Optional in MATLAB but improves efficiency.

It is obvious that we are thinking about 12 months per year and that we do not expect the number of months per year ever to change in other potential applications of this program.

8.1.1 Initializing Array Elements

Explicit lists of the initial elements in an array are allowed by C++, Fortran, and MATLAB. MATLAB is oriented to enter element values in the way that we read, that is, row by row. Fortran and C also allow array input by rows, but the default procedure is to accept values by ranging over its subscripts from left to right. That is, both F90 and C++ read by columns as their default mode. For example, consider the 2×3 array

$$A = \begin{bmatrix} 1 & 7 & -2 \\ 3 & 4 & 6 \end{bmatrix}.$$

This array could be typed as explicit input with the commands shown in Table 8.3. An alternative for F90 and MATLAB is to define the full array by column order as a vector that is then reshaped into a matrix with a specified number of rows and columns. The use of the RESHAPE operator is shown in Table 8.4.

Returning to the previous example, we see that the matrix A could have also been defined as

```
F90      A = reshape((/1,3,7,4, -2,6/), (/2,3/))
         A = reshape((/1,3,7,4, -2,6/),shape(A))
MATLAB   A = reshape([1,3,7,4, -2,6], 2,3)
```

To initialize the elements of an array to zero or unity, F90 and MATLAB have special constructs or functions that fill the bill. For example, for A to be zero and B to have unity

Table 8.4: Array Reshape Intrinsics

F90	MATLAB	Result
`data = (/(k, k=1,6)/)` `M = reshape(data,(/3,2/))`	`data = [1 : 6]` `M = reshape(data,3,2)`	$M = \begin{bmatrix} 1 & 4 \\ 2 & 5 \\ 3 & 6 \end{bmatrix}$
`N = reshape(data,(/2,3/))`	`N = reshape(data,2,3)`	$N = \begin{bmatrix} 1 & 3 & 5 \\ 2 & 4 & 6 \end{bmatrix}$

elements, we could use the following commands:

Action	F90	MATLAB
Define size	`integer :: A (2, 3)`	`A(2,3)=0;`
	`integer :: B (3)`	`B(3)=0;`
Zero A	`A=0`	`A=zeros(2,3);`
Initialize B	`B=1`	`B=ones(3);`

If we want to create a new array B with the first three even numbers, we would use *implied loops* as follows:

Action	F90	MATLAB
Even set	`B=(/(2*k,k=1,3)/)`	`B=2*[1:1:3];`
	`B=(/(k,k=2,6,2)/)`	`B=[2:2:6];`

Arrays can also be initialized by reading their element values from a stored data file. The two most common types of files are ASCII (standard characters) and binary (machine language) files. The former files are easy to read and edit, but binary files make more efficient use of storage and are read or written much faster than ASCII files. Often, ASCII files are denoted by the name extension of "dat." Binary files are denoted by the name extension "mat" in MATLAB, whereas in Fortran the extension "bin" is commonly employed.

For example, assume that the preceding `A(2,3)` array is to be initialized by reading its values from an ASCII file created by a text editor and given the name of `A.dat`. Further, assume that we wish to multiply all elements by 3 and store them as a new ASCII file. Then we could use `read` procedures like those in Table 8.5 in which the last MATLAB command associated a file name and a file type with the desired input/output (I/O) action. Fortran requires an OPEN statement to do this if the default I/O files (unit 5 to read and unit 6 to write) are not used in the read or write.

8.1.2 Intrinsic Array Functions

Note that MATLAB has intrinsic functions, `ones` and `zeros`, to carry out a task that F90 does with an operator. Often the reverse is true. MATLAB has several operators that in Fortran correspond to an intrinsic function or a CALLed function. A comparison of the similar F90 and MATLAB array mathematical operators is given in Table 8.5. They generally only differ slightly in syntax. For example, to transpose the matrix A, the F90 construct is `transpose(A)`, and in MATLAB it is simply A′.* In F90, the * operator means, for matrices, term-by-term multiplication: when A=$\begin{bmatrix}1&3&5\\2&4&6\end{bmatrix}$ and B=$\begin{bmatrix}1&2&4\\3&5&6\end{bmatrix}$, A*B yields $\begin{bmatrix}1&6&20\\6&20&36\end{bmatrix}$. In MATLAB, the same operation is expressed as `A.*B`. To multiply the matrices A and B, Fortran requires the intrinsic function `matmul` (i.e., `matmul(A,B)`), whereas MATLAB uses the * operator (A*B).

Another group of commonly used functions that operate on arrays in Fortran90 and MATLAB are briefly described in Table 8.6. Both languages have several other more specialized functions, but those in Table 8.6 are probably the most commonly used in programs.

* In MATLAB, A′ actually means conjugate transpose. If A is real, this operator performs the transpose as desired. If A is complex and we want its transpose, the MATLAB construct is A′.

Table 8.5: Array Operations in Programming Constructs. Lowercase letters denote scalars or scalar elements of arrays. MATLAB arrays are allowed a maximum of two subscripts, whereas Fortran allows seven. Uppercase letters denote matrices or scalar elements of matrices

Description	Equation	Fortran90 Operator	MATLAB Operator	Original Sizes	Result Size
Scalar plus scalar	$c = a \pm b$	$c = a \pm b$	$c = a \pm b;$	1, 1	1, 1
Element plus scalar	$c_{jk} = a_{jk} \pm b$	$c = a \pm b$	$c = a \pm b;$	m, n and 1, 1	m, n
Element plus element	$c_{jk} = a_{jk} \pm b_{jk}$	$c = a \pm b$	$c = a \pm b;$	m, n and m, n	m, n
Scalar times scalar	$c = a \times b$	$c = a * b$	$c = a * b;$	1, 1	1, 1
Element times scalar	$c_{jk} = a_{jk} \times b$	$c = a * b$	$c = a * b;$	m, n and 1, 1	m, n
Element times element	$c_{jk} = a_{jk} \times b_{jk}$	$c = a * b$	$c = a{\bullet} * b;$	m, n and m, n	m, n
Scalar divide scalar	$c = a/b$	$c = a/b$	$c = a/b;$	1, 1	1, 1
Scalar divide element	$c_{jk} = a_{jk}/b$	$c = a/b$	$c = a/b;$	m, n and 1, 1	m, n
Element divide element	$c_{jk} = a_{jk}/b_{jk}$	$c = a/b$	$c = a{\bullet}/b;$	m, n and m, n	m, n
Scalar power scalar	$c = a^b$	$c = a{*}{*}b$	$c = a \wedge b;$	1, 1	1, 1
Element power scalar	$c_{jk} = a_{jk}^b$	$c = a{*}{*}b$	$c = a \wedge b;$	m, n and 1, 1	m, n
Element power element	$c_{jk} = a_{jk}^{b_{jk}}$	$c = a{*}{*}b$	$c = a{\bullet} \wedge b;$	m, n and m, n	m, n
Matrix transpose	$C_{kj} = A_{jk}$	$C = \text{transpose}\ (A)$	$C = A';$	m, n	n, m
Matrix times matrix	$C_{ij} = \sum_k A_{ik} B_{kj}$	$C = \text{matmul}(A, B)$	$C = A * B;$	m, r and r, n	m, n
Vector dot vector	$c = \sum_k A_k B_k$	$c = \text{sum}(A * B)$	$c = \text{sum}(A{\bullet} * B);$	m, 1 and m, 1	1, 1
		$c = \text{dot\_product}(A, B)$	$c = A * B';$	m, 1 and m, 1	1, 1

Table 8.6: Equivalent Fortran90 and MATLAB Intrinsic Functions. The following KEY symbols are utilized to denote the TYPE of the intrinsic function, or subroutine, and its arguments: A-complex, integer, or real; I-integer; L-logical; M-mask (logical); R-real; X-real; Y-real; V-vector (rank 1 array); and Z-complex. Optional arguments are not shown. Fortran90 and MATLAB also have very similar array operations and colon operators

Type	Fortran90	MATLAB	Brief Description
A	ABS(A)	abs(a)	Absolute value of A.
R	ACOS(X)	acos(x)	Arccosine function of real X.
R	AIMAG(Z)	imag(z)	Imaginary part of complex number.
R	AINT(X)	real(fix(x))	Truncate X to a real whole number.
L	ALL(M)	all(m)	True if all mask elements M are true.
R	ANINT(X)	real(round(x))	Real whole number nearest to X.
L	ANY(M)	any(m)	True if any mask element M is true.
R	ASIN(X)	asin(x)	Arcsine function of real X.
R	ATAN(X)	atan(x)	Arctangent function of real X.
R	ATAN2(Y,X)	atan2(y,x)	Arctangent for complex number(X, Y).
I	CEILING(X)	ceil(x)	Least integer >= real X.
Z	CMPLX(X,Y)	(x+yi)	Convert real(s) to complex type.
Z	CONJG(Z)	conj(z)	Conjugate of complex number Z.
R	COS(R_Z)	cos(r_z)	Cosine of real or complex argument.
R	COSH(X)	cosh(x)	Hyperbolic cosine function of real X.
I	COUNT(M)	sum(m==1)	Number of true mask M elements.
R,L	DOT_PRODUCT(X,Y)	x'⋆y	Dot product of vectors X and Y.
R	EPSILON(X)	eps	Number, like X, $\ll 1$.
R,Z	EXP(R_Z)	exp(r_z)	Exponential of real or complex number.
I	FLOOR(X)	floor	Greatest integer $\leq$ X.
R	HUGE(X)	realmax	Largest number like X.
I	INT(A)	fix(a)	Convert A to integer type.
R	LOG(R_Z)	log(r_z)	Logarithm of real or complex number.
R	LOG10(X)	log10(x)	Base 10 logarithm function of real X.
R	MATMUL(X,Y)	x⋆y	Conformable matrix multiplication, X*Y.
I,V	I=MAXLOC(X)	[y,i]=max(x)	Location(s) of maximum array element.
R	Y=MAXVAL(X)	y=max(x)	Value of maximum array element.
I,V	I=MINLOC(X)	[y,i]=min(x)	Location(s) of minimum array element.
R	Y=MINVAL(X)	y=min(x)	Value of minimum array element.
I	NINT(X)	round(x)	Integer nearest to real X.
A	PRODUCT(A)	prod(a)	Product of array elements.
call	RANDOM_NUMBER(X)	x=rand	Pseudorandom numbers in (0, 1).
call	RANDOM_SEED	rand('seed')	Initialize random number generator.
R	REAL (A)	real(a)	Convert A to real type.
R	RESHAPE(X, (/ I, I2 /))	reshape(x, i, i2)	Reshape array X into I×I2 array.
I,V	SHAPE(X)	size(x)	Array (or scalar) shape vector.
R	SIGN(X,Y)		Absolute value of X times sign of Y.
R	SIGN(0.5,X)-SIGN(0.5,-X)	sign(x)	Signum, normalized sign, –1, 0, or 1.
R,Z	SIN(R_Z)	sin(r_z)	Sine of real or complex number.
R	SINH(X)	sinh(x)	Hyperbolic sine function of real X.
I	SIZE(X)	length(x)	Total number of elements in array X.
R,Z	SQRT(R_Z)	sqrt(r_z)	Square root of real or complex number.
R	SUM(X)	sum(x)	Sum of array elements.

Type	Fortran90	MATLAB	Brief Description
R	TAN(X)	tan(x)	Tangent function of real X.
R	TANH(X)	tanh(x)	Hyperbolic tangent function of real X.
R	TINY(X)	realmin	Smallest positive number like X.
R	TRANSPOSE(X)	x'	Matrix transpose of any type matrix.
R	X=1	x=ones(length(x))	Set all elements to 1.
R	X=0	x=zero(length(x))	Set all elements to 0.

For more detailed descriptions and sample uses of these intrinsic functions, see Adams, J.C et al., [1].

Often one needs to truncate a real number in some special fashion. Table 8.7 illustrates how to do that using some of the functions common to the languages of interest. That table also implies how one can convert reals to integers and vice versa.

8.1.3 Colon Operations on Arrays (Subscript Triplet)

The syntax of the colon operator, which is available in MATLAB and F90, is detailed in Table 4.6. What the colon operator concisely expresses is a sequence of numbers in an arithmetic progression. As shown in the table, the MATLAB expression `B:I:E` expresses the sequence `B, B+I, B+2*I, ..., B+`$\lfloor \frac{E-B}{I} \rfloor$`I`. The complicated expression for the sequence's last term simply means that the last value of the sequence does not exceed (in magnitude) the end value `E`.

You can also use the colon operator to extract smaller arrays from larger ones. If we wanted to extract the second row and third column of the array, $A = \left[\begin{smallmatrix} 1 & 7 & -2 \\ 3 & 4 & 6 \end{smallmatrix}\right]$, to get, re-

Table 8.7: Truncating Numbers

C++	-	int	-	-	floor	ceil
F90	aint	int	anint	nint	floor	ceiling
MATLAB	real (fix)	fix	real (round)	round	floor	ceil
Argument			**Value of Result**			
−2.000	−2.0	−2	−2.0	−2	−2	−2
−1.999	−1.0	−1	−2.0	−2	−2	−1
−1.500	−1.0	−1	−2.0	−2	−2	−1
−1.499	−1.0	−1	−1.0	−1	−2	−1
−1.000	−1.0	−1	−1.0	−1	−1	−1
−0.999	0.0	0	−1.0	−1	−1	0
−0.500	0.0	0	−1.0	−1	−1	0
−0.499	0.0	0	0.0	0	−1	0
0.000	0.0	0	0.0	0	0	0
0.499	0.0	0	0.0	0	0	1
0.500	0.0	0	1.0	1	0	1
0.999	0.0	0	1.0	1	0	1
1.000	1.0	1	1.0	1	1	1
1.499	1.0	1	1.0	1	1	2
1.500	1.0	1	2.0	2	1	2
1.999	1.0	1	2.0	2	1	2
2.000	2.0	2	2.0	2	2	2

spectively,

$$G = [3 \quad 4 \quad 6], \qquad C = \begin{Bmatrix} -2 \\ 6 \end{Bmatrix},$$

we could use the colon operator as follows:

Action	F90	MATLAB
Define size	`integer :: B (3)` `integer :: C (2)`	`B(3)=0;` `C(2)=0;`
Extract row	`B=A(2,:)`	`B=A(2,:);`
Extract columns	`C=A(:,3)`	`C=A(:,3);`

One can often use colon operators to avoid having loops act on arrays to define new arrays. For example, consider a square matrix

$$A = \begin{bmatrix} 1 & 2 & 3 \\ 4 & 5 & 6 \\ 7 & 8 & 9 \end{bmatrix}.$$

We can flip it left to right to create a new matrix (in F90 syntax)

$$\texttt{B=A(:, n:1:-1)} = \begin{bmatrix} 3 & 2 & 1 \\ 6 & 5 & 4 \\ 9 & 8 & 7 \end{bmatrix}$$

or flip it up to down

$$\texttt{C=A(n:1:-1, :)} = \begin{bmatrix} 7 & 8 & 9 \\ 4 & 5 & 6 \\ 1 & 2 & 3 \end{bmatrix}$$

or flip it up to down and then left to right

$$\texttt{D = A (n:1:-1, n:1:-1)} = \begin{bmatrix} 9 & 8 & 7 \\ 6 & 5 & 4 \\ 3 & 2 & 1 \end{bmatrix},$$

where $n = 3$ is the number of rows in the matrix A. In the MATLAB syntax, the second and third numbers would be interchanged in the colon operator. Actually, MATLAB has intrinsic operators to flip the matrices, and thus one could simply write

```
B = fliplr(A); C = flipud(A); D = rot90(A);
```

Table 8.8: F90 WHERE Constructs

```
WHERE (logical_array_expression)
    true_array_assignments
ELSEWHERE
    false_array_assignments
END WHERE
```
```
WHERE (logical_array_expression)
true_array_assignment
```

8.1.4 Array Logical Mask Operators

By default most MATLAB commands are designed to operate on arrays. Fortran77 and C++ have no built-in array operations, and it is necessary to program each loop. The Fortran90 standard has many of the MATLAB array commands – often with the identical syntax, as shown in Table 8.5 and 8.6. Frequently the F90 versions of these functions have optional features (arguments) that give the user more control than MATLAB does by including a logical control mask to be defined shortly.

To emphasize that an `IF` type of relational operator is to act on all elements of an array, Fortran90 also includes an array `WHERE` block or statement control (that is, an `IF` statement acting on all array elements), which is outlined in Table 8.8.

Note that the necessary loops are implied and need not be written. As an example, if

$$A = \begin{bmatrix} 0 & 3 & 5 \\ 7 & 4 & 8 \end{bmatrix}, \qquad B = \begin{bmatrix} 1 & 3 & 5 \\ 2 & 4 & 6 \end{bmatrix},$$

then, `WHERE (A > B) B = A` gives a new $B = \left[\begin{smallmatrix} 1 & 3 & 5 \\ 7 & 4 & 8 \end{smallmatrix}\right]$. By default, MATLAB always acts on matrices and considers scalars a special case. Thus, it would employ the standard syntax, `if A > B, B=A`, to do the same task.

A more sophisticated way to pick subscripts of an array selectively is to use a *mask* array. A mask array is the same size and shape as the array on which it will act. It is a Boolean array: all its elements have either true or false values. When associated with an operator, the operator will only act on those elements in the original array whose corresponding mask location is true (i.e., `.true.` in Fortran, `true` in C++, and `1` in MATLAB and C). Fortran90 has several operations that allow or require masks (Table 8.9). MATLAB functions with the same name exist in some cases, as seen in Table 8.6. Usually, they correspond to the F90 operator where the mask is true everywhere.

A general Fortran principle underlies the fact that the array mentioned in the `WHERE` mask may be changed within the `WHERE` construct. When an array appears in the `WHERE` statement mask, the logical test is executed first and the host system retains the result independent of whatever happens later inside the `WHERE` construct. Thus, in the program fragment

```
integer, parameter :: n = 5
real :: x (n) = (/ (k, k = 1, n) /)
  where (x > 0.0)
           x = -x
  end where
```

Table 8.9: F90 Array Operators with Logic Mask Control (*T* and *F* denote true and false, respectively). Optional arguments: b -- DIM & MASK, d -- DIM, m -- MASK, v-- VECTOR and DIM = 1 implies for any rows, DIM = 2 for any columns, and DIM = 3 for any plane.

Function	Description	Opt	Example
`all`	Find if all values are true for a fixed dimension.	d	`all (B = A, DIM = 1)` (true, false, false)
`any`	Find if any value is true for a fixed dimension.	d	`any (B > 2, DIM = 1)` (false, true, true)
`count`	Count number of true elements for a fixed dimension.	d	`count (A = B, DIM = 2)` (1, 2)
`maxloc`	Locate first element with maximum value given by mask.	m	`maxloc (A, A < 9)` (2, 3)
`maxval`	Max element for fixed dimension given by mask.	b	`maxval (B, DIM=1, B > 0)` (2, 4, 6)
`merge`	Pick true array A or false array B according to mask L.	–	`merge (A, B, L)` $\begin{bmatrix} 0 & 3 & 5 \\ 2 & 4 & 8 \end{bmatrix}$
`minloc`	Locate first element with minimum value given by mask.	m	`minloc (A, A > 3)` (2, 2)
`minval`	Min element for fixed dimension given by mask.	b	`minval (B, DIM = 2)` (1, 2)
`pack`	Pack array A into a vector under control of mask.	v	`pack (A, B < 4)` (0, 7, 3)
`product`	Product of all elements for fixed dimension; controlled by mask.	b	`product (B)` ; (720) `product (B, DIM = 1, T)` (2, 12, 30)
`sum`	Sum all elements for fixed dimension; controlled by mask.	b	`sum (B)` ;(21) `sum (B, DIM = 2, T)` (9, 12)
`unpack`	Replace the true locations in array B controlled by mask L with elements from the vector U.	–	`unpack (U, L, B)` $\begin{bmatrix} 7 & 3 & 8 \\ 2 & 4 & 9 \end{bmatrix}$

$A = \begin{bmatrix} 0 & 3 & 5 \\ 7 & 4 & 8 \end{bmatrix}, \quad B = \begin{bmatrix} 1 & 3 & 5 \\ 2 & 4 & 6 \end{bmatrix}, \quad L = \begin{bmatrix} T & F & T \\ F & F & T \end{bmatrix}, \quad U = (7, 8, 9)$

the sign is reversed for all elements of x because they all pass the initial logical mask. It is as if a classic DO sequence had been programmed

```
do i = 1, n, 1
    if (x(i) > 0.0) x(i) = -x(i)
end do
```

instead of the WHERE construct.

A more ominous and subtle issue surrounds the use of other transformational intrinsic functions listed in Table 8.10.

The danger is that when these intrinsics appear inside the body of a WHERE construct, the WHERE statement's initial mask may no longer apply. Hence, in the following example the transformational intrinsic function SUM operates over all five elements of X rather than just

Table 8.10: Intrinsic Functions Allowing Logical Mask Control

ALL	ANY	COUNT
CSHIFT	DOT_PRODUCT	EOSHIFT
MATMUL	MAXLOC	MAXVAL
MINLOC	MINVAL	PACK
PRODUCT	REPEAT	RESHAPE
SPREAD	SUM	TRANSFER
TRANSPOSE	TRIM	UNPACK

the two elements of X that exceed six:

```
integer, parameter :: n = 5
real :: x(n) = (/ 2, 4, 6, 8, 10 /)
  where (x > 6.0)
           x = x / sum(x)
  end where.
```

Thus, the new values for x are { 2, 4, 6, 8/30, 10/30 } rather than {2, 4, 6, 8/18, 10/18}. This standard-conforming, but otherwise "unexpected," result should raise a caution for the programmer. If one did not want the result illustrated above, it would be necessary to use the same mask of the WHERE as an optional argument to SUM: `sum(x, mask = x > 6.0)`. Much care needs to be taken to ensure that transformational intrinsics that appear in a WHERE construct use exactly the same mask.

8.1.5 User-Defined Operators

In addition to the many intrinsic operators and functions we have seen so far, the F90 user can also define new operators or extend existing ones. User-defined operators can employ intrinsic data types, user-defined data types, or both. The user-defined operators, or extensions, can be unary or binary (i.e., have one or two arguments). The operator symbol must be included between two periods such as '`.op.`'. As an example, consider a program to be used to create a shorthand notation to replace the standard F90 matrix transpose and matrix multiplication functions so that we could write

```
                B = .t. A
                C = B .x. D
or              C = (.t.A) .x. D

instead of      B = TRANSPOSE(A)
                C = MATMUL (B, D)
or              C = MATMUL(TRANSPOSE (A), D)
```

To do this, one must have a MODULE PROCEDURE to define the operator actions for all envisioned (and incorrect) inputs and an INTERFACE OPERATOR that informs F90 what your operation symbol is.

Figure 8.1 illustrates the code that would partially define the operator '`.t.`'. Note that, although TRANSPOSE accepts any type of matrix of any rank, our operator works only for real or integer rectangular arrays (of rank 2). It would not transpose LOGICAL arrays or vectors. That oversight can be extended by adding more functions to the interface.

```
MODULE Ops_Example   ! User defined matrix transpose example

IMPLICIT NONE
INTERFACE OPERATOR (.t.)                ! transpose operator
   MODULE PROCEDURE Trans_R, Trans_I ! for real or integer matrix
   ! Remember to add logicals and vectors later
END INTERFACE                           ! defining .t.

CONTAINS  ! the actual operator actions for argument types

FUNCTION  Trans_R ( A ) ! defines .t. for real rank 2 matrix
   REAL, DIMENSION (:,:), INTENT(IN)        :: A
   REAL, DIMENSION (SIZE(A,2), SIZE(A,1)) :: Trans_R
   Trans_R = TRANSPOSE (A)
END FUNCTION  Trans_R  ! for real rank 2 transpose via .t.

FUNCTION  Trans_I ( A ) ! defines .t. for integer rank 2 matrix
   INTEGER, DIMENSION (:,:), INTENT(IN)        :: A
   INTEGER, DIMENSION (SIZE(A,2), SIZE(A,1)) :: Trans_I
   Trans_I = TRANSPOSE (A)
END FUNCTION  Trans_I  ! for integer rank 2 transpose via .t.

END MODULE Ops_Example   ! User defined matrix transpose example

PROGRAM Demo_Trans       ! illustrate the .t. operator
  USE Ops_Example        ! module with user definitions
  IMPLICIT NONE
  INTEGER, PARAMETER   :: M = 3, N = 2  ! rows, columns
  REAL, DIMENSION (M,N) :: A ; REAL, DIMENSION (N,M) :: B

  ! define A, test operator, print results
  A = RESHAPE ( (/ ((I*J , I=1,M), J=1,N) /), SHAPE(A) )
  B = .t. A
  PRINT *, 'MATRIX A' ;  CALL M_print (A, M, N)
  PRINT *, 'MATRIX B' ;  CALL M_print (B, N, M)
  !                 Produces the result:
  !  MATRIX A
  !  RC      1         2
  !  1    1.000     2.000
  !  2    2.000     4.000
  !  3    3.000     6.000
  !
  !  MATRIX B
  !  RC      1         2         3
  !  1    1.000     2.000     3.000
  !  2    2.000     4.000     6.000
END PROGRAM Demo_Trans
```

Figure 8.1: Creating and applying user-defined operators.

If one works with matrices often, then it may be advisable to define a library of matrix operators. Such operators are not standard in F90 as they are in MATLAB but can be easily added. To provide a foundation for such a library, we provide a `Matrix_Operators` module with the operators defined in Table 8.11. The reader is encouraged to expand the initial support provided in that module.

Table 8.11: Definitions in Matrix Operators

Operator	Action	Use	Algebra
`.t.`	transpose	`.t.A`	A^T
`.x.`	multiplication	`A.x.B`	AB
`.i.`	inverse of matrix	`.i.A`	A^{-1}
`.ix.`	solution	`A.ix.B`	$A^{-1}B$
`.tx.`	transpose times matrix	`A.tx.B`	$A^T B$
`.xt.`	matrix times transpose	`A.xt.B`	AB^T
`.eye.`	identity matrix	`.eye.N`	I, $N \times N$

8.1.6 Connectivity Lists and Vector Subscripts

When using an array with constant increments in its subscripts, we usually provide its subscript in the form of a colon operator or a control variable in a DO or FOR loop. In either case, the array subscripts are integers. There are several practical programming applications for which the required subscripts are not known in advance. Typically, this occurs when we are dealing with an assemblage of components that can be connected in an arbitrary fashion by the user (e.g., electric circuits, truss structures, volume elements in a solid model). To get the subscripts necessary to build the assemblage we must read an integer data file that lists the junction numbers to which each component is attached. We call those data a *connectivity file*. If we assume each component has the same number of junction points, then the list can be inputted as a two-dimensional array. One subscript will range over the number of components, and the other will range over the number of possible junctions per component. For ease of typing these data, we usually assume that the kth row of the array contains the integer junction or connection points of that component. Such a row of connectivity data is often used in two related operations: `gather` and `scatter`. A `gather` operation uses the lists of connections to gather or collect information from the assembly necessary to describe the component or its action. The `scatter` operation has the reverse effect. It takes information about the component and sends it back to the assembly. Usually, values from the component are added into corresponding junction points of the assembly.

The main point of this discussion is that another way to define a nonsequential set of subscripts is to use an integer vector array that contains the set. Then one can use the array name as a way to range over the subscripts. This is a compact way to avoid an additional FOR or DO loop. The connectivity list for a component is often employed to select the subscripts needed for that component.

To illustrate the concept of vector subscripts, we will repeat the array flip example shown in Section 8.1.3 via the colon operators. Here we will define an integer vector called `Reverse` that has constant increments to be used in operating on the original array A. By using the vector name as a subscript, it automatically invokes an implied loop over the contents of that vector. As shown in Figure 8.2, this has the same effect as employing the colon operator directly.

The real power of the vector subscripts comes in the case in which it has integers in a random, or user input, order rather than in an order that has a uniform increment. For example, if we repeat the preceding example using a vector `Random=[3 1 2]`, then both MATLAB and F90 would give the result

$$\texttt{E = A (:, Random)} = \begin{bmatrix} 3 & 1 & 2 \\ 6 & 4 & 5 \\ 9 & 7 & 8 \end{bmatrix}.$$

$$A = \begin{bmatrix} 1 & 2 & 3 \\ 4 & 5 & 6 \\ 7 & 8 & 9 \end{bmatrix}, \quad \text{Reverse} = [3 \quad 2 \quad 1]$$

Flip left to right:

`B=A (: , Reverse)` $= \begin{bmatrix} 3 & 2 & 1 \\ 6 & 5 & 4 \\ 9 & 8 & 7 \end{bmatrix}$

Flip up to down:

`C = A (Reverse, :)` $= \begin{bmatrix} 7 & 8 & 9 \\ 4 & 5 & 6 \\ 1 & 2 & 3 \end{bmatrix}$

Flip up to down, left to right:

`D = A (Reverse,Reverse)` $= \begin{bmatrix} 9 & 8 & 7 \\ 6 & 5 & 4 \\ 3 & 2 & 1 \end{bmatrix}$

Figure 8.2: F90 and MATLAB vector subscripts and array shifts.

Although the `reshape` option of F90 and MATLAB allows the array elements to change from one rectangular storage mode to another, one can also move elements around in the fixed-shape array by utilizing the colon operators or by the use of "shift operators." The latter accept an integer to specify how many locations to move or shift an element. A positive number moves an element up a column, a negative value moves it down the column, and a zero leaves it unchanged. The elements that are moved out of the array either move from the head of the queue to the tail of the queue (called a "circular shift") or are replaced by a user-specified "pad" value (called an "end off shift"). If no pad is given, its value defaults to zero. These concepts are illustrated for F90 in Figures 8.3 and 8.4.

8.1.7 Component Gather and Scatter

Often the equations governing a system balance principle are assembled from the relative contributions of each component. When the answers for a complete system have been obtained, it is then possible to recover the response of each component. The automation of these processes has six basic requirements:

1. a component balance principle written in matrix form,
2. a joint connectivity data list that defines where a given component type connects into the system,

```
five  =  (/  1  2  3  4  5  /)
! without a pad
three =  eoshift(five,2) ! = (/  3  4  5  0  0  /)
three =  eoshift(five,-2) ! = (/  0  0  1  2  3  /)
! with a pad
pad = eoshift(five,2,9) ! = (/  3  4  5  9  9  /)
pad = eoshift(five,-2,9) ! = (/  9  9  1  2  3  /)
```

Figure 8.3: F90 end-off shift (`eoshift`) intrinsic.

```
five = (/  1  2  3  4  5  /)
left_3 = cshift(five,3) ! = (/  3  4  5  1  2  /)
right_3 = cshift(five,-3) ! = (/  4  5  1  2  3  /)
```

Figure 8.4: F90 circular shift (`cshift`) intrinsic.

3. a definition of a `scatter` operator that scatters the coefficients of the component matrices into corresponding locations in the governing system equations,
4. an efficient system equation solver,
5. a `gather` operator to gather the answers from the system for those joints connected to a component, and
6. a recovery of the internal results in the component.

The first of these is discipline dependent. We are primarily interested in the gather–scatter operations. These are opposites that both depend on the component connectivity list, which is often utilized as a vector subscript. The number of rows in the component equations is less than the number of rows in the assembled system except for the special case in which the system has only a single component. Thus, it is the purpose of the gather–scatter operators to define the relation between a system row number and a particular component row number. That is, they describe the relation that defines the subset of component unknowns, say $\mathbf{V}^e$ for component e, in terms of all the system unknowns, say $\mathbf{V}$: $\mathbf{V}^e \subset_e \mathbf{V}$. Here the containment $\subset$ is defined by the component's connection list and the number of unknowns per joint. If there is only one unknown per joint, then the subset involves only the connection list. The preceding process gathers the subset of component unknowns from the full set of system unknowns.

Let the list of joints or nodes connected to the component be called $\mathbf{L}^e$. The kth member in this list contains the corresponding system node number, K: that is `K = L_e(k)`. Thus, for a single unknown per joint, one simply has $\mathbf{V}^e = \mathbf{V}(\mathbf{L}^e) \subset_e \mathbf{V}$. Written in full loop form, the component gather operation would be

```
DO  k = 1,  size(L_e)
  V_e (k) = V(L_e (k))
END DO  !  OVER LOCAL JOINTS,
```

whereas in F90 or MATLAB vector subscript form, it is simply `V_e = V(L_e)` for a single unknown per joint. When there is more than one unknown per joint, the relation can be written in two ways.

We pick the one that counts (assigns equation numbers to) all unknowns at a joint before going on to the next joint. Let the number of unknowns per joint be N. Then by deduction, one finds that the equation number for the jth unknown at the Kth system node is

$$E(K, j) = N * (K - 1) + j, \qquad 1 \leq j \leq N.$$

But to find which equation numbers go with a particular component, we must use the connection list `L_e`. For the kth local node, `K = L_e (k)` and

$$E(k, j) = N * (L\_e(k) - 1) + j\ , \qquad 1 \leq j \leq N.$$

If we loop over all nodes on a component, we can build an index list, say I_e, that tells which equations relate to the component.

```
INTEGER, ALLOCATABLE :: I_e(:), V_e(:)
ALLOCATE(I_e(N * SIZE (L_e)), V_e (N*SIZE(L_e)))
DO  k = 1, SIZE(L_e) ! component nodes
  DO  j = 1, N  !  unknowns per node
    LOCAL  = N *(k-1) + j
    SYSTEM = N *(L_e (k) - 1) + j
    I_e (LOCAL) = SYSTEM
  END DO  !  on unknowns
END DO  !  on local nodes.
```

Therefore, the generalization of the component gather process is

```
DO  m = 1, SIZE(I_e)
  V_e (m) = V(I_e (m))
END DO  !  over local unknowns,
```

or in vector subscript form V_e = V(I_e) for an arbitrary number of unknowns per joint.

To illustrate the scatter concept, consider a system shown in Figure 8.5, which has six components and five nodes. If there is only one unknown at each joint (like voltage or axial displacement), then the system equations will have five rows. Since each component is connected to two nodes, each will contribute to (scatter to) two of the system equation rows. Which two rows? That is determined by the connection list shown in the figure. For example, component (4) is joined to nodes 4 and 3. Thus, the coefficients in the first row of the local component balance low would scatter into (be added to) the fourth row of the system, and the second row of the component would scatter to the third system equation row. If the component balance law is symmetric, then the column locations scatter in the same fashion.

8.2 Matrices

Matrices are very commonly used in many areas of applied mathematics and engineering. Although they can be considered a special case of the subscripted arrays given above, they have their own special algebra and calculus notations that are useful to know. In the following

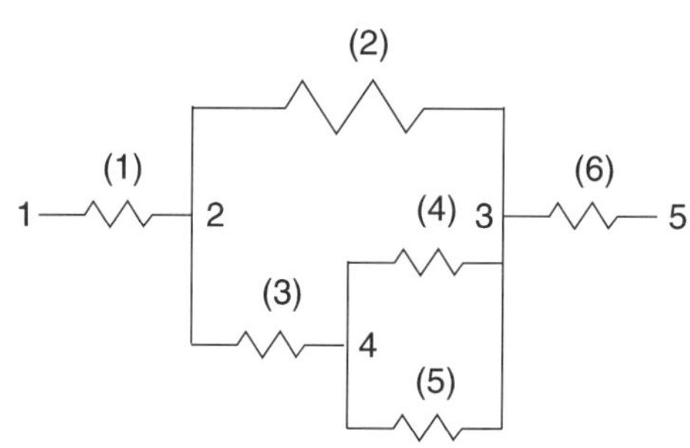

Component	Nodes	Property
(1)	1, 2	1
(2)	2, 3	2
(3)	2, 4	1
(4)	4, 3	3
(5)	4, 3	4
(6)	3, 5	1

Figure 8.5: Representative circuit or axial spring system.

sections we will describe matrices and the intrinsic operations on them that are included in F90 and MATLAB. Neither C nor C++ has such useful intrinsics but requires the programmer to develop them or extract them from a special library.

A *matrix* is a rectangular array of quantities arranged in rows and columns. The array is enclosed in brackets, and thus if there are m rows and n columns, the matrix can be represented by

$$\mathbf{A} = \begin{bmatrix} a_{11} & a_{12} & a_{13} & \cdots & a_{1j} & \cdots & a_{1n} \\ a_{21} & a_{22} & a_{23} & \cdots & a_{2j} & \cdots & a_{2n} \\ \vdots & & & & & & \vdots \\ a_{i1} & a_{i2} & a_{i3} & \cdots & a_{ij} & \cdots & a_{in} \\ \vdots & & & & & & \vdots \\ a_{m1} & a_{m2} & a_{m3} & \cdots & a_{mj} & \cdots & a_{mn} \end{bmatrix} = [\mathbf{A}], \tag{8.1}$$

where the typical element a_{ij} has two subscripts, of which the first denotes the row (ith) and the second denotes the column (jth) the element occupies in the matrix. A matrix with m rows and n columns is defined as a matrix of order $m \times n$, or simply an $m \times n$ matrix. The number of rows is always specified first. In Equation 8.1, the symbol **A** stands for the matrix of m rows and n columns, and it is usually printed in boldface type. If $m = n = 1$, the matrix is equivalent to a scalar. If $m = 1$, the matrix **A** reduces to the single row

$$\mathbf{A} = [a_{11} \quad a_{12} \quad a_{13} \quad \cdots \quad a_{1j} \quad \cdots \quad a_{1n}] = (\mathbf{A}),$$

which is called a *row matrix*. Similarly, if $n = 1$, the matrix **A** reduces to the single column

$$\mathbf{A} = \begin{bmatrix} a_{11} \\ a_{21} \\ \vdots \\ a_{m1} \end{bmatrix} = \text{col}[\, a_{11} \; a_{21} \; \cdots \; a_{m1} \,] = \{\mathbf{A}\},$$

which is called a *column matrix* or vector. When all the elements of matrix are equal to zero, the matrix is called *null* or *zero* and is indicated by **0**. A null matrix serves the same function as zero does in ordinary algebra. To set all the elements of **A** to zero, one writes $A = 0$ in F90 and $A = \text{zeros}\,[m,\ n]$ in MATLAB.

If $m = n$, the matrix is said to be *square*.

$$\mathbf{A} = \begin{bmatrix} a_{11} & a_{12} & \cdots & a_{1n} \\ \vdots & & & \vdots \\ a_{n1} & a_{n2} & \cdots & a_{nn} \end{bmatrix}$$

Before considering some of the matrix algebra implied by the equation above, a few other matrix types need definition. A *diagonal matrix* is a square matrix that has zero elements outside the principal diagonal. It follows, therefore, that for a diagonal matrix $a_{ij} = 0$ when $i \neq j$, and not all a_{ii} are zero. A typical diagonal matrix may be represented by

$$\mathbf{A} = \begin{bmatrix} a_{11} & 0 & \cdots & 0 \\ 0 & a_{22} & \cdots & 0 \\ \vdots & & & \vdots \\ 0 & 0 & \cdots & a_{nn} \end{bmatrix},$$

or more concisely as $\mathbf{A} = \text{diag}[a_{11}a_{22}\cdots a_{nn}]$.

A *unit* or *identity* matrix is a diagonal matrix whose elements are equal to 0 except those located on its main diagonal, which are equal to 1. That is, $a_{ij} = 1$ if $i = j$, and $a_{ij} = 0$ if $i \neq j$. The unit matrix will be given the symbol **I** throughout these notes. An example of a 3×3 unit matrix is

$$\mathbf{I} = \begin{bmatrix} 1 & 0 & 0 \\ 0 & 1 & 0 \\ 0 & 0 & 1 \end{bmatrix} = \text{diag}[1\ 1\ 1]\,.$$

A *Toeplitz* matrix has constant-valued diagonals. An identity matrix is a Toeplitz one, as is the following matrix:

$$\mathbf{A} = \begin{bmatrix} 1 & -2 & 3 & 5 \\ 4 & 1 & -2 & 3 \\ -1 & 4 & 1 & -2 \\ 10 & -1 & 4 & 1 \end{bmatrix}.$$

Note how the values of a Toeplitz matrix's elements are determined by the first row and the first column. MATLAB uses the Toeplitz function to create this unusual matrix.

A *symmetric matrix* is a square matrix whose elements $a_{ij} = a_{ji}$ for all i, j. For example,

$$\mathbf{A} = \begin{bmatrix} 12 & 2 & -1 \\ 2 & 33 & 0 \\ -1 & 0 & 15 \end{bmatrix}$$

is symmetric: The first row equals the first column, the second row the second column, and so forth.

An *antisymmetric* or *skew symmetric* matrix is a square matrix whose elements $a_{ij} = -a_{ji}$ for all i, j. Note that this condition means that the diagonal values of an antisymmetric matrix must equal zero. An example of such a matrix is

$$\mathbf{A} = \begin{bmatrix} 0 & 2 & -1 \\ -2 & 0 & 10 \\ 1 & -10 & 0 \end{bmatrix}.$$

The *transpose* of a matrix **A**, denoted by $\mathbf{A}^{\mathrm{T}}$, is obtained by interchanging the rows and columns. Thus, the transpose of an $m \times n$ matrix is an $n \times m$ matrix. For example,

$$\mathbf{A} = \begin{bmatrix} 2 & 1 \\ 3 & 5 \\ 0 & 1 \end{bmatrix} \qquad \mathbf{A}^{\mathrm{T}} = \begin{bmatrix} 2 & 3 & 0 \\ 1 & 5 & 1 \end{bmatrix}.$$

In MATLAB an appended prime is used to denote the transpose of any matrix, such as $\mathbf{B} = \mathbf{A}'$, whereas in F90 we employ the intrinsic function $\mathbf{B} = \text{transpose}\,(\mathbf{A})$ or a user-defined operator like **B** = `.t.`**A**, which we defined earlier.

If all the elements on one side of the diagonal of a square matrix are zero, the matrix is called a *triangular* matrix. There are two types of triangular matrices: (1) an upper triangular **U**, whose elements below the diagonal are all zero, and (2) a lower triangular **L**, whose elements above the diagonal are all zero. An example of a lower triangular matrix is

$$\mathbf{L} = \begin{bmatrix} 10 & 0 & 0 \\ 1 & 3 & 0 \\ 5 & 1 & 2 \end{bmatrix}.$$

A matrix may be divided into smaller arrays by horizontal and vertical lines. Such a matrix is then referred to as a *partitioned matrix*, and the smaller arrays are called *submatrices*. For example, we can partition a 3 × 3 matrix into four submatrices

$$\mathbf{A} = \left[\begin{array}{cc|c} a_{11} & a_{12} & a_{13} \\ a_{21} & a_{22} & a_{23} \\ \hline a_{31} & a_{32} & a_{33} \end{array}\right] = \begin{bmatrix} \mathbf{A}_{11} & \mathbf{A}_{12} \\ \mathbf{A}_{21} & \mathbf{A}_{22} \end{bmatrix} = \left[\begin{array}{cc|c} 2 & 1 & 3 \\ 10 & 5 & 0 \\ \hline 4 & 6 & 10 \end{array}\right],$$

where, in the F90 and MATLAB colon notation,

$$\mathbf{A}_{11} = \begin{bmatrix} a_{11} & a_{12} \\ a_{21} & a_{22} \end{bmatrix} = \begin{bmatrix} 2 & 1 \\ 10 & 5 \end{bmatrix} = \mathbf{A}(1:2,\quad 1:2)$$

$$\mathbf{A}_{12} = \begin{bmatrix} a_{13} \\ a_{23} \end{bmatrix} = \begin{bmatrix} 3 \\ 0 \end{bmatrix} = \mathbf{A}(1:2,\ 3)$$

$$\mathbf{A}_{21} = \begin{bmatrix} a_{31} & a_{32} \end{bmatrix} = \begin{bmatrix} 4 & 6 \end{bmatrix} = \mathbf{A}(3,\ 1:2)$$

$$\mathbf{A}_{22} = [a_{33}] = [10] = \mathbf{A}(3,\ 3).$$

Note that the elements of a partitioned matrix must be so ordered that they are compatible with the whole matrix **A** and with each other. That is, $\mathbf{A}_{11}$ and $\mathbf{A}_{12}$ must have an equal number of rows. Likewise, $\mathbf{A}_{21}$ and $\mathbf{A}_{22}$ must have an equal number of rows. Matrices $\mathbf{A}_{11}$ and $\mathbf{A}_{21}$ must have an equal number of columns; likewise for $\mathbf{A}_{12}$ and $\mathbf{A}_{22}$. Note that $\mathbf{A}_{22}$ is a matrix even though it consists of only one element. Provided the general rules for matrix algebra are observed, the submatrices can be treated as if they were ordinary matrix elements.

8.2.1 Matrix Algebra

To define what addition and multiplication means for matrices, we need to define an *algebra* for arrays of numbers so that they become useful to us. Without an algebra, all we have is a sequence of definitions without the ability to manipulate what they mean!

Addition of two matrices of the same order is accomplished by adding corresponding elements of each matrix. The matrix addition $\mathbf{C} = \mathbf{A} + \mathbf{B}$ (as we write it in F90 and MATLAB), where **A**, **B**, and **C** are matrices of the *same* order $m \times n$, can be indicated by the equation

$$c_{ij} = a_{ij} + b_{ij}, \quad 1 \le i \le m, \quad 1 \le j \le n,$$

where c_{ij}, a_{ij}, and b_{ij} are typical elements of the **C**, **A**, and **B** matrices, respectively. An example of matrix addition is

$$\begin{bmatrix} 3 & 0 & 1 \\ 2 & -1 & 2 \\ 1 & 1 & 1 \end{bmatrix} + \begin{bmatrix} -1 & 1 & -1 \\ 2 & 5 & 6 \\ -3 & 4 & 9 \end{bmatrix} = \begin{bmatrix} 2 & 1 & 0 \\ 4 & -4 & 8 \\ -2 & 5 & 10 \end{bmatrix}.$$

Matrix subtraction, $\mathbf{C} = \mathbf{A} - \mathbf{B}$, is performed in a similar manner.

Matrix addition and subtraction are *associative* and *commutative*. That is, with the previous definitions for matrix addition and subtraction, grouping and ordering with respect to these operations does not affect the result, that is,

$$\mathbf{A} \pm (\mathbf{B} \pm \mathbf{C}) = (\mathbf{A} \pm \mathbf{B}) \pm \mathbf{C} \qquad \text{and} \qquad \mathbf{C} \pm \mathbf{B} \pm \mathbf{A}.$$

Multiplication of the matrix **A** by a scalar c is defined as the multiplication of every element of the matrix by the scalar c. Thus, the elements of the product $\mathbf{B} = c\mathbf{A}$ are given by $b_{ij} = ca_{ij}$ and are written as $\mathbf{B} = C * \mathbf{A}$ in both F90 and MATLAB. Clearly, scalar multiplication distributes over matrix addition.

We could define special multiplication in the somewhat boring way as the term-by-term product of two identical-sized matrices: $\mathbf{C} = \mathbf{AB} \Longrightarrow c_{ij} = a_{ij}b_{ij}$. This feature is allowed in both F90 and MATLAB, where it is written as **C** = **A*****B** and **C** = **A**.***B**, respectively. Although this definition might be useful in some applications, this choice for what multiplication means in our algebra does not give us much power. Instead, we define the matrix product $\mathbf{C} = \mathbf{AB}$ to mean

$$c_{ij} = \sum_{k=1}^{p} a_{ik}b_{kj}, \quad 1 \le i \le m, 1 \le j \le n.$$

Matrices **A** and **B** can be multiplied together only when the number of columns in **A**, p, equals the number of rows in **B**. When this condition is fulfilled, the matrices **A** and **B** are said to be *conformable* for multiplication. Otherwise, matrix multiplication of two matrices cannot be defined. The product of two conformable matrices **A** and **B** having orders $m \times p$ and $p \times n$, respectively, yields an $m \times n$ matrix **C**. In MATLAB this is simply written as **C** = **A*****B**, where, as in F90, one would use the intrinsic function **C** = matmul (**A**, **B**) or a user-defined operator such as **C** = **A**.x.**B**, which we defined earlier.

This definition for matrix multiplication was chosen so that we can concisely represent a system of linear equations. The verbose form explicitly lists the equations as follows:

$$\begin{aligned}
a_{11}x_1 + a_{12}x_2 + a_{13}x_3 + \cdots + a_{1n}x_n &= c_1 \\
a_{21}x_1 + a_{22}x_2 + a_{23}x_3 + \cdots + a_{2n}x_n &= c_2 \\
a_{31}x_1 + a_{32}x_2 + a_{33}x_3 + \cdots + a_{3n}x_n &= c_3 \\
\vdots \qquad\qquad & \quad \vdots \\
a_{n1}x_1 + a_{n2}x_2 + a_{n3}x_3 + \cdots + a_{nn}x_n &= c_n,
\end{aligned}$$

where the a_{ij}'s and c_i's usually represent known coefficients and the x_i's unknowns. To express these equations more precisely, we define matrices for each of these arrays of numbers and lay them out as a matrix–vector product equaling a vector as follows:

$$\begin{bmatrix} a_{11} & a_{12} & a_{13} & \cdots & a_{1n} \\ a_{21} & a_{22} & a_{23} & \cdots & a_{2n} \\ a_{31} & a_{32} & a_{33} & \cdots & a_{3n} \\ & & \vdots & & \\ a_{n1} & a_{n2} & a_{n3} & \cdots & a_{nn} \end{bmatrix} \begin{bmatrix} x_1 \\ x_2 \\ x_3 \\ \vdots \\ x_n \end{bmatrix} = \begin{bmatrix} c_1 \\ c_2 \\ c_3 \\ \vdots \\ c_n \end{bmatrix}.$$

We thus obtain the more compact matrix form $\mathbf{AX} = \mathbf{C}$. **A** represents the square matrix of coefficients, **X** the vector (column matrix) of unknowns, and **C** the vector of known quantities.

Matrix multiplication is associative and distributive. For example,

$$\begin{aligned}
(\mathbf{AB})\mathbf{C} &= \mathbf{A}(\mathbf{BC}) \\
\mathbf{A}(\mathbf{B} + \mathbf{C}) &= \mathbf{AB} + \mathbf{AC}.
\end{aligned}$$

However, matrix multiplication is not commutative. In general, $\mathbf{AB} \neq \mathbf{BA}$. Consequently, the order in which matrix multiplication is specified is by no means arbitrary. Clearly, if the two matrices are not conformable, attempting to commute the product makes no sense (the matrix multiplication $\mathbf{BA}$ is not defined). In addition, when the matrices are conformable so that either product makes sense (the matrices are both square and have the same dimensions, for example), the product cannot be guaranteed to commute. You should try finding a simple example that illustrates this point. When two matrices $\mathbf{A}$ and $\mathbf{B}$ are multiplied, the product $\mathbf{AB}$ is referred to either as $\mathbf{B}$ *premultiplied* by $\mathbf{A}$ or as $\mathbf{A}$ *postmultiplied* by $\mathbf{B}$. When $\mathbf{AB} = \mathbf{BA}$, the matrices $\mathbf{A}$ and $\mathbf{B}$ are then said to be *commutable*. For example, the unit matrix $\mathbf{I}$ commutes with any square matrix of the same order: $\mathbf{AI} = \mathbf{IA} = \mathbf{A}$.*

The process of matrix multiplication can also be extended to partitioned matrices, provided the individual products of submatrices are conformable for multiplication. For example, the multiplication

$$\mathbf{AB} = \begin{bmatrix} \mathbf{A}_{11} & \mathbf{A}_{12} \\ \mathbf{A}_{21} & \mathbf{A}_{22} \end{bmatrix} \begin{bmatrix} \mathbf{B}_{11} & \mathbf{B}_{12} \\ \mathbf{B}_{21} & \mathbf{B}_{22} \end{bmatrix} = \begin{bmatrix} \mathbf{A}_{11}\mathbf{B}_{11} + \mathbf{A}_{12}\mathbf{B}_{21} & \mathbf{A}_{11}\mathbf{B}_{12} + \mathbf{A}_{12}\mathbf{B}_{22} \\ \mathbf{A}_{21}\mathbf{B}_{11} + \mathbf{A}_{22}\mathbf{B}_{21} & \mathbf{A}_{21}\mathbf{B}_{12} + \mathbf{A}_{22}\mathbf{B}_{22} \end{bmatrix}$$

is possible provided the products $\mathbf{A}_{11}\mathbf{B}_{11}$, $\mathbf{A}_{12}\mathbf{B}_{21}$, and so forth are conformable. For this condition to be fulfilled, it is only necessary for the vertical partitions in $\mathbf{A}$ to include a number of columns equal to the number of rows in the corresponding horizontal partitions in $\mathbf{B}$.

The transpose of a product of matrices equals $(\mathbf{AB} \cdots \mathbf{YZ})^{\mathrm{T}} = \mathbf{Z}^{\mathrm{T}}\mathbf{Y}^{\mathrm{T}} \cdots \mathbf{B}^{\mathrm{T}}\mathbf{A}^{\mathrm{T}}$. As an example of matrix multiplication, let $\mathbf{B} = \left[\begin{smallmatrix} 3 \\ 1 \\ 2 \end{smallmatrix}\right]$ and $\mathbf{A} = \left[\begin{smallmatrix} 2 & 1 & 0 \\ 1 & 0 & 1 \end{smallmatrix}\right]$; then

$$\mathbf{AB} = \begin{bmatrix} 2 & 1 & 0 \\ 1 & 0 & 1 \end{bmatrix} \begin{bmatrix} 3 \\ 1 \\ 2 \end{bmatrix} = \begin{bmatrix} 7 \\ 6 \end{bmatrix}$$

$$\mathbf{B}^{\mathrm{T}}\mathbf{A}^{\mathrm{T}} = \begin{bmatrix} 3 & 1 & 2 \end{bmatrix} \begin{bmatrix} 2 & 1 \\ 1 & 0 \\ 0 & 1 \end{bmatrix} = \begin{bmatrix} 7 & 6 \end{bmatrix}.$$

8.2.2 Inversion

Every (nonsingular) square matrix $\mathbf{A}$ has an *inverse*, indicated by $\mathbf{A}^{-1}$, such that by definition the product $\mathbf{AA}^{-1}$ is a unit matrix $\mathbf{I}$. The reverse is also true: $\mathbf{A}^{-1}\mathbf{A} = \mathbf{I}$. Inverse matrices are very useful in the solution of simultaneous equations $\mathbf{AX} = \mathbf{C}$ such as the one above, where $\mathbf{A}$ and $\mathbf{C}$ are known and $\mathbf{X}$ is unknown. If the inverse of $\mathbf{A}$ is known, the unknowns of the $\mathbf{X}$ matrix can be (symbolically) found by premultiplying both sides of the equation by the inverse $\mathbf{A}^{-1}\mathbf{AX} = \mathbf{A}^{-1}\mathbf{C}$ so that

$$\mathbf{X} = \mathbf{A}^{-1}\mathbf{C}.$$

In this way, in theory we have "solved" our system of linear equations. To employ this approach, we must find the inverse of the matrix $\mathbf{A}$, which is not any easy task. Despite this computational difficulty, using matrix algebra to express complicated linear combinations of quantities concisely often provides much insight into a problem and its solution techniques.

* This result is why **I** is called the identity matrix: It is the identity element with respect to matrix multiplication.

Various methods can be used to determine the inverse of a given matrix. For very large systems of equations it is probably more practical to avoid the calculation of the inverse and solve the equations by a procedure called *factorization*. Various procedures for computing an inverse matrix can be found in texts on numerical analysis. The inverse of 2×2 or 3×3 matrices can easily be written in closed form by using *Cramer's rule*. For a 2×2 matrix, we have the classic formula, which no engineering student should forget:

$$\begin{bmatrix} a & b \\ c & d \end{bmatrix}^{-1} = \frac{\begin{bmatrix} d & -b \\ -c & a \end{bmatrix}}{ad - bc}$$

However, finding the inverse of larger arrays using Cramer's rule is very inefficient computationally. In MATLAB, an inverse matrix of A is computed as `inv(A)`, but this is only practical for matrices of a small size, say those less than 100. There is no intrinsic matrix inversion function in F90, but we provide such a function, named `inv`, in our operator library.

8.2.3 Factorizations

We have indicated that we will frequently employ matrices to solve linear equation systems like $A * x = b$, where **A** is a known square matrix, **B** is a known vector, and **X** is an unknown vector. Although in theory the solution is simply the inverse of **A** times the vector **B**, $x = \mathbf{A}^{(-1)} * b$, that is computationally the least efficient way to find the vector **X**. In practice, one usually uses some form of factorization of the matrix **A**. A very common method is to define **A** to be the product of two triangular matrices, defined above, say $L * U = A$, where **L** is a square lower triangular matrix and **U** is a square upper triangular matrix. Skipping the details of this "**LU**-factorization," we could rewrite the original matrix system as $L * U * x = b$, which can be viewed as two matrix identities

$$\begin{aligned} L * h &= b \\ U * x &= h, \end{aligned}$$

where h is a new temporary vector, and where both **L** and **U** are much cheaper to compute than the inverse of **A**. We do not need the inverse of **L** or **U** since, as triangular matrices, their first or last row contains only one nonzero term. That allows us to find one term in the unknown vector from one scalar equation. The process of recovering the vectors from these two identities is called substitution.

We illustrate this process with a representative set of four equations with **A** and b given as

$$\mathbf{A} = \begin{bmatrix} 1800 & 600 & -360 & 900 \\ 0 & 4500 & -2700 & 2250 \\ 0 & -2700 & 2700 & -1890 \\ 6300 & 5250 & -1890 & 3795 \end{bmatrix}$$

$$\mathbf{b}^T = [\,6300 \quad -2250 \quad 1890 \quad 21405\,].$$

The **LU**-factorization process mentioned above gives the first of two lower triangular systems; $L * h = b$:

$$\begin{bmatrix} 60 & 0 & 0 & 0 \\ 0 & 150 & 0 & 0 \\ 0 & -90 & 36 & 0 \\ 210 & 105 & 42 & -10 \end{bmatrix} \begin{Bmatrix} h_1 \\ h_2 \\ h_3 \\ h_4 \end{Bmatrix} = \begin{Bmatrix} 6300 \\ -2250 \\ 1890 \\ 21405 \end{Bmatrix}.$$

Observe that the significant difference from $A * x = b$ is that the first row of this identity has one equation and one unknown:

$$60 * h_1 = 6300,$$

which yields $h_1 = 105$. This process continues through all the rows, solving for one unknown, h_k in row k, because all the h values above are known. For example, the next row gives $0 * 105 + 150 * h_2 = -2250$, which yields $h_2 = -15$. This process is known as "forward substitution." When completed, the substitution yields the intermediate answer:

$$h^T = [\,105 \quad -15 \quad 15 \quad -30\,].$$

Now that h is known we can write the upper triangular identity, $U * x = h$, as

$$\begin{bmatrix} 30 & 10 & -6 & 15 \\ 0 & 30 & -18 & 15 \\ 0 & 0 & 30 & -15 \\ 0 & 0 & 0 & 30 \end{bmatrix} \begin{Bmatrix} x_1 \\ x_2 \\ x_3 \\ x_4 \end{Bmatrix} = \begin{Bmatrix} 105 \\ -15 \\ 15 \\ -30 \end{Bmatrix}.$$

This time the bottom row has only one unknown, $30 * x_4 = -30$, and so the last unknown is $x_4 = -1$. Working backward up to the next row again, we find there is only one unknown:

$$30 * x_3 + -15 * (-1) = 15$$

so that $x_3 = 0$. Proceeding back up through the remaining rows to get all the unknowns is called "back substitution." It yields

$$x^T = [\,4 \quad 0 \quad 0 \quad -1\,].$$

By inspection you can verify that this satisfies the original system of linear equations, $A * x = b$. With a little more work one can employ matrix multiplication to verify that $L * U = A$. Although we have not given the simple algorithm for computing **L** and **U** from **A**, it is widely known as the "**LU** Factorization" and is in many texts on numerical analysis. Other common factorizations are the "QR factorization," the "Cholesky factorization" for a symmetric positive definite **A**, and the "SVD factorization" for the case in which **A** is rectangular or ill-conditioned and one is seeking a best approximation to **X**.

The factorization process is relatively expensive to compute but is much less expensive that an inversion. The forward and backward substitutions are very fast and cheap. In problems where you have many different b vectors (and corresponding x vectors, such as time-dependent problems), one carries out the expensive factorization process only once and then executes the cheap forward and back substitution for each b vector supplied.

8.2.4 Determinant of a Matrix

Every square matrix, say $\mathbf{A}$, has a single scalar quantity associated with it. That scalar is called the determinant $|\mathbf{A}|$ of the matrix. The determinant is important in solving equations and inverting matrices. A very important result is that the inverse $\mathbf{A}^{-1}$ exists if and only if $|\mathbf{A}| \neq 0$. If the determinant is zero, the matrix $\mathbf{A}$ (and the equivalent set of equations) is said to be *singular*. Simple conditions on a matrix's structure can be used to infer the determinant or its properties.

- If two rows or columns are equal, the determinant is zero.
- Interchanging two rows, or two columns, changes the sign of the determinant.
- The determinant is unchanged if any row, or column, is modified by adding to it a linear combination of any of the other rows, or columns.
- A singular square matrix may have nonsingular square partitions.

The last two items will become significant when we consider how to apply boundary conditions and how to solve a system of equations.

8.2.5 Matrix Calculus

At times you might find it necessary to differentiate or integrate matrices. These operations are simply carried out on each and every element of the matrix. Let the elements a_{ij} of $\mathbf{A}$ be a function of a parameter t. Then, the derivative and integral of a matrix simply equal term-by-term differentiation and integration, respectively as follows:

$$\mathbf{B} = \frac{d\mathbf{A}}{dt} \longleftrightarrow b_{ij} = \frac{da_{ij}}{dt}, \quad 1 \leq i \leq m, 1 \leq j \leq n$$

$$\mathbf{C} = \int \mathbf{A}\,dt \longleftrightarrow c_{ij} = \int a_{ij}\,dt, \quad 1 \leq i \leq m, 1 \leq j \leq n.$$

When dealing with functional relations, the concept of rate of change is often very important. If we have a function $f(\cdot)$ of a single independent variable, say x, then we call the rate of change the derivative with respect to x, which is written as df/dx. Generalizing this notion to functions of more than two variables, say $z = f(x, y)$, we may define two distinct rates of change. One is the function's rate of change with respect to one variable with the other held constant. We thus define *partial derivatives*. When x is allowed to vary, the derivative is called the *partial derivative with respect to* x and is denoted by $\partial f/\partial x$. By analogy with the usual definition of derivative, this partial derivative is mathematically defined as

$$f_x = \frac{\partial f}{\partial x} = \lim_{\Delta x \to 0} \frac{f(x + \Delta x, y) - f(x, y)}{\Delta x}.$$

A similar definition describes the partial derivative with respect to y denoted by $\partial f/\partial y$. The second notion of rate of change is the *total* derivative, which is expressed as df:

$$df = \frac{\partial f}{\partial x}dx + \frac{\partial f}{\partial y}dy.$$

These definitions can be extended to include a function of any number of independent variables.

Often one encounters a scalar u defined by a symmetric square $n \times n$ matrix, $\mathbf{A}$, a column vector $\mathbf{B}$, and a column vector $\mathbf{X}$ of n parameters. The combination we have in mind has the form

$$u = \frac{1}{2}\mathbf{X}^{\mathrm{T}}\mathbf{A}\mathbf{X} + \mathbf{X}^{\mathrm{T}}\mathbf{B} + \mathbf{C}. \tag{8.2}$$

If we calculate the derivative of the scalar u with respect to each x_i, the result is the column vector

$$\frac{\partial u}{\partial \mathbf{X}} = \mathbf{A}\mathbf{X} + \mathbf{B},$$

which is a result that can be verified by expanding Equation 8.2, differentiating with respect to every x_i in $\mathbf{X}$, and rewriting the result as a matrix product.

8.2.6 Computation with Matrices

Clearly, matrices are useful in representing systems of linear equations and expressing the solution. As said earlier, we need to be able to express linear equations in terms of matrix notation so that analytic manipulations become easy. Furthermore, calculations with linear equations become easy if we can directly express our matrix formulas in terms of programs. This section describes programming constructs for the simple matrix expressions and manipulations covered in this chapter.

In most languages, we must express the fact that a variable is an ordered array of numbers – a matrix – rather than a scalar (or some other kind of variable). Such *declaration* statements usually occur at the beginning of the program or function. Table 8.12 shows the declaration of an integer array for our suite of programming languages. Both Fortran and C++ require you

Table 8.12: Array Initialization Loop Constructs.

	MATLAB	C++	F90
Preallocate linear array	`A(100)=0`	`int A[100];`[a]	`integer A(100)`

Initialize to a constant value of 12	`for j=1:100 % slow`
	`A(j)=12`
	`end`
	`% better way`
	`A=12*ones(1,100)`
		`for (j=0; j<100; j++)`
		`A[j]=12;`
			`A=12`

Preallocate two-dimensional array	`A=ones(10,10)`	`int A[10][10];`	`integer A(10,10)`

[a] C++ has a starting subscript of 0, but the argument in the allocation statement is the array's size.

Table 8.13: Array Initialization Constructors

Action	MATLAB	C++	F90
Define size	`A=zeros(2,3)`[a]	`int A[2][3];`	`integer, dimension (2,3)::A`

Enter rows	`A=[1,7,-2;`
	`3, 4, 6];`
		`int A[2][3]={`
		`{1,7,2},`
		`{3,4,6}`
		`};`
			`A(1,:)=(/1,7,-2/)`
			`A(2,:)=(/3,4,6/)`

[a] Optional in MATLAB, but improves efficiency.

to specify the maximum range of each subscript of an array before the array or its elements are used. Such range specification is not required by MATLAB, but preallocating the array space can drastically improve the speed of MATLAB as well as make much more efficient use of the available memory. If you do not preallocate MATLAB arrays, the interpreter must check at each step if a position in a row or column is larger than the current maximum. If so, the maximum value is increased and the memory found to store the new element. Thus, failure to preallocate MATLAB arrays is permissible but inefficient.

Array initialization is concisely expressed in both Fortran and MATLAB; in C++, you must write a small program to initialize an array to a nonzero value.* If an array contains a variety of different numbers, we can concisely express the initialization; again, in C++, we must explicitly write statements for each array element.

An Aside: Matrix Storage

Most computer languages do not make evident how matrices are stored. More frequently than you might think, it becomes necessary to know how an array is actually stored in the computer's memory and retrieved. The procedure both Fortran and MATLAB use to store the elements of an array is known as *column major order*: all the elements of the first column are stored sequentially, then all of the second, and so forth Another way of saying this is that the first (leftmost) subscript ranges over all its values before the second is incremented. After the second subscript has been incremented, the first again ranges over all its values. In C++, *row major order* is used: The first row of an array is stored sequentially, then the second, and so forth Clearly, translating programs from Fortran to C++ or vice versa must be done with care.

However, this knowledge can be used to execute some operations more efficiently. For example, the matrix addition procedure could be written as $c_k = a_k + b_k$, $1 \le k \le m \times n$. One circumstance where knowing the storage format becomes crucial is extracting submatrices in partitioned arrays. Such a Fortran subroutine would have to `dimension` the arrays with a single subscript.

Expressing the addition, subtraction, or multiplication of arrays in Fortran or MATLAB is concise and natural. Explicit programs must be written in C++ to accomplish these

* Global arrays – those declared outside of any function definition – are initialized to zero in many versions of C++. Arrays declared within the scope of a function have no predefined values.

Table 8.14: Elementary Matrix Computational Routines (for $n \times n$ Matrices)

	MATLAB	C++	F90

Addition
$\mathbf{C} = \mathbf{A} + \mathbf{B}$
	`C=A+B`	`for (i=0; i<n; i++){`
		`  for (j=0; j<n; j++){`
		`    C[i][j]=A[i][j]+B[i][j];`
		`  }`
		`}`
			`C=A+B`

Multiplication
$\mathbf{C} = \mathbf{AB}$
	`C=A*B`	`for (i=0; i<n; i++){`
		`  for (j=0; j<n; j++){`
		`    C[i][j] = 0;`
		`    for (k=0; k<n; k++){`
		`      C[i][j] += A[i][k]*B[k][j];`
		`    }`
		`  }`
		`}`
			`C=matmul(A,B)`

Scalar multiplication
$\mathbf{C} = a\mathbf{B}$
	`C=a*B`	`for (i=0; i<n; i++){`
		`  for (j=0; j<n; j++){`
		`    C[i][j] = a*B[i][j];`
		`  }`
		`}`
			`C=a*B`

Matrix inverse $\mathbf{B} = \mathbf{A}^{-1}$	`B=inv(A)`	[a]	`B=inv(A)`[a]

[a] Neither C++ nor F90 has matrix inverse functions as part of its language definition nor as part of standard collections of mathematical functions (like those listed in Table 4.7). Instead, a special function, usually drawn from a library of numerical functions or a user-defined operation, must be used.

calculations. Table 8.14 displays what these constructs are for the special case of square matrices with n rows.

8.3 Exercises

1 Often it is necessary to check computer programs that invert matrices. One approach is to use test matrices for which the inverse is known analytically. Few such matrices are known, but one is the following $n \times n$ matrix:

$$\begin{bmatrix} \frac{n+2}{2n+2} & -\frac{1}{2} & 0 & 0 & \cdots & 0 & \frac{1}{2n+2} \\ -\frac{1}{2} & 1 & -\frac{1}{2} & 0 & \cdots & 0 & 0 \\ 0 & -\frac{1}{2} & 1 & -\frac{1}{2} & \cdots & 0 & 0 \\ \cdot & \cdot & \cdot & \cdot & \cdot & \cdot & \cdot \\ \cdot & \cdot & \cdot & \cdot & \cdot & \cdot & \cdot \\ \cdot & \cdot & \cdot & \cdot & \cdot & \cdot & \cdot \\ 0 & 0 & \cdots & \cdots & -\frac{1}{2} & 1 & -\frac{1}{2} \\ \frac{1}{2n+2} & 0 & \cdots & \cdots & 0 & -\frac{1}{2} & \frac{n+2}{2n+2} \end{bmatrix}^{-1} = \begin{bmatrix} n & n-1 & n-2 & \cdots & 2 & 1 \\ n-1 & n & n-1 & \cdots & 3 & 2 \\ n-2 & n-1 & n & \cdots & 4 & 3 \\ \cdot & & & & & \cdot \\ \cdot & & & & & \cdot \\ \cdot & & & & & \cdot \\ 2 & 3 & 4 & \cdots & n & n-1 \\ 1 & 2 & 3 & \cdots & n-1 & n \end{bmatrix}.$$

Develop two routines that will create each of these two matrices for a given `n` value and test them with a main program that uses `matmul` to compute their matrix product. The result should be the identity matrix.

2 The numerical accuracy in calculating an inverse is always an issue: To what extent can you believe the accuracy of the numbers that computer programs calculate? Because of the finite precision used to represent floating-point numbers, floating-point calculations can only rarely yield exact answers. We want to compute the difference between the inverse of the first matrix in the previous exercise empirically by using a library inversion routine and comparing its result with the exact answer. Because the error varies throughout the matrix, we need to summarize the error with a single quantity. Two measures are routinely used: the peak absolute error $\max_{i,j} \left|a_{ij} - b_{ij}\right|$ and the root-mean-squared (rms) error $\sqrt{\frac{1}{n^2}\Sigma_{i,j}\left(a_{ij} - b_{ij}\right)^2}$.* The first captures the biggest difference between the elements of two matrices, and the second summarizes the error throughout the entire difference. Clearly, the peak absolute error is always larger than the rms error. Comparing these two error measures provides some insight into the distribution of error: If the two are comparable, the errors have about the same size; if not, the errors deviate greatly throughout the matrix.

3 Combine the intrinsic array features of F90 with the concepts of OO classes to create a Vector class built around a type that has attributes consisting of the integer length of a vector and an array of its real components. Provide members to construct vectors, delete the arrays, read vectors, list vectors, and carry out basic mathematics operations. Overload the operators +, -, *, =, and ==. Avoid writing any serial loops.

4 Extend the Vector class concepts above to a Sparse Vector class in which it is assumed that most of the values in the vector are zero and that for efficiency only the nonzero entries are to be stored. This clearly exceeds the intrinsic array features of F90 and begins to show the usefulness of OOP. The defined type must be extended to include an integer array that contains the location (row number) of the nonzero values. In addition to changing the input and output routines to utilize the extra integer position list, all the mathematical member functions such as addition will have to be changed so that the resulting vector has nonzero terms in locations that are a union of the two given location sets (unless the operation creates new zero values). Use the concept of logical array masks in computing the dot product. Avoid writing any serial loops.

5 A tridiagonal matrix is a common special case of a square matrix that is zero except for its main diagonal and the adjacent diagonals above and below it. Plan software for a tridiagonal matrix object. For a matrix with n rows the main diagonal has n entries and the other two diagonals have $n-1$ entries. Often each diagonal has a constant value or constant except for a different value in a single row. Design a set of constructors that will (1) accept three vectors with which to populate the matrix, (2) accept three scalars with which to populate the matrix, and (3) accept two vectors with which to populate a symmetric matrix.

6 Applying the finite difference method to an ordinary differential equation is a common way to create a tridiagonal linear systems of equations to be solved by factorization.

* The $1/n^2$ term occurs in this expression because that equals the number of terms in the sum. The rms error is used frequently in practice to measure error; you average the squared error across the dataset and evaluate the square root of the result.

Extend the tridiagonal object software above to define an operator, say *.solve.*, to solve such a system. Note, for the ODE

$$x'' + p * x' + q * x = f$$

the terms in a typical row of the system of equations are

$$(1 - p * h/2),\ (-2 + q * h * h),\ (1 + p * h/2),\ (f * h * h)$$

for the three diagonal terms and right-hand side, respectively, for a grid-spacing distance of h.

CHAPTER NINE

Advanced Topics

9.1 Managing Dynamic Memory

9.1.1 Grouping Tasks

Fortran 90 includes several features to give the programmer the tools necessary to manage dynamic memory usage. However, one tends to think of these tools as completely free-standing statements or functions. In practice, a large code often has several related arrays or pointers that need to be created and released from memory at the same time. Basically, that means we should supply subprograms that generalize the operations provided by the intrinsic functions *allocated* and *associated*.

Here we illustrate this concept with a segment of a class that came from a classic finite element analysis system. The attributes are various types of allocatable arrays – local integers that will establish the array sizes. Additional items required to manage the memory are accessed through the *use* association of the module, called *system_constants*. The encapsulated members include initialization, debugging, and printing subprograms as well as the actual memory management members.

Figure 9.1 shows segments of the code *Elem_Type_Data_Class*. Here the word "type" is not used in the language sense but to identify one of about 18 possible finite elements from an existing library (such as a line, triangle, tetrahedron, etc.). Among the class attributes note that the local integer array *item*, line 5, serves the purpose of checking for local fatal error checks. It is sized to receive the number of subgroup allocations. Recall that the *allocate* function has an optional status return code, *stat=*, lines 36, 37, and so forth. It is given the value of zero if the memory allocation is successful. Different values are assigned if the item has already been allocated or if not enough memory is available. In our past examples we often did not utilize that error-checking status. It really should always be used – especially when dealing with very large allocatable data.

In this simplified module application there are about a dozen activities where related arrays or pointers must be allocated at the same time. The logical attributes in this class are used for testing the status of the grouped activities rather than checking each memory management act required by the related tasks. Those logical variables are assigned names that always end in *_alloc*. Two representative subroutines are *allocate_type_application* and *deallocate_type_application*. The former begins by testing the group allocation status, line 35, of the first subgroup. If a memory allocation is needed, the error flag is set to zero, line 34, and each array or pointer is allocated and its status flag returned. When finished with this subgroup task the allocation status is checked for any fatal allocation error, and aborts

```
module elem_type_data_class  ! for group memory management
 use system_constants ! for debug, dp, n_space
 implicit none
  integer :: lt_free, lt_n, lt_qp, lt_geom, lt_parm       ! sizes
  integer, parameter :: limit = 6 ; integer :: item (limit) ! status

  logical :: type_aply_alloc = .false., type_eqs_alloc  = .false.
  logical :: type_gaus_alloc = .false., type_topo_alloc = .false.

!  element type gauss quadrature points
  real(dp), allocatable :: wt (:), pt (:, :) ! quadratures

!  basic type geometry arrays
  integer,  allocatable :: el_nodes (:)    ! node numbers
  real(dp), allocatable :: coord    (:, :) ! coordinates

!  application specific element type arrays
  integer,  allocatable :: index (:)    ! equation numbers
  real(dp), allocatable :: d     (:)    ! element solution vector
  real(dp), allocatable :: c     (:)    ! element source vector
  real(dp), allocatable :: s     (:, :) ! element square matrix

contains

subroutine list_type_alloc_status
  print *, '** type allocation status **'
  print *, 'type_aply_alloc = ', type_aply_alloc ! overall
  print *, 'type_eqs_alloc  = ', type_eqs_alloc  ! equations
  print *, 'type_gaus_alloc = ', type_gaus_alloc ! quadratures
  print *, 'type_topo_alloc = ', type_topo_alloc ! topology
end subroutine list_type_alloc_status

subroutine allocate_type_application ! group allocate
  item = 0                           ! default to no allocate error
  if ( .not. type_topo_alloc ) then  ! 1st sub-group
    allocate ( el_nodes (lt_n),            stat=item(1) ) ! topology
    allocate ( coord    (lt_n,  n_space), stat=item(2) ) ! coordinates
    if ( any ( item (1:2) /= 0 ) ) stop 'type_topo_alloc failed'
      type_topo_alloc = .true.                            ! ok
      if ( debug ) print *, 'allocated type topology'
  else ; print *, 'warning: type topo already allocated' ; end if

  if ( .not. type_eqs_alloc ) then ! 2nd sub-group
    allocate ( index (lt_free),      stat=item(3) )  ! equations
    allocate ( d     (lt_free),      stat=item(4) )  ! solution
    allocate ( c     (lt_free),      stat=item(5) )  ! force
    allocate ( s (lt_free, lt_free), stat=item(6) )  ! stiffness
    if ( any ( item (3:6) /= 0 ) ) stop 'type_topo_alloc failed'
      type_eqs_alloc = .true.                        ! ok
      if ( debug ) print *, 'allocated type equations'
  else ; print *, 'warning: type eqs already allocated' ; end if

  if ( type_topo_alloc .and. &  ! now flag all groups
       type_eqs_alloc        ) type_aply_alloc = .true.
end subroutine allocate_type_application

```

```
[57] subroutine deallocate_type_application        ! group deallocates
[58]   if ( type_eqs_alloc ) then                  ! last sub-group
[59]     deallocate ( s ) ; deallocate ( c     )  ! reverse order
[60]     deallocate ( d ) ; deallocate ( index ) ! reverse order
[61]     type_eqs_alloc  = .false.                 ! ok
[62]     if ( debug ) print *, 'deallocated type equations'
[63]   else ; print *, 'warning: type eqs already deallocated' ; end if
[64]
[65]   if ( type_aply_alloc ) then                          ! first sub-group
[66]     deallocate ( coord ) ; deallocate ( el_nodes ) ! reverse order
[67]     type_topo_alloc = .false.                          ! ok
[68]     if ( debug ) print *, 'deallocated type topology'
[69]   else ; print *, 'warning: topology already deallocated' ; end if
[70]
[71]   if ( .not. type_topo_alloc .and. &  ! now flag all groups
[72]        .not. type_eqs_alloc        ) type_aply_alloc = .false.
[73] end subroutine  deallocate_type_application
[74]
[75] !  other similar members omitted
[76]
[77] end module elem_type_data_class
```

Figure 9.1: A grouping of memory management tasks.

if necessary. Here if the subgroup has already been allocated, a warning is issued. Usually that would be considered a fatal error. Additional subgroups are treated similarly.

In the latter routine, lines 57–73, the corresponding (but reverse) logic is employed to deallocate the subgroup of arrays or pointers. In theory, the order in which memory is released makes no difference. However, in practice it depends on the quality of the compiler. Compiler authors suggest that, to be safe, memory should be released (deallocated) by the programmer in the reverse order of creation. That practice is illustrated here.

Because memory management is a very common source of fatal errors in executing a program, one wants to be able to check allocation status easily. A debug tool is provided via subroutine *list_type_alloc_status*, lines 25–31. It presents a quick look at large groups of allocations without employing many *allocated* functions. Also, another subroutine (not shown) is provided to assign initial default values to all of the integer–element-type variables that appear in the *allocate* statements within this class.

9.1.2 Memory Leaks

Common serious problems with allocatable arrays and pointers are that they can be difficult to debug and can yield *memory leaks*. A memory leak, usually in a frequently invoked subprogram, causes the memory required to run the program to grow constantly with time. Press et al. [34] discuss this common problem and suggest how to avoid it for allocatable arrays and allocatable pointers. They give sample F90 codes to illustrate the approach. Memory leaks are common in any language that utilizes pointers or allocatable memory, and the programming advice is generally the same. Do not forget to deallocate and nullify the dynamic memory space of pointers and arrays after you are done with them. Do not assign a new address to an allocatable pointer before you either delete it or assign its address to another pointer. Failing to do so causes memory leaks.

Here we will simply illustrate a program that has a memory leak. It is given in Figure 9.2. Try to envision what happens after a subprogram that had been envoked inside a large loop. Note that the dynamic memory allocation status was checked for an error in lines 11, 12, and

```
[ 1] Program Memory_Leak
[ 2]  Implicit None
[ 3]   Integer          :: i, item (2)  ! loops, status
[ 4]   Integer, Pointer :: ptr_1 (:), ptr_2 (:)  ! allocatable
[ 5]
[ 6]    Print *, 'Are pointers associated ? ', & ! Initial associations
[ 7]      associated (ptr_1), associated (ptr_2)
[ 8]
[ 9]    ! Allocate and fill the arrays
[10]    item (1:2) = 0                           ! set error flags
[11]    Allocate ( ptr_1 (5), stat = item(1) )  ! first pointer
[12]    Allocate ( ptr_2 (5), stat = item(2) )  ! second pointer
[13]    If ( Any ( item /= 0 ) ) Stop 'Allocation failed' ! status
[14]
[15]    ptr_1 = (/ (i, i = 21,25) /) ; ptr_2 = (/ (i, i = 30,34) /)
[16]    Print *, 'Pointer 1 = ', ptr_1           ! echo data
[17]    Print *, 'Pointer 2 = ', ptr_2           ! echo data
[18]    Print *, 'Are pointers associated ? ', &  ! associations now
[19]      associated (ptr_1), associated (ptr_2)
[20]
[21]    ptr_2 => ptr_1 ; Print *, 'Now set ptr_2 => ptr_1'
[22]    Print *, 'Note: memory assigned to Pointer 2 is lost'
[23]    Print *, 'Pointer 1 = ', ptr_1           ! echo data
[24]    Print *, 'Pointer 2 = ', ptr_2           ! echo data
[25]    Print *, 'Are pointers associated ? ', & ! associations now
[26]      associated (ptr_1), associated (ptr_2)
[27]
[28]    Print *, 'Deallocate & Nullify all pointers'
[29]    Deallocate (ptr_1)               ! deallocate memory
[30]    Nullify    (ptr_1)               ! nullify after deallocate
[31]    Deallocate (ptr_2)               ! deallocate memory fails
[32]    Nullify    (ptr_2)               ! nullify after deallocate
[33]    Print *, 'Are pointers associated ? ', & ! associations now
[34]      associated (ptr_1), associated (ptr_2)
[35] End Program Memory_Leak     ! Running gives:
[36] ! Are pointers associated ?  F F
[37] ! Pointer 1 =  21 22 23 24 25
[38] ! Pointer 2 =  30 31 32 33 34
[39] ! Are pointers associated ?  T T
[40] ! Now set ptr_2 => ptr_1
[41] ! Note: memory assigned to Pointer 2 is lost
[42] ! Pointer 1 =  21 22 23 24 25
[43] ! Pointer 2 =  21 22 23 24 25
[44] ! Are pointers associated ?  T T
[45] ! Deallocate & Nullify all pointers
[46] !
[47] ! ******  FORTRAN RUN-TIME SYSTEM  ******
[48] ! Error 1185:  deallocating an object not allocated by
[49] !              an ALLOCATE statement
[50] ! Location:  DEALLOCATE statement at line 32 of ''memory_leak.f90"
[51] ! Abort
[52]
[53] ! Commenting out line 31 stops abort, but memory still leaks
[54] ! !b Deallocate (ptr_2) !b but adding stat= is better
[55] !
[56] ! Are pointers associated ?  T T
[57] ! Pointer 1 =  21 22 23 24 25
```

```
[58]  ! Pointer 2 =  30 31 32 33 34
[59]  ! Are pointers associated ?  T T
[60]  ! Now set ptr_2 => ptr_1
[61]  ! Note: memory assigned to Pointer 2 is lost
[62]  ! Pointer 1 =  21 22 23 24 25
[63]  ! Pointer 2 =  21 22 23 24 25
[64]  ! Are pointers associated ?  T T
[65]  ! Deallocate & Nullify all pointers
[66]  ! Are pointers associated ?  F T
```

Figure 9.2: Illustrating a memory leak.

13, but the corresponding actions were not taken at lines 29 and 31. That omission means that we were hoping the compiler would allow the operating system to catch our error rather than writing good code in the first place. Try adding the status checks and see what happens when you run the program.

It is possible to write code that will actually keep up with your memory usage. Although this will be educational for beginners, it is not necessary once you have learned to follow practices that avoid memory leaks. Such memory word counting software will be illustrated in the next section. If utilized here, the output in Figure 9.3 would show five integer words lost.

9.1.3 Reallocating Arrays and Pointers

There are times when we can only estimate the size of an allocatable array. Then we allocate the estimated size, and when we expect it to overflow we must then reallocate its memory. No language provides an intrinisic function for that purpose. Thus, we must develop our own tools for such a case. If you can afford the memory space to have two copies of the array (one small, one big), then it is not a difficult task. Press et al. [34] show several detailed ways to do that. However, in practice arrays needing to be reallocated are usually extremely large. Here we avoid two copies and thus avoid a likely memory crash by employing a binary write to auxiliary storage (an external scratch file) followed by a corresponding read. They are very fast operations (much faster than any formatted I/O) but not as fast as a memory access such as that used when the copy is retained in memory.

```
! Are pointers associated ?  F F
! INTEGER_WORDS =  5
! INTEGER_WORDS =  10
! Pointer 1 =  21 22 23 24 25
! Pointer 2 =  30 31 32 33 34
! Are pointers associated ?  T T
! Now set ptr_2 => ptr_1
! Note: memory assigned to Pointer 2 is lost
! Pointer 1 =  21 22 23 24 25
! Pointer 2 =  21 22 23 24 25
! Are pointers associated ?  T T
! Deallocate & Nullify all pointers
! INTEGER_WORDS =  5
! WARNING: Unable to Deallocate a call from Memory_Leak 2
! INTEGER_WORDS =  5
! Are pointers associated ?  F F
! Integer word memory leak =  5
```

Figure 9.3: Counting the memory leak.

```
Module Memory_Status_Count
 Implicit None
  Public   :: DOUBLE_WORDS, INTEGER_WORDS
  Integer, parameter :: Dp = kind(1.d0)
  Integer :: INTEGER_WORDS = 0 ! initially zero
  Integer :: DOUBLE_WORDS  = 0 ! initially zero

!  Add a generic interface here for double, etc

CONTAINS

Subroutine Alloc_Count_Int (status, sub, increment)
 Implicit None      ! Increase memory word count
 Integer,            Intent(In) :: status    ! of allocate
 Integer,            Intent(In) :: increment ! array size
 Character(Len=*), Intent(In) :: sub         ! prog name

  If ( status /= 0 ) Then                     ! error occured
     Print *, 'Unable to Allocate a call from ' // sub
     Stop 'Allocation failed'
  Else ; INTEGER_WORDS = INTEGER_WORDS + increment ; Endif
End Subroutine Alloc_Count_Int

Subroutine Dealloc_Count_Int (status, sub, decrement)
 Implicit None      ! Decrease memory word count
 Integer,            Intent(In) :: status    !of deallocate
 Integer,            Intent(In) :: decrement ! array size
 Character(Len=*), Intent(In) :: sub         ! prog name

   If ( status /= 0 ) Then                    ! error occured
     Print *, 'Unable to Deallocate a call from ' // sub
     Stop 'Deallocation failed'
   Else ; INTEGER_WORDS =  INTEGER_WORDS - decrement ; Endif
End Subroutine Dealloc_Count_Int

Subroutine Resize_Count_Int_OneD (Array, new)
 Implicit None ! Reallocates and Zeros new part of the array
 Integer,    Pointer :: Array (:) ! Intent (inout)
 Integer, Intent(in) :: new       ! new size
 Integer :: a_stat, d_stat         ! Status variables
 Integer :: old, unit             ! old size & unit

  If ( Associated (Array) ) Then
   old = Size (Array)
   If ( old /= new ) Then                           ! need to resize
    unit = get_next_io_unit ()                      ! get file
    Open (unit, form='unformatted', status='scratch') ! binary
    Write (unit) Array                              ! save old values
    Deallocate (Array, STAT=d_stat) ; Nullify (Array)
    Call Dealloc_Count_Int (d_stat, "Resize_Count_Int_OneD 1st", old)
    Allocate (Array(new), STAT=a_stat)      ! allocating to new size
    Call Alloc_Count_Int (a_stat, "Resize_Count_Int_OneD 1st", new)
    Array = 0 ; rewind (unit)               ! clear to refill
    If ( new >= old ) Then                  ! use all old values
      Read (unit) Array(1:old)              ! recover original values
      Array (old + 1:new) = 0               ! zero the rest
```

```
[57]        Else
[58]          Read (unit) Array(1:new)              ! recover first values
[59]        End If ! new array is bigger
[60]       End If ! need new size
[61]      Else                                      ! not associated
[62]       Allocate (Array(new), STAT=a_stat)      ! completely new
[63]       Call Alloc_Count_Int (a_stat, "Resize_Count_Int_OneD 1st", new)
[64]       Array = 0                                ! initialize
[65]      End If ! if not Associated
[66]    End Subroutine Resize_Count_Int_OneD
[67]    End Module Memory_Status_Count
[68]
[69]    Program No_Copy_Reallocate
[70]    Use Memory_Status_Count
[71]    Implicit none
[72]     Integer, Pointer :: Array (:) ! allocatable
[73]     Integer :: ten=10, more=20, a_stat, d_stat
[74]
[75]      INTEGER_WORDS = 0                               ! zero count
[76]      Print *, 'INTEGER_WORDS = ', INTEGER_WORDS
[77]      Allocate ( Array(ten), STAT=a_stat)             ! allocate 10
[78]      Call Alloc_Count_Int (a_stat,"Main", ten)      ! count 10
[79]      Print *, 'INTEGER_WORDS = ', INTEGER_WORDS
[80]      Array (1:ten) = 5 ; print *, Array             ! insert 5's
[81]      Call Resize_Count_Int_OneD (Array, more)       ! expand to 20, zero new part
[82]      Print *, 'INTEGER_WORDS = ', INTEGER_WORDS
[83]      Print *, Array                                  ! verify old
[84]      Print *, 'INTEGER_WORDS = ', INTEGER_WORDS
[85]      Array (ten:more) = 9 ; Print *, Array           ! change some to 9's
[86]      Deallocate (Array, STAT=d_stat)                  ! delete
[87]      Call Dealloc_Count_Int (d_stat,"Main", more) ! finalize word count
[88]      Print *, 'INTEGER_WORDS = ', INTEGER_WORDS
[89]      If ( INTEGER_WORDS == 0 ) Print *, 'No memory leak.'
[90]    End Program No_Copy_Reallocate              ! Running gives
[91]    ! INTEGER_WORDS =  0
[92]    ! INTEGER_WORDS =  10
[93]    ! 5 5 5 5 5 5 5 5 5 5
[94]    ! INTEGER_WORDS =  20
[95]    ! 5 5 5 5 5 5 5 5 5 5 0 0 0 0 0 0 0 0 0 0
[96]    ! INTEGER_WORDS =  20
[97]    ! 5 5 5 5 5 5 5 5 5 9 9 9 9 9 9 9 9 9 9 9
[98]    ! INTEGER_WORDS =  0
[99]    ! No memory leak.
```

Figure 9.4: Reallocating an array without copying it.

Figure 9.4 illustrates memory counting described in the previous section as well as memory reallocation. There in module *Memory_Status_Count* we use the partial name *alloc_Count* to indicate that we are both allocating and counting memory use in subroutines *Alloc_Count_Int Dealloc_Count_Int*, and so on. They rely on memory word counters as attributes (lines 5–6). They can be expanded to include any intrinsic or user-defined data types. These two subroutines are employed in turn to create the two reallocation operations in *Resize_Count_Int_OneD*, which keeps the contents of the original array and pads it with zeros if the new size is larger. Otherwise, the function fills the smaller array with the front section of the old array. Note that the binary write/read actions occur at lines 48, 55, and 58. A test program, *No_Copy_Reallocate*, validates the reallocation and counting operations.

9.2 Large-Scale Code Development

This section will describe the OO design and implementation of a typical engineering *number crunching* application: a P-Adaptive finite element method (FEM) employed to solve elliptical partial differential equations such as heat transfer and potential flow. We will demonstrate how various OO principles were successfully employed to achieve greater code reuse, flexibility, and easier maintainability and extensibility. This is helpful for a complex program like an adaptive finite element method. The p-adaptive application required a dozen classes, about 40 generic functions, 140 actual functions, about 20 classes, and over 200 subroutines. They combined to form about 10,000 lines of source code. That is too large a programming effort to cover in detail. Thus, only the highlights of its OOP implementation will be discussed here to give some insight into the practical application of the techniques covered in this book.

We will begin by giving a very brief outline of finite element analysis (FEA). For more extensive details the reader can review the finite element analysis text by Akin [4] or one of the dozens of texts in that field. The finite element method replaces a differential equation with an equivalent integral formulation, and then the integral form is solved approximately by using interpolation to convert it to a system of algebraic equations. The approximation gives the value of the primary unknown at every grid point in a mesh. The mesh consists of those grid points and their connections to a large group of quadrilateral or triangular cells (finite elements) that cover the original domain in a nonoverlapping fashion. The solution relies on a consistent set of interpolations over each cell space and along the corresponding edges of each cell (element). Usually all the elements have the same number of points on each edge. The number of points on any edge defines the degree of the polynomial interpolation to be used on that edge. For example, three points on an edge would define a quadratic interpolation because it takes three constants to define a unique one-dimensional quadratic function (along that edge).

Since its origin in the 1950s, the finite element method has matured and is now employed in a wide range of problems from solid mechanics to heat transfer, fluid mechanics, acoustics, and electromagnetism. The main advantage of finite element analysis is its ability to model complex and arbitrary shaped domains. It also supports modeling of general boundary conditions and nonhomogeneous materials. To achieve a greater degree of confidence in the accuracy of an FEA analysis, adaptive techniques have been developed. At the core of an adaptive FEA program is the error estimator, which provides numerical estimates of the errors in the solution and identifies where they occur in the mesh. Then, on the basis of this error information, the data structures are accordingly modified. Analysis points are added edges with high error and are removed from those with low errors. That cycle is repeated until the global error less than or equal to the specified threshold is achieved. There are four basic approaches for mesh adaptation that are known as h-, hp-, p-, and r-methods. H-refinement is based on changing the element geometric size h by subdividing the selected elements into smaller elements. It increases the number of elements, the number of points, and the number of equations to be solved. P-refinement reduces the error in the solution by increasing the polynomial order p of the element-interpolating functions. Although the number of elements might remain constant, the number of points or the number of unknowns per point is increased. R-refinement only relocates the position of points in a finite element mesh but does not increase the number of equations to be solved. The hp-refinement has been shown to be the best approach because it gives the maximum accuracy with the fewest equations to solve. However, it has by far the most complicated data structures and is the most difficult to program. This section will outline the implementation of a p-adaptive FEM in which the

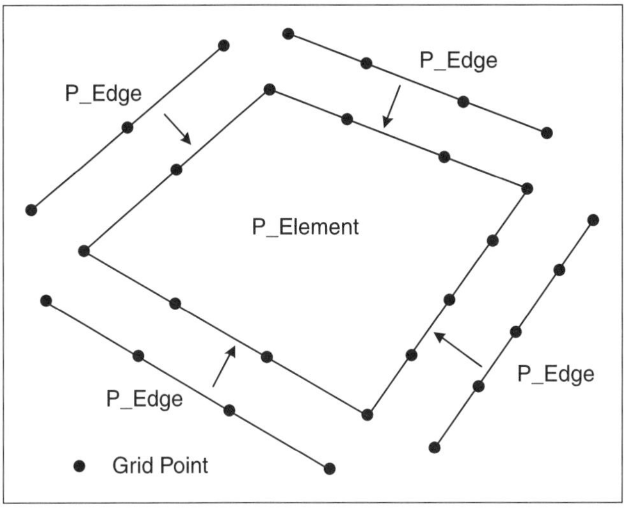

Figure 9.5: Adaptive polynomial edge and element interpolation.

number of elements is held constant but the number of points on any element edge can be increased to reduce the error. A typical p-adaptive element is shown in Figure 9.5. More details are available in the paper by Akin and Singh [2].

Here an adaptive solution is utilized in conjunction with an error estimator so as to obtain a more efficient iterative solution process until a user-specified level of accuracy is reached. It is called a *p-adaptive* method because it changes the polynomial interpolation degree. One algebraic equation must be solved for each point in the mesh. Since the number and location (connections) of the points constantly changes, a special dynamic data structure was required to establish the total system of algebraic equations to be solved to obtain the approximate solution for each adaptive mesh. In this example a linked list of pointers was selected to describe the polynomial degree (number of points) of all the edges in the mesh. Because most edges had a cell on either side it was also necessary to plan to search those edge data in two directions. That required a circular-linked list. In the usual finite element process the equation system is established by a constant integer array defined by the original connection order of the points to each cell.

Since finite element solutions are based on an integral over the domain, it is common to have the integral over each cell carried out by the Gaussian numerical integration technique. There a different set of points is used. Unlike the grid points that have attributes such as their physical coordinates and the solution value, the Gauss points each have tabulated nondimensional coordinates as well as a tabulated integration weight. The number of integration points in each cell had to be increased as the number of cell edge points (polynomial degree) increased. Thus, a p-adaptive finite element solution is much more complicated to program [2] than the classical nonadaptive approach [4] or an h-adaptive approach.

Rehak and Baugh [35] and Forde, Foschi, and Stiemer [16] probably first applied modern OO principles to finite element programming. In a series of papers Dubois-Pèlerin et al. [12–14] presented an OO finite element toolkit implemented in Smalltalk and C++. Dubois-P'elerin et al. [12] proposed further modularity by delineating two kinds of behavior of finite element software: analysis type (solvers used, static or dynamic analysis) and domain information (elements, grid points, boundary conditions). We will illustrate various concepts of OO programming in an FEA flavor with examples from the actual implementation.

9.2.1 Main OO Features in FEA

9.2.1.1 Classes. Figure 9.6 shows a *Point* class within a module; that class encapsulates the coordinates and number of dimensions of the point. The USE statement provides access to the methods of one object to other objects in different modules. This can be seen in the case of the *Point* class, located in *Point* module, which gets access to the data and methods in the *Utils_Module* and *Dbl_Precision_Module*. We can declare contents in a module as private or public to provide the outside user access only to relevant information and to hide the complexity within the module.

9.2.1.2 Polymorphism. It is the property of OO languages to allow the use of identical function names for logically similar methods in different types. This property can be seen in some intrinsic functions like *int(a)*, where *a* can be of integer, real, or complex type and the result is an integer. This can be extended to user-defined objects using generic programming, operator overloading, and the interface construct. For example, in Figure 9.6 *Init_Point* is bound to *Init* using the interface construct. This binding can be performed in all the classes in the program, with the result that the user only utilizes one call *Init* instead of *Init_Element*, *Init_Point* or *Init_Point_Vector*, and so forth. At compile time, the compiler uses the information about the unique argument types to determine which procedure to execute. Similarly, intrinsic operators can be overloaded for user-defined types, and additional operators can also be defined. Figure 9.6, shows how the '==' equality operator is defined for the *Point* class. The assignment operator '=' between two objects of same type is implicitly implemented by the language.

We employed inheritance by composition: This type of inheritance uses other classes to build bigger and complex classes. This is also known as 'has-a' inheritance. This is demonstrated in Figure 9.7 where the *Gauss_Type* class contains an instance of *Point* class to define its position in the space. The *Gauss_Type* class is granted access to contents of the *Point* class using public declarations and the *use* statement.

Finite element analysis requires many large arrays. The array syntax in F90 provides advanced numerical capabilities. Through the use of the assumed shape array, automatic array, and size command the procedures can be made independent of the length of the array arguments, lending more flexibility to the code. Fortran 90 also provides some safety features: pointers can be checked if they are associated (pointing to something valid), and dynamic arrays can be checked if they have been allocated.

9.2.1.3 Design of the Program. Design of an OO program is crucial to its success. First we determine the type of object needed, depending on the specific application. Next we define their interfaces, that is, what these objects need to do and how they will communicate with each other. After these specifications are ready, we can start implementing. It is a good habit to test various pieces of program as we are implementing them. Then the final testing is conducted.

For any application there is no one optimum design of the classes. A good design should exploit the benefits offered by the object-oriented approach. Along with that it needs to address issues like efficiency and ease of implementation. The design of this prototype program consists of several modules. Each module contains one or more logically related classes. There are eight major classes: *Problem, Adaptor, Solver, Domain, Element, Edge, Constraint* and *Grid_Point*. There are eight auxiliary classes: *Skyline* (sparse equation storage), *Patch* (superconvergent patch recovery), *Grid_Point_SubList*, *Gauss*, *Material*, *DOF* (degree of freedom), *Point*, and *Solution*. There are six modules containing data and procedures used

```
Module Point_Module  ! define a "point" in 1 or 2 dimensions
  Use Utils_Module
  Use DBL_Precision_Module   ! for Dp
  Implicit none

  Private                      ! All unless made public
  Public :: Point, Init, Set   ! Type, Constructor, Initializers
  Public :: MyPrint            ! Method
  Public :: GetX, GetY         ! Accessors
  Public :: operator (==)      ! Overloading

  Type Point
     Private
     Real (Dp) :: x, y
     Integer   :: Dimen
  End Type Point

  Interface Init
     Module Procedure Init_Point
     Module Procedure Init_Point_Vctr
     Module procedure Init_Point_Another
  End Interface

  Interface MyPrint
     Module Procedure MyPrint_Point ; End Interface

  Interface Set
     Module Procedure  Set_XY, Set_Point
     Module Procedure  Set_X,  Set_Vec   ; End Interface

  Interface operator (==)
     Module procedure equality_operator_point ; End Interface

Contains

Subroutine Init_Point (p1, x_val, y_val) ! Constructor
  Implicit none
  Type (Point),     Intent (InOut) :: p1
  Real (Dp), Intent (In), Optional :: x_val, y_val
    if  ( Present (x_val) .and. (Present (y_val) )) Then
       Call Set (p1, x_val, y_val)
    Else if  ( Present (x_val)) Then
       Call Set (p1, x_val)
    Else ; p1 % x= 0.0  ; p1 % y= 0.0  ; p1 % Dimen = 1 ; End if
End Subroutine Init_Point

Subroutine Init_Point_Vctr (p1, ptarr) ! Constructor
  Implicit none
  Type (Point), Intent (InOut) :: p1
  real (Dp),    Intent (in)    :: ptArr (:)
  Integer :: length  ! local
    length = Size (ptarr)
    select case (length)
      case (1) ; call Set (p1, ptarr (1))
      case (2) ; call Set (p1, ptarr (1), ptarr (2))
      case default ; stop 'Invalid space Init_Point_Vctr'
    end select
```

```
End Subroutine Init_Point_Vctr

Subroutine Init_Point_Another (p1, pos) ! Constructor
  Implicit none
  Type (Point), Intent (InOut) :: p1
  Type (Point), Intent (In)    :: pos
    p1 = pos ! Implicitly implemented in f90
End Subroutine Init_Point_Another

Subroutine MyPrint_Point (p1)
  implicit none
  Type (Point), Intent (In) :: p1
    if ( p1 % dimen == 1 ) then
      print *, p1 % x
    else ; print *, p1 % x, p1 % y ; end if
End Subroutine MyPrint_Point

Function equality_operator_point (p1, p2)  Result (res)
  Implicit none
  Type (Point), Intent (In) :: p1, p2
  Logical :: res
    if ( (p1 % X     == p2 % X)   .and. &
         (p1 % Y     == p2 % Y)   .and. &
         (p1 % Dimen == p2 % Dimen)) Then
       res = .true.
    else ; res = .false. ; End if
End Function equality_operator_point

Function GetX (p1)  Result (res)
  Implicit none
  Type (Point), Intent (In) :: p1
  Real (Dp) :: res
    res = p1 % x
End Function GetX

Function GetY (p1)  Result (res)
  Implicit none
  Type (Point), Intent (In) :: p1
  Real (Dp) :: res
    res = p1 % y
End Function GetY

Subroutine Set_X (p1, xval)
  Implicit none
  Type (Point), Intent (InOut) :: p1
  Real (Dp),    Intent (In)    :: xval
    p1 % x = xval ; p1 % y = 0.d0 ; p1 % Dimen = 1
End Subroutine Set_X

Subroutine Set_XY (p1, xval, yval)
  Implicit none
  Type (Point), Intent (InOut) :: p1
  Real (Dp),    Intent (In)    :: xval, yval
    p1 % x = xval  ; p1 % y = yval ; p1 % Dimen = 2
End Subroutine Set_XY

Subroutine Set_Point (this, inp_pt)
  Implicit none
```

```
  Type (Point), Intent (InOut) :: this
  Type (Point), Intent (In)    :: inp_pt
    this = inp_pt ! Since there is no pointer component
End Subroutine Set_Point

Subroutine Set_Vec (this, vec)
  Implicit none
  Type (Point), Intent (InOut) :: this
  Real (Dp),    Intent (in)    :: vec (:)
  Integer :: S   ! local
    S =  Size (vec)
    select case (S)
      case (1)
        this % x = vec (1) ; this % y = 0.d0    ; this % Dimen = 1
      case (2)
        this % x = vec (1) ; this % y = vec (2) ; this % Dimen = 2
      case default ; stop 'Invalid space Set_Vec'
    end select
End Subroutine Set_Vec
End Module Point_Module
```

Figure 9.6: A point class for simple grids.

by more than one class: *User_Specific*, *Interpolation*, *Element_Assembly*, *Control_Data*, *Utils*, and *Precision*. These common data and methods are grouped on the basis of logical or functional similarities. Figure 9.8 graphically depicts the design of this OO FEA system. The notation followed in that figure is that the class from where the arrow starts is either directly contained in, or its functions are used by, the class that is pointed to by the arrowhead. So, the higher-level class is at the top, the highest one being the *Problem* class.

Thus, relationships can be of containment of lower classes or only using their methods. This is an appropriate place to note an important detail. To remove confusion between a finite element point and a node in the link (and circular) lists, we note that the finite element

```
Module Gauss_Module
  Use Point_Module   ! for Dp and Point
  Implicit none

  Private
  Public :: Gauss_type, Init

  Type Gauss_type
     Real (Dp)    :: Weight
     Type (Point) :: pos
  End Type Gauss_type

  Interface Init
     Module Procedure Init_Gauss_Empty, Init_gauss
  End Interface

!  .... skipping details

End Module Gauss_Module
```

Figure 9.7: Example of inheritance by composition.

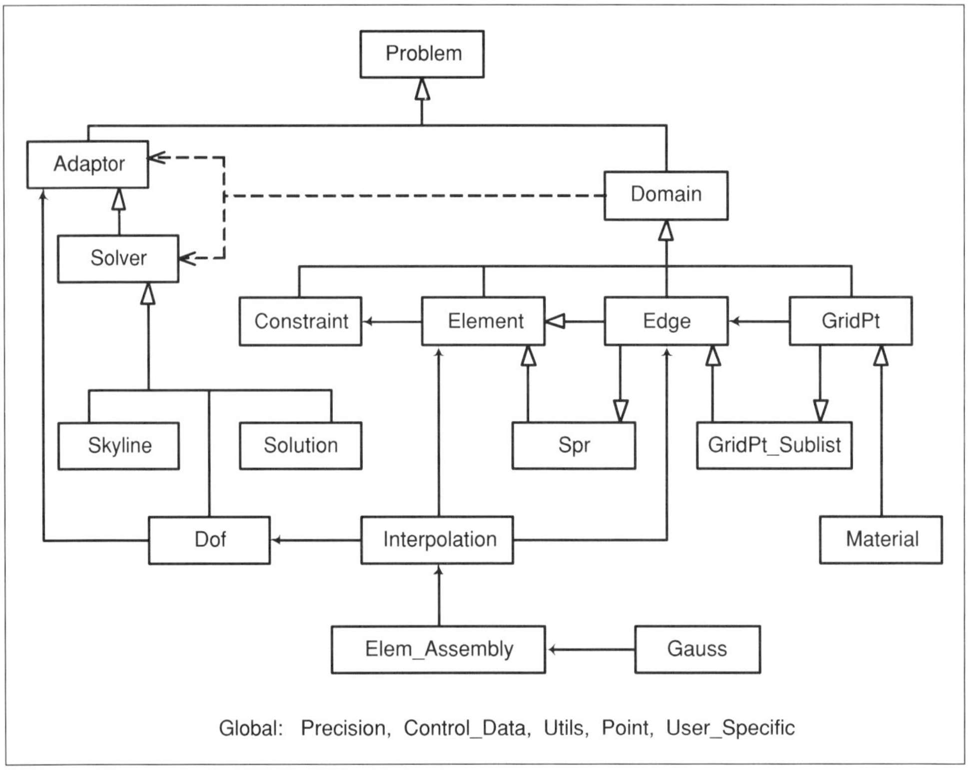

Figure 9.8: Graphical representation of OO adaptive FEA.

node is referred to as grid point whereas a list node is simply called a node. We will now discuss the role of these modules in more detail.

In this code design the information about the finite element model is separated from the details of finding the solution. In other words data are separated from the analysis method. This makes the program flexible and easy to debug. The highest level is the *Problem* class, its structure is shown in Figure 9.9. The model information is contained in the *Domain* class, and the adaptation and solver functionality is in the *Adaptor* and *Solver* classes.

The *Adaptor* and the *Solver* classes are illustrated in Figure 9.9. These classes need access to the data and methods in the *Domain* class to compute the solution. Thus, a pointer link to the Domain class is stored in these classes. The solver class contains the finite element stiffness matrix in variable *Stiff_Mat*, which is an instance of *Skyline* class. The class *DOF_*, an array of type *DOF*, stores the mapping between the local and the system numbering schemes. The class *Soln*, an instance of the *Solution* class, holds the solution values for each degree of freedom.

The *Domain* class contains data structures for the elements, edges, and grid points as well as the iterators for these lists. The iterators are used for implementing efficient traverse and query algorithms.

The *Element* module contains the *Element*, *Element_link_*, *Element_List_iterator*, and *Element_Pointer* classes. The *Element_List* class and the *Element_iterator* class provide methods for link list manipulation and traversal. The *Element* class is shown in Figure 9.10. In adaptive analysis, to recover an accurate gradient of an element, requires information about the neighboring elements. This information is stored in an array of

```
Problem Class
Attributes: Type; Variable
  Domain; Domain_1
  Adapter; Adapt_1
Tasks:
  Initialize the domain
  Run the program
  Perform higher level tasks
```

```
Adapter Class
Attributes: Typ Variable
    Domain, Pointer; Ptr_to_Domain_1
    Solve; Solve1
Tasks:
    Solve the system
    Recover superconvergent gradients
    Perform error estimation
    Perform adaptivity
    Perform postprocess
```

```
Solver Class
Attributes: Type; Variable
  Domain, Pointer; Ptr_to_Domain
  Skyline; Stiff_Matrix
  Array of Real; Sys_Col_Vctr
  Array of DOF; DOF_Arr
  Solution; Soln
  Integer; No_Sys_dof
Tasks:
  Assemble system matrix and vector
  Apply boundary conditions
  Solve the system of equations
```

```
Domain Class
Attributes: Type; Variable
    Grid pt circular list; GrdPtList
    Grid pt list iterator; GrdPtList_iter
    Edge link list; EdgeList
    Edge list iterator; EdgeList_iter
    Element link list; ElementList
    Element list iterator; ElementList_iter
    Constraint; Dirchlet_bc
    Boundary flux; Neumann_bc
Tasks:
    Read, store and manage the components
    Perform domain-level Postprocess
```

Figure 9.9: OO FEA adaptor, domain, problem, and solver classes.

pointers to the adjacent elements. Information about the edges is stored in another array of pointers.

The geometric grid point coordinates are calculated and stored in *Gm_GrdPt_Crds* to avoid expensive recomputation for each adaptivity iteration. *DOF_Map* contains the system degree of freedom numbers for the local element degree of freedom numbers. *Sample_Data* is a link list containing the sampling point data for the element used for accurate gradient recovery needed by the error estimator.

The *Edge* module contains the *Edge* class, *Edge_List* class, and the *Edge_List_iterator* class. The *Edge* class is depicted in Figure 9.10. Each edge contains a circular linked list, *GrdPtSubList*, which stores pointers to the grid points lying on the edge. *IsBndryFlux* is a logical field used to distinguish edges with a flux boundary condition from the rest of the edges.

The *Grid_Point* module also has a structure similar to the element and edge modules; it contains the *Grid_Point* class, *Grid_Point_List* class, and *Grid_Point_List_iterator* class. The *Grid_Point* class is shown in Figure 9.10. *Pos*, an instance of *Point* class, keeps track of the coordinates of the grid point. *DOF_Info* is an integer flag used to classify the analytic or geometric nature of the grid point. Given the use of different interpolation functions for the geometry and the solution, a grid point could be analytical, geometric, or both. The functions *Get_Is_PureGeometric()* and *Get_Is_PureAnalytic()* make this transparent to the user. *DOF_Info* also serves to identify each grid point uniquely. After each adaption iteration the *DOF_Info* is regenerated. The *Constraint* module contains the *Dirchlet* and *Boundary_Flux* classes. The *Dirchlet* class is outlined in Figure 9.10. The integer flag *Param* tells to which parameter of each grid point the boundary condition is applied.

The auxiliary classes also deserve some description. The *Skyline* class is used to implement the skyline storage of a square matrix. The functions like *Get (row,col)* hide the

```
Element Class
Attributes: Type; Variable
  Integer; Id
  Integer; No_An_GrdPt
  Material; Mat_Prop
  Array of integer; CrNrGrdPt_Seq
  Array of Edge pointers; Edg
  Array of Element pointers; Adj
  Array of Real; Gm_GrdPt_Crds
  Array of Real; Elem_Sq_Matrix
  Array of Real; Elem_Col_Vctr
  Array of Integer; DOF_Map
  Sampling data list Sample_data
Tasks:
  Read the element properties
  Generate DOF_Map
  Generate element stiffness matrix
  Find element bandwidth
  Find element column height
  Get number of analysis points
  Perform postprocess

Dirc_Bc Class
Attributes: Type; Variable
  Array of Real; values
  Array of Integer; GrdPtIds
  Array of Integer; Param
Tasks:
  Read and initialize itself
  Functionality for other classes
```

```
Edge Class
Attributes: Type; Variable
  Integer; Id
  Integer; No_An_GrdPt
  List of pointers to Grid_Pts; GridPtSubList
  Logical; IsBndryFlux
Tasks:
  Functionality for higher level classes
  Get number of analysis grid points on edge

Grid_Point Class
Attributes: Type; Variable
  Integer; Id
  Point; Pos
  Material; Mat_Prop
  Integer; DOF_Info
  Integer; Cnstrnt_Indicator
Tasks:
  Position itself in space
  Reset system degree of freedom
  Functionality for other classes
  Store information about a grid point.
```

Figure 9.10: OO FEA Dirc_Bc, Edge, Element, and Grid_Point Classes.

implementation complexity from the user. This allows us the flexibility to use a different matrix storage method, since by implementing the corresponding *Get (row,col)* method the rest of the program will remain unchanged. For recovering the superconvergent gradients we need a list to store the sampling point information of the element. The *Sampling_Point_Data* class and the corresponding list and iterator classes in the *Patch* module provide this functionality. The *GridPtSubList* class forms a circular list of grid point pointers. This list is used to represent the grid points on an edge. The *Gauss* class, outlined in Figure 9.7, stores the position and the weight associated with a Gauss point. The *Material* class is used to read and store the properties. The *DOF* (degree of freedom) class is used to form mapping between system and local degrees of freedom. The *DOF* class also provides equation renumbering algorithms. The *Point* class, which was illustrated in Figure 9.6 implements a point in one- or two-dimensional space. The *Solution* class is used to hold the system solution.

This FEA program also has some modules, which contain common data and methods. The *Interpolation* module provides methods for both geometric and solution interpolation. The *User_Specific* class holds procedures like exact solution for benchmark test cases and source functions. The *Element_Assembly* module provides the structures needed to generate the element stiffness matrix. The *Control_Data* module stores global level tags and flags, and the *Utils* module stores globally used procedures for implementing validation and error checking. The *Precision* module defines the precision type used in the program.

9.2.1.4 OOP Strengths and Weaknesses. In this section we will discuss using the OO approach and demonstrate that it is worth the effort. Some of the advantages of observing OO policies are as follows:

- The main advantage of an OO scheme lies in data encapsulation. First, the information is decentralized; as such, it may be stored at easily reachable places (no complicated pointing devices) and processed at suitable times. Second, objects possess more than integer identifiers; they can possess other objects. For example, the *Element* class does not contain the number of material properties but the material properties themselves.
- In OO programming we group data (attributes) and functions (methods) in a class. We do not have to pass all the arguments; just by passing the object we can use its methods to find information about its. For example, the element class has functions for constructing and initializing an element, generating an element stiffness matrix, and element-level postprocessing.
- The program is more organized and intuitive when objects present themselves to the external world in a more meaningful way (for example, "I am a beam on the third floor connecting such and such" as opposed to "I am an array element 5 in element array"). A finite element application maps very well into the computational domain using the OO design techniques.
- It is easier to debug and modify the implementation of one part of code without affecting the rest of it. This is of great relevance to scientific research, for the researcher can try new algorithms, new data structures, and different problems with less programming effort. In this application the solver is uncoupled from the domain information (element, edges, etc). The *Domain* is also independent of the sparse matrix storage technique and the data structures. These benefits were experienced in our research as we experimented with different element types, different solvers, different data structures, and different precisions with relative ease without affecting the rest of the program.
- It is easy for other people to understand the code written by us. This is gained by separating "what we are doing" from "how we are doing it."
- Concurrency issues: An OO approach encourages localized, distributed grouping of data and tasks. It is relatively natural to see how data and tasks can be distributed over processors (useful for parallel machines) and among individuals (good for a team-programming environment).
- By making use of the inheritance, we can add new components and reuse previously written code.

Now we will study some of the weakness and perceived weaknesses of using OO techniques:

- One of the main weaknesses of OO programming is its overhead, which makes it inherently inefficient with respect to speed mostly because of the addition of new procedure calls for implementing encapsulation and in some cases owing to late (run-time) binding typically associated with OO environments. An increase in overhead due to more function calls in many cases can be offset by the reduction in human time and effort, for human time is a more precious commodity than computer time. The number of function calls can be reduced by the use of pointers. In some instances, for the critical operations that are performed repeatedly, the encapsulation can be broken for efficiency.
- Another criticism of OO methodologies is creation of rigid hierarchies of classes. Too much emphasis on the code reuse coupled with the tendency to classify all objects into

an existing class hierarchy can lead to deep hierarchies of unrelated classes. This type of framework can break when an object that has multiple characteristics is encountered. This was also discussed in a posting on the C++ users mailing list [5], as Platypus effect. A platypus is a fur-bearing, egg-laying, aquatic creature, and to classify it in the class hierarchy of species using only "is-a" inheritance can lead to breakdown of the hierarchy. This is due to overuse of inheritance ("is-a") in the design and is not necessarily a weakness of OO method. With proper design – use of clear logical distinguishing classes and judicial use of inheritance ("is-a") and composition ("has-a") – a flexible infrastructure can be achieved. In this program we only used composition.

Fortran 90/95 provides good support for OO development; however, it lacks some of the features of other OO languages like C++ and Java. One of the missing features is the lack of direct intrinsic support for "is-a" inheritance. This type of inheritance can lead to code reuse and is more useful when there are multiple classes of similar kind. This type of inheritance is used successfully in places like GUI (Graphical User Interface) development but is not as useful in scientific computing. In the present application the OO infrastructure was constructed only using composition. One place where "is-a" inheritance could be used is to represent the element hierarchy by utilizing multiple types of elements without having to modify the rest of the code. However, this is achieved in the present code without inheritance by using parameters to distinguish the various element types. Integer parameters were used to make the methods of *Element* class general enough to be used by element objects with different geometric shape functions. The parameters were *N_Space* (dimension of computational domain), *GrdPt_per_El* (number of grid points in a element), and *No_Params_per_GrdPt* (number of degrees of freedom per grid point). We also use a function that generates element shape functions depending upon these parameters.

Another related feature absent in Fortran 90 is run-time polymorphism. This is a concept related to "is-a" inheritance. It can be useful in some situations, though it adds expense and makes it difficult for the compiler to optimize the code. This can also be implemented in F90 using Szymanski's method (see the dynamic dispatching section of Chapter 6). Fortran 90 has many other useful features missing in other languages – especially for scientific computing.

The p-adaptive finite element application developed during this study has shown good results. Benchmark problems were run to verify the adaptive analysis method applied to various Poisson equations like heat transfer and potential flow. Other tests were carried out to determine the effect of using even-degree polynomials versus odd-degree polynomials. Zienkiewicz-Zhu [40] suggested that even-degree polynomials give a faster rate of convergence. The results agree with the suggestion.

Much has been said about the ability of object orientation to make tasks easy for the software developer. However, OO programming does not obviate the need for forward thinking nor does it make it impossible to introduce a bug. The success of an OO program heavily depends on its design. Because the program is supposed to be flexible and easily extensible in the future, the developer needs to think beyond the present application. Initially the program design can consume a large amount of total application development time; this was also the case with this application. As the developer gains experience in OO principles, the subsequent projects will spend less time on the design board. The language selected for the development depends upon the type of application. Fortran 90/95 is well equipped to perform OO development for scientific and technical community.

9.3 Nonstandard Features

Elsewhere in this book only features of Fortran included in the 1995 standard have been utilized. It is common for compiler developers to provide addition enhancements that are hardware or environment specific and for the most useful of those features to appear in the next standard release. Compiler releases by Cray (®), Digitial (®), and Silicon Graphics (®) computers are examples of versions with extensive enhancements. Some compilers, like the Digitial (®) Visual Fortran (®), are designed to develop applications for the Microsoft (®) Windows (®) system and contain library modules for "standard" graphical displays via QuickWin (®), for dialog routines to the Graphical User Interface (GUI), for interfacing with multiple programming languages or the operating system, and for multiple "thread" operations. Threads are not currently in the F90 standard. They allow for response to the user interaction with any of a set of multiple buttons or dials in an active GUI.

Fortran 90 is a subset of the High Performance Fortran (HPF) standard that has been developed for use on massively parallel computers [26]. We have not discussed those enhancements.

Even without these special enhancements the OOP abilities of F90 provide an important tool in engineering and scientific programming. In support of that position we close with a quote from computer scientist Professor Boleslaw K. Szymanski's Web page [47] on High Performance Object-Oriented Programming in Fortran 90. His group concluded that "all of our Fortran 90 programs execute more quickly than the equivalent C++ versions, yet the abstraction modeling capabilities that we needed were comparably powerful."

9.4 Exercises

1 Employ the *Memory_Status_Count* module to convert program *Memory_Leak* to a new version, *Memory_Leak_Counted,* that will produce output similar to that in Figure 9.3. Note that this will require the use of the status code returned to the deallocate statement.

2 Modify the *Memory_Status_Count* module to add a generic interface to keep up also with the counts for single- and double-precision reals. Provide a test program to illustrate their validity.

3 Write a reallocation module for relatively small arrays that actually uses a temporary copy of the given array; that is, one where both the old- and new-size arrays exist in memory at the same time.

4 Write a reallocation module like *Realloc_Count_Int_OneD* for relatively large real vectors but without the counting features so we can get the maximum speed with the minimum memory use.

5 Write a reallocation module like *Realloc_Count_Int_OneD* for a relatively large doubly subscripted real array (matrix) but without the counting features so we can get the maximum speed with the minimum memory use.

APPENDIX A

Fortran 90 Overview

This overview of Fortran 90 (F90) features is presented as a series of tables that illustrate the syntax and abilities of F90. Frequently, comparisons are made with similar features in the C++ and F77 languages and the Matlab environment.

These tables show that F90 has significant improvements over F77 and matches or exceeds newer software capabilities found in C++ and Matlab for dynamic memory management, user-defined data structures, matrix operations, operator definition and overloading, intrinsics for vector and parallel processors and the basic requirements for object-oriented programming.

They are intended to serve as a condensed quick-reference guide for programming in F90 and for understanding programs developed by others.

A.1 List of Language Tables

Table A.1: Comment Syntax

Language	Syntax	Location
MATLAB	`% comment (to end of line)`	anywhere
C	`/*comment*/`	anywhere
F90	`! comment (to end of line)`	anywhere
F77	`* comment (to end of line)`	column 1

Table A.2: Intrinsic Data Types of Variables

Storage	MATLAB[a]	C++	F90	F77
byte		`char`	`character::`	`character`
integer		`int`	`integer::`	`integer`
single-precision		`float`	`real::`	`real`
double-precision		`double`	`real*8::`	`double precision`
complex		[b]	`complex::`	`complex`
Boolean		`bool`	`logical::`	`logical`
argument			`parameter::`	`parameter`
pointer		*	`pointer::`	
structure		`struct`	`type::`	

[a] MATLAB4 requires no variable-type declaration; the only two distinct types in MATLAB are strings and reals (which include complex). Booleans are just 0's and 1's treated as reals. MATLAB5 allows the user to select more types.

[b] There is no specific data type for a complex variable in C++; it must be created by the programmer.

Table A.3: Arithmetic Operators

Description	MATLAB[a]	C++	Fortran[b]
addition	+	+	+
subtraction[c]	-	-	-
multiplication	* and .*	*	*
division	/ and ./	/	/
exponentiation	^ and .^	pow[d]	**
remainder		%	
increment		++	
decrement		--	
parentheses (expression grouping)	()	()	()

[a] When doing arithmetic operations on matrices in MATLAB, a period ('.') must be put before the operator if scalar arithmetic is desired. Otherwise, MATLAB assumes matrix operations; figure out the difference between '*' and '.*'. Note that since matrix and scalar addition coincide, no '.+' operator exists (same holds for subtraction).

[b] Fortran 90 allows the user to change operators and to define new operator symbols.

[c] In all languages the minus sign is used for negation (i.e., changing sign).

[d] In C++ the exponentiation x^y is calculated by function *pow* (x, y).

Table A.4: Relational Operators (Arithmetic and Logical)

<table>
<tr><th>Description</th><th>MATLAB</th><th>C++</th><th>F90</th><th>F77</th></tr>
<tr><td>Equal to</td><td>==</td><td>==</td><td>==</td><td>.EQ.</td></tr>
<tr><td>Not equal to</td><td>~=</td><td>!=</td><td>/=</td><td>.NE.</td></tr>
<tr><td>Less than</td><td><</td><td><</td><td><</td><td>.LT.</td></tr>
<tr><td>Less or equal</td><td><=</td><td><=</td><td><=</td><td>.LE.</td></tr>
<tr><td>Greater than</td><td>></td><td>></td><td>></td><td>.GT.</td></tr>
<tr><td>Greater or equal</td><td>>=</td><td>>=</td><td>>=</td><td>.GE.</td></tr>
<tr><td>Logical NOT</td><td>~</td><td>!</td><td>.NOT.</td><td>.NOT.</td></tr>
<tr><td>Logical AND</td><td>&</td><td>&&</td><td>.AND.</td><td>.AND.</td></tr>
<tr><td>Logical inclusive OR</td><td>!</td><td>||</td><td>.OR.</td><td>.OR.</td></tr>
<tr><td>Logical exclusive OR</td><td>xor</td><td></td><td>.XOR.</td><td>.XOR.</td></tr>
<tr><td>Logical equivalent</td><td>==</td><td>==</td><td>.EQV.</td><td>.EQV.</td></tr>
<tr><td>Logical not equivalent</td><td>~=</td><td>!=</td><td>.NEQV.</td><td>.NEQV.</td></tr>
</table>

Table A.5: Precedence Pecking Order

<table>
<tr><th>MATLAB Operators</th><th>C++ Operators</th><th>F90 Operators[a]</th><th>F77 Operators</th></tr>
<tr><td>()</td><td>() [] -> .</td><td>()</td><td>()</td></tr>
<tr><td>+ -</td><td>! ++ -- +</td><td>**</td><td>**</td></tr>
<tr><td></td><td>- * & (type)</td><td></td><td></td></tr>
<tr><td></td><td>sizeof</td><td></td><td></td></tr>
<tr><td>* /</td><td>* / %</td><td>* /</td><td>* /</td></tr>
<tr><td>+ -[b]</td><td>+ -[b]</td><td>+ -[b]</td><td>+ -[b]</td></tr>
<tr><td>< <= > >=</td><td><< >></td><td>//</td><td>//</td></tr>
<tr><td>== ~=</td><td>< <= > =></td><td>== /= < <= ></td><td>.EQ. .NE.</td></tr>
<tr><td></td><td></td><td>>=</td><td>.LT. .LE.</td></tr>
<tr><td></td><td></td><td></td><td>.GT. .GE.</td></tr>
<tr><td>~</td><td>== !=</td><td>.NOT.</td><td>.NOT.</td></tr>
<tr><td>&</td><td>&&</td><td>.AND.</td><td>.AND.</td></tr>
<tr><td>|</td><td>||</td><td>.OR.</td><td>.OR.</td></tr>
<tr><td>=</td><td>|</td><td>.EQV. .NEQV.</td><td>.EQV. .NEQV.</td></tr>
<tr><td></td><td>?:</td><td></td><td></td></tr>
<tr><td></td><td>= += -= *= /=</td><td></td><td></td></tr>
<tr><td></td><td>%= &= ^= |=</td><td></td><td></td></tr>
<tr><td></td><td><<= >>=</td><td></td><td></td></tr>
</table>

[a] User-defined unary (binary) operators have the highest (lowest) precedence in F90.

[b] These are binary operators representing addition and subtraction. Unary operators + and - have higher precedence.

Table A.6: Colon Operator Syntax and Its Applications

Syntax	F90	MATLAB
Default	B:E:I	B:I:E
≥ B	B:	B:
≤ E	:E	:E
Full range	:	:

Use	F90	MATLAB
Array subscript ranges	yes	yes
Character positions in a string	yes	yes
Loop control	no	yes
Array element generation	no	yes

B = Beginning, E = Ending, I = Increment

Table A.7: Mathematical Functions

Description	MATLAB	C++	F90	F77
exponential	exp(x)	exp(x)	exp(x)	exp(x)
natural log	log(x)	log(x)	log(x)	log(x)
base 10 log	log10(x)	log10(x)	log10(x)	log10(x)
square root	sqrt(x)	sqrt(x)	sqrt(x)	sqrt(x)
raise to power (x^r)	x.^r	pow(x,r)	x**r	x**r
absolute value	abs(x)	fabs(x)	abs(x)	abs(x)
smallest integer>x	ceil(x)	ceil(x)	ceiling(x)	
largest integer<x	floor(x)	floor(x)	floor(x)	
division remainder	rem(x,y)	fmod(x,y)	mod(x,y)[a]	mod(x,y)
modulo			modulo(x,y)[a]	
complex conjugate	conj(z)		conjg(z)	conjg(z)
imaginary part	imag(z)		imag(z)	aimag(z)
drop fraction	fix(x)		aint(x)	aint(x)
round number	round(x)		nint(x)	nint(x)
cosine	cos(x)	cos(x)	cos(x)	cos(x)
sine	sin(x)	sin(x)	sin(x)	sin(x)
tangent	tan(x)	tan(x)	tan(x)	tan(x)
arccosine	acos(x)	acos(x)	acos(x)	acos(x)
arcsine	asin(x)	asin(x)	asin(x)	asin(x)
arctangent	atan(x)	atan(x)	atan(x)	atan(x)
arctangent[b]	atan2(x,y)	atan2(x,y)	atan2(x,y)	atan2(x,y)
hyperbolic cosine	cosh(x)	cosh(x)	cosh(x)	cosh(x)
hyperbolic sine	sinh(x)	sinh(x)	sinh(x)	sinh(x)
hyperbolic tangent	tanh(x)	tanh(x)	tanh(x)	tanh(x)
hyperbolic arccosine	acosh(x)			
hyperbolic arcsine	asinh(x)			
hyperbolic arctan	atanh(x)			

[a] Differ for $x < 0$.
[b] atan2(x,y) is used to calculate the arctangent of x/y in the range $[-\pi, +\pi]$. The one-argument function atan(x) computes the arctangent of x in the range $[-\pi/2, +\pi/2]$.

Table A.8: Flow Control Statements

Description	C++	F90	F77	MATLAB
Conditionally execute statements	`if` `{ }`	`if` `end if`	`if` `end if`	`if` `end`
Loop a specific number of times	`for k=1:n` `{ }`	`do k=1,n` `end do`	`do # k=1,n` `# continue`	`for k=1:n` `end`
Loop an indefinite number of times	`while` `{ }`	`do while` `end do`	— —	`while` `end`
Terminate and exit loop	`break`	`exit`	`go to`	`break`
Skip a cycle of loop	`continue`	`cycle`	`go to`	—
Display message and abort	`error()`	`stop`	`stop`	`error`
Return to invoking function	`return`	`return`	`return`	`return`
Conditional array action	—	`where`	—	`if`
Conditional alternate statements	`else` `else if`	`else` `elseif`	`else` `elseif`	`else` `elseif`
Conditional array alternatives	— —	`elsewhere` —	— —	`else` `elseif`
Conditional case selections	`switch { }`	`select case` `end select`	`if` `end if`	`if` `end`

Table A.9: Basic Loop Constructs

Loop	MATLAB	C++	Fortran

Indexed loop	`for index=matrix`
	statements
	`end`
		`for (init;test;inc)`
		`{`
		statements
		`}`
			`do index=b,e,i`
			statements
			`end do`

Pretest loop	`while (test)`
	statements
	`end`
		`while (test) {`
		statements
		`}`
			`do while (test)`
			statements
			`end do`

Posttest loop		`do {`
		statements
		`} while (test)`
			`do`
			statements
			`if (test) exit`
			`end do`

Table A.10: IF Constructs. The quantity l_expression means a logical expression having a value that is either TRUE of FALSE. The term true statement or true group means that the statement or group of statements, respectively, are executed if the conditional in the IF statement evaluates to TRUE.

MATLAB	Fortran	C++

if l_expression
  true group
end
	IF (l_expression) THEN
	  true group
	END IF
		if (l_expression)
		  true group;
		  }

	IF (l_expression) true statement	if (l_expression) *true statement;*

Table A.11: Nested IF Constructs

MATLAB	Fortran	C++

if l_expression1
  true group A
  if l_expression2
    true group B
  end
  true group C
end
statement group D
	IF (l_expression1) THEN
	  true group A
	  IF (l_expression2) THEN
	    true group B
	  END IF
	  true group C
	END IF
	statement group D
		if (l_expression1)
		  {
		  true group A
		  if (l_expression2)
		    {
		    true group B
		    }
		  true group C
		  }
		statement group D

Table A.12: Logical IF-ELSE Constructs

MATLAB	Fortran	C++

if l_expression
  true group A
else
  false group B
end
	IF (l_expression) THEN
	  true group A
	ELSE
	  false group B
	END IF
		if (l_expression)
		  {
		  true group A
		  }
		else
		  {
		  false group B
		  }

Table A.13: Logical IF-ELSE-IF Constructs

MATLAB	Fortran	C++

`if l_expression1`
  true group A
`elseif l_expression2`
  true group B
`elseif l_expression3`
  true group C
`else`
  default group D
`end`
	`IF (l_expression1) THEN`
	  true group A
	`ELSE IF (l_expression2) THEN`
	  true group B
	`ELSE IF (l_expression3) THEN`
	  true group C
	`ELSE`
	  default group D
	`END IF`
		`if (l_expression1)`
		  {
		  true group A
		  }
		`else if (l_expression2)`
		  {
		  true group B
		  }
		`else if (l_expression3)`
		  {
		  true group C
		  }
		`else`
		  {
		  default group D
		  }

Table A.14: Case Selection Constructs

F90	C++

`SELECT CASE (expression)`
  `CASE (value 1)`
    group 1
  `CASE (value 2)`
    group 2
    ⋮
  `CASE (value n)`
    group n
  `CASE DEFAULT`
    default group
`END SELECT`
	`switch (expression)`
	  {
	    `case value 1 :`
	      group 1
	      `break;`
	    `case value 2 :`
	      group 2
	      `break;`
	      ⋮
	    `case value n :`
	      group n
	      `break;`
	    `default:`
	      default group
	      `break;`
	  }

Table A.15: F90 Optional Logic Block Names

F90 Named IF

```
name: IF (logical_1) THEN
  true group A
ELSE IF (logical_2) THEN
  true group B
ELSE
  default group C
ENDIF name
```

F90 Named SELECT

```
name: SELECT CASE (expression)
  CASE (value 1)
    group 1
  CASE (value 2)
    group 2
  CASE DEFAULT
    default group
  END SELECT name
```

Table A.16: GO TO Break-out of Nested Loops. This Situation can be an Exception to the General Recommendation to Avoid GO TO Statements

F77

```
DO 1 ...
  DO 2 ...
    ...
    IF (disaster) THEN
      GO TO 3
    END IF
    ...
2  END DO
1 END DO
3 next statement
```

C++

```
for (...) {
  for (...) {
    ...
    if (disaster)
      go to error
    ...
  }
}
error:
```

Table A.17: Skip a Single Loop Cycle

F77

```
DO 1 I = 1,N
  ...
  IF (skip condition) THEN
    GO TO 1
  ELSE
    false group
  END IF
1 continue
```

F90

```
DO I = 1,N
  ...
  IF (skip condition) THEN
    CYCLE ! to next I
  ELSE
    false group
  END IF
END DO
```

C++

```
for (i=1; i<n; i++)
  {
  if (skip condition)
    continue; // to next
  else if
    false group
  end
  }
```

Table A.18: Abort a Single Loop

F77	F90	C++
DO 1 I = 1,N	DO I = 1,N	for (i=1; i<n; i++)
IF (exit condition) THEN	IF (exit condition) THEN	{
GO TO 2	EXIT ! this do	if (exit condition)
ELSE	ELSE	break;// out of loop
false group	*false group*	else if
END IF	END IF	*false group*
1 CONTINUE	END DO	end
2 *next statement*	*next statement*	}
		next statement

Table A.19: F90 DO's Named for Control

```
main: DO ! forever
  test: DO k=1,k_max
    third: DO m=m_max,m_min,-1
      IF (test condition) THEN
        CYCLE test ! loop on k
      END IF
    END DO third ! loop on m
    fourth: DO n=n_min,n_max,2
      IF (main condition) THEN
        EXIT main ! forever loop
    END DO fourth ! on n
  END DO test ! over k
END DO main
next statement
```

Table A.20: Looping While a Condition is True

MATLAB	C++
initialize test	*initialize test*
while l_expression	while (l_expression)
true group	{
change test	*true group*
end	*change test*
	}

F77	F90
initialize test	initialize test
# continue	do while (l_expression)
IF (l_expression) THEN	*true group*
true group	*change test*
change test	end do
go to #	
END IF	

Table A.21: Function Definitions. In Each Case, the Function Being Defined is Named `f` and is Called with `m` Arguments `a1,...,am`.

Function Type	MATLAB[a]	C++	Fortran

program	*statements*
	[y1...yn]=f(a1,...,am)
	[end of file]
		main(argc,char **argv)
		{
		statements
		y = f(a1,I,am);
		}
			program main
			type y
			type a1,...,type am
			statements
			y = f(a1,...,am)
			call s(a1,...,am)
			end program

subroutine		void f
		(type a1,...,type am)
		{
		statements
		}
			subroutine s(a1,...,am)
			type a1,...,type am
			statements
			end

function	function [r1...rn]
	=f(a1,...,am)
	statements
		type f
		(type a1,...,type am)
		{
		statements
		}
			function f(a1,...,am)
			type f
			type a1,...,type am
			statements
			end

[a] Every function or program in MATLAB must be in separate files.

Table A.22: Arguments and Return Values of Subprograms

	One-Input, One-Result Procedures
MATLAB	function out = name (in)
F90	function name (in) ! name = out
	function name (in) result (out)
C++	name (in, out)
	Multiple-Input, Multiple-Result Procedures
MATLAB	function [inout, out2] = name (in1, in2, inout)
F90	subroutine name (in1, in2, inout, out2)
C++	name(in1, in2, inout, out2)

Table A.23: Defining and Referring to Global Variables

	Global Variable Declaration
MATLAB	`global` list of variables
F77	`common` /set_name/ list of variables

F90	`module` set_name
	  `save`
	  `type` (type_tag) :: list of variables
	`end module` set_name

C++	`extern` list of variables
	Access to Variable Declaration
MATLAB	`global` list of variables
F77	`common` /set_name/ list of variables
F90	`use` set_name, `only` subset of variables `use` set_name2 list of variables
C++	`extern` list of variables

Table A.24: Bit Function Intrinsics

Action	C++	F90
Bitwise AND	&	`iand`
Bitwise exclusive OR	^	`ieor`
Bitwise exclusive OR	|	`ior`
Circular bit shift		`ishftc`
Clear bit		`ibclr`
Combination of bits		`mvbits`
Extract bit		`ibits`
Logical complement	~	`not`
Number of bits in integer	`sizeof`	`bit_size`
Set bit		`ibset`
Shift bit left	$\ll$	`ishft`
Shift bit right	$\gg$	`ishft`
Test on or off		`btest`
Transfer bits to integer		`transfer`

Table A.25: The ASCII Character Set

<table>
<tr><td>0</td><td>NUL</td><td>1</td><td>SOH</td><td>2</td><td>STX</td><td>3</td><td>ETX</td><td>4</td><td>EOT</td><td>5</td><td>ENQ</td><td>6</td><td>ACK</td><td>7</td><td>BEL</td></tr>
<tr><td>8</td><td>BS</td><td>9</td><td>HT</td><td>10</td><td>NL</td><td>11</td><td>VT</td><td>12</td><td>NP</td><td>13</td><td>CR</td><td>14</td><td>SO</td><td>15</td><td>SI</td></tr>
<tr><td>16</td><td>DLE</td><td>17</td><td>DC1</td><td>18</td><td>DC2</td><td>19</td><td>DC3</td><td>20</td><td>DC4</td><td>21</td><td>NAK</td><td>22</td><td>SYN</td><td>23</td><td>ETB</td></tr>
<tr><td>24</td><td>CAN</td><td>25</td><td>EM</td><td>26</td><td>SUB</td><td>27</td><td>ESC</td><td>28</td><td>FS</td><td>29</td><td>GS</td><td>30</td><td>RS</td><td>31</td><td>US</td></tr>
<tr><td>32</td><td>SP</td><td>33</td><td>!</td><td>34</td><td>"</td><td>35</td><td>#</td><td>36</td><td>$</td><td>37</td><td>%</td><td>38</td><td>&</td><td>39</td><td>’</td></tr>
<tr><td>40</td><td>(</td><td>41</td><td>)</td><td>42</td><td>*</td><td>43</td><td>+</td><td>44</td><td>,</td><td>45</td><td>-</td><td>46</td><td>.</td><td>47</td><td>/</td></tr>
<tr><td>48</td><td>0</td><td>49</td><td>1</td><td>50</td><td>2</td><td>51</td><td>3</td><td>52</td><td>4</td><td>53</td><td>5</td><td>54</td><td>6</td><td>55</td><td>7</td></tr>
<tr><td>56</td><td>8</td><td>57</td><td>9</td><td>58</td><td>:</td><td>59</td><td>;</td><td>60</td><td><</td><td>61</td><td>=</td><td>62</td><td>></td><td>63</td><td>?</td></tr>
<tr><td>64</td><td>@</td><td>65</td><td>A</td><td>66</td><td>B</td><td>67</td><td>C</td><td>68</td><td>D</td><td>69</td><td>E</td><td>70</td><td>F</td><td>71</td><td>G</td></tr>
<tr><td>72</td><td>H</td><td>73</td><td>I</td><td>74</td><td>J</td><td>75</td><td>K</td><td>76</td><td>L</td><td>77</td><td>M</td><td>78</td><td>N</td><td>79</td><td>O</td></tr>
<tr><td>80</td><td>P</td><td>81</td><td>Q</td><td>82</td><td>R</td><td>83</td><td>S</td><td>84</td><td>T</td><td>85</td><td>U</td><td>86</td><td>V</td><td>87</td><td>W</td></tr>
<tr><td>88</td><td>X</td><td>89</td><td>Y</td><td>90</td><td>Z</td><td>91</td><td>[</td><td>92</td><td>\</td><td>93</td><td>]</td><td>94</td><td>^</td><td>95</td><td>_</td></tr>
<tr><td>96</td><td>‘</td><td>97</td><td>a</td><td>98</td><td>b</td><td>99</td><td>c</td><td>100</td><td>d</td><td>101</td><td>e</td><td>102</td><td>f</td><td>103</td><td>g</td></tr>
<tr><td>104</td><td>h</td><td>105</td><td>i</td><td>106</td><td>j</td><td>107</td><td>k</td><td>108</td><td>l</td><td>109</td><td>m</td><td>110</td><td>n</td><td>111</td><td>o</td></tr>
<tr><td>112</td><td>p</td><td>113</td><td>q</td><td>114</td><td>r</td><td>115</td><td>s</td><td>116</td><td>t</td><td>117</td><td>u</td><td>118</td><td>v</td><td>119</td><td>w</td></tr>
<tr><td>120</td><td>x</td><td>121</td><td>y</td><td>122</td><td>z</td><td>123</td><td>{</td><td>124</td><td>|</td><td>125</td><td>}</td><td>126</td><td>~</td><td>127</td><td>DEL</td></tr>
</table>

Table A.26: F90 Character Functions

Function	Description
ACHAR (I)	Character number I in ASCII collating set
ADJUSTL (STRING)	Adjust left
ADJUSTR (STRING)	Adjust right
CHAR (I) *	Character I in processor collating set
IACHAR (C)	Position of C in ASCII collating set
ICHAR (C)	Position of C in processor collating set
INDEX (STRING, SUBSTRING)[a]	Starting position of a substring
LEN (STRING)	Length of a character entity
LEN_TRIM (STRING)	Length without trailing blanks
LGE (STRING_A, STRING_B)	Lexically greater than or equal
LGT (STRING_A, STRING_B)	Lexically greater than
LLE (STRING_A, STRING_B)	Lexically less than or equal
LLT (STRING_A, STRING_B)	Lexically less than
REPEAT (STRING, NCOPIES)	Repeated concatenation
SCAN (STRING, SET)[a]	Scan a string for a character in a set
TRIM (STRING)	Remove trailing blank characters
VERIFY (STRING, SET)[a]	Verify the set of characters in a string
STRING_A//STRING_B	Concatenate two strings

[a] Optional arguments not shown.

Table A.27: How to Type Nonprinting Characters

Action	ASCII Character	F90 Input[a]	C++ Input
Alert (Bell)	7	Ctrl-G	\a
Backspace	8	Ctrl-H	\b
Carriage Return	13	Ctrl-M	\r
End of Transmission	4	Ctrl-D	Ctrl-D
Form Feed	12	Ctrl-L	\f
Horizontal Tab	9	Ctrl-I	\t
New Line	10	Ctrl-J	\n
Vertical Tab	11	Ctrl-K	\v

[a] "Ctrl-" denotes control action; That is, simultaneous pressing of the CONTROL key and the letter following.

Table A.28: Referencing Structure Components

C, C++	`Variable.component.sub_component`
F90	`Variable%component%sub_component`

Table A.29: Defining New Types of Data Structure

C, C++
```
struct data_tag {
    intrinsic_type_1 component_names;
    intrinsic_type_2 component_names;
} ;
```
F90
```
type data_tag
    intrinsic_type_1 :: component_names;
    intrinsic_type_2 :: component_names;
end type data_tag
```

Table A.30: Nested Data Structure Definitions

C, C++
```
struct data_tag {
    intrinsic_type_1 component_names;
    struct tag_2 component_names;
} ;
```
F90
```
type data_tag
    intrinsic_type :: component_names;
    type (tag_2) :: component_names;
end type data_tag
```

Table A.31: Declaring, Initializing, and Assigning Components of User-defined Data Types

C, C++
```
struct data_tag variable_list; /* Definition */
struct data_tag variable = {component_values}; /* Initialization */
variable.component.sub_component = value; /* Assignment */
```
F90
```
type (data_tag) :: variable_list ! Definition
variable = data_tag (component_values) ! Initialization
variable%component%sub_component = value ! Assignment
```

Table A.32: F90-Derived-type Component Interpretation

```
INTEGER, PARAMETER :: j_max = 6
TYPE meaning_demo
  INTEGER, PARAMETER :: k_max = 9, word = 15
  CHARACTER (LEN = word) :: name(k_max)
END TYPE meaning_demo
TYPE (meaning_demo) derived(j_max)
```

Construct	Interpretation
`derived`	All components of all `derived`'s elements
`derived(j)`	All components of jth element of `derived`
`derived(j)%name`	All `k_max` components of `name` within j^{th} element of `derived`
`derived%name(k)`	Component `k` of the `name` array for all elements of `derived`
`derived(j)%name(k)`	Component `k` of the `name` array of jth element of `derived`

Table A.33: Definition of Pointers and Accessing their Targets

	C++	F90
Declaration	`type_tag *pointer_name;`	`type (type_tag), pointer :: pointer_name`
Target	`&target_name`	`type (type_tag), target :: target_name`
Examples	`char *cp, c;`	`character, pointer :: cp`
	`int *ip, i;`	`integer, pointer :: ip`
	`float *fp, f;`	`real, pointer :: fp`
	`cp = & c;`	`cp => c`
	`ip = & i;`	`ip => i`
	`fp = & f;`	`fp => f`

Table A.34: Nullifying a Pointer to Break Association with Target

C, C++	`pointer_name = NULL`
F90	`nullify (list_of_pointer_names)`
F95	`pointer_name = NULL()`

Table A.35: Special Array Characters

Purpose	F90	MATLAB
Form subscripts	( )	( )
Separate subscripts and elements	,	,
Generate elements and subscripts	:	:
Separate commands	;	;
Form arrays	(/ /)	[ ]
Continue to new line	&	...
Indicate comment	!	%
Suppress printing	default	;

Table A.36: Array Operations in Programming Constructs. Lowercase letters denote scalars or scalar elements of arrays. MATLAB arrays are allowed a maximum of two subscripts, whereas Fortran allows seven. Uppercase letters denote matrices or scalar elements of matrices

Description	Equation	Fortran 90 Operator	MATLAB Operator	Original Sizes	Result Size
Scalar plus scalar	$c = a \pm b$	$c = a \pm b$	$c = a \pm b;$	$1, 1$	$1, 1$
Element plus scalar	$c_{jk} = a_{jk} \pm b$	$c = a \pm b$	$c = a \pm b;$	m, n and $1, 1$	m, n
Element plus element	$c_{jk} = a_{jk} \pm b_{jk}$	$c = a \pm b$	$c = a \pm b;$	m, n and m, n	m, n
Scalar times scalar	$c = a \times b$	$c = a * b$	$c = a * b;$	$1, 1$	$1, 1$
Element times scalar	$c_{jk} = a_{jk} \times b$	$c = a * b$	$c = a * b;$	m, n and $1, 1$	m, n
Element times element	$c_{jk} = a_{jk} \times b_{jk}$	$c = a * b$	$c = a_\bullet * b;$	m, n and m, n	m, n
Scalar divide scalar	$c = a/b$	$c = a/b$	$c = a/b;$	$1, 1$	$1, 1$
Scalar divide element	$c_{jk} = a_{jk}/b$	$c = a/b$	$c = a/b;$	m, n and $1, 1$	m, n
Element divide element	$c_{jk} = a_{jk}/b_{jk}$	$c = a/b$	$c = a./b;$	m, n and m, n	m, n
Scalar power scalar	$c = a^b$	$c = a{**}b$	$c = a \wedge b;$	$1, 1$	$1, 1$
Element power scalar	$c_{jk} = a_{jk}^b$	$c = a{**}b$	$c = a \wedge b;$	m, n and $1, 1$	m, n
Element power element	$c_{jk} = a_{jk}^{b_{jk}}$	$c = a{**}b$	$c = a_\bullet \wedge b;$	m, n and m, n	m, n
Matrix transpose	$C_{kj} = A_{jk}$	$C = \text{transpose}\ (A)$	$C = A';$	m, n	n, m
Matrix times matrix	$C_{ij} = \sum_k A_{ik} B_{kj}$	$C = \text{matmul}(A, B)$	$C = A * B;$	m, r and r, n	m, n
Vector dot vector	$c = \sum_k A_k B_k$	$c = \text{sum}(A * B)$	$c = \text{sum}(A. * B);$	$m, 1$ and $m, 1$	$1, 1$
		$c = \text{dot\_product}(A, B)$	$c = A * B';$	$m, 1$ and $m, 1$	$1, 1$

Table A.37: Equivalent Fortran 90 and MATLAB Intrinsic Functions. The following KEY symbols are utilized to denote the TYPE of the intrinsic function, or subroutine, and its arguments: A-complex, integer, or real; I-integer; L-logical; M-mask (logical); R-real; X-real; Y-real; V-vector (rank 1 array); and Z-complex. Optional arguments are not shown. Fortran 90 and MATLAB also have very similar array operations and colon operators

Type	Fortran 90	MATLAB	Brief Description
A	ABS(A)	abs(a)	Absolute value of A
R	ACOS(X)	acos(x)	Arc cosine function of real X
R	AIMAG(Z)	imag(z)	Imaginary part of complex number
R	AINT(X)	real(fix(x))	Truncate X to a real whole number
L	ALL(M)	all(m)	True if all mask elements M are true
R	ANINT(X)	real(round(x))	Real whole number nearest to X
L	ANY(M)	any(m)	True if any mask element M is true
R	ASIN(X)	asin(x)	Arcsine function of real X
R	ATAN(X)	atan(x)	Arctangent function of real X
R	ATAN2(Y,X)	atan2(y,x)	Arctangent for complex number(X, Y)
I	CEILING(X)	ceil(x)	Least integer >= real X
Z	CMPLX(X,Y)	(x+yi)	Convert real(s) to complex type
Z	CONJG(Z)	conj(z)	Conjugate of complex number Z
R	COS(R_Z)	cos(r_z)	Cosine of real or complex argument
R	COSH(X)	cosh(x)	Hyperbolic cosine function of real X
I	COUNT(M)	sum(m==1)	Number of true mask M elements
R,L	DOT_PRODUCT(X,Y)	x'⋆y	Dot product of vectors X and Y
R	EPSILON(X)	eps	Number, like X, $\ll 1$
R,Z	EXP(R_Z)	exp(r_z)	Exponential of real or complex number
I	FLOOR(X)	floor	Greatest integer $\leq$ X
R	HUGE(X)	realmax	Largest number like X
I	INT(A)	fix(a)	Convert A to integer type
R	LOG(R_Z)	log(r_z)	Logarithm of real or complex number
R	LOG10(X)	log10(x)	Base 10 logarithm function of real X
R	MATMUL(X,Y)	x⋆y	Conformable matrix multiplication, X*Y
I,V	I=MAXLOC(X)	[y,i]=max(x)	Location(s) of maximum array element
R	Y=MAXVAL(X)	y=max(x)	Value of maximum array element
I,V	I=MINLOC(X)	[y,i]=min(x)	Location(s) of minimum array element
R	Y=MINVAL(X)	y=min(x)	Value of minimum array element
I	NINT(X)	round(x)	Integer nearest to real X
A	PRODUCT(A)	prod(a)	Product of array elements
call	RANDOM_NUMBER(X)	x=rand	Pseudorandom numbers in (0, 1)
call	RANDOM_SEED	rand('seed')	Initialize random number generator
R	REAL(A)	real(a)	Convert A to real type
R	RESHAPE(X, (/ I, I2 /))	reshape(x, i, i2)	Reshape array X into I×I2 array
I,V	SHAPE(X)	size(x)	Array (or scalar) shape vector
R	SIGN(X,Y)		Absolute value of X times sign of Y
R	SIGN(0.5,X)-SIGN(0.5,-X)	sign(x)	Signum, normalized sign, –1, 0, or 1
R,Z	SIN(R_Z)	sin(r_z)	Sine of real or complex number
R	SINH(X)	sinh(x)	Hyperbolic sine function of real X
I	SIZE(X)	length(x)	Total number of elements in array X
R,Z	SQRT(R_Z)	sqrt(r_z)	Square root, of real or complex number

(continued)

(continued)

Type	Fortran 90	MATLAB	Brief Description
R	SUM(X)	sum(x)	Sum of array elements
R	TAN(X)	tan(x)	Tangent function of real X
R	TANH(X)	tanh(x)	Hyperbolic tangent function of real X
R	TINY(X)	realmin	Smallest positive number like X
R	TRANSPOSE(X)	x'	Matrix transpose of any type matrix
R	X=1	x=ones(length(x))	Set all elements to 1
R	X=0	x=zero(length(x))	Set all elements to 0

For more detailed descriptions and sample uses of these intrinsic functions see [1].

Table A.38: Truncating Numbers

C++	--	int	--	--	floor	ceil
F90	aint	int	anint	nint	floor	ceiling
MATLAB	real (fix)	fix	real (round)	round	floor	ceil
Argument			**Value of Result**			
–2.000	–2.0	–2	–2.0	–2	–2	–2
–1.999	–1.0	–1	–2.0	–2	–2	–1
–1.500	–1.0	–1	–2.0	–2	–2	–1
–1.499	–1.0	–1	–1.0	–1	–2	–1
–1.000	–1.0	–1	–1.0	–1	–1	–1
–0.999	0.0	0	–1.0	–1	–1	0
–0.500	0.0	0	–1.0	–1	–1	0
–0.499	0.0	0	0.0	0	–1	0
0.000	0.0	0	0.0	0	0	0
0.499	0.0	0	0.0	0	0	1
0.500	0.0	0	1.0	1	0	1
0.999	0.0	0	1.0	1	0	1
1.000	1.0	1	1.0	1	1	1
1.499	1.0	1	1.0	1	1	2
1.500	1.0	1	2.0	2	1	2
1.999	1.0	1	2.0	2	1	2
2.000	2.0	2	2.0	2	2	2

Table A.39: F90 WHERE Constructs

```
WHERE (logical_array_expression)
    true_array_assignments
ELSEWHERE
    false_array_assignments
END WHERE
```

```
WHERE (logical_array_expression) true_array_assignment
```

Table A.40: F90 Array Operators with Logic Mask Control. `T` and `F` denote true and false, respectively. Optional arguments: b `-- DIM & MASK`, d `-- DIM`, m `-- MASK`, v `-- VECTOR` and `DIM = 1` implies for any rows, `DIM = 2` for any columns, and `DIM = 3` for any plane

Function	Description	Opt	Example
`all`	Find if all values are true for a fixed dimension.	d	`all(B = A, DIM = 1)` (true, false, false)
`any`	Find if any value is true for a fixed dimension.	d	`any (B > 2, DIM = 1)` (false, true, true)
`count`	Count number of true elements for a fixed dimension.	d	`count(A = B, DIM = 2)` (1, 2)
`maxloc`	Locate first element with maximum value given by mask.	m	`maxloc(A, A < 9)` (2, 3)
`maxval`	Max element for fixed dimension given by mask.	b	`maxval (B, DIM=1, B > 0)` (2, 4, 6)
`merge`	Pick true array A or false array B according to mask L.[a]	–	`merge(A, B, L)` $\begin{bmatrix} 0 & 3 & 5 \\ 2 & 4 & 8 \end{bmatrix}$
`minloc`	Locate first element with minimum value given by mask.	m	`minloc(A, A > 3)` (2, 2)
`minval`	Min element for fixed dimension given by mask.	b	`minval(B, DIM = 2)` (1, 2)
`pack`	Pack array A into a vector under control of mask.	v	`pack(A, B < 4)` (0, 7, 3)
`product`	Product of all elements for fixed dimension controlled by mask.	b	`product(B)`; (720) `product(B, DIM = 1, T)` (2, 12, 30)
`sum`	Sum all elements for fixed dimension controlled by mask.	b	`sum(B)`; (21) `sum(B, DIM = 2, T)` (9, 12)
`unpack`	Replace the true locations in array B controlled by mask L with elements from the vector U.[a]	–	`unpack(U, L, B)` $\begin{bmatrix} 7 & 3 & 8 \\ 2 & 4 & 9 \end{bmatrix}$

[a] $A = \begin{bmatrix} 0 & 3 & 5 \\ 7 & 4 & 8 \end{bmatrix}$, $B = \begin{bmatrix} 1 & 3 & 5 \\ 2 & 4 & 6 \end{bmatrix}$, $L = \begin{bmatrix} T & F & T \\ F & F & T \end{bmatrix}$, $U = (7, 8, 9)$

Table A.41: Array Initialization Loop Constructs

	MATLAB	C++	F90

Preallocate linear array Initialize to a constant value of 12	`A(100)=0`
	`for j=1:100 % slow`
	`A(j)=12`
	`end`
	`% better way`
	`A=12*ones(1,100)`
		`int A[100];`[a]
		`for (j=0; j<100; j++)`
		`A[j]=12;`
			`integer A(100)`
			`A=12`

Preallocate two-dimensional array	`A=ones(10,10)`	`int A[10][10];`	`integer A(10,10)`

[a] C++ has a starting subscript of 0, but the argument in the allocation statement is the array's size.

Table A.42: Array Initialization Constructors

Action	MATLAB	C++	F90
Define size	A=zeros(2,3)[a]	int A[2][3];	integer,dimension(2,3)::A

Enter rows	A=[1,7,-2;
	3, 4, 6];
		int A[2][3]={
		  {1,7,2}
		  {3, 4, 6}
		};
			A(1,:)=(/1,7,-2/)
			A(2,:)=(/3,4,6/)

[a] Optional in MATLAB but improves efficiency.

Table A.43: Elementary Matrix Computational Routines

	MATLAB	C++	F90

Addition
$\mathbf{C} = \mathbf{A} + \mathbf{B}$
	C=A+B	for (i=0; i<10; i++){
		  for (j=0; j<10; j++){
		    C[i][j]=A[i][j]+B[i][j];
		  }
		}
			C=A+B

Multiplication
$\mathbf{C} = \mathbf{AB}$
	C=A*B	for (i=0; i<10; i++){
		  for (j=0; j<10; j++){
		    C[i][j] = 0;
		    for (k=0; k<10; k++){
		      C[i][j] += A[i][k]*B[k][j];
		    }
		  }
		}
			C=matmul(A,B)

Scalar multiplication
$\mathbf{C} = a\mathbf{B}$
	C=a*B	for (i=0; i<10; i++){
		  for (j=0; j < 10; j++){
		    C[i][j] = a*B[i][j];
		  }
		}
			C=a*B

Matrix inverse $\mathbf{B} = \mathbf{A}^{-1}$	B=inv(A)	[a]	B=inv(A)[a]

[a] Neither C++ nor F90 has matrix inverse functions as part of language definitions or as part of standard collections of mathematical functions (like those listed in Table 4.7). Instead, a special function, usually drawn from a library of numerical functions, or a user-defined operation, must be used.

Table A.44: Dynamic Allocation of Arrays and Pointers

```
C++  int* point, vector, matrix
     ...
     point = new type_tag
     vector = new type_tag [space_1]
     if (vector == 0) {error_process}
     matrix = new type_tag [space_1 * space_2]
     ...
     delete matrix
     ...
     delete vector
     delete point
F90  type_tag, pointer, allocatable :: point
     type_tag, allocatable :: vector (:), matrix (:,:)
     ...
     allocate (point)
     allocate (vector (space_1), STAT = my_int)
     if (my_int /= 0) error_process
     allocate (matrix (space_1, space_2))
     ...
     deallocate (matrix)
     if (associated (point, target_name)) pointer_action ...
     if (allocated (matrix)) matrix_action ...
     ...
     deallocate (vector)
     deallocate (point)
```

Table A.45: Automatic Memory Management of Local Scope Arrays

```
SUBROUTINE AUTO_ARRAYS (M,N, OTHER)
USE GLOBAL_CONSTANTS ! FOR INTEGER K
   IMPLICIT NONE
   INTEGER, INTENT (IN) :: M,N
   type_tag, INTENT (OUT) :: OTHER (M,N) ! dummy array
! Automatic array allocations
   type_tag :: FROM_USE (K)
   type_tag :: FROM_ARG (M)
   type_tag :: FROM_MIX (K,N)
   ...
! Automatic deallocation at end of scope
END SUBROUTINE AUTO_ARRAYS
```

Table A.46: F90 Single Inheritance Form

```
module derived_class_name
     use base_class_name
! new attribute declarations, if any
          ...
contains
   ! new member definitions
          ...
end module derived_class_name
```

Table A.47: F90 Selective Single Inheritance Form

```
module derived_class_name
        use base_class_name, only: list_of_entities
! new attribute declarations, if any
                    ...
contains
      ! new member definitions
                    ...
end module derived_class_name
```

Table A.48: F90 Single Inheritance Form with Local Renaming

```
module derived_class_name
        use base_class_name, local_name => base_entity_name
! new attribute declarations, if any
                    ...
contains
      ! new member definitions
                    ...
end module derived_class_name
```

Table A.49: F90 Multiple Selective Inheritance with Renaming

```
module derived_class_name
        use base1_class_name
        use base2_class_name
        use base3_class_name, only: list_of_entities
        use base4_class_name, local_name => base_entity_name
! new attribute declarations, if any
                    ...
contains
        ! new member definitions
                    ...
end module derived_class_name
```

A.2 Alphabetical Table of Fortran 90 Intrinsic Routines

The following KEY symbols are utilized to denote the TYPE of the intrinsic function, or subroutine, and its arguments: A-complex, integer, or real; B-integer bit; C-character; D-dimension; I-integer; K-kind; L-logical; M-mask (logical); N-integer, or real; P-pointer; R-real; S-string; T-target; V-vector (rank-one array); X-real; Y-real; Z-complex; and *-any type. For more detailed descriptions and sample uses of these intrinsic functions, see [1].

Alphabetical Table of Fortran 90 Intrinsic Functions

Type	Intrinsic	Description
A	ABS (A)	Absolute value of A
C	ACHAR (I)	Character in position I of ASCII collating sequence
R	ACOS (X)	Arc cosine (inverse cosine) function of real X
C	ADJUSTL (S)	Adjust S left; move leading blanks to trailing blanks
C	ADJUSTR (S)	Adjust S right; move trailing blanks to leading blanks
R	AIMAG (Z)	Imaginary part of complex number Z
R	AINT (X [,K])	Truncate X to a real whole number of the given kind
L	ALL (M [,D])	True if all mask M elements are true in dimension D
L	ALLOCATED (*_ARRAY_P)	True if the array or pointer is allocated
R	ANINT (X [,K])	Real whole number nearest to X of the given kind
L	ANY (M [,D])	True if any mask M element is true in dimension D
R	ASIN (X)	Arcsine (inverse sine) function of real X
L	ASSOCIATED (P [,T])	True if pointer P is associated with any target or T
R	ATAN (X)	Arctangent (inverse tangent) function of real X
R	ATAN2 (Y,X)	Arctangent for argument of complex number (X, Y)
I	BIT_SIZE (I)	Maximum number of bits integer I can hold (e.g., 32)
L	BTEST (I,I_POS)	True if bit location I_POS of integer I has value 1
I	CEILING (X)	Least integer $\geq$ real X of the given kind
C	CHAR (I [,K])	Character in position I of processor collating sequence
Z	CMPLX (X [,Y][,K])	Convert real(s) to complex type of given kind
Z	CONJG (Z)	Conjugate of complex number Z
R	COS (R_Z)	Cosine function of real or complex argument
R	COSH (X)	Hyperbolic cosine function of real X
I	COUNT (M [,D])	Number of true mask M elements in dimension D
*	CSHIFT (*_ARAY,I_SHIF [,D])	Circular shift out and in for I_SHIF elements
call	DATE_AND_TIME ([S_DATE] [,S_TIME] [,S_ZONE] [,I_V_VALUES])	Real-time clock date, time, zone, and vector with year, month, day, UTC, hour, minutes, seconds, and milliseconds
R	DBLE (A)	Convert A to double-precision real
N	DIGITS (N)	Number of significant digits for N (e.g., 31)
R	DIM (X,Y)	The difference, MAX (X – Y, 0.0)
N,L	DOT_PRODUCT (V,V_2)	Dot product of vectors V and V_2
R	DPROD (X,Y)	Double-precision real product of two real scalars
*	EOSHIFT (*_ARRAY, I_SHIFT [,*_FILL][,D])	Perform vector end-off shift by ± I_shift terms and fill in dimension D
R	EPSILON (X)	Number $\ll$ 1 for numbers like X (e.g. 2**–23)
R,Z	EXP (R_Z)	Exponential function of real or complex argument
I	EXPONENT (X)	Exponent part of the model for real X
I	FLOOR (X)	Greatest integer less than or equal to X
R	FRACTION (X)	Fractional part of the model for real X
N	HUGE (N)	Largest number for numbers like N (e.g., 2**128)
I	IACHAR (C)	Position of character C in ASCII collation
B	IAND (I,I_2)	Logical AND on the bits of I and I_2
B	IBCLR (I,I_POS)	Clear bit I_POS to zero in integer I
B	IBITS (I,I_POS,I_LEN)	Extract an I_LEN sequence of bits at I_POS in I
B	IBSET (I,I_POS)	Set bit I_POS to one in integer I
I	ICHAR (C)	Position of character C in processor collation
B	IEOR (I,I_2)	Exclusive OR on the bits of I and I_2
I	INDEX (S,S_SUB [,L_BACK])	Left starting position of S_SUB within S (right)

(continued)

(continued)

Type	Intrinsic	Description
I	INT (A [,K])	Convert A to integer type of given kind
B	IOR (I,I_2)	Inclusive OR on the bits of I and I_2
B	ISHFT (I,I_SHIFT)	Logical shift of bits of I by I_SHIFT pad with 0
B	ISHFTC (I,I_SHIFT [,I_SIZE])	Logical circular shift of I_SIZE rightmost bits of I
I	KIND (ANY)	Kind type integer parameter value for any argument
I,V	LBOUND (⋆_ARRAY [,D])	ARRAY lower bound(s) vector along dimension D
I	LEN (S)	Total character string length
I	LEN_TRIM (S)	Length of S without trailing blanks
L	LGE (S,S_2)	True if S > or equal to S_2 in ASCII sequence
L	LGT (S,S_2)	True if S follows S_2 in ASCII collating sequence
L	LLE (S,S_2)	True if S < or equal to S_2 in ASCII sequence
L	LLT (S,S_2	True if S precedes S_2 in ASCII collating sequence
R	LOG (R_Z)	Natural (base e) logarithm of real or complex number
L	LOGICAL (L [,K])	Convert L to logical of kind K
R	LOG10 (X)	Common (base 10) logarithm function of real X
N,L	MATMUL (MATRIX,MATRIX_2)	Conformable matrix multiplication
N	MAX (N,N_2 [,N_3,...])	Maximum value of two or more numbers of the same type
I	MAXEXPONENT (X)	Maximum exponent for real numbers like X (e.g. 128)
I,V	MAXLOC (N_ARRAY [,M])	Location(s) of maximum ARRAY element passing M
N	MAXVAL (N_ARRAY [,D] [,M])	Maximum ARRAY term in dimension D passing M
⋆	MERGE (⋆_TRUE,⋆_FALSE,M)	Use ⋆_TRUE when M is true; ⋆_FALSE otherwise
N	MIN (N,N_2 [,N_3,...])	Minimum value of two or more same type numbers
I	MINEXPONENT (X)	Minimum exponent for real numbers like X (e.g., –125)
I,V	MINLOC (N_ARRAY [,M])	Location(s) of minimum ARRAY term, passing M
N	MINVAL (N_ARRAY [,D] [,M])	Minimum ARRAY term in dimension D passing M
N	MOD (N,N_2)	Remainder for N_2. That is, N–INT(N/N_2)⋆ N_2
N	MODULO (N,N_2)	Modulo, that is, N–FLOOR(N/N_2)⋆N_2
call	MVBITS (I_FROM,I_LOC, I_LEN,I_TO,I_POS)	Copy I_LEN bits at I_LOC in I_FROM to I_TO at I_POS
R	NEAREST (X,Y)	Nearest number at X in the direction of sign Y
I	NINT (X [,K])	Integer nearest to real X of the stated kind
I	NOT (I)	Logical complement of the bits of integer I
⋆,V	PACK (⋆_ARRAY,M [,V_PAD])	Pack ARRAY at true M into vector using V_PAD
I	PRECISION (R_Z)	Decimal precision for a real or complex R_Z (e.g., 6)
L	PRESENT (OPTIONAL)	True if optional argument is present in call
A	PRODUCT (A_ARRAY [,D] [,M])	Product of ARRAY elements along D for mask M
I	RADIX (N)	Base of the model for numbers like N (e.g., 2)
call	RANDOM_NUMBER (X)	Pseudorandom numbers in range $0 < X < 1$
call	RANDOM_SEED ([I_SIZE] [,I_V_PUT][,I_V_GET])	Initialize random number generator; defaults to processor initialization
I	RANGE (A)	Decimal exponent range in the model for A (e.g., 37)
R	REAL (A [,K])	Convert A to real type of type K
S	REPEAT (S,I_COPIES)	Concatenates I_COPIES of string S
⋆	RESHAPE (⋆_ARAY,I_V_SHAP [,⋆_PAD] [,V_ORDER])	Reshape ARAY using vector SHAP pad from an array and reorder
R	RRSPACING (X)	Relative spacing reciprocal of numbers near X
R	SCALE (X,I)	Return X times b⋆⋆I, for base of b = RADIX (X)
I	SCAN (S,S_SET [,L_BACK])	Leftmost character index in S found in S_SET; (rightmost)
I	SELECTED_INT_KIND (I_r)	Integer kind with range, –(10⋆⋆I_r) to (10⋆⋆I_r)

Type	Intrinsic	Description
I	SELECTED_REAL_KIND	Kind for real of decimal precision I and exponent
I	([I] [,I_r])	range I_r
R	SET_EXPONENT (X,I)	Number with mantissa of X and exponent of I
I,V	SHAPE (⋆_ARRAY)	ARRAY (or scalar) shape vector
N	SIGN (N,N_2)	Absolute value of N times sign of same type N_2
R,Z	SIN (R_Z)	Sine function of real or complex number
R	SINH (X)	Hyperbolic sine function of real X
I	SIZE (⋆_ARRAY [,D])	ARRAY size along dimension D
R	SPACING (X)	Absolute spacing of numbers near real X (e.g., 2⋆⋆–17)
⋆	SPREAD (⋆_ARAY,D,I_COPIES)	I_COPIES along dimension D of ARAY into an array of rank 1 greater
R,Z	SQRT (R_Z)	Square root function of real or complex number
A	SUM (A_ARRAY [,D] [,M])	Sum of ARRAY elements along D passing mask M
call	SYSTEM_CLOCK ([I_NOW] [,I_RATE] [,I_MAX])	Integer data from real-time clock. CPU time is (finish_now - start_now) / rate
R	TAN (X)	Tangent function of real X
R	TANH (X)	Hyperbolic tangent function of real X
R	TINY (N)	Smallest positive number, like N (e.g., 2⋆⋆–126)
⋆	TRANSFER (⋆_ARAY, V_MOLD [,I_SIZE])	Same representation as ARAY but type of MOLD in vector of length SIZE
⋆	TRANSPOSE (MATRIX)	Matrix transpose of any type matrix
S	TRIM (S)	Remove trailing blanks from a single string
I,V	UBOUND (⋆_ARRAY [,D])	ARRAY upper bound(s) vector along dimension D
⋆	UNPACK (V,M,⋆_USE)	Unpack vector V at true elements of M into USE
I	VERIFY (S,S_SET [,L_BACK])	First position in S not found in S_SET (or last)

A.3 Subject Table of Fortran 90 Intrinsic Routines

The following KEY symbols are utilized to denote the TYPE of the intrinsic function, or subroutine, and its arguments: A-complex, integer, or real; B-integer bit; C-character; D-dimension; I-integer; K-kind; L-logical; M-mask (logical); N-integer, or real; P-pointer; R-real; S-string; T-target; V-vector (rank one array); X-real; Y-real; Z-complex; and *-any type. For more detailed descriptions and illustrative uses of these intrinsic functions, see Adams, J.C. et al., [1].

Subject Table of Fortran 90 Intrinsic Routines

Type	Intrinsic	Description
ALLOCATION		
L	ALLOCATED (⋆_ARRAY)	True if the array is allocated
ARGUMENT		
L	PRESENT (OPTIONAL)	True if optional argument is present in the call
ARRAY: CONSTRUCTION		
⋆	MERGE (⋆_TRUE,⋆_FALSE,M)	Use ⋆_TRUE if M is true; ⋆_FALSE otherwise
⋆,V	PACK (⋆_ARRAY,M [,V_PAD])	Pack ARRAY for true M into vector and pad from V_PAD
⋆	RESHAPE (⋆_ARRAY,I_V_SHAPE [,⋆_PAD] [,V_ORDER])	Reshape ARRAY using vector SHAPE, pad from an array, and reorder

(continued)

(continued)

Type	Intrinsic	Description
*	SPREAD (*_ARRAY,D,I_COPIES)	I_COPIES along D of ARRAY to rank 1 greater array
*	UNPACK (V,M,*_USE)	Unpack V at true elements of M into USE
ARRAY: DIMENSIONS		
I,V	LBOUND (*_ARRAY [,D])	ARRAY lower bound(s vector) along dimension D
I,V	SHAPE (*_ARRAY)	ARRAY (or scalar) shape vector
I	SIZE (*_ARRAY [,D])	ARRAY size along dimension D
I,V	UBOUND (*_ARRAY [,D])	ARRAY upper bound(s vector) along dimension D
ARRAY: INQUIRY		
L	ALL (M [,D])	True if all mask M elements are true along D
L	ALLOCATED (*_ARRAY)	True if the array is allocated
L	ANY (M [,D])	True if any mask M element is true along D
I,V	LBOUND (*_ARRAY [,D])	ARRAY lower bound(s) vector along dimension D
I,V	SHAPE (*_ARRAY)	ARRAY (or scalar) shape vector
I,V	UBOUND (*_ARRAY [,D])	ARRAY upper bound(s) vector along dimension D
ARRAY: LOCATION		
I,V	MAXLOC (N_ARRAY [,M])	Location(s) of maximum ARRAY term passing M
I,V	MINLOC (N_ARRAY [,M])	Location(s) of minimum ARRAY term passing M
ARRAY: MANIPULATION		
*	CSHIFT (*_ARRAY,I_SHIFT [,D])	Circular shift out and in for I_SHIFT elements
*	EOSHIFT (*_ARRAY,I_SHIFT [,*_FIL][,D])	End-off shift ARRAY and fill in dimension D
*	TRANSPOSE (MATRIX)	Matrix transpose of any type matrix
ARRAY: MATHEMATICS		
N,L	DOT_PRODUCT (V,V_2)	Dot product of vectors V and V_2
N,L	MATMUL (MATRIX,MATRIX_2)	Conformable matrix multiplication
N	MAXVAL (N_ARRAY [,D] [,M])	Value of max ARRAY term along D passing M
N	MINVAL (N_ARRAY [,D] [,M])	Value of min ARRAY term along D passing M
A	PRODUCT (A_ARRAY [,D] [,M])	Product of ARRAY terms along D for mask M
A	SUM (A_ARRAY [,D] [,M])	Sum of ARRAY terms along D passing mask M
ARRAY: PACKING		
*,V	PACK (*_ARRAY,M [,V_PAD])	Pack ARRAY for true M into vector and pad from V_PAD
*	UNPACK (V,M,*_USE)	Unpack V at true elements of M into USE
ARRAY: REDUCTION		
L	ALL (M [,D])	True if all mask M terms are true along D
L	ANY (M [,D])	True if any mask M term is true along D
I	COUNT (M [,D])	Number of true mask M terms along dimension D
N	MAXVAL (N_ARRAY [,D] [,M])	Value of max ARRAY term along D passing M
N	MINVAL (N_ARRAY [,D] [,M])	Value of min ARRAY term along D passing M
A	PRODUCT (A_ARRAY [,D] [,M])	Product of ARRAY terms along D for mask M
A	SUM (A_ARRAY [,D] [,M])	Sum of ARRAY terms along D passing mask M
BACK SCAN		
I	INDEX (S,S_SUB [,L_BACK])	Left starting position of S_SUB within S (or right)
I	SCAN (S,S_SET [,L_BACK])	Left character index in S also in S_SET (or right)
I	VERIFY (S,S_SET [,L_BACK])	First position in S not belonging to S_SET (or last)
BIT: INQUIRY		
I	BIT_SIZE (I)	Max number of bits possible in integer I (e.g., 32)
BIT: MANIPULATION		
L	BTEST (I,I_POS)	True if bit location I_POS of integer I has value 1

Type	Intrinsic	Description
B	IAND (I,I_2)	Logical AND on the bits of I and I_2
B	IBCLR (I,I_POS)	Clear bit I_POS to zero in integer I
B	IBITS (I,I_POS,I_LEN)	Extract I_LEN bits at I_POS in integer I
B	IBSET (I,I_POS)	Set bit I_POS to one in integer I
B	IEOR (I,I_2)	Exclusive OR on the bits of I and I_2
B	IOR (I,I_2)	Inclusive OR on the bits of I and I_2
B	ISHFT (I,I_SHIFT)	Logical shift of bits of I by I_SHIFT, pad with 0
B	ISHFTC (I,I_SHIFT [,I_SIZE])	Logical circular shift of I_SIZE rightmost bits of I
call	MVBITS (I_GET, I_LOC, I, I_TO,I_POS)	Copy I bits at I_LOC in I_GET to I_TO at I_POS
I	NOT (I)	Logical complement of the bits of integer I
⋆	TRANSFER (⋆_ARRAY, V_MOLD [,I_SIZE])	Same representation as ARRAY but type of MOLD
BOUNDS		
I	CEILING (X)	Least integer greater than or equal to real X
I	FLOOR (X)	Greatest integer less than or equal to X
I,V	LBOUND (⋆_ARRAY [,D])	ARRAY lower bound(s) vector along dimension D
N	MAX (N,N_2 [,N_3,...])	Maximum value of two or more numbers same type
N	MAXVAL (N_ARRAY [,D] [,M])	Value of max ARRAY term along D passing M
N	MINVAL (N_ARRAY [,D] [,M])	Value of min ARRAY term along D passing M
I,V	UBOUND (⋆_ARRAY [,D])	ARRAY upper bound(s) vector along dimension D
CALLS		
call	MVBITS (I_GET,I_LOC,I, I_TO,I_POS)	Copy I bits at I_LOC in I_GET to I_TO at I_POS
call	DATE_AND_TIME ([S_DATE] [,S_TIME] [,S_ZONE] [,I_V_VALUES])	Real-time clock data
call	RANDOM_NUMBER (X)	Pseudorandom numbers in range $0 < X < 1$
call	RANDOM_SEED ([I_SIZE] [,I_V_P] [,I_V_G])	Initialize random number generator
call	SYSTEM_CLOCK ([I_NOW] [,I_RAT] [,I_MX])	Integer data from real-time clock
CHARACTERS		
C	ACHAR (I)	Character in position I of ASCII collating sequence
C	CHAR (I [,K])	Character in position I of processor collation
I	IACHAR (C)	Position of character C in ASCII collating sequence
I	ICHAR (C)	Position of character C in processor collation
CLOCK		
call	SYSTEM_CLOCK ([I_NOW] [,I_RAT] [,I_MX])	Integer data from real-time clock
COMBINING		
⋆	MERGE (⋆_TRUE,⋆_FALSE,M)	Use ⋆_TRUE term if M is true or ⋆_FALSE otherwise
COMPLEX		
R	AIMAG (Z)	Imaginary part of complex number
Z	CMPLX (X [,Y][,K])	Convert real(s) to complex type of given kind
Z	CONJG (Z)	Conjugate of complex number Z
R	COS (R_Z)	Cosine function of real or complex argument
R,Z	EXP (R_Z)	Exponential function of real or complex argument
R	LOG (R_Z)	Natural (base e) logarithm of real or complex number
I	PRECISION (R_Z)	Decimal precision of real or complex value (e.g. 6)
R,Z	SIN (R_Z)	Sine function of real or complex number

(continued)

(continued)

Type	Intrinsic	Description
R,Z	SQRT (R_Z)	Square root function of real or complex number
CONVERSIONS		
R	AIMAG (Z)	Imaginary part of complex number
R	AINT (X [,K])	Truncate X to a real whole number
Z	CMPLX (X [,Y][,K])	Convert real (s) to complex type of given kind
R	DBLE (A)	Convert A to double-precision real
R	DPROD (X,Y)	Double-precision product of two default real scalars
I	INT (A [,K])	Convert A to integer type of given kind
L	LOGICAL (L [,K])	Convert L to logical of kind K
I	NINT (X [,K])	Integer nearest to real X of the stated kind
R	REAL (A [,K])	Convert A to real type of type K
N	SIGN (N,N_2)	Absolute value of N times sign of same type N_2
⋆	TRANSFER (⋆_ARRAY, V_MOLD [,I_SIZ])	Same representation as ARRAY but type of MOLD
COPIES		
⋆	MERGE (⋆_TRUE,⋆_FALSE,M)	Use ⋆_TRUE if M is true or ⋆_FALSE otherwise
call	MVBITS (I_FROM,I_LOC, I, I_TO,I_POS)	Copy I bits at I_LOC in I_FROM to I_TO at I_POS
S	REPEAT (S,I_COPIES)	Concatenate I_COPIES of string S
⋆	SPREAD (⋆_ARRAY,D,I_COPIES)	I_COPIES along D of ARRAY to rank 1 greater array
COUNTING		
I	COUNT (M [,D])	Number of true mask M terms along dimension D
DATE		
call	DATE_AND_TIME ([S_DATE] [,S_TIME] [,S_ZONE] [,I_V_VALUES])	Real-time clock data
DIMENSION OPTIONAL ARGUMENT		
L	ALL (M [,D])	True if all mask M terms are true along D
L	ANY (M [,D])	True if any mask M term is true along D
I	COUNT (M [,D])	Number of true mask M terms along dimension D
⋆	CSHIFT (⋆_ARRAY,I_SHIFT [,D])	Perform circular shift out and in for I_SHIFT terms
⋆	EOSHIFT (⋆_ARRAY, I_SHIFT [,⋆_FIL][,D])	Perform end-off shift and fill in dimension D
I,V	LBOUND (⋆_ARRAY [,D])	ARRAY lower bound(s) vector along dimension D
N	MAXVAL (N_ARRAY [,D] [,M])	Value of max ARRAY term along D passing M
N	MINVAL (N_ARRAY [,D] [,M])	Value of min ARRAY term along D passing M
A	PRODUCT (A_ARRAY [,D] [,M])	Product of ARRAY terms along D for mask M
I	SIZE (⋆_ARRAY [,D])	ARRAY size along dimension D
A	SUM (A_ARRAY [,D] [,M])	Sum of ARRAY terms along D passing mask M
I,V	UBOUND (⋆_ARRAY [,D])	ARRAY upper bound(s) vector along dimension D
DIMENSIONS		
I,V	LBOUND (⋆_ARRAY [,D])	ARRAY lower bound(s) vector along dimension D
I,V	SHAPE (⋆_ARRAY)	ARRAY (or scalar) shape vector
I	SIZE (⋆_ARRAY [,D])	ARRAY size along dimension D
I,V	UBOUND (⋆_ARRAY [,D])	ARRAY upper bound(s) vector along dimension D
DOUBLE PRECISION		(see SELECTED_REAL_KIND)
R	DBLE (A)	Convert A to double-precision real
R	DPROD (X,Y)	Double-precision product of two default real scalars

Type	Intrinsic	Description
EXISTENCE		
L	ALLOCATED (⋆_ARRAY)	True if the array is allocated
L	ASSOCIATED (P [,T])	True if pointer P is associated with any target or T
L	PRESENT (OPTIONAL)	True if optional argument is present in call
FILE		
FILL IN		
⋆	EOSHIFT (⋆_ARRAY,I_SHIFT [,⋆_FIL][,D])	End-off shift ARRAY and fill in dimension D
INQUIRY: ARRAY		
L	ALL (M [,D])	True if all mask M terms are true along D
L	ALLOCATED (⋆_ARRAY)	True if the array is allocated
L	ANY (M [,D])	True if any mask M term is true along D
I,V	LBOUND (⋆_ARRAY [,D])	ARRAY lower bound(s) vector along dimension D
I,V	SHAPE (⋆_ARRAY)	ARRAY (or scalar) shape vector
I	SIZE (⋆_ARRAY [,D])	ARRAY size along dimension D
I,V	UBOUND (⋆_ARRAY [,D])	ARRAY upper bound(s) vector along dimension D
INQUIRY: BIT		
I	BIT_SIZE (I)	Max number of bits possible in integer I (e.g., 32)
INQUIRY: CHARACTER		
I	LEN (S)	Total character string length
I	LEN_TRIM (S)	Length of S without trailing blanks
INQUIRY: NUMBER MODEL		
N	DIGITS (N)	Number of significant digits in number N (e.g., 31)
R	EPSILON (X)	Number ≪ 1 for numbers like X (e.g., 2⋆⋆–23)
N	HUGE (N)	Largest number for numbers like N (e.g. 2⋆⋆128)
I	MAXEXPONENT (X)	Max exponent for real numbers like X (e.g., 128)
I	MINEXPONENT (X)	Min exponent for real numbers like X (e.g., –125)
I	PRECISION (R_Z)	Decimal precision for real or complex value (e.g., 6)
I	RADIX (N)	Base of the model for numbers like N (e.g., 2)
I	RANGE (A)	Decimal exponent range for A (e.g., 37)
I,V	SHAPE (⋆_ARRAY)	ARRAY (or scalar) shape vector
I	SIZE (⋆_ARRAY [,D])	ARRAY size along dimension D
R	TINY (N)	Smallest positive number like N (e.g., 2⋆⋆–126)
INQUIRY: MISCELLANEOUS		
I	COUNT (M [,D])	Number of true mask M elements along D
I	INDEX (S,S_SUB [,L_BACK])	Left starting position of S_SUB within S (or right)
I	SCAN (S,S_SET [,L_BACK])	Left character index in S also in S_SET; (or right)
I	VERIFY (S,S_SET [,L_BACK])	First position in S not belonging to S_SET, (or last)
INTEGERS		
I	CEILING (X)	Least integer greater than or equal to real X
I	FLOOR (X)	Greatest integer less than or equal to X
I	MAX1 (X,X2 [,X3])	Maximum integer from list of reals
I	MIN1 (X,X2 [,X3])	Minimum integer from list of reals
N	MODULO (N,N_2)	Modulo, N-FLOOR(N/N_2)⋆N_2
I	SELECTED_INT_KIND (I_r)	Integer with exponent, –(10⋆⋆I_r) to (10⋆⋆I_r)
KIND: INQUIRY		
I	KIND (ANY)	Kind type integer parameter value for any argument
KIND: DEFINITION		
I	SELECTED_INT_KIND (I_r)	Integer with exponent, –(10⋆⋆I_r) to (10⋆⋆I_r)

(continued)

(continued)

Type	Intrinsic	Description
I	SELECTED_REAL_KIND ([I] [,I_r])	Real with precision I and exponent range I_r
KIND: USE OPTION		
R	AINT (X [,K])	Truncate X to a real whole number
R	ANINT (X [,K])	Real whole number nearest to X
C	CHAR (I [,K])	Character in position I of processor collation
Z	CMPLX (X [,Y][,K])	Convert real(s) to complex type of given kind
I	INT (A [,K])	Convert A to integer type of given kind
L	LOGICAL (L [,K])	Convert L to logical of kind K
I	NINT (X [,K])	Integer nearest to real X of the stated kind
R	REAL (A [,K])	Convert A to real type of type K
LOCATION		
I	IACHAR (C)	Position of character C in ASCII collating sequence
I	ICHAR (C)	Position of character C in processor collation
I	INDEX (S,S_SUB [,L_BACK])	Left starting position of S_SUB within S (or right)
I,V	MAXLOC (N_ARRAY [,M])	Vector location(s) of ARRAY maximum passing M
I,V	MINLOC (N_ARRAY [,M])	Vector location(s) of ARRAY minimum passing M
I	SCAN (S,S_SET [,L_BACK])	Left character index in S found in S_SET; (or right)
LOGICAL		
L	ALL (M [,D])	True if all mask M terms are true along D
L	ALLOCATED (⋆_ARRAY)	True if the array is allocated
L	ANY (M [,D])	True if any mask M term is true along D
L	ASSOCIATED (P [,T])	True if pointer P is associated with any target or T
L	BTEST (I,I_POS)	True if bit location I_POS of integer I has value one
N,L	DOT_PRODUCT (V,V_2)	Dot product of vectors V and V_2
B	IAND (I,I_2)	Logical AND on the bits of I and I_2
B	IEOR (I,I_2)	Exclusive OR on the bits of I and I_2
B	IOR (I,I_2)	Inclusive OR on the bits of I and I_2
B	ISHFT (I,I_SHIFT)	Logical shift of bits of I by I_SHIFT; pad with 0
L	LGE (S,S_2)	True if S is ≥ S_2 in ASCII collating sequence
L	LGT (S,S_2)	True if S follows S_2 in ASCII collating sequence
L	LLE (S,S_2)	True if S is ≤ to S_2 in ASCII collating sequence
L	LLT (S,S_2)	True if S precedes S_2 in ASCII collating sequence
N,L	MATMUL (MATRIX,MATRIX_2)	Conformable matrix multiplication
L	LOGICAL (L [,K])	Convert L to logical of kind K
I	NOT (I)	Logical complement of the bits of integer I
L	PRESENT (OPTIONAL)	True if optional argument is present in call
MASK, or MASK OPTIONAL ARGUMENT		
L	ALL (M [,D])	True if all mask M terms are true along D
L	ANY (M [,D])	True if any mask M term is true along D
I	COUNT (M [,D])	Number of true mask M terms, along dimension D
I,V	MAXLOC (N_ARRAY [,M])	Vector of location(s) of ARRAY max's passing M
N	MAXVAL (N_ARRAY [,D] [,M])	Value of ARRAY maximum along D passing M
⋆	MERGE (⋆_TRUE,⋆_FALSE,M)	Use ⋆_TRUE if M is true or ⋆_FALSE otherwise.
I,V	MINLOC (N_ARRAY [,M])	Vector location(s) of ARRAY minimum passing M
N	MINVAL (N_ARRAY [,D] [,M])	Value of ARRAY minimum along D passing M
⋆,V	PACK (⋆_ARRAY,M [,V_PAD])	Pack ARRAY for true M into vector; pad from V_PAD
A	PRODUCT (A_ARRAY [,D] [,M])	Product of ARRAY terms along D for mask M
A	SUM (A_ARRAY [,D] [,M])	Sum of ARRAY terms along D passing mask M

Type	Intrinsic	Description
MATHEMATICAL FUNCTIONS		
R	ACOS (X)	Arccosine (inverse cosine) function of real X
R	ASIN (X)	Arcsine (inverse sine) function of real X
R	ATAN (X)	Arctangent (inverse tangent) function of real X
R	ATAN2 (Y,X)	Arctangent for argument of complex number (X, Y)
R	COS (R_Z)	Cosine function of real or complex argument
R	COSH (X)	Hyperbolic cosine function of real X
R,Z	EXP (R_Z)	Exponential function of real or complex argument
R	LOG (R_Z)	Natural logarithm of real or complex number
R	LOG10 (X)	Common (base 10) logarithm function of real X
R,Z	SIN (R_Z)	Sine function of real or complex number
R	SINH (X)	Hyperbolic sine function of real X
R	TAN (X)	Tangent function of real X
R	TANH (X)	Hyperbolic tangent function of real X
MATRICES (See ARRAYS)		
N,L	DOT_PRODUCT (V,V_2)	Dot product of vectors V and V_2
N,L	MATMUL (MATRIX,MATRIX_2)	Conformable matrix multiplication
⋆	TRANSPOSE (MATRIX)	Matrix transpose of any type matrix
NUMBER MODEL		
N	DIGITS (N)	Number of significant digits for N (e.g., 31)
R	EPSILON (X)	Number $\ll$ 1 for numbers like X (e.g., 2⋆⋆–23)
I	EXPONENT (X)	Exponent part of the model for real X
R	FRACTION (X)	Fractional part of the model for real X
N	HUGE (N)	Largest number for numbers like N (e.g., 2⋆⋆128)
R	NEAREST (X,Y)	Nearest number at X in the direction of sign Y
I	RADIX (N)	Base of the model for numbers like N (e.g., 2)
I	RANGE (A)	Decimal exponent range for A (e.g., 37)
R	RRSPACING (X)	Reciprocal of relative spacing of numbers near X
R	SCALE (X,I)	Return X times b⋆⋆I, where base b = RADIX (X)
R	SET_EXPONENT (X,I)	Real with mantissa part of X and exponent part of I
R	SPACING (X)	Absolute spacing of numbers near X (e.g., 2⋆⋆-17)
R	TINY (N)	Smallest positive number like N (e.g., 2⋆⋆–126)
NUMERIC FUNCTIONS		
A	ABS (A)	Absolute value of A
R	AIMAG (Z)	Imaginary part of complex number
R	ANINT (X [,K])	Real whole number nearest to X
I	CEILING (X)	Least integer greater than or equal to real X
Z	CMPLX (X [,Y][,K])	Convert real(s) to complex type of given kind
Z	CONJG (Z)	Conjugate of complex number Z
R	DBLE (A)	Convert A to double-precision real
R	DPROD (X,Y)	Double-precision real product of two real scalars
I	FLOOR (X)	Greatest integer less than or equal to X
I	INT (A [,K])	Convert A to integer type of given kind
N	MAX (N,N_2 [,N_3,...])	Maximum value of two or more numbers same type
N	MIN (N,N_2 [,N_3,...])	Minimum value of two or more same type numbers
N	MOD (N,N_2)	Remainder for N_2, i.e., N-INT(N/N_2)⋆N_2
N	MODULO (N,N_2)	Modulo, N-FLOOR(N/N_2)⋆N_2
R	REAL (A [,K])	Convert A to real type of type K
N	SIGN (N,N_2)	Absolute value of N times sign of same type N_2
PADDING		
B	ISHFT (I,I_SHIFT)	Logical shift of bits of I by I_SHIFT; pad with 0

(continued)

(continued)

Type	Intrinsic	Description
⋆,V	PACK (⋆_ARRAY,M [,V_PAD])	Pack ARRAY for true M into vector; pad from V_PAD
⋆	RESHAPE (⋆_ARRAY,I_V_SHAPE [,⋆_PAD] [,V_ORDER])	Reshape ARRAY to vector SHAPE, pad, reorder
POINTER		
L	ASSOCIATED (P [,T])	True if pointer P is associated with any target or T
PRESENCE		
L	PRESENT (OPTIONAL)	True if optional argument is present in call
RANDOM NUMBER		
call	RANDOM_NUMBER (X)	Pseudorandom numbers in range $0 < X < 1$
call	RANDOM_SEED ([I_SIZE] [,I_V_P][,I_V_G])	Initialize random number generator
REALS		
R	AINT (X [,K])	Truncate X to a real whole number
R	ANINT (X [,K])	Real whole number nearest to X
R	AMAX0 (I,I2 [,I3])	Maximum real from list of integers
R	AMIN0 (I,I2 [,I3])	Minimum real from list of integers
R	REAL (A [,K])	Convert A to real type, of type K
I	SELECTED_REAL_KIND ([I] [,I_r])	Real with precision I and exponent range I_r
REDUCTION		
L	ALL (M [,D])	True if all mask M terms are true along D
L	ANY (M [,D])	True if any mask M term is true along D
I	COUNT (M [,D])	Number of true mask M terms along dimension D
N	MAXVAL (N_ARRAY [,D] [,M])	Value of max ARRAY term along D passing M
N	MINVAL (N_ARRAY [,D] [,M])	Value of min ARRAY term along D passing M
A	PRODUCT (A_ARRAY [,D] [,M])	Product of ARRAY terms along D for mask M
A	SUM (A_ARRAY [,D] [,M])	Sum of ARRAY terms along D passing mask M
RESHAPING ARRAYS		
⋆	CSHIFT (⋆_ARRAY,I_SHIFT [,D])	Perform circular shift out and in for I_SHIFT terms.
⋆	EOSHIFT (⋆_ARRAY,I_SHFT [,⋆_FIL] [,D])	End-off shift ARRAY and fill in dimension D
⋆,V	PACK (⋆_ARRAY,M [,V_PAD])	Pack ARRAY for true M into vector; pad from V_PAD
⋆	RESHAPE (⋆_ARRAY,I_V_SHAPE [,⋆_PAD] [,V_ORDER])	Reshape ARRAY to vector SHAPE, pad, reorder
⋆	UNPACK (V,M,⋆_USE)	Unpack V for true elements of M into USE
REVERSE ORDER		
I	INDEX (S,S_SUB [,L_BACK])	Left starting position of S_SUB within S (rightmost)
I	SCAN (S,S_SET [,L_BACK])	Left character index in S found in S_SET; (rightmost)
I	VERIFY (S,S_SET [,L_BACK])	First position in S not found in S_SET, (or last)
SHIFTS		
⋆	CSHIFT (⋆_ARRAY,I_SHIFT [,D])	Perform circular shift out and in for I_SHIFT terms
⋆	EOSHIFT (⋆_ARRAY,I_SHIFT [,⋆_FILL][,D])	Perform end-off shift, and fill, in dimension D
B	ISHFT (I,I_SHIFT)	Logical shift of bits of I by I_SHIFT; pad with 0
B	ISHFTC (I,I_SHIFT [,I_SIZE])	Logical circular shift of I_SIZE rightmost bits of I
STRING		
C	ADJUSTL (S)	Adjust S left; move leading blanks to trailing blanks
C	ADJUSTR (S)	Adjust S right; move trailing to leading blanks

Type	Intrinsic	Description
I	INDEX (S,S_SUB [,L_BACK])	Left starting position of S_SUB within S (or right)
I	LEN (S)	Total character string length
I	LEN_TRIM (S)	Length of S without trailing blanks
L	LGE (S,S_2)	True if S is ≥ to S_2 in ASCII collating sequence
L	LGT (S,S_2)	True if S follows S_2 in ASCII collating sequence
L	LLE (S,S_2)	True if S is ≤ to S_2 in ASCII collating sequence
L	LLT (S,S_2)	True if S precedes S_2 in ASCII collating sequence
S	REPEAT (S,I_COPIES)	Concatenates I_COPIES of string S
I	SCAN (S,S_SET [,L_BACK])	Left character index in S found in S_SET; (or right)
S	TRIM (S)	Remove trailing blanks from a single string
I	VERIFY (S,S_SET [,L_BACK])	First position in S not found in S_SET, (or last)
TARGET		
L	ASSOCIATED (P [,T])	True if pointer P is associated with any target or T
TIME		
call	DATE_AND_TIME ([S_DATE] [,S_TIME] [,S_ZONE] [,I_V_VALUES])	Real-time clock data
call	SYSTEM_CLOCK ([I_NOW] [,I_RAT] [,I_MX])	Integer data from real-time clock
VECTOR (See ARRAYS)		
N,L	DOT_PRODUCT (V,V_2)	Dot product of vectors V and V_2
I,V	LBOUND (⋆_ARRAY [,D])	ARRAY lower bound(s) vector along D
I,V	MAXLOC (N_ARRAY [,M])	Location(s) of maximum ARRAY term passing M
I,V	MINLOC (N_ARRAY [,M])	Location(s) of minimum ARRAY term passing M
⋆,V	PACK (⋆_ARRAY,M [,V_PAD])	Pack ARRAY for true M into vector; pad from V_PAD
⋆	RESHAPE (⋆_ARRAY,I_V_SHAPE [,⋆_PAD] [,V_ORDER])	Reshape ARRAY to vector SHAPE, pad, reorder
I,V	SHAPE (⋆_ARRAY)	ARRAY (or scalar) shape vector
⋆	TRANSFER (⋆_ARRAY, V_MOLD [,I_SIZE])	Same representation as ARRAY but type of MOLD
I,V	UBOUND (⋆_ARRAY [,D])	ARRAY upper bound(s) vector along dimension D

A.4 Syntax of Fortran 90 Statements

The following is a list of the recommended Fortran 90 statements. Additional statements are allowed but have been declared obsolete and are expected to be deleted in future standards. Thus, they should not be utilized in new programs. They are appended to the end of this list. Below we list the standard syntax for the Fortran 90 statements. In some cases the most common simple form of a statement is shown before its more general options. Such optional features are shown included in brackets, [ ], and a vertical bar | means "or." Note that the new attribute terminator symbol :: is always optional, but its use is recommended.

The following abbreviations are employed: arg=argument, attr=attribute, exp=expression, i_=integer, r_=real, s_=string, spec=specifier, and here [type] means CHARACTER | COMPLEX | INTEGER | LOGICAL | REAL or a user-defined name given in a TYPE statement. Recall that F90 allows variable names to be 31 characters long, and they may include an underscore (but F77 allows only 6 characters and no underscore); F90 lines may contain up to 132 characters (but just 72 in F77). All standard F77 statements are a subset of F90. Attribute options, and their specifiers, for each statement are given in the companion table "Fortran 90 Attributes and Specifiers." The numerous options for the INQUIRE statement are given in the table entitled "Options for F90 INQUIRE."

In addition to the statements given below, F90 offers intrinsic array operations, implied do loops, vector subscripts, and about 160 intrinsic functions. Those functions, with their arguments, are given in the tables "Alphabetical Table of Fortran 90 Intrinsic Functions and Subroutines," and "Subject Table of Fortran 90 Intrinsic Functions and Subroutines."

F90 Syntax

```
! preceeds a comment in F90
 in column one denotes a comment line in F77
& continues a line in F90 (must be in column 6 for F77)
; terminates a statement in F90 (allows multiple statements per line)
variable = expression_or_statement ! is an assignment (column 7 in F77)
```

```
ALLOCATABLE [::] array_name[(extents)] [, array_name[(extents)]]
ALLOCATE (array_name)
ALLOCATE (array_name [, STAT=status] [,array_name [, STAT=status]])
BACKSPACE i_exp ! file unit number
BACKSPACE ([UNIT=]i_value [, IOSTAT=i_variable] [, ERR=i_label])
C in column one denotes a comment line in F77
CALL subroutine_name [([args])]
CASE (range_list) [select_name] ! purpose
CASE DEFAULT [select_name] ! purpose
CHARACTER LEN=i_value [::] s_list
CHARACTER [(LEN=i_value | * [, KIND=]i_kind)] [[, attr_list] ::] s_list
CHARACTER [(i_value | *, [KIND=]i_kind)] [[, attr_list] ::] s_list
CHARACTER [([KIND=i_kind] [, LEN=i_value | *])] [[, attr_list] ::] s_list
CLOSE (i_value) ! unit number
CLOSE ([UNIT=]i_value [, ERR=i_label] [, IOSTAT=i_variable] [, STATUS=exp])
COMPLEX [::] variable_list
COMPLEX [([KIND=]i_kind)] [[, attr_list] ::] variable_list
CONTAINS ! internal definitions follow
CYCLE ! current do only for a purpose
CYCLE [nested_do_name] ! and terminate its sub_do's for a purpose
DEALLOCATE (array_name)
DEALLOCATE (array_name [, STAT=status] [, array_name [, STAT=status]])
DIMENSION array_name(extents) [, array_name(extents)]
DO ! forever
DO i_variable = i_start, i_stop ! loop_name_or_purpose
DO [i_variable = i_start, i_stop [, i_inc]] ! loop_name_or_purpose
DO [i_label,] [i_variable = i_start, i_stop [, i_inc]] ! loop_name
[loop_name:] DO [i_variable = i_start, i_stop [, i_inc]] ! purpose
[loop_name:] DO [i_label,] [i_variable = i_start, i_stop [, i_inc]]
DO WHILE (logical_expression) ! obsolete, use DO-EXIT pair
DO [i_label,] WHILE (logical_expression) ! obsolete-obsolete
[name:] DO [i_label,] WHILE (logical_expression) ! obsolete
ELSE [if_name]
ELSE IF (logical_expression) THEN [if_name]
ELSE WHERE (logical_expression)
END [name] ! purpose
```

```
END DO [do_name]  ! purpose
END FUNCTION [function_name]  ! purpose
END IF [if_name]  ! purpose
END INTERFACE  ! purpose
END MODULE [module_name]  ! purpose
END PROGRAM [program_name]  ! purpose
END SELECT [select_name]  ! purpose
END SUBROUTINE [name]  ! purpose
END TYPE [type_name]  ! purpose
END WHERE  ! purpose
ENDFILE i_exp  ! for file unit number
ENDFILE ([UNIT=]i_value [, IOSTAT=i_variable] [, ERR=i_label])
ENTRY entry_name [([args])] [RESULT(variable_name)]
EXIT  ! current do only for a purpose
EXIT [nested_do_name]  ! and its sub_do's for a purpose
EXTERNAL program_list
i_label FORMAT (specification_and_edit_list)
FUNCTION name ([args])  ! purpose
FUNCTION name ([args]) [RESULT(variable_name)]  ! purpose
[type] [RECURSIVE] FUNCTION name ([args]) [RESULT(variable_name)]
[RECURSIVE] [type] FUNCTION name ([args]) [RESULT(variable_name)]
GO TO i_label  ! for_a_reason
IF (logical_expression) executable_statement
[name:] IF (logical_expression) THEN  ! state_purpose
IMPLICIT type (letter_list)  ! F77 (a-h,o-z) real, (i-n) integer
IMPLICIT NONE  ! F90 recommended default
INCLUDE source_file_path_name  ! purpose
INQUIRE ([FILE=]'name_string' [, see_INQUIRE_table])  ! re file
INQUIRE ([NAME=]s_variable [, see_INQUIRE_table])  ! re file
INQUIRE (IOLENGTH=i_variable [, see_INQUIRE_table])  ! re output
INQUIRE ([UNIT=]i_value [, see_INQUIRE_table])  ! re unit
INTEGER [::] variable_list
INTEGER [([KIND=]i_kind)] [[, attr_list] ::] variable_list
INTENT ([IN | INOUT | OUT]) argument_list
INTERFACE ASSIGNMENT (+ | - | * | / | = | **)  ! user extension
INTERFACE OPERATOR (.operator.)  ! user defined
INTERFACE [interface_name]
INTRINSIC function_list
LOGICAL [::] variable_list
LOGICAL [([KIND=]i_kind)] [[, attr_list] ::] variable_list
MODULE PROCEDURE program_list
MODULE module_name  ! purpose
NULLIFY (pointer_list)
OPEN (i_value)  ! unit number
OPEN ([UNIT=]i_value [, ERR=i_label] [, IOSTAT=i_variable] [, other_spec])
OPTIONAL [::] argument_list
PARAMETER (variable=value [, variable=value])
POINTER [::] name[(extent)] [, name[(extent)]]  ! purpose
PRINT * , output_list  ! default free format
PRINT * , (io_implied_do)  ! default free format
PRINT '(formats)' , output_list  ! formatted
PRINT '(formats)' , (io_implied_do)  ! formatted
```

(continued)

(continued)

```
PRIVATE [[::] module_variable_list]  ! limit access
PROGRAM [program_name]  ! purpose
PUBLIC [[::] module_variable_list]  ! default access
READ * , input_list  ! default free format
READ * , (io_implied_do)  ! default free format
READ '(formats)' input_list  ! formatted
READ '(formats)' (io_implied_do)  ! formatted
READ ([UNIT=]i_value, [FMT=]i_label [, io_spec_list]) input_list  ! formatted
READ ([UNIT=]i_value, s_variable [, io_spec_list]) input_list  ! formatted
READ ([UNIT=]i_value, '(formats)' [, io_spec_list]) input_list  ! formatted
READ (i_value) input_list  ! binary read
READ ([UNIT=]i_value, [, io_spec_list]) input_list  ! binary read
READ (s_variable, [FMT=]i_label) input_list  ! internal file type change
READ ([UNIT=]s_variable, [FMT=]i_label [, io_spec_list]) input_list  ! internal file change
REAL [::] variable_list
REAL [([KIND=]i_kind)] [[, attr_list] ::] variable_list
RECURSIVE FUNCTION name ([args]) [RESULT(variable_name)]  ! purpose
[type] RECURSIVE FUNCTION name ([args]) [RESULT(variable_name)]  ! purpose
RECURSIVE SUBROUTINE name [([args])]  ! purpose
RETURN  ! from subroutine_name
REWIND i_exp  ! file unit number
REWIND ([UNIT=]i_value [, IOSTAT=i_variable] [, ERR=i_label])
SAVE [[::] variable_list]
[name:] SELECT CASE (value)
SEQUENCE
STOP ['stop_message_string']
SUBROUTINE name [([args])]  ! purpose
SUBROUTINE name [([args])] [args, optional_args]  ! purpose
[RECURSIVE] SUBROUTINE name [([args])]  ! purpose
TARGET [::] name[(extent)] [, name[(extent)]]
TYPE (type_name) [[, attr_list] ::] variable_list
TYPE [, PRIVATE | PUBLIC] name
USE module_name [, ONLY: list_in_module_name]  ! purpose
USE module_name [, new_var_or_sub=>old_name]  ! purpose
WHERE (logical_array_expression)  ! then
WHERE (logical_array_expression) array_variable = array_expression
WRITE * , output_list  ! default free format
WRITE * , (io_implied_do)  ! default free format
WRITE '(formats)' output_list  ! formatted write
WRITE '(formats)' (io_implied_do)  ! formatted write
WRITE ([UNIT=]i_value, [FMT=]i_label [, io_spec_list]) output_list  ! formatted write
WRITE ([UNIT=]i_value, s_variable [, io_spec_list]) output_list  ! formatted write
WRITE ([UNIT=]i_value, '(formats)' [, io_spec_list]) output_list  ! formatted write
WRITE (i_value) output_list  ! binary write
WRITE (i_value) (io_implied_do)  ! binary write
WRITE ([UNIT=]i_value, [, io_spec_list]) output_list  ! binary write
WRITE (s_variable, [FMT=]i_label) output_list  ! internal file type change
WRITE ([UNIT=]s_variable, [FMT=]i_label [, io_spec_list]) output_list  ! internal file change
```

The attributes lists for the type declarations (e.g., REAL) are ALLOCATABLE, DIMENSION, INTENT, OPTIONAL, KIND, POINTER, PARAMETER, PRIVATE, PUBLIC, SAVE, and TARGET; those for OPEN and CLOSE are ACCESS, ACTION, BLANK, and DELIM; whereas those for READ and WRITE are ADVANCE, END, EOR, ERR, and FMT.

Obsolescent statements are those from Fortran 77 that are redundant and for which better methods are available in both Fortran 77 and Fortran 90.

Obsolete Syntax

ASSIGN i_label TO i_variable
BLOCK DATA [block_data_name]
COMMON [/common_block_name/] r_variable_list, i_variable_list
[i_label] CONTINUE ! from do [do_name]
DATA variable_list / value_list /
DATA (array_implied_do) / value_list /
DOUBLE PRECISION [[, attr_list] ::] variable_list
DO [i_label,] [r_variable = r_start, r_stop [, r_inc]] ! real control
DO_CONTINUE_pair
[name:] DO [i_label,] WHILE (logical_expression) ! obsolete
END BLOCK DATA [block_data_name]
EQUIVALENCE (variable_1, variable_2) [, (variable_3, variable_4)]
GO TO (i_label_1,i_label_2,...,i_label_n)[,] i_variable
IF (arithmetic_exp) i_label_neg, i_label_zero, i_label_pos
NAMELIST /group_name/ variable_list
PAUSE ! for human action
RETURN alternates
statement_function (args) = expression

A.5 Examples of F90 Statements

The following is a list of examples of the recommended Fortran90 statements. Some have been declared obsolete and are expected to be deleted in future standards. Thus, they should not be used in new programs. They are noted in the comments. In some cases the most common simple form of a statement is shown along with its more general options. Note that the new attribute terminator symbol :: is always optional, but its use is recommended. Although Fortran is not case-sensitive, this table employs uppercase letters to denote standard features and lowercase letters for user-supplied information. The following abbreviations are employed: arg=argument, attr=attribute, exp=expression, i_=integer, l_=logical, r_=real, s_=string, spec=specifier, z_=complex.

Recall that F90 allows variable names to be 31 characters long, and they may include an underscore (but F77 allows only 6 characters and no underscore). The F90 lines may contain up to 132 characters (but just 72 in F77). All standard F77 statements are a subset of F90.

The attributes lists for the type declarations (e.g., REAL) are ALLOCATABLE, DIMENSION, INTENT, OPTIONAL, KIND, POINTER, PARAMETER, PRIVATE, PUBLIC, SAVE, and TARGET. Those optional attributes for OPEN are ACCESS = [DIRECT, SEQUENTIAL], ACTION = [READ, READWRITE, WRITE], BLANK = [NULL, ZERO], DELIM = [APOSTROPHE, NONE, QUOTE], ERR = i_label, FILE = s_name, FORM = [FORMATTED, UNFORMATTED],

IOSTAT = i_var, PAD = [NO, YES], POSITION = [APPEND, ASIS, REWIND], RECL = i_len, STATUS = [NEW, OLD, REPLACE, SEARCH, UNKNOWN], and UNIT = i_unit; whereas CLOSE utilizes only ERR, IOSTAT, STATUS, and UNIT.

The io_spec_list options for READ and WRITE are ADVANCE = [NO, YES], END = i_label, EOR = i_label, ERR = i_label, FMT = [*, i_label, s_var], IOSTAT = i_var, NML = var_list, REC = i_exp, SIZE = i_size, and UNIT = i_unit.

Fortran Statement Examples

Name	Examples	Comments
Allocatable	ALLOCATABLE :: force, stiffness	By name
	ALLOCATABLE :: force(:), stiffness(:,:)	Ranks
Allocate	ALLOCATE (hyper_matrix(5, 10, 3))	
	ALLOCATE (force(m))	
	ALLOCATE (array_name(3, 3, 3, 3), STAT=i_err)	Error status
Assign	ASSIGN 9 TO k	Obsolete
Assignment	c = 'b'	Character
	s = "abc"	String
	s = c // 'abc'	Concatenation
	s = string(j:m)	Substring
	s_fmt = '(2F5.1)'	Stored format
	l = l_1 .OR. l_2	Logical
	l = m < = 80	
	poor = (final > = 60) .AND. (final < 70)	
	proceed = .TRUE.	
	n = n + 1	Arithmetic
	x = b'1010'	Binary
	z = (0.0, 1.0)	Complex
	r = SQRT (5.)	Function
	converged = (ABS (x0 – x) < 2*SPACING (x))	
	x = z'B'	Hexadecimal
	k = 123	Integer
	x = o'12'	Octal
	r = 321.	Real
	a = 23. ; j = 120 ; ans = .TRUE.;	Semicolon
	k = SELECTED_INTEGER_KIND (20)	Kind
	m = SELECTED_REAL_KIND (16, 30)	
	long = SELECTED_REAL_KIND (9, 20)	
	pi = 3.1459265_long	
	a = b + c	Matrix add
	d = MATMUL (a, b)	Matrix multiply
	e = TRANSPOSE (d)	Matrix transpose
	f = 0 ; g = (/ 2. , 4. , 6. /)	Matrix initialize
	B = Al:, n:(:–1)	Matrix flipped
	x = (/ (k, k = 0, n) /) * d	Implied do
	kth_row => a(k,:)	Pointer
	corners => a(1:n:(n-1), 1:m:(m-1))	
	p_2 => r	

Name	Examples	Comments
	student_record % rank = 51	Defined type
	patient_data % city = 'houston'	
	sqrt(x) = DSQRT(x) ! function statement	Obsolete
Backspace	BACKSPACE i_exp	Compute unit
	BACKSPACE 8	Unit
	BACKSPACE (UNIT=9, IOSTAT=i, ERR=5)	Error go to
	BACKSPACE (9, IOSTAT=io_ok, ERR=99)	
	BACKSPACE (UNIT=9, IOSTAT=io_ok, ERR=99)	
	BACKSPACE (8, IOSTAT=io_ok)	I/O status
Block Data	BLOCK DATA ! Obsolete	
	BLOCK DATA winter ! Obsolete	Named
C	C in column one denotes a comment line in F77	Obsolete
	* in column one denotes a comment line in F77	Obsolete
	! anywhere starts a comment line in F90	
Call	CALL sub1 (a, b)	
	CALL sub2 (a, b, *5) ! Obsolete, use CASE	Alt return to 5
	CALL sub3	No arguments
	CALL subroutine_name (args, optional_args)	Optional arg
Case	CASE (range_list)	See SELECT
	CASE (range_list) select_name	Named
Case	CASE DEFAULT	See SELECT
Default	CASE DEFAULT select_name	Named
Character	CHARACTER (80) s, s_2*3(4)	
	CHARACTER *16 a, b, c	
	CHARACTER * home_team	:: recommended
	CHARACTER (*), INTENT(IN) :: home_team	Intent
	CHARACTER (LEN=3) :: b = 'xyz'	Initialize b
	CHARACTER LEN=40 :: monday, wednesday, friday	
	CHARACTER (LEN=40), attr_list :: last, first, middle	
	CHARACTER (40), attr_list :: name, state	
	CHARACTER (*), PARAMETER :: reply = "Invalid Data"	
	CHARACTER (*, KIND=greek), attr_list :: s1_list	Kind
	CHARACTER (*, KIND=greek), attr_list :: last, first, middle	
	CHARACTER (KIND=cyrillic, LEN=40) :: name, state	
	CHARACTER (KIND=cyrillic, *), attr_list :: s_list	
Close	CLOSE (7)	Unit number
	CLOSE (UNIT=k)	
	CLOSE (UNIT=8, ERR=90, IOSTAT=i)	Error go to
	CLOSE (8, ERR=99, IOSTAT=io_ok, STATUS='KEEP')	I/O status
	CLOSE (9, ERR=99, IOSTAT=io, STATUS='DELETE')	File status
	CLOSE (UNIT=8, ERR=95, IOSTAT=io_ok)	
Common	COMMON / name / h, p, t ! Obsolete	Named common
	COMMON p, d, q(m,n) ! Obsolete	Blank common
Complex	COMPLEX u, v, w(3, 6)	:: recommended
	COMPLEX :: u = (1.0,1.0), v = (1.0,10.0)	Initialize u and v
	COMPLEX :: variable_list	

(continued)

(continued)

Name	Examples	Comments
	COMPLEX attr_list :: variable_list	
	COMPLEX (KIND=i2_kind), attr_list :: variable_list	Kind
Contains	CONTAINS	Internal definitions
	CONTAINS	
	FUNCTION mine (b)	Or subroutines
	...	
	END FUNCTION mine	
Continuation	! any non-block character in column 6 flags continuation	F77 obsolete
	& at the end flags continuation to next line	F90 standard
	& at the beginning flags continuation from above line	
	a_long_name = a_constant_value* &	
	another_value ! on following line	
	a_long_name_here_is_set_to = value	
	& * another_value ! continued from above	
Continue	100 CONTINUE	Obsolete
Cycle	CYCLE	Current do only
	CYCLE nested_do_name	Terminate sub_dos
Data	DATA a, s / 4.01, 'z' /	Obsolete
	DATA s_fmt / '(2F5.1)' /	Stored format
	DATA (r(k), k=1,3) / 0.7, 0.8, 1.9 /	Implied do
	DATA array (4,4) / 1.0 /	Single value
	DATA bit_val / b'0011111' /	Binary
Deallocate	DEALLOCATE (force)	File name
	DEALLOCATE (force, STAT=i_err)	Error status
Dimension	DIMENSION array (4, 4)	
	DIMENSION v(1000), w(3) = (/ 1., 2., 4. /)	Initialize w
	DIMENSION force(20), stiffness(:,:)	
	DIMENSION (5,10,3) :: triplet	:: recommended
	INTEGER, DIMENSION (:,:) :: material, nodes_list	Typed
	REAL, DIMENSION (m, n) :: a, b	
	REAL, DIMENSION (:,:) :: force, stiffness	
	REAL, DIMENSION(5,10,3), INTENT(IN) :: triplet	Intent
Do	DO 100 j = init, last, incr ! Obsolete	Labeled do
	...	
	100 CONTINUE	Obsolete
	DO j = init, last	Unlabeled do
	...	
	END DO	
	DO ! forever	Unlabeled do
	...	
	END DO ! forever	
	DO WHILE (diff <= delta)	Unlabeled while
	...	
	END DO	
	DO 100 WHILE (diff < = delta) ! Obsolete	Labeled while
	...	
	100 CONTINUE	Obsolete
	DO	Forever
	DO k = i_start, i_stop	Integer range

Name	Examples	Comments
	DO k = i_start, i_stop, i_inc	Increment
	DO 10, k = i_start, i_stop	Obsolete
	do_name: DO k = i_start, i_stop, i_inc	Named
	do_name: DO 10, k = i_start, i_stop, i_inc	Named label
	DO 10, r_variable = r_start, r_stop, r_inc ! Obsolete	Real range
Do While	DO WHILE (.NOT. converged)	Use DO-EXIT pair
	DO 10, WHILE (.NOT. converged)	Obsolete
	do_name: DO 10, WHILE (.NOT. converged)	Obsolete
Double	DOUBLE PRECISION a, d, y(2)	Obsolete
Precision	DOUBLE PRECISION :: a, d = 1.2D3, y(2)	Initialize D
	DOUBLE PRECISION, attr_list :: variable_list	Obsolete
Else	ELSE	Then
	ELSE leap_year	Named
Else If	ELSE IF (k > 50) THEN	
	ELSE IF (days_in_year == 364) THEN	
	ELSE IF (days_in_year == 364) THEN leap_year	Named
Elsewhere	ELSEWHERE	See WHERE
End	END	
	END name	Named
End Block	END BLOCK DATA	Obsolete
Data	END BLOCK DATA block_data_name	Obsolete
End Do	END DO	
	END DO do_name	Named
End Function	END FUNCTION function_name	
	END FUNCTION	
End If	END IF leap_year	Named
	END IF	
End Interface	END INTERFACE	
End Module	END MODULE my_matrix_operators	
	END MODULE	
End Program	END PROGRAM program_name	
	END PROGRAM	
End Select	END SELECT select_name	Named
	END SELECT	
End	END SUBROUTINE name	
Subroutine	END SUBROUTINE	
End Type	END TYPE type_name	See TYPE
	END TYPE	
End Where	END WHERE	See WHERE
Endfile	ENDFILE i_exp	Compute unit
	ENDFILE (UNIT=k)	Unit number
	ENDFILE k	
	ENDFILE (UNIT=8, ERR=95)	Error go to
	ENDFILE (7, IOSTAT=io_ok, ERR=99)	I/O status

(continued)

(continued)

Name	Examples	Comments
	ENDFILE (UNIT=8, IOSTAT=k, ERR=9)	
	ENDFILE (UNIT=9, IOSTAT=io_ok, ERR=99)	
Entry	ENTRY sec1 (x, y)	Arguments
	ENTRY sec2 (a1, a2, *4) ! Obsolete, use CASE	Alternate return to 4
	ENTRY section	No arguments
	ENTRY entry_name RESULT(variable_name)	Result
Equivalence	EQUIVALENCE (v (1), a (1,1))	Obsolete
	EQUIVALENCE (v, a)	
	EQUIVALENCE (x, v(10)), (p, q, d)	
Exit	EXIT	Current do only
	EXIT nested_do_name	Current and subdos
External	EXTERNAL my_program	
Format	10 FORMAT (2X, 2I3, 3F6.1, 4E12.2, 2A6, 3L2)	X I F E A L
	10 FORMAT (// 2D6.1, 3G12.2)	D, G
	10 FORMAT (2I3.3, 3G6.1E3, 4E12.2E3)	Exponent w
	10 FORMAT ('a quoted string', "another", I2)	Strings
	10 FORMAT (1X, T10, A1, T20, A1)	Tabs
	10 FORMAT (5X, TR10, A1, TR10, A1, TL5, A1)	Tab right, left
	10 FORMAT ("Init=", I2, :, 3X, "Last=", I2)	: stop if empty
	10 FORMAT ('Octal ', o6, ', Hex ' z6)	Octal, hex
	10 FORMAT (specification_and_edit_list)	
Function	FUNCTION z (a, b)	Arguments
	FUNCTION w (e, d) RESULT (a)	Result
	FUNCTION name (args)	
	FUNCTION name	No argument
	FUNCTION name (args) RESULT(variable_name)	
	INTEGER FUNCTION n (j, k)	Type
	INTEGER FUNCTION name (args)	
	COMPLEX RECURSIVE FUNCTION dat (args)	
	RECURSIVE REAL FUNCTION name (args)	
Go To	GO TO 99	Unconditional
	GO TO (10,20,35,95), i_variable ! Obsolete	Computed
If	IF (arithmetic_exp) 95, 10, 20 ! Obsolete	Arithmetic
	IF (logic) RETURN	Logical if
	IF (logic) n = n + 2	
	IF (logic) THEN	if block
	n = n + 1	
	k = k + 1	
	END IF	
	leap_year: IF (logical_expression) THEN	Named
	IF (logic) THEN	if else block
	n = n + 1	
	ELSE	
	k = k + 1	
	END IF	
	IF (c == 'a') THEN	if else-if block
	na = na + 1	
	CALL sub_a	

Name	Examples	Comments
	ELSE IF (c == 'b') THEN	(Use CASE)
	nb = nb + 1	
	ELSE IF (c == 'c') THEN	
	nc = nc + 1	
	CALL sub_c	
	END IF	
Implicit	IMPLICIT INTEGER (i-n)	F77 default
Type	IMPLICIT REAL (a-h,o-z)	F77 default
	IMPLICIT NONE	Recommended F90
	IMPLICIT CHARACTER *10 (f,l)	Character
	IMPLICIT COMPLEX (a-c,z)	Complex
	IMPLICIT TYPE (color) (b,g,r)	Derived type
	IMPLICIT LOGICAL (KIND=bit) (m)	Logical
Include	INCLUDE 'path/source.f'	
Inquire	INQUIRE (UNIT=3, OPENED=t_or_f)	Opened
	INQUIRE (FILE='mydata', EXIST=t_or_f)	Exists
	INQUIRE (UNIT=3, OPENED=ok, IOSTAT=k)	I/O status
	INQUIRE (FILE='name_string', see_INQUIRE_table)	Refile
	INQUIRE (NAME=s_variable, see_INQUIRE_table)	Refile
	INQUIRE (IOLENGTH=i_var, see_INQUIRE_table)	Reoutput
	INQUIRE (7, see_INQUIRE_table)	Reunit
	INQUIRE (UNIT=8, see_INQUIRE_table)	Reunit
Integer	INTEGER c, d(4)	:: Recommended
	INTEGER (long), attr_list :: variable_list	
	INTEGER, DIMENSION (4) :: a, d, e	
	INTEGER, ALLOCATABLE, DIMENSION (:,:) :: a, b	Allocatable
	INTEGER :: a = 100, b, c = 9	Initialize a & c
	INTEGER :: i, j, k, l, m, n, month, year = 1996	
	INTEGER, attr_list :: variable_list	
	INTEGER (KIND=i2_kind), attr_list :: variable_list	Kind
Intent	INTENT (IN) :: credit_card_owners	
	INTENT (INOUT) :: amount_due	
	INTENT (OUT) income_rank	
Interface	INTERFACE ASSIGNMENT (=)	User extension
	INTERFACE OPERATOR (+)	User extension
	INTERFACE OPERATOR (–)	User extension
	INTERFACE OPERATOR (/)	User extension
	INTERFACE OPERATOR (*)	User extension
	INTERFACE OPERATOR (**)	User extension
	INTERFACE OPERATOR (.operator.)	User-defined
	INTERFACE	
	INTERFACE interface_name	
Intrinsic	INTRINSIC SQRT, EXP	Functions
Logical	LOGICAL c	:: recommended
	LOGICAL, ALLOCATABLE :: mask(:), mask_2(:,:)	Allocatable
	LOGICAL (KIND = byte) :: flag, status	Kind
	LOGICAL :: b = .FALSE., c	Initialize b

(continued)

(continued)

Name	Examples	Comments
Module	MODULE PROCEDURE mat_x_mat, mat_x_vec	Generics
	MODULE my_matrix_operators	
Namelist	NAMELIST /data/ s, n, d	Obsolete
Nullify	NULLIFY (pointer_list)	
Open	OPEN (7)	Unit number
	OPEN (UNIT=3, FILE="data.test")	Name
	OPEN (UNIT=2, FILE="data", STATUS = "old")	File status
	OPEN (UNIT=3, IOSTAT=k)	I/O status
	OPEN (9, ERR = 12, ACCESS ="direct")	Access type
	OPEN (8, ERR=99, IOSTAT=io_ok)	Error go to
	OPEN (UNIT=8, ERR=99, IOSTAT=io_ok)	
Optional	OPTIONAL slow, fast	Argument list
	OPTIONAL :: argument_list	
Parameter	PARAMETER (a="xyz"), (pi=3.14159)	Character
	PARAMETER (a="z", pi=3.14159)	Real
	PARAMETER (x=11, y = x/3)	Computed
	PARAMETER, REAL :: weight = 245.6	Type
Pause	PAUSE ! for human action	Obsolete
Pointer	POINTER current, last	:: recommended
	POINTER :: name(4,5)	Rank
	REAL, POINTER :: y(:), x(:,:,:)	Type
Print	PRINT *, a, j	List-directed
	PRINT *, output_list	Default unformatted
	PRINT *, (io_implied_do)	Implied do
	PRINT *, "The squre root of", n, 'is', SQRT(n)	Function
	PRINT *, (4*k-1, k=1,10,3)	
	PRINT 10, a, j	Formatted
	PRINT 10, m_array	Array
	PRINT 10, (m(i), i = j,k)	Implied do
	PRINT 10, s(j:k)	Substring
	PRINT '(A6, I3)', a, j	Character, integer
	PRINT FMT='(A6, I3)', a, j	Included format
	PRINT data_namelist ! Obsolete	Name list
	PRINT '(formats)', output_list	Formatted
	PRINT '(formats)', (io_implied_do)	Implied do
	PRINT '(I4)', (2*k, k=1,5)	
Private	PRIVATE	
	PRIVATE :: module_variable_list	Specific items
Program	PROGRAM my_job	
	PROGRAM	
Public	PUBLIC	
	PUBLIC :: module_variable_list	Specific items
Read	READ *, a, j	List-directed
	READ 1, a , j	Formatted
	READ 10, m_array	Formatted array
	READ 10, (m(i), i=j, k)	Implied do

Name	Examples	Comments
	READ 10, s(i:k)	Substring
	READ '(A6, I3)' a, i	Character, integer
	READ (1, 2) x, y	Formatted file
	READ (UNIT=1, FMT=2) x, y	
	READ (1, 2, ERR=8, END=9) x, y	End of file go to
	READ (UNIT=1, FMT=2, ERR=8, END=9) x, y	Error go to
	READ (*, 2) x, y	Formatted, std out
	READ (*, 10) m_array	Unformatted array
	READ (*, 10) (m(i), i=j, k)	Implied do
	READ (*, 10) s(i:k)	Substring
	READ (1, *) x, y	Unformatted file
	READ (*, *) x, y	Unformatted, std out
	READ (1, '(A6, I3)') x, y	Character, integer
	READ (1, FMT='(A6, I3)') x, y	Included format
	READ (1, s_fmt) x, y	Format in a string
	READ (1, FMT=s_fmt) x, y	
	READ (*, NML=data) ! Obsolete	Name list read
	READ (1, NML=data) ! Obsolete	Name list from a file
	READ (1, END=8, ERR=9) x, y	Unformatted
	READ (s2, 1, ERR=9) x	Internal, formatted
	READ (s2, *, ERR=9) x	Unformatted
	READ (s2, REC=4, END=8) x	Internal, direct
	READ (1, REC=3) v	Unformatted direct
	READ (1, 2, REC=3) v	Formatted direct
	READ *, input_list	Default unformatted
	READ *, (io_implied_do)	Implied do
	READ *, (a(j,:), j=1, rows)	
	READ '(formats)' input_list	Formatted read
	READ '(formats)' (io_implied_do)	Formatted read
	READ '(5I5, (5I5))', (num(k), k=1, n)	
	READ (8, FMT=20) input_list	Formatted
	READ (8, FMT=20, ADVANCE='NO') input	Advance
	READ (9, FMT=20, io_spec_list) input_list	I/O Specification
	READ (UNIT=7, 20, io_spec_list) input_list	
	READ (UNIT=8, FMT=10, io_spec_list) input	
	READ (7, s_fmt, io_spec_list) input_list	Stored format
	READ (UNIT=7, s_fmt, io_spec_list) input	
	READ (9, '(formats)' io_spec_list) input_list	Inline format
	READ (UNIT=9, '(formats)' io_spec_list) input	
	READ (8) input_list	Binary read
	READ (UNIT=7) input_list	
	READ (8, io_spec_list) input_list	I/O Specification
	READ (UNIT=9, io_spec_list) input_list	
	READ (s_variable, FMT=20) input_list	Internal file,
	READ (UNIT=s_variable, 10, io_spec_list) input	type change
Real	REAL*4	:: recommended
	REAL :: r, m(9)	
	REAL*16 :: a, b, c	Quad Precision
	REAL*8, DIMENSION (n) :: a, b, c	Double Precision

(continued)

(continued)

Name	Examples	Comments
	REAL :: a = 3.14, b, c = 100.0	Initialize a & c
	REAL :: variable_list	
	REAL, attr_list :: variable_list	
	REAL, POINTER :: a(:,:)	
	REAL (KIND=i2_kind), attr_list :: variable_list	Kind
	REAL (double), attr_list :: variable_list	
Recursive	RECURSIVE FUNCTION name	Function
	RECURSIVE FUNCTION a(n) RESULT(fac)	Result
	INTEGER RECURSIVE FUNCTION name (args)	
	RECURSIVE SUBROUTINE name (args)	Subroutine
	RECURSIVE SUBROUTINE name	
Return	RETURN	Standard return
Rewind	REWIND i_exp	Compute unit
	REWIND 2	Unit number
	REWIND k	
	REWIND (UNIT=8, IOSTAT=k, ERR=9)	Error go to
	REWIND (UNIT=8, ERR=95)	
	REWIND (8, IOSTAT=io_ok, ERR=99)	I/O status
Save	SAVE a, /name/, c	Scalars, common
	SAVE	Everything
	SAVE :: variable_list	
Select Case	SELECT CASE (value)	
	name: SELECT CASE (value)	Named
	u_or_l SELECT CASE (letter)	Block
	CASE ("a":"z") ! lower case	
	lower = .TRUE.	
	CASE ("A":"Z") ! upper case	
	lower = .FALSE.	
	CASE DEFAULT ! not a letter	
	PRINT *, "Symbol is not a letter", letter	
	lower = .FALSE.	
	END SELECT u_or_l	
Sequence	SEQUENCE	Forced storage
Stop	STOP	
	STOP "invalid data"	With message
Subroutine	SUBROUTINE sub1 (a, b)	
	SUBROUTINE sub1	No arguments
	SUBROUTINE name (args, optional_args)	Optional arguments
	SUBROUTINE sub3 (a, b, *9) ! Obsolete, use CASE	Return to 9
	RECURSIVE SUBROUTINE sub2 (a, b)	Recursive
Target	TARGET :: name, name_2	See Pointer
	TARGET :: name(4,5), name_2(3)	
Type Declaration	TYPE (person) car_pool(5)	User-defined type
	TYPE (color), DIMENSION (256) :: hues	
	TYPE (type_name), attr_list :: variable_list	

Name	Examples	Comments
	TYPE (person), DIMENSION (n) :: address_book	
	TYPE (type_name) :: variable_list	
	TYPE (student_record)	Definition block
	CHARACTER (name_len) :: last, first	
	INTEGER :: rank	
	END TYPE student_record	
Type	TYPE, PRIVATE name	Access
Statement	TYPE, PUBLIC :: name	
Use	USE module_name	
	USE module_name, ONLY: list_in_module_name	Only
	USE module_name, var_subr_fun_name => old_name	Rename
Where	WHERE (logical_array_mask)	Then
	WHERE (a_array > 0.0)	Where block
	sqrt_a = SQRT(a_array)	
	END WHERE	
	WHERE (mask > 0.0)	Elsewhere block
	a_array = mask	
	ELSEWHERE	
	a_array = 0.0	
	END WHERE	
	WHERE (a_array>0) b_array = SQRT(a_array)	Statement
Write	WRITE (*, 10) s(j:k)	Substring
	WRITE (1, *) x, y	Unformatted file
	WRITE (*, *) x, y	Unformatted
	WRITE (1, '(A6, I3)') x, y	Character, integer
	WRITE (1, FMT='(A6, I3)') x, y	Included format
	WRITE (1, s_fmt) x, y	Stored format string
	WRITE (1, FMT=s_fmt) x, y	
	WRITE (*, NML=data) ! Obsolete	Namelist to stdout
	WRITE (1, NML=data) ! Obsolete	Namelist to a file
	WRITE (1, END=8, ERR=9) x, y	Unformatted
	WRITE (1, REC=3) v	Unformatted direct
	WRITE (1, 2, REC=3) v	Formatted direct
	WRITE (s2, 1, ERR=9) x	Internal, format
	WRITE (s2, *, ERR=9) x	Unformatted
	WRITE (s2, REC=4, END=8) x	Internal, direct
	WRITE *, output_list	Unformatted
	WRITE *, (io_implied_do)	Implied do
	WRITE *, ((a(i, j), j=1, cols) i=1, rows)	
	WRITE '(formats)' output_list	Formatted write
	WRITE '(formats)' (io_implied_do)	Implied do
	WRITE (7, 10, ADVANCE='NO') output_list	Advance
	WRITE (8, 10, io_spec_list) output_list	I/O specification
	WRITE (9, FMT=20, io_spec_list) output_list	
	WRITE (UNIT=7, 10, io_spec_list) output_list	
	WRITE (9, s_fmt, io_spec_list) output_list	Stored format
	WRITE (UNIT=8, s_fmt, io_spec_list) output	

(continued)

(continued)

Name	Examples	Comments
	WRITE (9, '(formats)' io_spec_list), output_list	Inline format
	WRITE (UNIT=7, '(formats)' io_spec_list), output	
	WRITE (8), output_list	Binary write
	WRITE (7), (io_implied_do)	Implied do
	WRITE (8, ADVANCE='NO'), output_list	Advance
	WRITE (9, io_spec_list), output_list	I/O specification
	WRITE (UNIT=9, io_spec_list), output_list	
	WRITE (s_variable, FMT=20), output_list	Internal file
	WRITE (UNIT=s_variable, FMT=20), output_list	
	WRITE (s_variable, 20, io_spec_list), output_list	I/O specification
	WRITE (UNIT=s_var, FMT=20, io_spec), output	

APPENDIX B

Selected Exercise Solutions

B.1 Problem 1.8.1 : Checking Trigonometric Identities

The Fortran 90 program and output follow. The error levels reflect that F90 defaults to single-precision reals; however, F90 is easily extended to double precision and in theory supports any level of user-specified precision. For simplicity, the F77 default-naming convention for integers and reals is used. That is not a good practice since safety dictates declaring the type of each variable at the beginning of each program. (Try changing the reals to double precision to verify that the error is indeed reduced.)

```
implicit none
integer :: k,n = 16
real, parameter :: pi = 3.141592654 ! set constant
real :: cost, sint, theta, test
 print *,' Theta          sin^2+cos^2          error'
 do k = 0, n                 ! Loop over (n+1) points
   theta = k*pi/n
   sint  = sin( theta )
   cost  = cos( theta )
   test  = sint*sint + cost*cost
   write (*, '( 3(1pe14.5) )') theta, test, 1.-test
 end do ! over k
```

```
Theta          sin^2+cos^2    error
0.00000E+00    1.00000E+00    0.00000E+00
1.96350E-01    1.00000E+00    5.96046E-08
3.92699E-01    1.00000E+00    0.00000E+00
5.89049E-01    1.00000E+00    0.00000E+00
7.85398E-01    1.00000E+00    5.96046E-08
9.81748E-01    1.00000E+00    0.00000E+00
1.17810E+00    1.00000E+00    5.96046E-08
1.37445E+00    1.00000E+00    0.00000E+00
1.57080E+00    1.00000E+00    0.00000E+00
1.76715E+00    1.00000E+00    5.96046E-08
1.96350E+00    1.00000E+00    0.00000E+00
2.15985E+00    1.00000E+00    0.00000E+00
2.35619E+00    1.00000E+00    5.96046E-08
2.55254E+00    1.00000E+00    0.00000E+00
2.74889E+00    1.00000E+00    0.00000E+00
2.94524E+00    1.00000E+00    0.00000E+00
3.14159E+00    1.00000E+00    0.00000E+00
```

B.2 Problem 1.8.2 : Newton–Raphson Algorithm

The most convenient form of loop is the posttest loop, which allows each iteration to be calculated and the error checked at the end.

```
xnew = x
do {
    x = xnew
    xnew = x - f(x)/fprime(x)
    }
    while (abs(xnew-x) < tolerance)
```

The alternate logic constructs employ tests at the end of the loop and transfer out the end of the loop when necessary. MATLAB and C++ transfer using the "break" command, whereas F90 uses the "exit" command.

An F90 program with an infinite loop named `testnewton.f90` and its result are given below. Be warned that this version uses the IMPLICIT name styles for integers and reals instead of the better strong typing that results from the recommended use of IMPLICIT NONE.

```
function f(x) result(y)
  real, intent (in) :: x
  real              :: y
    y = exp(2*x) - 5*x - 1
end function f

function fprime(x) result(y)
  real, intent (in) :: x
  real              :: y
    y = 2*exp(2*x) - 5
end function fprime

program Newton
implicit none
real, parameter :: tolerance = 1.e-6  ! set constant
real :: f, fprime, x, xnew = 3.   ! Initial value
integer :: iteration
  iteration = 0
! Iteration count
  do ! forever until true
    iteration = iteration + 1
    x         = xnew
    xnew      = x - f(x)/fprime(x)
    if ( abs(xnew - x) < tolerance ) exit ! converged is true
  end do ! forever
  print *, 'Solution: ', xnew, ', Iterations:', iteration
end program Newton
```

```
>>f90 -o newton testnewton.f90
>>newton
 Solution:    0.8093941 , Iterations: 10
```

B.3 Problem 1.8.3 : Game of Life

```
program game_of_life   ! procedural version
implicit none
```

```
  integer, parameter :: boardsize = 10
  integer            :: board    (boardsize, boardsize) = 0
  integer            :: newboard (boardsize, boardsize)
  character(len=1)   :: ok          ! page prompt
  integer            :: k, number   ! loops

!           Initial life data, the "Glider"
   board (3, 3) = 1; board (4, 4) = 1; board (5, 4) = 1
   board (5, 3) = 1; board (5, 2) = 1

   print *, "Initial Life Display:"
   call spy (board) ! show initial lifeforms
   print *, "Initially alive = ", sum (board); print *, " "

   print *, "Enter number of generations to display:"
   read  *, number
   do k = 1, number
     newboard = next_generation (board)
     board    = newboard ! save current lifeforms
     call spy (board)    ! show current lifeforms
     print * ; print *, "Generation number = ", k
     print *, "Currently alive = ", sum (newboard)

     print *, 'continue? (y, n)'
     read *, ok ! read any character to continue
     if ( ok == 'n' ) exit ! this do loop only
   end do ! on k for number of generations

contains  ! internal (vs external) subprograms

  function next_generation (board) result (newboard)
!  Compute the next generation of life
  integer, intent(in) :: board   (:, :)
  integer             :: newboard (size(board, 1), size(board, 2))
  integer             :: i, j, neighbors  ! loops

   newboard = 0  ! initialize next generation
   do i = 2, boardsize - 1
     do j = 2, boardsize - 1
       neighbors = sum (board (i - 1:i + 1, j - 1:j + 1))  %
                 -  board (i, j)
       if ( board (i, j) == 1 ) then ! life in the cell
         if ( (neighbors > 3 .or. neighbors < 2) ) then
           newboard (i, j) = 0       ! it died
         else
           newboard (i, j) = 1       ! newborn
         end if ! on number of neighbors
       else ! no life in the cell
         if ( neighbors == 3 ) then
           newboard (i, j) = 1       ! newborn
         else
           newboard (i, j) = 0       ! died
         end if ! on number of neighbors
       end if ! life status
     end do ! on column j
   end do ! on row i
  end function next_generation
```

```
  Subroutine spy (board)    ! model matlab spy function
! Show an X at each non-zero entry of board, else show -
  integer, intent(in) :: board (:, :)
  character (len=1)   :: line (size(board, 1))   ! a line on screen
  integer             :: i                       ! loops

   line = ' '                                  ! blank out the line
   do i = 1, size (board, 1 )                  ! loop over each row
     line (1:size (board, 2 )) = '-'          ! current board width
     where ( board (i, :) /= 0 ) line = 'X'   ! mark non-zero columns
     write (*, '(80a1)') line                 ! print current row
   end do ! over all rows
  end subroutine spy
end program  ! game_of_life

! Running gives:
!  Initial Life Display:
! ----------
! ----------
! --X-------
! ---X------
! -XXX------
! ----------
! ----------
! ----------
! ----------
! ----------
!  Initially alive = 5
!
!  Enter number of generations to display: 4
! ----------
! ----------
! ----------
! -X-X------
! --XX------
! --X-------
! ----------
! ----------
! ----------
! ----------
!
!  Generation number = 1
!  Currently alive = 5
!   continue? (y, n) n
```

B.4 Problem 2.5.1 : Conversion Factors

This code illustrates the type of global units conversion factors you can define for your field of study. They can be accessed by any program that includes a use `Conversion_Constants` line and cites a parameter name, as shown on line 16.

```
[ 1]  Module Conversion_Constants      ! DefineUnits Conversion
[ 2]  ! Define selected precision
[ 3]     INTEGER, PARAMETER :: DP = KIND (1.d0) ! Alternate form
[ 4]  ! ========== Metric Conversions ==========
[ 5]  real(DP), parameter:: cm_Per_Inch       = 2.54_DP
[ 6]  real(DP), parameter:: kg_Per_Pound      = 0.45359237_DP
```

```
real(DP), parameter:: kg_Per_Short_Ton = 907.18474_DP
real(DP), parameter:: kg_Per_Long_Ton  = 1016.0469088_DP
real(DP), parameter:: m_Per_Foot        = 3.048_DP
real(DP), parameter:: m_Per_Mile        = 1609.344_DP
real(DP), parameter:: m_Per_Naut_Mile  = 1852.0_DP
real(DP), parameter:: m_Per_Yard        = 0.9144_DP
end Module Conversion_Constants
Program Test_Conversion
  use Conversion_Constants
  print *, 'cm_Per_Inch = ', cm_Per_Inch ; End Program
! Running gives:  cm_Per_Inch = 2.54000000000000004
```

This code illustrates the type of common physical constants that can be made available as global variables you can define for your field of study. They can be accessed by any program that includes a use Physical_Constants line and cites a parameter name, as shown on line 60 below.

```
[ 1] Module Physical_Constants      ! Define Physical Constants
[ 2] ! Define selected precision
[ 3]     INTEGER, PARAMETER :: DP = KIND (1.d0) ! Alternate form
[ 4]
[ 5] ! ========== Physics Constants and units ==========
[ 6] real(DP), parameter:: AMU_Value            = 1.6605402E-27_DP    ! kg
[ 7] real(DP), parameter:: Atmosphere_Pres      = 9.80665E+04_DP      ! Pa
[ 8] real(DP), parameter:: Avogadro            = 6.0221367E+23_DP    ! 1/mol
[ 9] real(DP), parameter:: Bohr_Magneton        = 9.2740154E-24_DP    ! J/T
[10] real(DP), parameter:: Bohr_Radius          = 5.29177249E-11_DP   ! m
[11] real(DP), parameter:: Boltzmann           = 1.380657E-23_DP     ! J/K
[12] real(DP), parameter:: c_Light              = 2.997924580E+8_DP   ! m/s
[13] real(DP), parameter:: Electron_Compton     = 2.42631058E-12_DP   ! m
[14] real(DP), parameter:: Electron_Angular     = 5.2729E-35_DP       ! J*s
[15] real(DP), parameter:: Electron_Charge      =-1.60217738E-19_DP   ! coul
[16] real(DP), parameter:: Electron_Mass_Rest = 9.1093897E-31_DP     ! kg
[17] real(DP), parameter:: Electron_Moment      = 9.2847700E-24_DP    ! J/T
[18] real(DP), parameter:: Electron_Radius      = 2.81794092E-15_DP   ! m
[19] real(DP), parameter:: Faraday             = 9.6485309E+04_DP    ! C/mo
[20] real(DP), parameter:: G_Universal          = 6.67260E-11_DP      ! m^3/(s^2*kg)
[21] real(DP), parameter:: Light_Year           = 9.46073E+15_DP      ! m
[22] real(DP), parameter:: Mech_equiv_Heat       = 4.185E+3_DP        ! J/kcal
[23] real(DP), parameter:: Molar_Volume         = 0.02241410_DP       ! m^3/mol
[24] real(DP), parameter:: Neutron_Mass         = 1.6749286E-27_DP    ! kg
[25] real(DP), parameter:: Permeability        = 1.25663706143E-06_DP ! H/m
[26] real(DP), parameter:: Permittivity        = 8.85418781762E-12_DP ! F/m
[27] real(DP), parameter:: Planck_Const         = 6.6260754E-34_DP    ! J*s
[28] real(DP), parameter:: Proton_Mass          = 1.6726230E-27_DP    ! kg
[29] real(DP), parameter:: Proton_Moment        = 1.41060761E-26_DP   ! J/T
[30] real(DP), parameter:: Quantum_charge_r      = 4.13556E+12_DP      ! J*s/C
[31] real(DP), parameter:: Rydberg_inf          = 1.0973731534E+07_DP! 1/m
[32] real(DP), parameter:: Rydberg_Hydrogen     = 1.09678E+07_DP      ! 1/m
[33] real(DP), parameter:: Std_Atmosphere       = 1.01325E+05_DP      ! Pa
[34] real(DP), parameter:: Stefan_Boltzmann     = 5.67050E-08_DP      ! W/(m^2*K^4)
[35] real(DP), parameter:: Thomson_cross_sect = 6.6516E-29_DP         ! m^2
[36] real(DP), parameter:: Universal_Gas_C       = 8.314510_DP         ! J/mol*K
[37]
[38] ! ========== Astronomy Constants and units ==========
[39] real(DP), parameter:: AU_Earth_Sun          = 1.4959787E+11_DP ! m
[40] real(DP), parameter:: Anomal_Month          = 27.5546_DP        ! days
[41] real(DP), parameter:: Anomal_Year           = 365.2596_DP       ! days
```

```
real(DP), parameter:: Dracon_Month       = 27.2122_DP       ! days
real(DP), parameter:: Earth_G            = 9.80665_DP       ! m/s^2
real(DP), parameter:: Earth_Mass         = 5.974E+24_DP     ! kg
real(DP), parameter:: Earth_Radius_Eq     = 6.37814E+6_DP    ! m
real(DP), parameter:: Earth_Radius_Mean   = 6.371E+6_DP      ! m
real(DP), parameter:: Earth_Radius_Polar = 6.356755E+6_DP   ! m
real(DP), parameter:: Julian_Year        = 365.25_DP        ! days
real(DP), parameter:: Rotation_Day       = 23.93447222_DP   ! hours
real(DP), parameter:: Sidereal_Day       = 23.93446944_DP   ! hours
real(DP), parameter:: Sidereal_Month     = 27.3217_DP       ! days
real(DP), parameter:: Sidereal_Ratio     = 1.0027379092558_DP
real(DP), parameter:: Sidereal_Year      = 365.2564_DP      ! days
real(DP), parameter:: Solar_Day          = 24.06571111_DP   ! hours
real(DP), parameter:: Synodic_Month      = 29.5306_DP       ! days
real(DP), parameter:: Tropical_Year      = 365.2422_DP      ! days
end Module Physical_Constants     ! Define Physical Constants
Program Test_Physical
  use Physical_Constants
  print *, 'Avogadro = ', Avogadro ; End Program Test_Physical
! Running gives: Avogadro =  0.602213669999999967E+24
```

B.5 Problem 3.5.3 : Creating a Vector Class

We begin by defining the components to be included in our vector object. They include the length of each vector and a corresponding real array of pointers to the vector components:

```
module class_Vector    ! filename: class_Vector.f90
! public, everything by default, but can specify any
 implicit none
  type Vector
     private
     integer                         :: size    ! vector length
     real, pointer, dimension(:) :: data    ! component values
  end type Vector
```

For persons familiar with vectors the use of overloaded operators makes sense (but it often does not make sense). Thus, we overload the addition, subtraction, multiplication, assignment, and logical equal to operators by defining the correct class members to be used for different argument types:

```
!              Overload common operators
interface operator (+)                    ! add others later
 module procedure add_Vector, add_Real_to_Vector; end interface
interface operator (-)                    ! add unary versions later
 module procedure subtract_Vector, subtract_Real; end interface
interface operator (*)                    ! overload *
 module procedure dot_Vector, real_mult_Vector, Vector_mult_real
end interface
interface assignment (=)                  ! overload =
 module procedure equal_Real; end interface
interface operator (==)                   ! overload ==
 module procedure is_equal_to; end interface

```

Then we encapsulate the supporting member functions, beginning with two constructors, assign and make_Vector:

```
[ 22]  contains  ! functions & operators
[ 23]
[ 24]  function assign (values) result (name) ! array to vector constructor
[ 25]    real, intent(in) :: values(:)        ! given rank 1 array
[ 26]    integer          :: length           ! array size
[ 27]    type (Vector)    :: name             ! Vector to create
[ 28]     length = size(values); allocate ( name%data(length) )
[ 29]     name % size = length; name % data = values; end function assign
[ 30]
[ 31]  function make_Vector (len, values) result(v) ! Optional Constructor
[ 32]    integer, optional, intent(in) :: len       ! number of values
[ 33]    real,    optional, intent(in) :: values(:) ! given values
[ 34]    type (Vector)                 :: v
[ 35]     if ( present (len) ) then                 ! create vector data
[ 36]       v%size = len ; allocate ( v%data(len) )
[ 37]       if ( present (values)) then ; v%data = values    ! vector
[ 38]         else                      ; v%data = 0.d0      ! null vector
[ 39]       end if ! values present
[ 40]     else                                      ! scalar constant
[ 41]       v%size = 1                  ; allocate ( v%data(1) ) ! default
[ 42]       if ( present (values)) then ; v%data(1) = values(1)  ! scalar
[ 43]         else                      ; v%data(1) = 0.d0       ! null
[ 44]       end if ! value present
[ 45]     end if ! len present
[ 46]  end function make_Vector
[ 47]
```

The remainder of the members are given in alphabetical order:

```
[ 48]   function add_Real_to_Vector (v, r) result (new) ! overload +
[ 49]    type (Vector), intent(in) :: v
[ 50]    real,          intent(in) :: r
[ 51]    type (Vector)             :: new         ! new = v + r
[ 52]     if ( v%size < 1 ) stop "No sizes in add_Real_to_Vector"
[ 53]     allocate ( new%data(v%size) ) ; new%size = v%size
[ 54]   ! new%data = v%data + r        ! as array operation
[ 55]     new%data(1:v%size) = v%data(1:v%size) + r ; end function
[ 56]
[ 57]  function add_Vector (a, b) result (new)    ! vector + vector
[ 58]    type (Vector), intent(in) :: a, b
[ 59]    type (Vector)             :: new         ! new = a + b
[ 60]     if ( a%size /= b%size ) stop "Sizes differ in add_Vector"
[ 61]     allocate ( new%data(a%size) ) ; new%size = a%size
[ 62]     new%data = a%data + b%data    ; end function add_Vector
```

Note that lines 55 and 62 above are similar ways to avoid writing serial loops that would have to be used in most languages. This keeps the code cleaner and shorter and, more important, it lets the compiler carry out those operations in parallel on some machines.

Although copy members are very important to C++ programmers, the following `copy_Vector` should probably be omitted since you would not usually pass big arrays as copies and F90 defaults to passing-by reference unless forced to pass by value.

```
[ 63]
[ 64]  function copy_Vector (name) result (new)
[ 65]    type (Vector), intent(in) :: name
[ 66]    type (Vector)             :: new
[ 67]     allocate ( new%data(name%size) ) ; new%size = name%size
[ 68]     new%data = name%data              ; end function copy_Vector
```

The routine delete_Vector is the destructor for this class. In some sense it is incomplete because it does not delete the size attribute. It was decided that, although the actual array of data may take a huge amount of storage, the single integer is not important. To be more complete one would need to make size an integer pointer and allocate and deallocate it at numerous locations within this module.

```

subroutine  delete_Vector (name) ! deallocate allocated items
  type (Vector), intent(inout) :: name
  integer                      :: ok ! check deallocate status
   deallocate (name%data, stat = ok )
   if ( ok /= 0 ) stop "Vector not allocated in delete_Vector"
     name%size = 0 ; end subroutine delete_Vector

function dot_Vector (a, b) result (c)      ! overload *
  type (Vector), intent(in) :: a, b
  real                      :: c
   if ( a%size /= b%size ) stop "Sizes differ in dot_Vector"
     c = dot_product(a%data, b%data); end function dot_Vector

subroutine equal_Real (new, R)   ! overload =, real to vector
  type (Vector), intent(inout) :: new
  real,          intent(in)    :: R
   if ( associated (new%data) ) deallocate (new%data)
   allocate ( new%data(1) ); new%size = 1
    new%data = R            ; end subroutine equal_Real

logical function is_equal_to (a, b) result (t_f) ! overload ==
  type (Vector), intent(in) :: a, b        ! left & right of ==
   t_f = .false.                           ! initialize
   if ( a%size /= b%size ) return          ! same size ?
     t_f = all ( a%data == b%data )        ! and all values match
end function is_equal_to

function length (name) result (n)          ! accessor member
  type (Vector), intent(in) :: name
  integer                   :: n
   n = name % size ; end function length

subroutine list (name)  ! accessor member, for prettier printing
  type (Vector), intent(in) :: name
   print *,"[", name % data(1:name%size), "]"; end subroutine list

function normalize_Vector (name)  result (new)
  type (Vector), intent(in) :: name
  type (Vector)             :: new
  real                      :: total, nil = epsilon(1.0) ! tolerance
   allocate ( new%data(name%size) ) ; new%size = name%size
   total = sqrt ( sum ( name%data**2 ) )     ! intrinsic functions
   if ( total < nil ) then ; new%data = 0.d0 ! avoid division by 0
     else                  ; new%data = name%data/total
   end if                  ; end function normalize_Vector

subroutine read_Vector (name)              ! read array, assign
  type (Vector), intent(inout) :: name
  integer, parameter           :: max = 999
  integer                      :: length
   read (*,'(i1)', advance = 'no') length
```

```
[121]     if ( length <= 0 )   stop "Invalid length in read_Vector"
[122]     if ( length >= max ) stop "Maximum length in read_Vector"
[123]      allocate ( name % data(length) ) ; name % size = length
[124]      read *, name % data(1:length)     ; end subroutine read_Vector
[125]
[126]  function real_mult_Vector (r, v) result (new) ! overload *
[127]    real,            intent(in) :: r
[128]    type (Vector), intent(in) :: v
[129]    type (Vector)               :: new         ! new = r * v
[130]     if ( v%size < 1 ) stop "Zero size in real_mult_Vector"
[131]      allocate ( new%data(v%size) ) ; new%size = v%size
[132]      new%data = r * v%data          ; end function real_mult_Vector
[133]
[134]  function size_Vector (name) result (n)      ! accessor member
[135]    type (Vector), intent(in) :: name
[136]    integer                     :: n
[137]     n = name % size ; end function size_Vector
[138]
[139]  function subtract_Real(v, r) result(new) ! vector-real, overload -
[140]    type (Vector), intent(in) :: v
[141]    real,            intent(in) :: r
[142]    type (Vector)               :: new         ! new = v + r
[143]     if ( v%size < 1 ) stop "Zero length in subtract_Real"
[144]      allocate ( new%data(v%size) ) ; new%size = v%size
[145]      new%data = v%data - r          ; end function subtract_Real
[146]
[147]  function subtract_Vector (a, b) result (new) ! overload -
[148]    type (Vector), intent(in) :: a, b
[149]    type (Vector)               :: new
[150]     if ( a%size /= b%size ) stop "Sizes differ in subtract_Vector"
[151]      allocate ( new%data(a%size) ) ; new%size = a%size
[152]      new%data = a%data - b%data     ; end function subtract_Vector
[153]
[154]  function values (name) result (array)         ! accessor member
[155]    type (Vector), intent(in) :: name
[156]    real                        :: array(name%size)
[157]     array = name % data ; end function values
```

The routine delete_Vector is the manual constructor for this class. It has no optional arguments, and so both arguments must be supplied; it duplicates the constructor on line 31 but uses the naming convention preferred by the author.

```
[158]
[159]  function Vector_ (length, values) result(name) ! constructor
[160]    integer,        intent(in) :: length          ! array size
[161]    real, target, intent(in) :: values(length)   ! given array
[162]    real, pointer              :: pt_to_val(:)     ! pointer to array
[163]    type (Vector)              :: name            ! Vector to create
[164]    integer                    :: get_m           ! allocate flag
[165]      allocate ( pt_to_val (length), stat = get_m )  ! allocate
[166]      if ( get_m /= 0 ) stop 'allocate error'        ! check
[167]      pt_to_val = values                       ! dereference values
[168]      name      = Vector(length, pt_to_val) ! intrinsic constructor
[169]  end function Vector_
[170]
[171]  function Vector_max_value (a) result (v)       ! accessor member
[172]    type (Vector), intent(in) :: a
[173]    real                        :: v
```

```
    v = maxval ( a%data(1:a%size) ) ; end function Vector_max_value

 function Vector_min_value (a) result (v)       ! accessor member
   type (Vector), intent(in) :: a
   real                     :: v
    v = minval ( a%data(1:a%size) ) ; end function Vector_min_value

 function Vector_mult_real(v, r) result(new) ! vec*real, overload *
   type (Vector), intent(in) :: v
   real,          intent(in) :: r
   type (Vector)             :: new             ! new = v * r
    if ( v%size < 1 ) stop "Zero size in Vector_mult_real"
      new = Real_mult_Vector(r, v); end function Vector_mult_real

 end module class_Vector
```

A first test of this class is given below along with comments that give the verifications of the members.

```
!         Testing Vector Class Constructors & Operators
include 'class_Vector.f90'         ! see previous figure
program check_vector_class
 use class_Vector
 implicit none

 type (Vector) :: x, y, z

!          test optional constructors: assign, and copy
 x = make_Vector ()                     ! single scalar zero
 write (*,'("made scalar x = ")',advance='no'); call list(x)

 call delete_Vector (x) ; y = make_Vector (4)  ! 4 zeros
 write (*,'("made null y = ")',advance='no'); call list(y)

 z = make_Vector (4, (/11., 12., 13., 14./) )  ! 4 non-zeros
 write (*,'("made full z = ")',advance='no'); call list(z)
 write (*,'("assign [ 31., 32., 33., 34. ] to x")')

 x = assign( (/31., 32., 33., 34./) )          ! (4) non-zeros
 write (*,'("assigned  x = ")',advance='no'); call list(x)

 x = Vector_(4, (/31., 32., 33., 34./) )       ! 4 non-zeros
 write (*,'("public    x = ")',advance='no'); call list(x)
 write (*,'("copy x to y =")',advance='no')
 y = copy_Vector (x) ; call list(y)                        ! copy

!                    test overloaded operators
 write (*,'("z * x gives ")',advance='no'); print *, z*x  ! dot
 write (*,'("z + x gives ")',advance='no'); call list(z+x) ! add
 y = 25.6                                ! real to vector
 write (*,'("y = 25.6 gives ")',advance='no'); call list(y)
 y = z                                   ! equality
 write (*,'("y = z gives y as ")',  advance='no'); call list(y)
 write (*,'("logic y == x gives ")',advance='no'); print *, y==x
 write (*,'("logic y == z gives ")',advance='no'); print *, y==z

!                    test destructor, accessors
 call delete_Vector (y)                         ! destructor
```

```
  write (*,'("deleting y gives y = ")',advance='no'); call list(y)
  print *, "size of x is ", length (x)            ! accessor
  print *, "data in x are [", values (x), "]"     ! accessor
  write (*,'("2. times x is ")',advance='no'); call list(2.0*x)
  write (*,'("x times 2. is ")',advance='no'); call list(x*2.0)
  call delete_Vector (x); call delete_Vector (z)  ! clean up
end program check_vector_class
!  Running gives the output:     ! made scalar x = [0]
! made null y = [0, 0, 0, 0]     ! made full z = [11, 12, 13, 14]
! assign [31, 32, 33, 34] to x ! assigned x  = [31, 32, 33, 34]
! public  x = [31, 32, 33, 34] ! copy x to y = [31, 32, 33, 34]
! z * x gives 1630             ! z + x gives   [42, 44, 46, 48]
! y = 256 gives [256000004]    ! y = z,    y =  [11, 12, 13, 14]
! logic y == x gives F         ! logic y == z gives T
! deleting y gives y = []      ! size of x is 4
! data in x : [31, 32, 33, 34] ! 2 times x is [62, 64, 66, 68]
! x times 2 is [62, 64, 66, 68]
```

Having tested the vector class, we will now use it in some typical vector operations. We want a program that will work with arrays of vectors to read in the number of vectors. The array of vectors will use an automatic storage mode. That could be risky because, if the system runs out of memory, we will get a fatal error message and the run will abort. If we make the alternate choice of allocatable arrays, then we can check the allocation status and have a chance (but not a good chance) of closing down the code is some "friendly" manner. Once the code reads the number of vectors, then, for each one it reads the number of components and the the component values. After testing some simple vector math, we compute a more complicated result known as the orthonormal basis for the given set of vectors:

```
!     Test Vector Class Constructors, Operators and Basis
include 'class_Vector.f'

program check_basis ! demonstrate a typical Vector class
  use class_Vector
  implicit none

  interface
     subroutine testing_basis (N_V)
       integer, intent(in) :: N_V
     end subroutine testing_basis
  end interface

  print *, "Test automatic allocate, deallocate"
  print *, " " ; read  *, N_V
  print *, "The number of vectors to be read is: ", N_V
  call  testing_basis ( N_V) ! to use automatic arrays
end program check_basis

subroutine testing_basis (N_V)
! test vectors AND demo automatic allocation/deallocation
  use class_Vector

  integer, intent(in) :: N_V
  type (Vector)       :: Input(N_V) ! automatic array
  type (Vector)       :: Ortho(N_V) ! automatic array
  integer             :: j
  real                :: norm

```

```
interface
  subroutine  orthonormal_basis (Input, Ortho, N_given)
    use class_Vector
    type (Vector), intent(in)  :: Input(N_given)
    type (Vector), intent(out) :: Ortho(N_given)
    integer, intent(in)        :: N_given
  end subroutine  orthonormal_basis
end interface

  print *, " " ; print *, "The given ", N_V, " vectors:"
  do j = 1, N_V
     call read_Vector ( Input(j) )
     call list        ( Input(j) )
  end do ! for j

  print *, " "
  print *, "The Orthogonal Basis of the original set is:"

  call orthonormal_basis (Input, Ortho, N_V)
  do j = 1, N_V                ! list new orthogonal basis
     call list ( Ortho(j) )
  end do ! for j

       ! use vector class features & operators
  print *, ' ' ; print *,"vector 1 + vector 2 = "
  call list (Input(1)+Input(2))
  print *,"vector 1 - vector 2 = "
  call list (Input(1)-Input(2))
  print *,"vector 1 dot vector 2 = ", Input(1)*Input(2)
  print *,"vector 1 * 3.5 = "
  call list (3.5*Input(1))
  norm = sqrt ( dot_Vector( Input(1), Input(1) ))
  print *,"norm(vector 1) = ", norm
  print *,"normalized vector 1 = "
  call list (normalize_Vector(Input(1)))
  print *,"max(vector 1) = ", vector_max_value (Input(1))
  print *,"min(vector 1) = ", vector_min_value (Input(1))
  print *,"length of vector 1 = ", length ( Input(1) )
end subroutine testing_basis

subroutine  orthonormal_basis (Input, Ortho, N_given)
!     Find Orthonormal Basis of a Set of Vector Classes
  use class_Vector
!********************************************************
! =, -, +, * are overloaded operators from class_Vector
!********************************************************

  type (Vector), intent(in)  :: Input(N_given)
  type (Vector), intent(out) :: Ortho(N_given)
  integer, intent(in)        :: N_given
  integer                    :: i, j  ! loops
  real                       :: dot
  do i = 1, N_given          ! original set of vectors
    Ortho(i) = Input(i)      ! copy input vector class
    do j = 1, i              ! for previous copies
      dot      = dot_Vector(Ortho(i), Ortho(j))
      Ortho(i) = Ortho(i) - (dot*Ortho(j))
    end do ! for j
```

```
    Ortho(i) = normalize_Vector ( Ortho(i) )
  end do ! over i
end subroutine  orthonormal_basis

! Compiling and inputting :
! 4
! 3 0.625 0 0
! 3 7.5 3.125 0
! 3 13.25 -7.8125 6.5
! 3 14.0 3.5 -7.5
!               Gives:
! Test automatic allocate, deallocate
!
! The number of vectors to be read is:  4
! The given  4  vectors:
! [  0.6250   0.0000   0.0000 ]
! [  7.5000   3.1250   0.0000 ]
! [ 13.2500  -7.8125   6.5000 ]
! [ 14.0000   3.5000  -7.5000 ]
!
! The Orthogonal Basis of the original set is:
! [  1.0000   0.0000   0.0000 ]
! [  0.0000  -1.0000   0.0000 ]
! [  0.0000   0.0000  -1.0000 ]
! [  0.0000   0.0000   0.0000 ]
!
! vector 1 + vector 2    = [ 8.1250   3.1250   0.0000 ]
! vector 1 - vector 2    = [-6.8750  -3.1250   0.0000 ]
! vector 1 dot vector 2  =   4.6875
! vector 1 * 3.5         = [ 2.1875   0.0000   0.0000 ]
! norm(vector 1)         =   0.6250
! normalized vector 1    = [ 1.0000   0.0000   0.0000 ]
! max(vector 1)          =   0.6250
! min(vector 1)          =   0.0000
! length of vector 1     =  3
```

B.6 Problem 3.5.4 : Creating a Sparse Vector Class

This class begins like the previous vector class except that we must add a row entry (line 5) for each data value entry (line 6). This is done for efficiency since we expect most values in sparse vectors to be zero (and hence their name). The attribute non_zero is the size of both rows and values.

```
[  1]  module class_sparse_Vector
[  2]   implicit none
[  3]    type sv              ! a sparse vector
[  4]     integer             :: non_zeros
[  5]     integer, pointer :: rows(:)
[  6]     real,     pointer :: values(:)
[  7]    end type
[  8]
```

The overloading process is similar, but now we will see that much more logic is required to deal with the zero entries and new zeros created by addition or multiplication.

```
[  8]    interface assignment (=)
[  9]      module procedure equal_Vector ; end interface
```

```
[ 10]     interface operator (.dot.) ! define dot product operator
[ 11]       module procedure dot_Vector ; end interface
[ 12]     interface operator (==) ! Boolean equal to
[ 13]       module procedure is_equal_to ; end interface
[ 14]     interface operator (*) ! term by term product
[ 15]       module procedure el_by_el_Mult, real_mult_Sparse
[ 16]       module procedure Sparse_mult_real
[ 17]     end interface
[ 18]     interface operator (-)    ! for sparse vectors
[ 19]        module procedure Sub_Sparse_Vectors ; end interface
[ 20]     interface operator (+)    ! for sparse vectors
[ 21]        module procedure Sum_Sparse_Vectors ; end interface
[ 22]
[ 23]   contains  ! operators and functionality
```

In the following constructor for the class note that both of the pointer array attributes are allocated (line 32) the same amount of storage in memory. One should also include the allocation status flag here and check its value to raise a possible exception (as seen in lines 41–46).

```
[ 24]     subroutine make_Sparse_Vector (s,n,r,v)
[ 25]     !       allows zero length vectors
[ 26]       type (sv)             :: s      ! name
[ 27]       integer, intent(in) :: n      ! size
[ 28]       integer, intent(in) :: r(n)   ! rows
[ 29]       real,    intent(in) :: v(n)   ! values
[ 30]         if ( n < 0 ) stop &
[ 31]           "Error, negative rows in make_Sparse_Vector"
[ 32]           allocate (s%rows(n), s%values(n))
[ 33]           s%non_zeros = n       ! copy size
[ 34]           s%rows      = r       ! row   array assignment
[ 35]           s%values    = v       ! value array assignment
[ 36]     end subroutine make_Sparse_Vector
[ 37]
```

This is really a destructor. Again, it is incomplete because the integer array size was not made allocatable for simplicity.

```
[ 38]     subroutine delete_Sparse_Vector (s)
[ 39]       type (sv) :: s        ! name of sparse vector
[ 40]       integer   :: error    ! deallocate status flag, 0 no error
[ 41]         deallocate (s%rows, s%values, stat = error) ! memory released
[ 42]         if ( error == 0 ) then
[ 43]           s%non_zeros = 0                         ! reset size
[ 44]         else ! never created
[ 45]           stop "Sparse vector to delete does not exist"
[ 46]         end if ; end subroutine delete_Sparse_Vector
[ 47]
```

This creates a user-defined operator called `.dot.` to be applied to sparse vectors.

```
[ 48]     function dot_Vector (u, v) result (d) ! defines .dot.
[ 49]     ! dot product of sparse vectors
[ 50]       type (sv), intent(in) :: u, v ! sparse vectors
[ 51]       type (sv)             :: w    ! sparse vector, temporary
[ 52]       real                  :: d    ! dot product value
[ 53]         d = 0.0                                            ! default
[ 54]         if ( u%non_zeros < 1 .or. v%non_zeros < 1 ) return  ! null
```

```
[ 55]         w = el_by_el_Mult (u, v) ! element by element sparse product
[ 56]         if ( w%non_zeros > 0 ) &
[ 57]         d = sum( w%values(1:w%non_zeros) ) ! summed
[ 58]         call delete_Sparse_Vector (w)              ! delete temp
[ 59]     end function dot_Vector
[ 60]
```

The `dot_Vector` above is more complicated in this format because it is likely that stored nonzero values will be multiplied by (unstored) zeros. Thus, the real work is done in the following member function that employs Boolean logic. The terms for the summation that creates the scalar dot product are first computed in a full vector equal in length to the minimum row number given. Observe that its size is established through the use of the `min` intrinsic acting on the two given sizes within the `dimension` attribute for the full array (lines 67,68). Three logical arrays (line 68) are used as "masks," which are `true` when a nonzero exists in the corresponding row of their associated sparse vector (down to the minimum row cited above). The three logical vectors are initialized in lines 77 to 92. That process ends with the third vector's being created as a Boolean product (line 91), and the maximum possible number of nonzero products is found from the `count` intrinsic (line 92).

It is also important to note that the working space vector `full` is an `automatic array`, and memory for it is automatically allocated for it each time the function is called. It could be an extremely long vector, and thus it is possible (but not likely) that there would not be enough memory available. Then the system would abort with an error message. To avoid that possibility one could have declared `full` to be an `allocatable` vector and then allocated its memory by using a similar `min` construct. That allocation request should (always) include the STAT flag so that, if the memory allocation fails, it would be possible to issue an exception to try to avoid a fatal crash of the system (not likely).

```
[ 61]     function el_by_el_Mult (u, v) result (w) ! defines * operator
[ 62]     ! element by element product of sparse vectors: 0 * real ?
[ 63]       type (sv), intent(in) :: u, v               ! given vectors
[ 64]       type (sv)             :: w                  ! new vector
[ 65]       real :: full( min( u%rows(u%non_zeros),    & ! automatic
[ 66]            &              v%rows(v%non_zeros) ) )  ! workspace
[ 67]       logical, dimension( min( u%rows(u%non_zeros), &
[ 68]         v%rows(v%non_zeros))) :: u_m, v_m, w_m ! logical product masks
[ 69]       integer :: j, k, last, n, row
[ 70]         !  is either u or v null ?
[ 71]         if ( u%non_zeros < 1 .or. v%non_zeros < 1 ) then ! w is null
[ 72]           allocate ( w%rows(0), w%values(0) )
[ 73]           w%non_zeros = 0
[ 74]           return  ! a null sparse vector
[ 75]         end if ! no calculation necessary
[ 76]
[ 77]         !               Initialize logic masks
[ 78]         last = min( u%rows(u%non_zeros), v%rows(v%non_zeros) ) ! max size
[ 79]         u_m = .false.                          ! assume no contributions
[ 80]         do j = 1, size(u%rows)
[ 81]           row = u%rows(j)                     ! get row number to flag
[ 82]           if ( row > last ) exit ! j loop
[ 83]             u_m(row) = .true.                  ! possible contribution
[ 84]         end do  ! to initialize u mask
[ 85]         v_m = .false.                          ! assume no contributions
[ 86]         do j = 1, size(v%rows)
[ 87]           row = v%rows(j)                     ! get row number to flag
[ 88]           if ( row > last ) exit ! j loop
```

```
[ 89]         v_m(row) = .true.                  ! possible contribution
[ 90]       end do  ! to initalize v mask
[ 91]       w_m = (u_m .and. v_m )                ! Boolean product logic
[ 92]       n   = count ( w_m )                  ! count possible products
[ 93]       ! if ( n == 0 ) print *,"Warning: zero length sparse" ! debug
[ 94]
```

The vector `full` is set to zero (line 96) and comparison DO loops (lines 97,101) over the two given vectors are minimized (lines 100,103) by testing where the mask vector `w_m` is `true` (thereby indicating a nonzero product). When all the products are stored in the `full` vector it is converted to the sparse vector storage mode (line 109) for release as the return result. Because `full` is an `automatic array`, its memory is automatically released when the function is exited.

```
[ 95]       !             Fill the product workspace, full
[ 96]       full = 0.0                                       ! initialize
[ 97]       do j = 1, size(u%rows)                           ! loop over u
[ 98]         row = u%rows(j)                                ! row in u
[ 99]         if ( row > last ) exit ! this loop in u        ! past end of w
[100]         if ( .not. w_m(row) ) cycle ! to next j         ! not in product
[101]         do k = 1, size(v%rows)                           ! loop over v
[102]           if ( v%rows(k) > last ) exit ! this loop       ! past end of w
[103]           if ( .not. w_m(v%rows(k)) ) cycle ! to k+1     ! not in product
[104]             if ( row == v%rows(k) ) then                 ! same row, u & v
[105]               full(row) = u%values(j)*v%values(k)        ! get product
[106]             end if
[107]         end do ! on k in v
[108]       end do ! on j in u
[109]       w = Vector_To_Sparse (full)                          !delete any zeros
[110]     end function el_by_el_Mult ! deletes full & 3 masks
[111]
```

The operator overloading members are given with the next function (line 112) as well as in lines 140, 231, and 320.

```
[112]     subroutine equal_Vector (new, s) ! overload =
[113]       type (sv), intent(inout) :: new
[114]       type (sv), intent(in)    :: s
[115]         allocate ( new%rows(s%non_zeros) )
[116]         allocate ( new%values(s%non_zeros) )
[117]         new%non_zeros = s%non_zeros
[118]         if ( s%non_zeros > 0 ) then
[119]           new%rows (1:s%non_zeros) = s%rows (1:s%non_zeros) ! array copy
[120]           new%values(1:s%non_zeros) = s%values(1:s%non_zeros) ! copy
[121]         end if ; end subroutine equal_Vector
[122]
[123]     function get_element (name, row) result (v)
[124]       type (sv), intent(in) :: name     ! sparse vector
[125]       integer,   intent(in) :: row      ! row in sparse vector
[126]       integer               :: j        ! loops
[127]       real                  :: v        ! value at row
[128]         v = 0.0                                    ! default
[129]         if ( row < 1 ) stop "Invalid row number, get_element"
[130]         if ( name%non_zeros < 1 ) return             ! not here
[131]         if ( row > name%rows(name%non_zeros) ) return ! not here
[132]           do j = 1, name%non_zeros
[133]             if ( row == name%rows(j) ) then
[134]               v = name%values(j)                   ! found the value
```

```
[135]             return                                    ! search done
[136]           end if ! in the vector
[137]         end do ! over possible values
[138]   end function get_element
[139]
[140]   function is_equal_to (a, b) result (t_or_f)  ! define ==
[141]    type (sv), intent(in) :: a, b    ! two sparse vectors
[142]    logical               :: t_or_f
[143]    integer               :: i       ! loops
[144]      t_or_f = .true.                          ! default
[145]    if ( a%non_zeros == b%non_zeros ) then ! also check values
[146]     do i = 1, a%non_zeros  ! or use count function for simplicity
[147]       if (a%rows(i) /= b%rows(i) .or. &
[148]           a%values(i) /= b%values(i)) then
[149]           t_or_f = .false.   ! because rows and/or values differ
[150]           return            ! no additional checks needed
[151]       end if ! same values
[152]     end do ! over sparse rows
[153]    else                 ! sizes differ so vectors must be different
[154]      t_or_f = .false.
[155]    end if ! sizes match
[156]   end function is_equal_to
[157]
[158]   function  largest_index (s) result(row)
[159]     type (sv), intent(in) :: s    ! sparse vector
[160]     integer               :: row  ! last non-zero in full vector
[161]     integer               :: j    ! loops
[162]       row = 0                          ! initalize
[163]       if ( s%non_zeros < 1 ) return     ! null vector
[164]       do j = s%non_zeros, 1, -1         ! loop backward
[165]         if ( s%values(j) /= 0.0 ) then  ! last non-zero term
[166]           row = s%rows(j)               ! actual row number
[167]           return                        ! search done
[168]         end if
[169]       end do
[170]   end function  largest_index
[171]
[172]   function  length (name) result (n)
[173]     type (sv), intent(in) :: name
[174]     integer               :: n
[175]       n = name % non_zeros  ! read access to size, if private
[176]   end function  length
[177]
```

Once again we observe that the next two functions employ the colon operator (lines 185,196,199, and 201) to avoid explicit serial loops, which would make them faster on certain vector and parallel computers.

```
[178]  function  norm (name)  result (total)
[179]    type (sv), intent(in) :: name
[180]    real                  :: total
[181]      if ( name%non_zeros < 1 ) then
[182]        ! print *, "Warning: empty vector in norm"
[183]        total = 0.0
[184]      else
[185]        total = sqrt( sum( name%values(1:name%non_zeros)**2 ))
[186]      end if ! a null vector
[187]  end function  norm
```

```

function  normalize_Vector (s)  result (new)
  type (sv), intent(in) :: s
  type (sv)             :: new
  real                  :: total, epsilon = 1.e-6
    allocate ( new%rows   (s%non_zeros) )
    allocate ( new%values(s%non_zeros) )
    new%non_zeros             = s%non_zeros           ! copy size
    new%rows(1:s%non_zeros) = s%rows(1:s%non_zeros)  ! copy rows
    total = sqrt( sum( s%values(1:s%non_zeros)**2 )) ! norm
    if ( total <= epsilon ) then                ! divide by 0 ?
      new%values(1:s%non_zeros) = 0.d0          ! set to zero
    else                                        ! or real values
      new%values(1:s%non_zeros) = s%values(1:s%non_zeros)/total
    end if ! division by zero
end function  normalize_Vector

subroutine pretty (s)   ! print all values if space allows
  type (sv), intent(in) :: s           ! sparse vector
  integer, parameter    :: limit = 20 ! for print size
  integer               :: n
  real                  :: full( s%rows(s%non_zeros) ) ! temp
    n = s%non_zeros
    if ( s%non_zeros < 1 .or. s%rows(s%non_zeros) > limit ) then
      print *, "Wrong size to pretty print"
    else
      full = 0.                              ! initialize to zero
      if ( n > 0 ) full(s%rows) = s%values ! array copy non zeros
      print *,"[", full,"]"                  ! pretty print
    end if ; end subroutine pretty ! automatic deallocate of full

subroutine read_Vector (name)      ! sparse vector data on unit 1
  type (sv), intent(inout) :: name
  integer                  :: length, j
    read (1,'(i1)', advance = 'no') length
    if ( length <= 0 )   stop "Invalid length in read_Vector"
    name % non_zeros = length
    allocate ( name % rows    (length) )
    allocate ( name % values (length) )
    read (1,*) ( name%rows(j), name%values(j), j = 1, length)
    name%rows = name%rows + 1 ! default to 1 not 0 in F90
end subroutine read_Vector

  function  real_mult_Sparse (a, b) result (new)
  !  scalar * vector
    real,      intent(in) :: a
    type (sv), intent(in) :: b
    type (sv)             :: new
      allocate ( new%rows   (b%non_zeros) )
      allocate ( new%values(b%non_zeros) )
      new%non_zeros = b%non_zeros
      if ( b%non_zeros < 1 ) then
        print *, "Warning: zero size in real_mult_Sparse "
      else  ! copy array components
        new%rows   (1:b%non_zeros) =     b%rows   (1:b%non_zeros)
        new%values(1:b%non_zeros) = a * b%values(1:b%non_zeros)
      end if ! null vector
  end function  real_mult_Sparse
```

```

    function rows_of (s)  result(n)  ! copy rows array of s
      type (sv) :: s                  ! sparse vector
      integer   :: n(s%non_zeros)     ! standard array
        if ( s%non_zeros < 1 ) stop "No rows to extract, rows_of"
        n = s%rows                      ! array copy
      end function rows_of

  subroutine set_element  (s, row, value)
   ! Set, or insert, value into row of a sparse vector, s
      type (sv), intent(inout) :: s          ! sparse vector
      integer,   intent(in)    :: row        ! full vector row
      real,      intent(in)    :: value      ! full vector value
      type (sv)                :: new        ! workspace
      logical                  :: found      ! true if row exists
      integer                  :: j, where ! loops, locator
        found = .false.                        ! initialize
        where = 0                              ! initialize
        do  j = 1, s%non_zeros
          if ( s%rows(j) == row ) then         ! found it
            s%values(j) = value                ! value changed
            return                             ! no insert needed
          end if
          if ( s%rows(j) > row ) then
            where = j                          ! insert before j
            exit ! the loop search
          else ! s%rows(j) < row,               may be next or last
            where = j + 1
          end if
        end do ! over current rows in s
        if ( .not. found ) then ! expand and insert at where
          if ( where == 0 ) stop "Logic error, set_element"
          new%non_zeros = s%non_zeros + 1
          allocate ( new%rows   (new%non_zeros) )
          allocate ( new%values(new%non_zeros) )
          !   copy preceeding rows
          if ( where > 1 ) then   ! copy to front of new
            new%rows   (1:where-1) = s%rows   (1:where-1) ! array copy
            new%values(1:where-1) = s%values(1:where-1) ! array copy
          end if ! copy to front of new
          !   insert, copy following rows of s
          new%rows   (where    ) = row                    ! insert
          new%values(where    ) = value                   ! insert
          new%rows   (where+1:) = s%rows   (where:)       ! array copy
          new%values(where+1:) = s%values(where:)         ! array copy
          !   deallocate s, move new to s, deallocate new
          call delete_Sparse_Vector (s)                     ! delete s
          call equal_Vector          (s, new)              ! s <- new
          call delete_Sparse_Vector (new)                   ! delete new
        end if ! an insert is required
    end subroutine set_element

    subroutine show (s) ! alternating row number and value
      type (sv) :: s     ! sparse vector
      integer   :: j, k ! implied loops
        k = length (s)
        if ( k == 0 ) then
          print *, k ; else ;           ! print in C++ style rows
```

```
[304]         print *, k, ( (s%rows(j)-1), s%values(j), j = 1, k )
[305]       end if ; end subroutine show
[306]
[307]   subroutine show_r_v (s) ! all rows then all values
[308]     type (sv) :: s          ! sparse vector
[309]       print *, "Vector has ", s%non_zeros, " non_zero terms."
[310]       if ( s%non_zeros > 0 ) then
[311]         print *, "Rows:     ", s%rows - 1      ! to look like C++
[312]         print *, "Values: ", s%values
[313]       end if ; end subroutine show_r_v
[314]
[315]   function size_of (s)  result(n)
[316]     type (sv) :: s
[317]     integer   :: n
[318]       n = s%non_zeros ; end function size_of
[319]
[320]   function  Sparse_mult_real (a, b) result (new)
[321]   !  vector * scalar
[322]     real,       intent(in) :: b
[323]     type (sv), intent(in) :: a
[324]     type (sv)              :: new
[325]       new = real_mult_Sparse ( b, a)  ! reverse the order
[326]   end function  Sparse_mult_real
[327]
```

In the following subtraction and addition functions we again note that sparse terms with the same values but opposite signs can yield new zero terms in the resulting vector. A temporary automatic workspace vector, `full`, is used to hold the preliminary results. In this case it must have a size that is the maximum of the two given vectors. Thus, the `max` intrinsic is employed in its `dimension` attribute (lines 331, 344), which is opposite the earlier multiplication example (line 65).

```
[328]   function Sub_Sparse_Vectors (u, v) result (w) ! defines -
[329]     type (sv), intent(in) :: u, v
[330]     type (sv)             :: w
[331]     real :: full( max( u%rows(u%non_zeros),    & ! automatic
[332]         &              v%rows(v%non_zeros) ) )  ! workspace
[333]       if ( u%non_zeros <= 0 ) stop "First vector doesn't exist"
[334]       if ( v%non_zeros <= 0 ) stop "Second vector doesn't exist"
[335]       full          = 0.0                      ! set to zero
[336]       full(u%rows) = u%values                 ! copy first values
[337]       full(v%rows) = full(v%rows) - v%values ! less second values
[338]       w = Vector_To_Sparse (full)              ! delete any zeros
[339]   end function Sub_Sparse_Vectors ! automatically deletes full
[340]
[341]   function Sum_Sparse_Vectors (u, v) result (w) ! defines +
[342]     type (sv), intent(in) :: u, v
[343]     type (sv)             :: w
[344]       real :: full( max( u%rows(u%non_zeros),    & ! automatic
[345]           &              v%rows(v%non_zeros) ) )  ! workspace
[346]       if ( u%non_zeros <= 0 ) stop "First vector doesn't exist"
[347]       if ( v%non_zeros <= 0 ) stop "Second vector doesn't exist"
[348]       full          = 0.                        ! set to zero
[349]       full(u%rows) = u%values                  ! copy first values
[350]       full(v%rows) = full(v%rows) + v%values  ! add second values
[351]       w = Vector_To_Sparse (full)               ! delete any zeros
[352]   end function Sum_Sparse_Vectors ! automatically deletes full
[353]
[354]   function values_of (s)  result(v)  ! copy values of s
```

```
    type (sv) :: s                     ! sparse vector
    real      :: v(s%non_zeros)        ! standard array
      if ( s%non_zeros < 1 ) &
         stop "No values to extract, in values_of"
      v = s%values                     ! array copy
  end function values_of

  function Vector_max_value (a) result (v)
    type (sv), intent(in) :: a
    real                  :: v
      v = maxval (a%values(1:a%non_zeros)) ! intrinsic function
      !  is it a sparse vector with a false negative maximum ?
      if ( a%non_zeros < a%rows(a%non_zeros) .and. v < 0. ) v = 0.0
  end function Vector_max_value

  function Vector_min_value (a) result (v)
    type (sv), intent(in) :: a
    real                  :: v
      v = minval ( a%values(1:a%non_zeros) ) ! intrinsic function
      !  is it a sparse vector with a false positive minimum ?
      if ( a%non_zeros < a%rows(a%non_zeros) &
           .and. v > 0. ) v = 0.0
  end function Vector_min_value

```

This function is invoked several times in other member functions. It simply accepts a standard (dense) vector and converts it to the sparse storage mode in the return result.

```
  function Vector_To_Sparse (full) result (sparse)
    real, intent(in) :: full(:)       ! standard array
    type (sv)        :: sparse        ! sparse vector copy
    integer          :: j, n, number  ! loops and counters
      n = count ( full /= 0.0 )       ! count non_zeros
      ! if ( n == 0 ) print *, "Warning: null full vector "
      allocate ( sparse%rows(n), sparse%values(n) )
      sparse%non_zeros = n             ! sparse size
      number           = 0            ! non zeros inserted
      do j = 1, size(full)
        if ( full(j) == 0.0 ) cycle          ! to next j value
          number                = number + 1 ! non zeros inserted
          sparse%rows(number)   = j          ! row number in full
          sparse%values(number) = full(j)    ! value
          if ( number == n ) exit            ! all non_zeros found
      end do ; end function Vector_To_Sparse

  function zero_sparse ()  result (s)
    type (sv) :: s   ! create sparse null vector
      s%non_zeros = 0
      allocate (s%rows(0), s%values(0)); end function zero_sparse
end module class_sparse_Vector
```

B.7 Problem 3.5.5 : Creating an Inventory Object

We begin with the given components for the object and the initialization process.

```
module inventory_object
 implicit none

```

```
  public ! all member functions

  type inventory
   private
    character(len=50) :: name
    real              :: cost
    real              :: price
    integer           :: in_stock    ! number in stock
    integer           :: lead_time   ! work days to re-stock
  end type inventory

contains

function initialize_item () result (item)
  type (inventory) :: item
    item % name      = ""
    item % cost      = 0.0
    item % in_stock  = 0
    item % lead_time = 0
end function initialize_item

```

The next group of functions provide access to the private attributes.

```
function get_item_name (item) result (name)
  type (inventory), intent(in) :: item
  character(len=50) :: name
    name = item % name
end function get_item_name

function get_item_cost (item) result (cost)
  type (inventory), intent(in) :: item
  real :: cost
    cost = item % cost
end function get_item_cost

function get_item_count (item) result (count)
  type (inventory), intent(in) :: item
  integer :: count
    count = item % in_stock
end function get_item_count

function get_item_delay (item) result (delay)
  type (inventory), intent(in) :: item
  integer :: delay
    delay = item % in_stock
end function get_item_delay

```

If we are going to list or save items it makes sense to do so only for nonempty items; thus, access to an empty test is included.

```
function is_item_empty (item) result (t_f)
  type (inventory), intent(in) :: item
  logical :: t_f
    t_f = ((get_item_name (item)) == '')
end function is_item_empty

```

A standard input–output interface is provided for

```
subroutine enter_item (one)
  type (inventory), intent(inout) :: one
    one = initialize_item ()   ! initialize
    print *, "Enter the requested data:"
    print *, "Product (name) : "; read *, one % name
    print *, "Cost ($)       : "; read *, one % cost
    print *, "Price ($)      : "; read *, one % price
    print *, "In Stock (#)   : "; read *, one % in_stock
    print *, "Re-Stock (days): "; read *, one % lead_time
end subroutine enter_item
subroutine print_item (one)
  type (inventory), intent(in) :: one
    print *, "Current Inventory Status:"
    print *, "Product (name) : ", one % name
    print *, "Cost ($)       : ", one % cost
    print *, "Price ($)      : ", one % price
    print *, "In Stock (#)   : ", one % in_stock
    print *, "Re-Stock (days): ", one % lead_time
end subroutine print_item
```

For long-term storage it is desirable to keep the information in its most compact (binary) form. Thus, file access with status checking is a useful option.

```
subroutine file_read (unit, one, ok)
  integer,           intent(in)  :: unit
  type (inventory), intent(out) :: one
  integer,           intent(out) :: ok ! status
    read (unit, iostat=ok) one ! private components
end subroutine file_read
subroutine file_write (unit, one, ok)
  integer,           intent(in)  :: unit
  type (inventory), intent(in)  :: one
  integer,           intent(out) :: ok ! status
    write (unit, iostat=ok) one ! private components
end subroutine file_write
end module inventory_object
```

Later we will use this object in building an inventory system.

B.8 Problem 4.11.1 : Count the Lines in an External File

```
function inputCount(unit) result(linesOfInput)
!-----------------------------------------------------------
! takes a file number, counts the number of lines in that
! file, and returns the number of lines.
!-----------------------------------------------------------
implicit none
integer, intent(in) :: unit         ! file unit number
integer             :: linesOfInput ! result
integer ioResult     ! system I/O action error code
character temp       ! place to hold the character read
```

```

   rewind (unit)                ! go to the front of the file
   linesOfInput = 0             ! initially, there are 0 lines

   do  ! Until iostat says we've hit the end_of_file
     read (unit,'(A)', iostat = ioResult) temp    ! one char

     if ( ioResult == 0 ) then           ! there were no errors
       linesOfInput = linesOfInput + 1   ! increment lines
     else if ( ioResult < 0 ) then       ! we've hit end-of-file
       exit                              ! so exit this loop.
     else   ! ioResult is positive, which is a user error
       write (*,*) 'inputCount: no data at unit =', unit
       stop 'user read error'
     end if
   end do
   rewind(unit)                 ! go to the front of the file
 end Function inputCount
```

B.9 Problem 4.11.3 : Computing CPU Time Usage

Although this is mainly designed to show the use of the module tic_toc, you should note that the intrinsic way of printing a date or time is not "pretty" and could easily be improved.

```
 program watch
 ! ---------------------------------------------------
 ! Exercise DATE_AND_TIME and SYSTEM_CLOCK functions.
 ! ---------------------------------------------------
   use tic_toc
   implicit none
   character* 8   :: the_date
   character*10   :: the_time
   integer        :: j, k
 !
    call date_and_time ( DATE = the_date )
    call date_and_time ( TIME = the_time )
    print *, 'The date is ', the_date, &
   &         ' and the time is now ', the_time
 !   Display facts about the system clock.
    print *, ' '
    call system_clock ( COUNT_RATE  =  rate )
    print *, 'System clock runs at ', rate,&
   &         ' ticks per second'
 !
 !   Call the system clock to start an execution timer.
    call  tic
 !
 !  call run_the_job, or test with next 3 lines
     do k = 1, 9999
        j = sqrt ( real(k*k) )
     end do
 !   Stop the execution timer and report execution time.
    print *, ' '
    print *, 'Job took ', toc (), ' seconds to execute.'
  end program watch                    ! Running gives
 ! The date is 19980313 and the time is now 171837.792
 ! System clock runs at  100  ticks per second
 ! Job took  0.9999999776E-02  seconds to execute.
```

B.10 Problem 4.11.4 : Converting a String to Uppercase

The change from the to_lower should be obvious here. It seems desirable to place these two routines and others that deal with strings into a single strings utility module.

```
function  to_upper (string)  result (new_string) ! like C
! -------------------------------------------------------------
!         Convert a string or character to upper case
!          (valid for ASCII or EBCDIC processors)
! -------------------------------------------------------------
implicit none
character (len = *), intent(in) :: string      ! unknown length
character (len = len(string))    :: new_string ! same length
character (len = 26), parameter ::                  &
          UPPER = 'ABCDEFGHIJKLMNOPQRSTUVWXYZ',     &
          lower = 'abcdefghijklmnopqrstuvwxyz'
integer :: k    ! loop counter
integer :: loc  ! position in alphabet
  new_string = string        ! copy everything
  do k = 1, len(string)      ! to change letters
    loc = index ( lower, string(k:k))              ! locate
    if (loc /= 0 ) new_string(k:k) = UPPER(loc:loc) ! convert
  end do ! over string characters
end function to_upper
```

B.11 Problem 4.11.8 : Read two Values from Each Line of an External File

```
subroutine readData (inFile, lines, x, y)
! -------------------------------------------------------
!   Take a file number, the number of lines to be read,
!      and put the data into the arrays x and y
! -------------------------------------------------------
! inFile     is unit number to be read
! lines      is number of lines in the file
! x          is independent data
! y          is dependent data
  implicit none
  integer, intent(in)  :: inFile,   lines
  real,    intent(out) :: x(lines), y(lines)
  integer              :: j

  rewind (inFile)                 ! go to front of the file
  do j = 1, lines                 ! for the entire file
    read (inFile, *) x(j), y(j) ! get the x and y values
  end do ! over all lines
end subroutine readData
```

B.12 Problem 4.11.14 : Two-line Least-square Fits

The extension of the single-line least-squares fit shown in Figure 4.21 is rather straightforward in that we will call subroutine lsq_fit multiple times. In line 37 we first call it in case a single-line fit may be more accurate than the expected two-line fit.

```
[  1]  program two_line_lsq_fit
[  2]  !------------------------------------------------------
[  3]  ! Best two-line linear least-squares fit of data in
```

```
[  4]  ! file specified by the user, and split in two sets
[  5]  !-----------------------------------------------
[  6]    implicit none
[  7]    real, allocatable :: x (:)  ! independent data
[  8]    real, allocatable :: y (:)  ! dependent data
[  9]
[ 10]    real    :: fit(3),  fit1(3), fit2(3) ! error results
[ 11]    real    :: left(3), right(3)         ! best results
[ 12]    real    :: error                     ! current error
[ 13]    real    :: error_min                  ! best error
[ 14]    integer :: split                     ! best division
[ 15]
[ 16]    integer, parameter   :: filenumber = 1 ! input unit
[ 17]    character (len = 64) :: filename       ! input file
[ 18]    integer              :: lines          ! of input
[ 19]    integer              :: inputCount, j  ! loops
[ 20]
[ 21]  !  Get the name of the file containing the data.
[ 22]     write (*, *) 'Enter the data input filename:'
[ 23]     read  (*, *) filename
[ 24]
[ 25]  !       Open that file for reading.
[ 26]     open (unit = filenumber, file = filename)
[ 27]
[ 28]  !       Find the number of lines in the file
[ 29]     lines = inputCount (filenumber)
[ 30]     write (*, *) 'There were ',lines,' records read.'
[ 31]
[ 32]  !  Allocate that many entries in the x and y array
[ 33]     allocate (x(lines), y(lines))
[ 34]     call read_xy_file (filenumber, lines, x, y) ! Read data
[ 35]     close (filenumber)
[ 36]
[ 37]     call lsq_fit (lines, x, y, fit)   ! single line fit
[ 38]     print *, "Single line fit"
[ 39]     print *, "the slope is     ", fit(1)
[ 40]     print *, "the intercept is ", fit(2)
[ 41]     print *, "the error is     ", fit(3)
[ 42]
```

After that we want to try all the reasonable choices for reading the dataset into two adjacent regions that are each to be fitted with a different straight line. Trial variables were defined in lines 10 and 12, whereas the best results found are in variables declared in lines 11, 13, and 14. Note that on line 48 we have required that at least three points be used to define an approximate straight line. If we allowed two points to be employed we would get a false (or misleading) indication of zero error for such a choice. Thus, in line 48 we begin a loop over all possible sets of three or more data points and call lsq_fit for each of the two segments, as seen in lines 50 and 51.

```
[ 43]  ! Loop to determine the mean squared error for each
[ 44]  ! of the possible two divisions of the data
[ 45]  !
[ 46]     error_min = HUGE(error_min)   ! initialize the error_min
[ 47]     split = 3                    ! initialize split point
[ 48]     do j = 3, lines-3            ! 3 pts to approximate a line
[ 49]  !        least-squares fit of two data subsets
```

```
[ 50]        call lsq_fit (j,       x(1:j),        y(1:j),        fit1)
[ 51]        call lsq_fit (lines-j, x(j+1:lines), y(j+1:lines), fit2)
[ 52]        error = fit1(3) + fit2(3)
[ 53]
```

In splitting up the two data regions note that it was not necessary to copy segments of the independent and dependent data. Instead the colon operator, or implied do loops, were used in lines 50 and 51 to pass vectors with j and *(lines – j)* entries, respectively to the two calls to lsq_fit. After combining the two errors in line 52, we update the current best choice for the dataset division point in lines 55 through 58.

```
[ 54]  !        does this division gives you a smaller error ?
[ 55]         if ( error < error_min ) then
[ 56]           error_min = error ; split = j
[ 57]           left      = fit1  ; right = fit2
[ 58]         end if ! current best choice
[ 59]       end do ! of split choices
```

After we exit the loop, at line 59 we simply list the best results obtained. In line 73 we have also deallocated the data arrays even though it is just a formality at this point since all memory is released because the program terminates immediately afterwards. Had this been a subroutine or function, then we would need to have been sure that allocated variables were released when their access scope terminated. Later versions of Fortran will do that for you, but good programmers should keep up with memory allocations.

```
[ 60]  !        Display the results
[ 61]       print *, "Two line best fit; combined error is ", error_min
[ 62]       print *, "Best division of the data is:"
[ 63]       print *, "data(:j), data(j+1:), where j = ", split
[ 64]       print *, "Left line fit:"
[ 65]       print *, "the slope is      ", left(1)
[ 66]       print *, "the intercept is ", left(2)
[ 67]       print *, "the error is      ", left(3)
[ 68]       print *, "Right line fit:"
[ 69]       print *, "the slope is      ", right(1)
[ 70]       print *, "the intercept is ", right(2)
[ 71]       print *, "the error is      ", right(3)
[ 72]
[ 73]       deallocate (y, x)
[ 74]  end program two_line_lsq_fit
[ 75]
```

For completeness an input routine, read_xy_file is illustrated. It is elementary since it does not check for any read errors and thus does not allow for any exception control if the read somehow fails.

```
[ 76]  subroutine read_xy_file (infile, lines, x, y)
[ 77]  !--------------------------------------------------
[ 78]  ! Take a file number, the number of lines to be read,
[ 79]  !   and put the data into the arrays x and y
[ 80]  !--------------------------------------------------
[ 81]    implicit none
[ 82]    integer, intent(in)  :: inFile      ! unit to read
[ 83]    integer, intent(in)  :: lines       ! length of the file
[ 84]    real,    intent(out) :: x(lines)    ! independent data
```

```
[ 85]    real,    intent(out) :: y(lines)   ! dependent data
[ 86]    integer :: j
[ 87]      rewind (inFile)  ! go to front of the file
[ 88]      do j = 1, lines                 ! for the entire file
[ 89]        read (infile, *) x(j), y(j) ! get the x and y values
[ 90]      end do ! over all lines
[ 91]  end subroutine read_xy_file
[ 92]
```

If the supplied data file were huge, say the argument lines have a value of ten million, then such data would probably have been stored in a binary rather than a formatted file. In that case we would simply invoke a binary read by rewriting line 89 as

```
[ 89]        read (infile) x(j), y(j) ! binary read of x and y
```

Such a change would yield a much faster input but would still be relatively slow owing to its being in the loop starting at line 88. To get the fastest posible input we would have needed to save the binary data on the file such that all the x values were stored first followed by all the corresponding y values. In that case, we avoid the loop and get the fastest possible input by replacing lines 88–90 with

```
[ 88]      ! sequential binary read of x and y values
[ 89]        read (infile) x, y
[ 90]      ! input complete, add iostat for exceptions
```

Here we will not go into the details about how we would have to replace subroutine inputCount with an equivalent one for binary files. To do that you will have to study the Fortran INQUIRE statement for files and its IOLENGTH option to get a hardware-independent record length of a real variable.

```
[ 93]  !  Given test data in file two_line.dat:
[ 94]  !  0.0000000e+00   1.7348276e+01
[ 95]  !  1.0000000e+00   6.5017349e+01
[ 96]  !  2.0000000e+00   8.7237749e+01
[ 97]  !  3.0000000e+00   1.2433478e+02
[ 98]  !  4.0000000e+00   1.5456681e+02
[ 99]  !  5.0000000e+00   1.8956219e+02
[100]  !  6.0000000e+00   2.1740486e+02
[101]  !  7.0000000e+00   2.3138619e+02
[102]  !  8.0000000e+00   2.7995041e+02
[103]  !  9.0000000e+00   3.1885162e+02
[104]  !  1.0000000e+01   3.4628642e+02
[105]  !  1.1000000e+01   3.3522546e+02
[106]  !  1.2000000e+01   3.7626218e+02
[107]  !  1.3000000e+01   3.9577060e+02
[108]  !  1.4000000e+01   4.2217988e+02
[109]  !  1.5000000e+01   4.3388828e+02
[110]  !  1.6000000e+01   4.5897959e+02
[111]  !  1.7000000e+01   4.9506511e+02
[112]  !  1.8000000e+01   5.0747649e+02
[113]  !  1.9000000e+01   5.2168101e+02
[114]  !  2.0000000e+01   5.2976511e+02
```

Assuming the formatted data are stored in file two_line.dat as shown above, we obtain the best two straight-line fits.

```
[115]  ! Running the program gives:
[116]  !
```

```
! Enter the data input filename: two_line.dat
! There were 21 records read.
! Single line fit
! the slope is      25.6630135
! the intercept is 53.2859993
! the error is      343.854675
! Two line best fit; combined error is 126.096634
! Best division of the data is:
! data(:j), data(j+1:), where j = 11
! Left line fit:
! the slope is      31.9555302
! the intercept is 24.9447269
! the error is      46.060421
! Right line fit:
! the slope is      21.6427555
! the intercept is 112.166664
! the error is      80.0362091
```

Verify this by plotting the data points and the three straight-line segments. Just remember that the first line covers the whole domain, whereas the second goes only up to halfway between points 11 and 12 and the third line runs from there to the end of the independent data.

B.13 Problem 4.11.15 : Find the Next Available File Unit

The INQUIRE statement has many very useful features that return information based on the unit number or the file name. It can also tell you how much storage a particular type of record requires (like the sizeof function in C and C++). Here we use only the ability to determine if a unit number is currently open. To do that we begin by checking the unit number that follows the last one we used. Line 9 declares that variable, last_unit, and initializes it to 0. The save attribute in that line ensures that the latest value of last_unit will always be saved and available on each subsequent use of the function. Since the standard input–output units have numbers less that 10, we allow the unit numbers to be used to range from 10 to 999, as seen in line 8. However, the upper limit could be changed.

Lines 14–18 determine if the unit after last_unit is closed. If so, that unit will be used and we are basically finished. We set the return value, next, update last_unit, and return.

```
[ 1]  function get_next_io_unit () result (next)
[ 2]  ! * * * * * * * * * * * * * * * * * * * * * * * * * * * * * *
[ 3]  !       find a unit number available for i/o action
[ 4]  ! * * * * * * * * * * * * * * * * * * * * * * * * * * * * * *
[ 5]    implicit none
[ 6]    integer :: next    ! the next available unit number
[ 7]
[ 8]    integer, parameter :: min_unit = 10, max_unit = 999
[ 9]    integer, save      :: last_unit = 0    ! initialize
[10]    integer            :: count           ! number of failures
[11]    logical            :: open            ! file status
[12]
[13]    count = 0 ; next = min_unit - 1
[14]    if ( last_unit > 0 ) then ! check next in line
[15]      next = last_unit + 1
[16]      inquire (unit=next, opened=open)
[17]      if ( .not. open ) last_unit = next ! found it
[18]      return
```

Otherwise, if the unit after last_unit is open, we must loop over all the higher-unit numbers in search of one that is closed. If we succeed, then we update last_unit and return by exiting the forever loop, as seen in lines 24 and 25.

```
[19]     else ! loop through allowed units
[20]       do ! forever
[21]         next = next + 1
[22]         inquire (unit=next, opened=open)
[23]         if ( .not. open ) then
[24]           last_unit = next       ! found it
[25]           exit ! the unit loop
[26]         end if
```

At this point it may be impossible to find a unit. However, with 999 units available it is likely that one that was previously in use has now been closed and is available again. Before aborting we reset the search and allow three cycles to find a unit that is now free. That is done in lines 27–31.

```
[27]         if ( next == max_unit ) then ! attempt reset 3 times
[28]           last_unit = 0
[29]           count     = count + 1
[30]           if ( count <= 3 ) next = min_unit - 1
[31]         end if ! reset try
```

In the unlikely event that all allowed units are still in use, we abort the function after giving some insight into the reason.

```
[32]         if ( next > max_unit ) then ! abort
[33]           print *,'ERROR: max unit exceeded in get_next_io_unit'
[34]           stop    'ERROR: max unit exceeded in get_next_io_unit'
[35]         end if ! abort
[36]       end do ! over unit numbers
[37]     end if ! last_unit
[38]   end function get_next_io_unit
```

B.14 Problem 5.4.4 : Polymorphic Interface for the Class 'Position_Angle'

```
module class_Position_Angle  ! file: class_Position_Angle.f90
  use class_Angle
  implicit none
  type Position_Angle          ! angle in deg, min, sec
    private
    integer   :: deg, min     ! degrees, minutes
    real      :: sec          ! seconds
    character :: dir          ! N | S, E | W
  end type
```

The type definitions above are unchanged. The only new part of the module for this class is the INTERFACE given in the following five lines.

```
  interface Position_Angle_    ! generic constructor
    module procedure Decimal_sec, Decimal_min
    module procedure Int_deg, Int_deg_min, Int_deg_min_sec
  end interface
contains  . . .
```

Returning to the original main program

```
[ 1] program Another_Great_Arc
[ 2]  use class_Great_Arc
[ 3]  implicit none
[ 4]   type (Great_Arc)        :: arc
[ 5]   type (Global_Position) :: g1, g2
[ 6]   type (Position_Angle)  :: a1, a2
[ 7]   type (Angle)           :: ang
[ 8]   real                   :: deg, rad
```

we simply replace all the previous constructor calls with the generic function Position_Angle_ as shown on lines 9 through 18 below.

```
[ 9]     a1 = Position_Angle_ (10, 30, 0., "N")  ! note decimal point
[10]     call List_Position_Angle (a1)
[11]     a1 = Position_Angle_ (10, 30, 0,  "N")
[12]     call List_Position_Angle (a1)
[13]     a1 = Position_Angle_ (10, 30,     "N")
[14]     call List_Position_Angle (a1)
[15]     a1 = Position_Anglc_ (20,         "N")
[16]     call List_Position_Angle (a1)
[17]     a2 = Position_Angle_ (30, 48, 0., "N")
[18]     call List_Position_Angle (a2)
```

B.15 Problem 5.4.5 : Building an Object Inventory System

```
module inventory_system
 use inventory_object
 implicit none

  public ! members
  integer,         save, private :: Size = 0, old_size = 0
  integer,         save, private :: Saved = 0
  integer, parameter, private :: save_file = 9

```

The preceding private integers keep up with the current and previous size of the allocatable arrays to be created. Among the methods below *set_Size* is used only once, whereas *increase_Size* is used every time the system gets full and needs to be reallocated.

```
contains

subroutine set_Size (n)
  integer, intent (in) :: n
    if ( Size == 0 ) then ; Size = n
    else ! inventory already exists
      print *, 'System exists with a size = ', Size
      print *, 'You must save the system, resize it, '
      print *, 'and restore present system.'
    end if
end subroutine set_Size

subroutine increase_Size (n)
  integer, intent (in) :: n
    print *, 'Increased size from ', Size, ' to ', n
    if ( Size == 0 ) then ; Size = n
```

```
[ 26]      else ! inventory already exists
[ 27]        old_size = Size
[ 28]        Size     = n
[ 29]      end if
[ 30]  end subroutine increase_Size
[ 31]
```

We assign the name *inventory.bin* to a binary file that can serve either to back up the contents for long-term storage or as a very short-term storage while the inventory list is being reallocated. Note that the private status of an item's components requires that the item object have methods for binary file I/O as seen at lines 42 and 66. Additional logic is provide to process only nonempty items in the array.

```
[ 32]  subroutine save_system (inv)
[ 33]    type (inventory), intent(in) :: inv(Size)
[ 34]    integer :: j, total, ok
[ 35]      open (save_file, file='inventory.bin', form='unformatted', &
[ 36]            status='unknown')  ! for a binary sequential write
[ 37]      ! if public components: write (save_file) inv
[ 38]      total = 0
[ 39]      print *,'Saving inventory to file inventory.bin'
[ 40]      do j = 1, Size ! save used items
[ 41]        if (.not. is_item_empty (inv(j)) ) then
[ 42]          call file_write (save_file, inv(j), ok)
[ 43]          if ( ok == 0 ) then ! write ok
[ 44]            total = total + 1
[ 45]          else ; print *,'Abort at record ', total
[ 46]            stop 'Write to inventory.bin failed'
[ 47]          end if ! write error
[ 48]        end if ! not empty
[ 49]      end do ! of private component attribute
[ 50]      old_size = Size
[ 51]      print *, total, 'inventory items saved to file inventory.bin'
[ 52]      saved = total ; close (save_file)
[ 53]  end subroutine save_system
[ 54]
```

Note that the *saved* counter attribute has been used, at lines 52 and 65, to compress the binary copy by accessing only nonempty items.

```
[ 55]  subroutine restore_system (inv)
[ 56]    type (inventory), intent(out) :: inv(Size)
[ 57]    integer :: exists, j, ok
[ 58]      open (save_file, file='inventory.bin', form='unformatted', &
[ 59]            status='old', iostat=exists)  ! for a binary read
[ 60]      if ( exists > 0 ) stop 'Error: file inventory.bin not found'
[ 61]      if ( Size >= old_size ) then ! restore old part
[ 62]        call initialize_sys (inv)
[ 63]        ! iff public: read (save_file, iostat=ok) inv (1:old_size)
[ 64]        print *,'Restoring from inventory.bin'
[ 65]        do j = 1, saved
[ 66]          call file_read (save_file, inv(j), ok)
[ 67]          if ( ok /= 0 ) then ! read not ok
[ 68]            print *,'Abort at record ', j
[ 69]            stop 'Read from inventory.bin failed'
[ 70]          end if
[ 71]        end do
[ 72]        old_size = Size  ! no read error
```

```
        print *,'Restored ', saved, ' non-empty items'
      end if ! new size larger
      close (save_file)
  end subroutine restore_system

```

Likewise, the display feature only shows nonempty objects. The display would be prettier if formatted output were used for the dollar values.

```
  subroutine display_all (inv)
    type (inventory), intent(in) :: inv(Size)
    integer                      :: j
      do j = 1, Size    ! to find a non-empty product
        if (.not. is_item_empty (inv(j))) call print_item ( inv(j) )
      end do
  end subroutine display_all

```

The following is a rather inefficent way to change all components in an object interactively even if only one needs revision. Propose a more efficient approach.

```
  subroutine enter_update (inv)
    type (inventory), intent(inout) :: inv(Size)
    character(len=50)               :: name
    integer                         :: j, k
      print *, "Enter product name:" ; read *, name
      k = 0
      do j = 1, Size
        if ( name == get_item_name (inv(j)) ) then
          k = j
          call print_item ( inv(k) ) ! echo status
          call enter_item  ( inv(k) ) ! input status
          exit ! this loop
        end if
      end do
      if ( k == 0 ) print *, "Item not present. Try again."
  end subroutine enter_update

```

We must be able to initialize the system at the beginning and after memory has been reallocated.

```
  subroutine initialize_sys (inv)
    type (inventory), intent(out) :: inv(Size)
    integer                       :: j
      do j = 1, Size
        inv (j) = initialize_item ()
      end do ! on products
  end subroutine initialize_sys

```

The interactive filling of an item is fairly efficient. Note that the name (or description) must be inputted in between quotes if it contains blanks or commas because we have employed a default-free format read.

```
  subroutine enter_entry (inv) ! place new item in inventory
    type (inventory), intent (inout) :: inv(Size)
    integer :: j, k
```

```
      k = 0              ! initialize
      do j = 1, Size     ! to find an empty product
        if ( is_item_empty (inv(j)) ) then
          k = j ; exit ! empty slot at k
        end if
      end do
      if ( k == 0 )  then
        print *, "Sorry, system is full."
      else       ! room for more
        call enter_item( inv(k) )
      end if
  end subroutine enter_entry

  end module inventory_system
```

Now we provide a simple test program to verify most of the features of the initial system design:

```
program test_inventory_system
use inventory_system
use inventory_object
 implicit none
 integer                           :: start = 2, new
 type (inventory), allocatable :: inv_sys(:)
 character                         :: c

   print *, "Welcome to the Inventory System"
   allocate (inv_sys (start) )
   call set_Size (start) ; print *,'System size = ', start
   call initialize_sys (inv_sys)

   print *, "Choose inventory action. Enter Q to quit."
!  loop until done
   do ! forever
```

Note the next line employs a simple screen menu feature supplied as an internal subprogram at the end.

```
      c = get_menu () ! get interactive user input
      select case (c)
        case ('E', 'e') ! Enter new data
          call enter_entry ( inv_sys )
        case ('D', 'd') ! Display all entries
          call display_all (inv_sys)
        case ('U', 'u') ! Update an entry
          call enter_update ( inv_sys )
        case ('Q', 'q') ! Quit
          exit ! the do forever
        case ('S', 's') ! Save the inventory
          call save_system (inv_sys)
        case ('N', 'n') ! Give a new larger size
          print *,'Give new size greater than ', start
          read *, new ; new = max0 (new, start)
          call save_system (inv_sys)
          deallocate (inv_sys) ; allocate (inv_sys (new) )
          call increase_size (new) ! to test restore
          call restore_system (inv_sys) ; start = new
        case ('R', 'r') ! Restore the inventory
          call restore_system (inv_sys)
```

```
        case default
          print *, 'Unknown response, Exiting'
          exit ! the do forever
      end select
    end do

  contains
```

A simple character-driven menu function is defined here. It is based on the *index* function for operating on strings. Clearly, a case-selection process might be more efficient for a large number of choices (as seen in the main program above).

```

  function get_menu () result (c)
    character :: c
      print *, "(D)isplay  (E)nter (R)estore (S)ave (U)pdate:"
      do ! forever
        read  *, c
        if ( index ('EeDdUuQq', c) > 0 ) exit ! acceptable input
        if ( index ('SsRrNn',    c) > 0 ) exit ! acceptable input
        print *, 'Enter Q to quit' ! if you got here
      end do ! for user input
  end function get_menu

  end program test_inventory_system    ! Running gives
```

Validation results:

```
  ! Welcome to the Inventory System
  ! System size =  9
  ! Choose inventory action. Enter Q to quit.
  ! (D)isplay  (E)nter (R)estore (S)ave (U)pdate: E
  ! Enter the requested data:
  ! Product (name) :  "Drill, Electric"
  ! Cost ($)       :  45
  ! Price ($)      :  23
  ! In Stock (#)   :  9
  ! Re-Stock (days):  11
  ! (D)isplay  (E)nter (R)estore (S)ave (U)pdate: e
  ! Enter the requested data:
  ! Product (name) :  Hammer
  ! Cost ($)       :  4.5
  ! Price ($)      :  5.6
  ! In Stock (#)   :  5
  ! Re-Stock (days):  3
  ! (D)isplay  (E)nter (R)estore (S)ave (U)pdate: s
  ! Saving inventory to file inventory.bin
  ! 2 inventory items saved to file inventory.bin
  ! (D)isplay  (E)nter (R)estore (S)ave (U)pdate: r
  ! Restoring from inventory.bin
  ! Restored  2  non-empty items
  ! (D)isplay  (E)nter (R)estore (S)ave (U)pdate: d
  ! Current Inventory Status:
  ! Product (name) : Drill, Electric
  ! Cost ($)       :   45.0000000
  ! Price ($)      :   23.0000000
  ! In Stock (#)   :  9
  ! Re-Stock (days):  11
  ! Current Inventory Status:
```

```
! Product (name) : Hammer
! Cost ($)       :     4.5000000
! Price ($)      :     5.5999999
! In Stock (#)   :  5
! Re-Stock (days):  3
! (D)isplay  (E)nter (R)estore (S)ave (U)pdate: q
```

B.16 Problem 6.4.1 : Using a Function With the Same Name in two Classes

```
include 'class_X.f90'
include 'class_Y.f90'
program Revise_employee_manager  ! modified from Fig. 4.6.2-3F
  use class_Y, Y_f => f ! renamed in main
  implicit none
  type (X_) :: x, z ; type (Y_) :: y
    x%a = 22                ! assigns 22 to the a defined in X
    call X_f(x)             ! invokes the f() defined in X
    print *,"x%a = ", x%a ! lists the a defined in X
    y%a = 44                ! assigns 44 to the a defined in Y
    x%a = 66                ! assigns 66 to the a defined in X
    call Y_f(y)             ! invokes the f() defined in Y
    call X_f(x)             ! invokes the f() defined in X
    print *,"y%a = ", y%a ! lists the a defined in X
    print *,"x%a = ", x%a ! lists the a defined in X
    z%a = y%a               ! assign Y a to z in X
    print *,"z%a = ", z%a ! lists the a defined in X
end program Revise_employee_manager                        ! Running gives:
! X_ f() executing                 ! x%a = 22
! Y_ f() executing                 ! X_ f() executing
! y%a = 44                         ! x%a = 66
! z%a = 44
```

B.17 Problem 6.4.3 : Revising the Employee–manager Classes

The changes are relatively simple. First we add two lines in the Employee class:

```
interface setData                    ! a polymorphic member
  module procedure setDataE          ; end interface
```

Then we change two other lines:

```
  empl = setData ( "Burke", "John", 25.0 )
. . .
  mgr = Manager_ ( "Kovacs", "Jan", 1200.0 ) ! constructor
```

The generic setData could not also contain setDataM because it has the same argument signature as setDataE, and the compiler would not be able to tell which dynamic binding to select.

B.18 Problem 8.3.5 : Design a Tridiagonal Matrix Class

We begin by defining the attributes needed in a triadiagonal matrix system, the three diagonals, and their size. However, the reader is warned that there are two common ways of implementing such matrices. One is to use three equal-sized arrays in which the off diagonals each have one term that is always zero. The other is to have the off diagonals with a length that is one smaller than the main diagonal. We use the latter except for one routine in which we illustrate changing storage modes.

```
MODULE tridiagonal_matrix_class
  IMPLICIT NONE
  PUBLIC  :: tri_diag_matrix, tri_diag_maker
  PUBLIC  :: tri_diag_free,   tri_diag_print
  PUBLIC  :: OPERATOR (*), OPERATOR (.solve.), transpose
  PRIVATE :: tri_diag_by_vector, tri_diag_solve
  PRIVATE ! components accessed by these methods only

   TYPE :: tri_diag_matrix    ! tridiagonal matrix
     INTEGER                          :: size       ! dimension
     DOUBLE PRECISION, POINTER :: lower (:)  ! lower diagonal
     DOUBLE PRECISION, POINTER :: main  (:)  ! main  diagonal
     DOUBLE PRECISION, POINTER :: upper (:)  ! upper diagonal

!   Warning: the above allocatable vectors will have sizes of
!            lower (size - 1), main (size), upper (size - 1).
!    Some logic might be simpler if we waste two reals and make
!    them all the same length with lower(1) = upper(size) = 0

! | b(1)   c(1)    0       0   0   0           | | u(1) |   | r(1) |
! | a(1)   b(2)   c(2)     0   0   0           | | u(2) |   | r(2) |
! |                .........                   | |  ..  |   |  ..  |
! |  0    a(I-1)  b(I)   c(I)  0   0           | | u(I) | = | r(I) |
! |                .........                   | |  ..  |   |  ..  |
! |                        a(L-2) b(L-1) c(L-1)| |u(L-1)|   |r(L-1)|
! |                               a(L-1)  b(L) | | u(L) |   | r(L) |
!
   END TYPE tri_diag_matrix

```

Here we overload only the most obvious operators and define a few of the generic operations that are common to matrix operations in general.

```
   INTERFACE TRANSPOSE ! interface for transpose function
     MODULE PROCEDURE tri_diag_trans ; END INTERFACE

   INTERFACE tri_diag_maker ! generic constructor
     MODULE PROCEDURE tri_diag_alloc   ! null matrix
     MODULE PROCEDURE tri_diag_scalars ! build from scalars
     MODULE PROCEDURE tri_diag_vectors ! build from vectors
   END INTERFACE

   INTERFACE OPERATOR (*) ! matrix times vector
     MODULE PROCEDURE tri_diag_by_vector ; END INTERFACE

   INTERFACE OPERATOR (.solve.)  ! by factorization
     MODULE PROCEDURE tri_diag_solve ; END INTERFACE

CONTAINS

```

Here we overload the common transpose operation.

```
FUNCTION tri_diag_trans (S) RESULT (T)  ! T = transpose (S)
  TYPE (tri_diag_matrix), INTENT(IN) :: S
  TYPE (tri_diag_matrix)             :: T ! intent (out)
    T = tri_diag_alloc (S % size)         ! allocate T
```

```
    T % upper = S % lower                ! lower --> upper
    T % main  = S % main                 ! same main diagonal
    T % lower = S % upper                ! upper --> lower
END FUNCTION tri_diag_trans

```

Next we provide subprograms to allocate, deallocate, and print a tridiagonal matrix.

```
FUNCTION tri_diag_alloc (n) RESULT (T) ! allocate tri_diag_matrix
  INTEGER,     INTENT(IN) :: n          ! desired size
  TYPE (tri_diag_matrix) :: T           ! intent(out)
    T % size = n                        ! (consider all size n)
    ALLOCATE (T % lower (n-1), T % main (n), T % upper (n-1))
END FUNCTION tri_diag_alloc

SUBROUTINE tri_diag_print (T) ! print tri_diag_matrix
  TYPE (tri_diag_matrix), INTENT(IN) :: T  ! matrix
  INTEGER :: n, j                          ! work
    n = T % size                           ! size
    print *, 1, 0.d0, T % main (1), T % upper (1)
    if ( n > 2 ) then                      ! more rows
      do j = 2, n-1                        ! row loop
        print *, j, T % lower (j-1), T % main (j), T % upper (j)
      end do
    end if                                 ! add last row
    print *, n, T % lower (n-1), T % main (n), 0.d0
END SUBROUTINE tri_diag_print

SUBROUTINE tri_diag_free (A) ! deallocate tri_diag_matrix
  TYPE (tri_diag_matrix), INTENT(INOUT) :: A  ! destroy
    A % size = 0 ; DEALLOCATE (A % lower, A % main, A % upper)
END SUBROUTINE tri_diag_free

```

We need basic constructors. The first is for a common special case in which each diagonal contains a single scalar constant. The second employes three vectors to copy onto the diagonals. We may also want a default construction that is an identity matrix.

```
FUNCTION tri_diag_scalars (n, sl, sm, su) RESULT (T)
  INTEGER,          INTENT(IN) :: n          ! size from scalars
  DOUBLE PRECISION, INTENT(IN) :: sl, sm, su ! scalars
  TYPE (tri_diag_matrix)       :: T          ! matrix, intent(out)
    T = tri_diag_alloc (n) ; T % lower = sl  ! allocate
    T % main = sm          ; T % upper = su  ! fill
END FUNCTION tri_diag_scalars

FUNCTION tri_diag_vectors (n, vl, vm, vu) RESULT (T)
  INTEGER,          INTENT(IN) :: n                         ! size
  DOUBLE PRECISION, INTENT(IN) :: vl(n-1), vm(n), vu(n-1) ! vectors
  TYPE (tri_diag_matrix)       :: T                          ! intent(out)
    T = tri_diag_alloc (n) ; T % lower = vl                  ! allocate
    T % main = vm          ; T % upper = vu                 ! fill
END FUNCTION tri_diag_vectors

```

We often need to multiply a matrix by a vector and to solve a linear equation system, and thus we give two members that are used to overload common symbols for those operations.

We have not provided other common operations like adding two tridiagonals, pre- and postmultiplying by a scalar, multiplying two tridiagonals, and so forth.

```
FUNCTION tri_diag_by_vector (T, v) RESULT (w)
  TYPE (tri_diag_matrix), INTENT(IN) :: T
  DOUBLE PRECISION, INTENT(IN)  :: v (T % size)
  DOUBLE PRECISION              :: w (T % size)   ! intent(out)
  INTEGER :: i, n                                 ! loops
    n = T % size                                  ! system size
    w(1) = T % main (1)*v(1) + T % upper (1)*v(2) ! first row
    DO i = 2, n-1                                 ! middle rows
       w(i) = T % lower (i-1) * v(i-1) &
            + T % main  (i)   * v(i)   &
            + T % upper (i)   * v(i+1) ; END DO
    w(n) = T % lower (n-1)*v(n-1) + T % main (n)*v(n) ! last row
END FUNCTION tri_diag_by_vector

FUNCTION tri_diag_solve (T, b) RESULT (x)               ! linear system
  TYPE (tri_diag_matrix), INTENT(IN) :: T               ! matrix
  DOUBLE PRECISION,        INTENT(IN) :: b (T % size) ! rhs
  DOUBLE PRECISION                    :: x (T % size) ! intent(out)
!            Copies to be destroyed (note size)
  DOUBLE PRECISION :: dl (T % size), dm (T % size), &
                      du (T % size), r  (T % size)
  INTEGER :: n                                ! system size
    n = T % size ; x = 0.d0                   ! initialize
    dl(1) = 0.d0 ; du(n) = 0.d0 ; r = b       ! initialize
!            Copies to be expanded and destroyed
    dl(2:n) = T % lower ; dm = T % main ; du(1:n-1) = T % upper
    x = Thomas_tri_diag (du, dm, dl, r) ! Solve the system for x
END FUNCTION tri_diag_solve

```

The arguments of the preceding solver are not destroyed, but it employed the Thomas algorithm below that (as written) does destroy its input arguments. Also, the function *Thomas_tri_diag* uses three equal-length diagonals and thus differs from our class. āāEither observation requires the definition of copied diagonals used above. The code below is an old procedural code, and so the interfacing above illustrates how to reuse codes and update their interface.

```
FUNCTION Thomas_tri_diag (a, d, b, r) result (x)
! WARNING all input vectors are destroyed herein
! Solve Tridiagonal matrix system, T x = r for x
! Where a = upper diagonal of T, a(n) = 0
!       d = main  diagonal of T
!       b = lower diagonal of T, b(1) = 0
!       r = right hand side vector
  Implicit none                          ! note size change below
  DOUBLE PRECISION, INTENT(INOUT) :: a (:),       d (size(a)), &
                                     b (size(a)), r (size(a))
  DOUBLE PRECISION :: x (size(a))     ! intent (out)
  DOUBLE PRECISION :: denom, tol = epsilon (1.d0)
  INTEGER :: n, i

! | d(I)   a(I)     0       0    0    0        | | x(I) |    | r(I) |
! |b(I+1) d(I+1) a(I+1)     0    0    0        | |x(I+1)|    |r(I+1)|
! |  0    b(I+2) d(I+2) a(I+2) 0    0          | |x(I+2)|    |r(I+2)|
! |                   ..........               | |  ..  | =  |  ..  |
```

```
! |                  b(n-1) d(n-1) a(n-1)| |x(n-1)|    |r(n-1)|
! |                         b(n)   d(n) | | x(n) |    | r(n) |
!     NOTE: all vectors are equal length, b(1)=a(n)=0 always
    n = size(a)                                   ! system size
!     factor the upper triangle
    a(1) = a(1) / d(1) ; r(1) = r(1) / d(1)      ! first row
    do i = 2, n-1                                 ! down rows
      denom = d(i) - b(i) * a(i-1)                ! pivot
      if ( abs(denom) <= tol ) stop 'zero pivot in Thomas'
      a(i) = a(i) / denom
      r(i) = (r(i) - b(i) * r(i-1)) / denom
    end do ! down rows
    denom = d(n) - b(n) * a(n-1)                  ! pivot
    if ( abs(denom) <= tol ) stop 'zero pivot in Thomas'
    r(n) = (r(n) - b(n)*r(n-1)) / denom          ! last row
!     back substitute for solution
    x(n) = r(n)                                   ! last row
    do i = n-1,1,-1
      x(i) = r(i) - a(i) * x(i+1)                 ! up rows
    end do ! up rows
END FUNCTION Thomas_tri_diag

END MODULE tridiagonal_matrix_class

```

Finally, we test most but not all of this incomplete tridiagonal_class.

```
PROGRAM Test_tridiagonal_class
 USE tridiagonal_matrix_class
   IMPLICIT NONE
   INTEGER, PARAMETER :: n_eqs = 3    ! define matrix system data
   DOUBLE PRECISION :: rhs  (n_eqs)   = (/ 3.d0, 8.d0, 16.d0 /)
   DOUBLE PRECISION :: low  (n_eqs-1) = (/ 1.d0, 3.d0 /)
   DOUBLE PRECISION :: high (n_eqs-1) = (/ 2.d0, 4.d0 /)
   DOUBLE PRECISION :: mid  (n_eqs)   = (/ 1.d0, 3.d0, 13.d0 /)
   DOUBLE PRECISION :: ans  (n_eqs)   ! to be found
   TYPE (tri_diag_matrix) :: A

     A = tri_diag_maker (n_eqs, low, mid, high)       ! allocate and fill
     print *, 'Given tridiagonal matrix diagonals:'
     call tri_diag_print (A)                          ! verify data
     print *, 'Given right hand side:' ; print *, rhs ! verify data

     ans = A .solve. rhs                              ! solve system
     print *, 'Computed solution is:' ; print *, ans  ! answer
     print *, 'Error is:'                             ! verify answer
     print *, sum ( abs ((A * ans) - rhs) )           ! overloaded *

     CALL tri_diag_free (A)    ! free tridiagonal_matrix memory
END PROGRAM Test_tridiagonal_class    ! Running gives
! Given tridiagonal matrix diagonals:
! 1   0.0E+0   1.0    2.0
! 2   1.0      3.0    4.0
! 3   3.0      13.0   0.0E+0
! Given right hand side: 3.0   8.0   16.0
! Computed solution is:  1.0   1.0   1.0
! Error is: 0.0E+0
```

B.19 Problem 9.1 : Count the Integer Word Memory Leak

```
Program Memory_Leak_Counted
Use Memory_Status_Count
 Implicit None
  Integer           :: i, item (2)  ! loops, status
```

Note that *item* will now be used for both allocations and deallocations.

```
  Integer, Pointer :: ptr_1 (:), ptr_2 (:)

   Print *, 'Are pointers associated ? ', & ! Initial associations
     associated (ptr_1), associated (ptr_2)

   ! Allocate and fill the arrays
   item (1:2) = 0                          ! set error flags
   Allocate ( ptr_1 (5), stat = item(1) )  ! first pointer
```

The following line uses a successful allocation to increase the memory count. A failure to allocate gives a warning here but almost always would be a fatal error.

```
   Call Alloc_Count_Int (item(1), "Memory_Leak 1", 5)
   Print *, 'INTEGER_WORDS = ', INTEGER_WORDS
   Allocate ( ptr_2 (5), stat = item(2) )  ! second pointer
   Call Alloc_Count_Int (item(2), "Memory_Leak 2", 5)
   Print *, 'INTEGER_WORDS = ', INTEGER_WORDS
   If ( Any ( item /= 0 ) ) Stop 'Allocation failed' ! status

   ptr_1 = (/ (i, i = 21,25) /) ; ptr_2 = (/ (i, i = 30,34) /)
   Print *, 'Pointer 1 = ', ptr_1              ! echo data
   Print *, 'Pointer 2 = ', ptr_2              ! echo data
   Print *, 'Are pointers associated ? ', & ! associations now
     associated (ptr_1), associated (ptr_2)

   ptr_2 => ptr_1 ; Print *, 'Now set ptr_2 => ptr_1'
   Print *, 'Note: memory assigned to Pointer 2 is lost'
   Print *, 'Pointer 1 = ', ptr_1              ! echo data
   Print *, 'Pointer 2 = ', ptr_2              ! echo data
   Print *, 'Are pointers associated ? ', & ! associations now
     associated (ptr_1), associated (ptr_2)

   Print *, 'Deallocate & Nullify all pointers'
```

This is where the reduction-in-memory count occurs. Except in this case it happens to fail and a warning is issued.

```
   Deallocate (ptr_1, stat = item(1) ) ! deallocate memory fails
   Call Dealloc_Count_Int (item(1), "Memory_Leak 1", 5)
   Print *, 'INTEGER_WORDS = ', INTEGER_WORDS
   Nullify    (ptr_1)                ! nullify after deallocate
   Deallocate (ptr_2, stat = item(2) ) ! deallocate memory fails
   Call Dealloc_Count_Int (item(2), "Memory_Leak 2", 5)
   Print *, 'INTEGER_WORDS = ', INTEGER_WORDS
   Nullify    (ptr_2)                ! nullify after deallocate
   Print *, 'Are pointers associated ? ', & ! associations now
     associated (ptr_1), associated (ptr_2)
```

```
    If ( INTEGER_WORDS == 0 ) Then
      Print *, 'No memory leak.'
    Else
      Print *, 'Integer word memory leak = ', INTEGER_WORDS
    End If
End Program Memory_Leak_Counted    ! Running gives:
! Are pointers associated ?  F F
! INTEGER_WORDS =  5
! INTEGER_WORDS =  10
! Pointer 1 =  21 22 23 24 25
! Pointer 2 =  30 31 32 33 34
! Are pointers associated ?  T T
! Now set ptr_2 => ptr_1
! Note: memory assigned to Pointer 2 is lost
! Pointer 1 =  21 22 23 24 25
! Pointer 2 =  21 22 23 24 25
! Are pointers associated ?  T T
! Deallocate & Nullify all pointers
! INTEGER_WORDS =  5
! WARNING: Unable to Deallocate a call from Memory_Leak 2
! INTEGER_WORDS =  5
! Are pointers associated ?  F F
! Integer word memory leak =  5
```

APPENDIX C

Companion C++ Examples

C.1 Introduction

It is necessary to be multilingual in computer languages today. Since C++ is often used in the OOP literature, it should be useful to have C++ versions of the same code given earlier in F90. In most cases these examples have the same variable names and the line numbers are usually very close to each other. This appendix will allow you to flip from F90 examples in Chapter 4 of the main body of the text to see similar operations in C++.

```
#include <iostream.h> // system i/o files
#include <math.h>     // system math files
main ()
// Examples of simple arithmetic in C++
{
 int    Integer_Var_1, Integer_Var_2;  // user inputs
 int    Mult_Result, Div_Result, Add_Result
 int    Sub_Result, Mod_Result;
 double Pow_Result, Sqrt_Result;
 cout << "Enter two integers: ";
 cin >>  Integer_Var_1, Integer_Var_2;

 Add_Result = Integer_Var_1 + Integer_Var_2;
 cout << Integer_Var_1 << " + " << Integer_Var_2 << " = "
      << Add_Result << endl;
 Sub_Result = Integer_Var_1 - Integer_Var_2 ;
 cout << Integer_Var_1 << " - " << Integer_Var_2 << " = "
      << Sub_Result << endl;
 Mult_Result = Integer_Var_1 * Integer_Var_2 ;
 cout << Integer_Var_1 << " * " << Integer_Var_2 << " = "
      << Mult_Result << endl;
 Div_Result = Integer_Var_1 / Integer_Var_2 ;
 cout << Integer_Var_1 << " / " << Integer_Var_2 << " = "
      << Div_Result << endl;
 Mod_Result = Integer_Var_1 % Integer_Var_2; // remainder
 cout << Integer_Var_1 << " % " << Integer_Var_2 << " = "
      << Mod_Result << endl;
 Pow_Result = pow ((double)Integer_Var_1, (double)Integer_Var_2);
 cout << Integer_Var_1 << " ^ " << Integer_Var_2 << " = "
      << Pow_Result << endl;
 Sqrt_Result = sqrt( (double)Integer_Var_1 );
```

```
  cout << "Square root of " << Integer_Var_1 << " is "
       << Sqrt_Result << endl;
} // end main, Running produces:
// Enter two integers: 25 4
// 25  +  4  =  29
// 25  -  4  =  21
// 25  *  4  =  100
// 25  /  4  =  6, note integer
// 25  %  4  =  1
// 25  ^  4  =  390625
// Square root of  25  =  5
```

Figure C.1: Typical math and functions in C++.

```
#include <iostream.h> // system i/o files
main ()
// Examples of a simple loop in C++
{
  int  Integer_Var;

  for (Integer_Var = 0; Integer_Var < 5; Integer_Var ++)
  {
    cout << "The loop variable is: " << Integer_Var << endl;
  } // end for

  cout << "The final loop variable is: " << Integer_Var << endl;

} // end main                              // Running produces:
// The loop variable is: 0
// The loop variable is: 1
// The loop variable is: 2
// The loop variable is: 3
// The loop variable is: 4
// The final loop variable is: 5 <- NOTE
```

Figure C.2: Typical looping concepts in C++.

```
#include <iostream.h> // system i/o files
main ()
//  Examples of simple array indexing in C++
{
  int MAX = 5, loopcount;
  int  Integer_Array[5] ;
  // or, int  Integer_Array[5] = {10, 20, 30, 40, 50 };

  Integer_Array[0] = 10 ;   // C arrays start at zero
  Integer_Array[1] = 20 ; Integer_Array[2] = 30 ;
  Integer_Array[3] = 40 ; Integer_Array[4] = 50 ;

  for ( loopcount = 0; loopcount < MAX; loopcount ++)
    cout << "The loop counter is: " << loopcount
         << " with an array value of: " << Integer
  // end for loop
  cout << "The final loop counter is: " << loopcount << endl ;

} // end main

```

```
// Running produces:
// The loop counter is: 0 with an array value of: 10
// The loop counter is: 1 with an array value of: 20
// The loop counter is: 2 with an array value of: 30
// The loop counter is: 3 with an array value of: 40
// The loop counter is: 4 with an array value of: 50
// The final loop counter is: 5
```

Figure C.3: Simple array indexing in C++.

```
#include <iostream.h> // system i/o files
main ()
// Examples of relational "if" operator, via C++
{
  int     Integer_Var_1, Integer_Var_2; // user inputs

  cout << "\nEnter two integers: ";
  cin >> Integer_Var_1, Integer_Var_2;

  if ( Integer_Var_1 > Integer_Var_2 )
    cout << Integer_Var_1 << " is greater than " << Integer_Var_2;

  if ( Integer_Var_1 < Integer_Var_2 )
    cout << Integer_Var_1 << " is less than " << Integer_Var_2;

  if ( Integer_Var_1 == Integer_Var_2 )
    cout << Integer_Var_1 << " is equal to " << Integer_Var_2;

} // end main

// Running with 25 and 4 produces: 25 4
// Enter two integers:
// 25 is greater than  4
```

Figure C.4: Typical relational operators in C++.

```
#include <iostream.h>
main ()
// Illustrate a simple if-else logic in C++
{
  int Integer_Var;

  cout << "Enter an integer: ";
  cin  >>  Integer_Var;

  if ( Integer_Var > 5 && Integer_Var < 10 )
   {
     cout << Integer_Var << " is greater than 5 and less than 10"
    << endl; }
   else
   {
     cout << Integer_Var << " is not greater than 5 and less than 10"
    << endl; } // end of range of input

} // end program main

// Running with 3 gives: 3 is not greater than 5 and less than 10
// Running with 8 gives: 8 is greater than 5 and less than 10
```

Figure C.5: Typical if-else uses in C++.

```
#include <iostream.h>
main ()
// Examples of Logical operators in C++
{
  int Logic_Var_1, Logic_Var_2;
  cout << "Enter logical value of A (1 or 0): ";
  cin >> Logic_Var_1;
  cout << "Enter logical value of B (1 or 0): ";
  cin >> Logic_Var_2;
  cout << "NOT A is " << !Logic_Var_1 << endl;
  if ( Logic_Var_1  && Logic_Var_2 )
   {
    cout << "A ANDed with B is true " << endl;
   }
  else
   {
    cout << "A ANDed with B is false " << endl;
   } // end if for AND
  if ( Logic_Var_1 || Logic_Var_2 )
   {
    cout << "A ORed with B is true " << endl;
   }
  else
   {
    cout << "A ORed with B is false " << endl;
   } // end if for OR
  if ( Logic_Var_1 == Logic_Var_2 )
   {
    cout << "A EQiValent with B is true " << endl;
   }
  else
   {
    cout << "A EQiValent with B is false " << endl;
   } // end if for EQV
  if ( Logic_Var_1 != Logic_Var_2 )
   {
    cout << "A Not EQiValent with B is true " << endl;
   }
  else
   {
    cout << "A Not EQiValent with B is false " << endl;
   } // end if for NEQV
} // end main
// Running with 1 and 0 produces:
// Enter logical value of A (1 or 0): 1
// Enter logical value of B (1 or 0): 0
// NOT A is 0
// A ANDed with B is false
// A ORed with B is true
// A EQiValent with B is false
// A Not EQiValent with B is true
```

Figure C.6: Typical logical operators in C++.

```
// Program to find the maximum of a set of integers
#include <iostream.h>
#include <stdlib.h> // for exit
#define ARRAYLENGTH 100
long integers[ARRAYLENGTH];

// Function interface prototype
long maxint(long [], long);

// Main routine

main() { // Read in the number of integers
long i, n;

 cout << "Find maximum; type n: "; cin >> n;
 if ( n > ARRAYLENGTH || n < 0 ) {
   cout << "Value you typed is too large or negative." << endl;
   exit(1);
   } // end if

 for (i = 0; i < n; i++) { // Read in the user's integers
    cout << "Integer " << (i+1) << ": "; cin >> integers[i]; cout
    << endl;  } // end for
 cout << "Maximum: ",  cout << maxint(integers, n); cout << endl;
} // end main

// Find the maximum of an array of integers
long maxint(long input[], long input_length) {
long i, max;

 for (max = input[0], i = 1; i < input_length; i++) {
   if ( input[i] > max ) {
     max = input[i]; } // end if
  } // end for
 return(max);
} // end maxint                     // produces this result
// Find maximum; type n: 4
// Integer 1: 9
// Integer 2: 6
// Integer 3: 4
// Integer 4: -99
// Maximum: 9
```

Figure C.7: Search for largest value in C++.

```
#include <iostream.h>

// declare the interface prototypes
void  Change    ( int& Input_Val);
void  No_Change ( int  Input_Val);

main ()
//  illustrate passing by reference and by value in C++
{
  int Input_Val;
```

```
   cout << "Enter an integer: ";
   cin >> Input_Val;
   cout << "Input value was " <<  Input_Val << endl;

   //  pass by value
   No_Change ( Input_Val );  // Use but do not change
   cout << "After No_Change it is " <<  Input_Val << endl;

   //  pass by reference
   Change ( Input_Val );  // Use and change
   cout << "After Change it is " <<  Input_Val << endl;
 }

 void  Change (int& Value)
 {
 //  changes Value in calling code IF passed by reference
   Value = 100;
   cout << "Inside Change it is set to " << Value << endl;
 }

 void  No_Change (int Value)
 {
 //  does not change Value in calling code IF passed by value
   Value  = 100;
   cout << "Inside No_Change it is set to " << Value << endl;
 }
 //   Running gives:
 // Enter an integer: 12
 // Input value was 12
 // Inside No_Change it is set to 100
 // After No_Change it is 12
 // Inside Change it is set to 100
 // After Change it is 100
```

Figure C.8: Passing arguments by reference and by value in C++.

```
#include <iostream.h>
main ()
// Compare two character strings in C++
// Concatenate two character strings together
{
  char String1[40];
  char String2[20];
  int  length;

  cout << "Enter first string (20 char max):";
  cin >> String1;

  cout << "Enter second string (20 char max):";
  cin >> String2;

  // Compare
```

```
    if ( !strcmp(String1, String2) ) {
      cout << "They are the same." << endl;
      }
      else {
      cout << "They are different." << endl;
      } // end if the same

    // Concatenate
    strcat(String1, String2) ; // add onto String1

    cout << "The combined string is: " << String1 << endl;
    length = strlen( String1 );
    cout << "The combined length is: " << length << endl;
    length = strlen( String1 );

  } // end main
  // Running with "red" and "bird" produces:
  // Enter first string (20 char max): red
  // Enter second string (20 char max): bird
  // They are different.
  // The combined string is: redbird
  // The combined length is: 7
  // But, "the red" and "bird" gives unexpected results
```

Figure C.9: Using two strings in C++.

```
#include <iostream.h>
#include <stdlib.h>
#include <math.h>  // system math files

main()
// Convert a character string to an integer in C++
{
  char Age_Char[5];
  int  age;

  cout << "Enter your age: ";
  cin >> Age_Char;

  // convert with intrinsic function
  age = atoi(Age_Char);

  cout << "Your integer age is "              << age << endl;
  cout << "Your hexadecimal age is " << hex << age << endl;
  cout << "Your octal age is "        << oct << age << endl;

} // end of main

// Running gives:
// Enter your age: 45
// Your integer age is 45.
// Your hexadecimal age is 2d.
// Your octal age is 55.
```

Figure C.10: Converting a string to an integer with C++.

```
#include <iostream.h>

// Define structures and components in C++

struct Person      // define a person structure type
 {
  char   Name[20];
  int    Age;
 };

struct Who_Where   // use person type in a new structure
 {
  struct Person Guest;
  char   Address[40];
 };

// Fill a record of the Who_Where type components
main ()
{
   struct Who_Where  Record;

   cout << "Enter your name: ";
   cin  >>  Record.Guest.Name;

   cout << "Enter your city: ";
   cin  >>  Record.Address;

   cout << "Enter your age: ";
   cin  >>  Record.Guest.Age;

   cout << "Hello " << Record.Guest.Age << " year old "
        << Record.Guest.Name << " in " << Record.Address << endl;
}
// Running with input: Sammy, Houston, 104 gives
// Hello 104 year old Sammy in Houston
//
// But try: Sammy Owl, Houston, 104 for a bug
```

Figure C.11: Using multiple structures in C++.

Bibliography

1. Adams, J.C., Brainerd, W.S., Martin, J.T., Smith, B.T., Wagener, J.L., *Fortran 90 Handbook: Complete ANSI/ISO Reference*, Intertext Publications, McGraw-Hill Book Company, New York, 1992.
2. Akin, J.E., *Finite Elements for Analysis and Design,* Academic Press, London, 1996.
3. Akin, J.E., "Object-Oriented Programming via Fortran 90," *Engineering Computations*, 16(1) 26–48, 1999.
4. Akin, J.E., and Singh, M., "Object-Oriented Fortran 90 P-Adaptive Finite Element Method," *Developments in Engineering Computational Technology*, (Ed. B.H.V. Topping), Civil-Comp Press, Edinburgh, 141–149, 2000.
5. Anonymous, "Encapsulation, Inheritance and the Platypus Effect," *The C++ developer discussion diary*, May 2000, www.advogato.org/article/83.html.
6. Bar-David, T., *Object-Oriented Design for C++*, Prentice-Hall, Englewood Cliffs, NJ, 1993.
7. Barton, J.J., and Nackman L.R., *Scientific and Engineering C++*, Addison-Wesley, Reading, MA, 1994.
8. Cary, J.R., Shasharina, S.G., Cummings, J.C., Reynders, J.V.W., Hinker, P.J., "A Comparison of C++ and Fortran 90 for Object-Oriented Scientific Programming," *Computer Phys. Comm.*, 105, 20, 1997.
9. Coad, P., and Yourdon, E., *Object Oriented Design*, Prentice-Hall, Englewood Cliffs, NJ, 1991.
10. Decyk, V.K., Norton, C.D., Szymanski, B.K., "Expressing Object-Oriented Concepts in Fortran90," *ACM Fortran Forum*, 16(1), April 1997.
11. Decyk, V.K., Norton, C.D., Szymanski, B.K., "How to Express C++ Concepts in Fortran90," *Scientific Programming*, 6, 363–390, 1997.
12. Dubois-Pèlerin, Y., and Pegon, P., "Improving Modularity in Object-Oriented Finite Element Programming," *Communications in Numerical Methods in Engineering*, 13, 193–198, 1997.
13. Dubois-Pèlerin, Y., and Zimmermann, T., "Object-Oriented Finite Element Programming: III. An efficient implementation in C++," *Comp. Meth. Appl. Mech. Engr.*, 108, 165–183, 1993.
14. Dubois-Pèlerin, Y., Zimmermann, T., Bomme, P., "Object-Oriented Finite Element Programming: II A Prototype Program in Smalltalk" *Comp. Meth. Appl. Mech. Engr.*, 98, 361–397, 1992.
15. Filho, J.S.R.A., and Devloo, P.R.B. "Object Oriented Programming in Scientific Computations," *Engineering Computations*, 8(1), 81–87, 1991.
16. Forde, B.W.R., Foschi, R.B., Stiemer, S.F., "Object-oriented Finite Element Analysis," *Comput. & Struct.*, 34, 355–374, 1990.
17. Gehrke, W., *Fortran 90 Language Guide*, Springer, Verlag London, 1995.
18. George, A., and Liu, J., "An Object-Oriented Approach to the Design of a User Interface for a Sparse Matrix Package," *SIAM J. Matrix Anal. Appl.*, 20(4), 953–969, 1999.

19. Graham, I., *Object Oriented Methods*, Addison-Wesley, Reading, MA, 1991.
20. Gray, M.G., and Roberts, R.M., "Object-Based Programming in Fortran 90," *Computers in Physics*, 11, 355, 1997.
21. Hahn, B.D., *Fortran 90 for Scientists and Engineers*, Edward Arnold, London, 1994.
22. Hanly, J.R., *Essential C++ for Engineers and Scientists*, Addison-Wesley, 1997.
23. Hanselman, D., and Littlefield, B., *Mastering Matlab 5*, Prentice-Hall, Englewood Cliffs, NJ, 1998.
24. Hubbard, J.R., *Programming with C++*, McGraw-Hill, New York, NY, 1994.
25. Kerrigan, J., *Migrating to Fortran 90*, O'Reilly & Associates, Sebastopol, CA, 1993.
26. Koelbel, C.H., Loveman, D.B., Schreiber, R.S., Steele, G.L., Jr., Zosel, M.E., *The High Performance Fortran Handbook*, MIT Press, Cambridge, MA, 1994.
27. Machiels, L., and Deville, M.O., "Fortran 90: On Entry to Object Oriented Programming for the Solution of Partial Differential Equations," *ACM Trans. Math. Software*, 23(1), 32–49, March 1997.
28. Meyer, B., *Object-Oriented Software Construction*, Prentice-Hall, Englewood Cliffs, NJ, 1988.
29. Mossberg, E., Otto, K., Thune, M. "Object-Oriented Software Tools for the Construction of Preconditioners" *Scientific Programming*, 6, 285–295, 1997.
30. Nielsen, K., *Object-Oriented Development with C++*, International Thomson Computer Press, 1997.
31. Norton, C.D., Decyk, V.K., Szymanski, B.K., "High Performance Object-Oriented Scientific Programming in Fortran 90," *Proc. Eighth SIAM Conf. on Parallel Processing for Scientific Programming*, (Ed. Heath et al.), March 1997.
32. Norton, C.D., Szymanski, B.K., Decyk, V.K., "Object Oriented Parallel Computation for Plasma Simulation," *Comm. ACM*, 38(10), 88, 1995.
33. Pratap, R., *Getting Started with* MATLAB, Saunders College Publishing, Ft. Worth, TX, 1996.
34. Press, W.H., Teukolsky, S.A., Vetterling, W.T., Flannery, B.P., *Numerical Recipes in Fortran 90*, 2nd ed., Cambridge University Press, Cambridge, 1996.
35. Rehak, D.R., and Baugh, J.W., Jr., "Alternative Programming Techniques for Finite Element Program Development," *Proc. IABSE Colloquium on Expert Systems in Civil Engineering*, Bergamo, Italy, 1989.
36. Rumbaugh, J., Blaha, M., Premerlani, W., Eddy, F., Lorensen, W., *Object Oriented Modeling and Design*, Prentice-Hall, Englewood Cliffs, NJ, 1991.
37. Szymanski, B.K., Decyk, V.K., Norton, C.D., "Expressing Object-Oriented Concepts in Fortran90," *ACM Fortran Forum*, 16, 1, April 1997.
38. Szymanski, B.K., Decyk, V.K., Norton, C.D., "How to Support Inheritance and Run-Time Polymorphism in Fortran 90," *Computer Physics Communications*, 115, 9–17, 1998.
39. Thomas, P., and Weedon, R., *Object-Oriented Programming in Eiffel*, Addison-Wesley, Reading, MA, 1995.
40. Zienkiewicz, O.C., and Zhu, J.Z., "The Superconvergent Patch Recovery (SPR) and Adaptive Finite Element Refinement," *Comp. Meth. Appl. Mech. Engr.*, 101, 207–224, 1992. Links to Worldwide Websites (as of January 2002, subject to change):
41. http:/blas.mcmaster.ca/f̃red/oo.html
42. http://citeseer.nj.nec.com/242268.html
43. http://epubs.siam.org/sam-bin/dbq/article/31773
44. http://kanaima.ciens.ucv.ve/hpf/HTMLNotesnode29.html
45. http://webserv.gsfc.nasa.gov/ESS/annual.reports/ess98/cdn.html
46. http://www.amath.washington.edu/l̃f/software/CompCPP_F90SciOOP.html
47. http://www.cs.rpi.edu/s̃zymansk/oof90.html
48. http://www.nasatech.com/Briefs/Mar98/NPO20180.html
49. http://www.ssec.wisc.edu/r̃obert/Software/F90-ObjOrientProg.html
50. http://www.tdb.uu.se/ñgssc/OOP00/module2/
51. http://www.ticra.dk/ooa.htm

Glossary of Object-Oriented Terms

abstract class: A class primarily intended to define an instance but one that cannot be instantiated without additional methods.

abstract data type: An abstraction that describes a set of items in terms of a hidden data structure and operations on that structure.

abstraction: A mental facility that permits one to view problems with varying degrees of detail depending on the current context of the problem.

accessor: A public member subprogram that provides query access to a private data member.

actor: An object that initiates behavior in other objects but cannot be acted upon itself.

ADT: Abstract data type.

agent: An object that can initiate behavior in other objects and be operated upon by other objects.

AKO: A kind of. The inheritance relationship between classes and their superclasses.

allocatable array: A named array having the ability to obtain memory dynamically. Only when space has been allocated for it does it have a shape and may it be referenced or defined.

argument: A value, variable, or expression that provides input to a subprogram.

array: An ordered collection that is indexed.

array constructor: A means of creating a part of an array by a single statement.

array overflow: An attempt to access an array element with a subscript outside the array size bounds.

array pointer: A pointer whose target is an array or an array section.

array section: A subobject that is an array and is not a defined type component.

assertion: A programming means to cope with errors and exceptions.

assignment operator: The equal symbol, "=," which may be overloaded by a user.

assignment statement: A statement of the form "variable = expression."

association: Host association, name association, pointer association, or storage association.

attribute: A property of a variable that may be specified in a type declaration statement.

automatic array: An explicit-shape array in a procedure, which is not a dummy argument, some or all of whose bounds are provided when the procedure is invoked.

base class: A previously defined class whose public members can be inherited by another class. (Also called a super class.)

behavior sharing: A form of polymorphism, when multiple entities have the same generic interface. This is achieved by inheritance or operator overloading.

binary operator: An operator that takes two operands.

bintree: A tree structure in which each node has two child nodes.

browser: A tool to find all occurrences of a variable, object, or component in a source code.

call-by-reference: A language mechanism that supplies an argument to a procedure by passing the address of the argument rather than its value. If it is modified, the new value will also take effect outside of the procedure.

call-by-value: A language mechanism that supplies an argument to a procedure by passing a copy of its data value. If it is modified, the new value will not take effect outside of the procedure that modified it.

class: An abstraction of an object that specifies the static and behavioral characteristics of it, including their public and private nature. A class is an ADT with a constructor template from which object instances are created.

class attribute: An attribute whose value is common to a class of objects rather than a value peculiar to each instance of the class.

class descriptor: An object representing a class containing a list of its attributes and methods as well as the values of any class attributes.

class diagram: A diagram depicting classes, their internal structure and operations, and the fixed relationships between them.

class inheritance: Defining a new derived class in terms of one or more base classes.

client: A software component that uses services from another supplier class.

concrete class: A class having no abstract operations and can be instantiated.

compiler: Software that translates a high-level language into machine language.

component: A data member of a defined type within a class declaration.

constructor: An operation by a class member function that initializes a newly created instance of a class. (See default and intrinsic constructor.)

constructor operations: Methods that create and initialize the state of an object.

container class: A class whose instances are container objects. Examples include sets, arrays, and stacks.

container object: An object that stores a collection of other objects and provides operations to access or iterate over them.

control variable: The variable that controls the number of loop executions.

data abstraction: The ability to create new data types together with associated operators and to hide the internal structure and operations from the user, thus allowing the new data type to be used in a fashion analogous to intrinsic data types.

data hiding: The concept that some variables, operations, or both in a module may not be accessible to a user of that module; a key element of data abstraction.

data member: A public data attribute, or instance variable, in a class declaration.

data type: A named category of data characterized by a set of values together with a way to denote these values and a collection of operations that interpret and manipulate the values. For an intrinsic type, the set of data values depends on the values of the type parameters.

deallocation statement: A statement that releases dynamic memory that has previously been allocated to an allocatable array or a pointer.

debugger software: A program that allows one to execute a program in segments up to selected break points and to observe the program variables.

debugging: The process of detecting, locating, and correcting errors in software.

declaration statement: A statement that specifies the type and, optionally, attributes of one or more variables or constants.

default constructor: A class member function with no arguments that assigns default initial values to all data members in a newly created instance of a class.

defined operator: An operator that is not an intrinsic operator and is defined by a subprogram associated with a generic identifier.

deque: A container that supports inserts or removals from either end of a queue.

dereferencing: The interpretation of a pointer as the target to which it is pointing.

derived attribute: An attribute that is determined from other attributes.

derived class: A class whose declaration indicates that it is to inherit the public members of a previously defined base class.

derived type: A user-defined data type with components, each of which is either of the intrinsic type or of another derived type.

destructor: An operation that cleans up an existing instance of a class that is no longer needed.

destructor operations: Methods that destroy objects and reclaim their dynamic memory.

domain: The set over which a function or relation is defined.

dummy argument: An argument in a procedure definition that will be associated with the actual (reference or value) argument when the procedure is invoked.

dummy array: A dummy argument that is an array.

dummy pointer: A dummy argument that is a pointer.

dummy procedure: A dummy argument that is specified or referenced as a procedure.

dynamic binding: The allocation of storage at run time rather than compile time or the run time association of an object and one of its generic operations.

edit descriptor: An item in an input–output format that specifies the conversion between internal and external forms.

encapsulation: A modeling and implementation technique (information hiding) that separates the external aspects of an object from its internal implementation details.

exception: An unexpected error condition causing an interruption to the normal flow of program control.

explicit interface: For a procedure referenced in a scoping unit, the property of being an internal procedure, a module procedure, an external procedure that has an interface (prototype) block, a recursive procedure reference in its own scoping unit, or a dummy procedure that has an interface block.

explicit shape array: A named array that is declared with explicit bounds.

external file: A sequence of records that exists in a medium external to the program.

external procedure: A procedure defined by an external subprogram.

FIFO: First-in, first-out storage; a queue.

friend: A method, in C++ that is allowed privileged access to the private implementation of another object.

function body: A block of statements manipulating parameters to accomplish the subprogram's purpose.

function definition: A program unit that associates a return type, a list of arguments, and a sequence of statements with a subprogram name that manipulate the arguments to accomplish the subprogram's purpose

function header: A line of code at the beginning of a function definition; it includes the argument list and the function return variable name.

generic function: A function that can be called with different types of arguments.

generic identifier: A lexical token that appears in an INTERFACE statement and is associated with all the procedures in the interface block.

generic interface block: A form of interface block used to define a generic name for a set of procedures.

generic name: A name used to identify two or more procedures, the required one being determined by the types of the nonoptional arguments in the procedure invocation.

generic operator: An operator that can be invoked with different types of operands.

Has-A: A relationship in which the derived class has a property of the base class.

hashing technique: A technique used to create a hash table in which the array element where an item is to be stored is determined by converting some item feature into an integer in the range of the size of the table.

heap: A region of memory used for data structures dynamically allocated and deallocated by a program.

host: The program unit containing a lower (hosted) internal procedure.

host association: Data and variables automatically available to an internal procedure from its host.

information hiding: The principle that the state and implementation of an object should be private to that object and only accessible via its public interface.

inheritance: The relationship between classes whereby one class inherits part or all of the public description of another base class and instances inherit all the properties and methods of the classes they contain.

instance: An individual example of a class invoked via a class constructor.

instance diagram: A drawing showing the instance connection between two objects along with the number or range of mapping that may occur.

instantiation: The process of creating (giving a value to) instances from classes.

intent: An attribute of a dummy argument that indicates whether it may be used to transfer data into the procedure, out of the procedure, or both.

interaction diagram: A diagram that shows the flow of requests or messages between objects.

interface: The set of all signatures (public methods) defined for an object.

internal file: A character string used to transfer and convert data from one internal storage mode to a different one.

internal procedure: A procedure contained within another program unit or class that can only be invoked from within that program unit or class.

internal subprogram: A subprogram contained in a main program or another subprogram.

intrinsic constructor: A class member function with the same name as the class that receives initial values of all the data members as arguments.

Is-A: A relationship in which the derived class is a variation of the base class.

iterator: A method that permits all parts of a data structure to be visited.

keyword: A programming language word already defined and reserved for a single special purpose.

LIFO: Last-in, first-out storage; a stack.

link: The process of combining compiled program units to form an executable program.

linked list: A data structure in which each element identifies its predecessor and successor by some form of pointer.

linker: Software that combines object files to create an executable machine language program.

list: An ordered collection that is not indexed.

map: An indexed collection that may be ordered.

matrix: A rank-two array.

member data: Variables declared as components of a defined type and encapsulated in a class.

member function: Subprograms encapsulated as members of a class.

message: A request, from another object, for an object to carry out one of its operations.

message passing: The philosophy that objects only interact by sending messages to each other that request some operations to be performed.

method: A class member function encapsulated with its class data members.

method resolution: The process of matching a generic operation on an object to the unique method appropriate to the object's class.

module: A program unit that allows other program units to access variables, derived type definitions, classes, and procedures declared within it by USE association.

module procedure: A procedure contained within a module and usually used to define generic interfaces and to overload or define operators.

nested: Placement of a control structure inside another control structure.

object: A concept or thing with crisp boundaries and meanings for the problem at hand; an instance of a class.

object diagram: A graphical representation of an object model showing relationships, attributes, and operations.

object-oriented (OO): A software development strategy that organizes software as a collection of objects that contain both data structure and behavior (abbreviated OO).

object-oriented analysis (OOA): A method that examines the requirements of an application from the perspective of the classes and objects in the domain.

object-oriented design (OOD): A method that takes the results of an OOA and shifts its emphasis from the application domain to the computational (and language) domain.

object-oriented programming (OOP): Programming approach that is object- and class-based and supports inheritance between classes and base classes and allows objects to send and receive messages.

object-oriented programming language: A language that supports objects (encapsulating identity, data, and operations), method resolution, and inheritance.

octree: A tree structure in which each node has eight child nodes.

OO (acronym): Object-oriented.

operand: An expression or variable that precedes or succeeds an operator.

operation: Manipulation of an object's data by its member function when it receives a request.

operator overloading: A special case of polymorphism; attaching more than one meaning to the same operator symbol. "Overloading" is also sometimes used to indicate using the same name for different objects.

overflow: An error condition arising from an attempt to store a number that is too large for the storage location specified; typically caused by an attempt to divide by zero.

overloading: Using the same name for multiple functions or operators in a single scope.

overriding: The ability to change the definition of an inherited method or attribute in a subclass.

parameterized classes: A template for creating real classes that may differ in well-defined ways as specified by parameters at the time of creation. The parameters are often data types or classes but may include other attributes such as the size of a collection (also called generic classes).

pass-by-reference: Method of passing an argument that permits the function to refer to the memory holding the original copy of the argument.

pass-by-value: Method of passing an argument that evaluates the argument and stores this value in the corresponding formal argument so the function has its own copy of the argument value.

pointer: A single data object that stands for another (a "target"), which may be a compound object such as an array or defined type.

pointer array: An array declared with the pointer attribute. Its shape and size may not be determined until they are created for the array by means of a memory allocation statement.

pointer assignment statement: A statement of the form "pointer-name ⇒ target."

polymorphism: The ability of a function/operator with one name to refer to arguments or return types of different classes at run time.

postcondition: Specifies what must be true after the execution of an operation.

precondition: Specifies the condition(s) that must be true before an operation can be executed.

private: That part of a class, methods or attributes, that may not be accessed by other classes but only by instances of that class.

protected: (Referring to an attribute or operation of a class in C++) accessible by methods of any descendent of the current class.

prototype: A statement declaring a function's return type, name, and list of argument types.

pseudocode: A language of structured English statements used in designing a step-by-step approach to solving a problem.

public: That part of an object, methods or attributes, that may be accessed by other objects and thus constitutes its interface.

quadtree: A tree structure in which each tree node has four child nodes.

query operation: An operation that returns a value without modifying any objects.

rank: Number of subscripted variables an array has. A scalar has rank zero, a vector has rank one, and a matrix has rank two.

scope: That part of an executable program within which a lexical token (name) has a single interpretation.

section: Part of an array.

sequential: A kind of file in which each record is written (read) after the previously written (read) record.

server: An object that can only be operated upon by other objects.

service: A class member function encapsulated with its class data members.

shape: The rank of an array and the extent of each of its subscripts. It is often stored in a rank-one array.

side effect: A change in a variable's value as a result of using it as an operand or argument.

signature: The combination of a subprogram's (operator's) name and its argument (operand) types; it does not include function result types.

size: The total number of elements in an array.

stack: Region of memory used for allocation of function data areas; allocation of variables on the stack occurs automatically when a block is entered, and deallocation occurs when the block is exited

stride: The increment used in a subscript triplet.

strong typing: The property of a programming language such that the type of each variable must be declared.

structure component: The part of a data object of derived type corresponding to a component of its type.

subobject: A portion of a data object that may be referenced or defined independently of other portions. It may be an array element, an array section, a structure component, or a substring.

subprogram: A function or subroutine subprogram.

subprogram header: A block of code at the beginning of a subprogram definition; includes the name and the argument list if any.

subscript triplet: A method of specifying an array section by means of the initial and final subscript integer values and an optional stride (or increment).

super class: A class from which another class inherits. (See base class.)

supplier: Software component that implements a new class with services to be used by a client software component.

target: The data object pointed to by a pointer or reference variable.

template: An abstract recipe with parameters for producing concrete code for class definitions or sub-program definitions.

thread: The basic entity to which the operating system allocates CPU time.

tree: A form of linked list in which each node points to at least two other nodes, thus defining a dynamic data structure.

unary operator: An operator that has only one operand.

undefined: A data object that does not have a defined value.

underflow: An error condition in which a number is too close to zero to be distinguished from zero in the floating-point representation being used.

utility function: A private subprogram that can only be used within its defining class.

vector: A rank-one array. An array with one subscript.

vector subscript: A method of specifying an array section by means of a vector containing the subscripts of the elements of the parent array that are to constitute the array section.

virtual function: A genetic function with a specific return type extended later for each new argument type.

void subprogram: A C++ subprogram with an empty argument list, a subroutine with no returned argument, or both.

work array: A temporary array used for the storage of intermediate results during processing.

Index